A Publication of the Horace Mann–Lincoln
Institute of School Experimentation
TEACHERS COLLEGE, COLUMBIA UNIVERSITY

EDUCATION AND AMERICAN CIVILIZATION

GEORGE S. COUNTS
Professor of Education
Teachers College, Columbia University

GREENWOOD PRESS, PUBLISHERS
WESTPORT, CONNECTICUT

Library of Congress Cataloging in Publication Data

Counts, George Sylvester, 1889-
  Education and American civilization.

  Reprint of the ed. published by Bureau of Publications, Teachers College, Columbia University, New York.
  "A publication of the Horace Mann-Lincoln Institute of School Experimentation."
  1. Education--United States. 2. United States--Civilization--20th century. I. Title.
[LA210.C63 1974]   370'.973   73-19569
ISBN 0-8371-7293-4

Copyright 1952 by Teachers College, Columbia University

Originally published in 1952 by Teachers College, Columbia University, New York

Reprinted with the permission of Teachers College, Columbia University

Reprinted in 1974 by Greenwood Press,
a division of Williamhouse-Regency Inc.

Library of Congress Catalogue Card Number 73-19569

ISBN 0-8371-7293-4

Printed in the United States of America

FOREWORD

The Horace Mann–Lincoln Institute of School Experimentation was established in 1943. At that time the staff initiated three related studies which it believed were basic to school experimentation. Publications resulting from inquiries into the nature of child development and of the curriculum have already appeared.[1] The present volume is about our American civilization, and has been prepared by George S. Counts.

Mr. Counts begins by noting our need for a great education. Here we are, he says, at the end of an era, "between two civilizations, one that is passing away and another that is in birth." The tasks before us are urgent, and we must have schools for our children that are equal to these tasks.

Then, beginning with an analysis of the relationship between a culture and the education it provides its children and youth, the author proceeds to describe, sensitively and lucidly, what he believes to be the American heritage. We are a nation of varied people, and most of us are common people. For more than a century we developed our conception of a free society of farmers and tradesmen in a land rich in natural resources, and beautiful to behold.

---

[1] *See* Arthur T. Jersild and Associates, *Child Development and the Curriculum* (1946); and Florence B. Stratemeyer, Hamden L. Forkner, and Margaret G. McKim, *Developing a Curriculum for Modern Living* (1947), Bureau of Publications, Teachers College, Columbia University.

Then came the technological revolution which, at an ever-accelerating rate, is changing the character of our civilization and ourselves. New modes of livelihood have come and are coming into being, new social relationships, new forms of communication, new fantastic sources of power, and the possibility of a rich and abundant life for all.

But the gap between this emerging industrial culture and our customs, loyalties, and outlooks is tremendous. And such is our perversity that we seem at times to strive to widen it. We cling tenaciously to a host of myths that are contradicted by the most significant of contemporary events.

This clinging blindly to the past, Mr. Counts believes, is the surest way to lose the future. Holding fast to that which is good in our heritage, we must re-examine our values, our opinions, our points of view, our actions. The new American way of life must rest upon a new synthesis of the values that are inherent in the Hebraic-Christian ethic, the humanistic spirit, the scientific method, the rule of law, and the democratic faith.

This analysis of American civilization and the problems it faces implies schools that are different in many respects from those we have. We do not lack the resources, material and spiritual, for building a great education—one that develops individual excellence, preserves the principles of equality and political liberty, achieves an economy of security and plenty, and supports an enduring world civilization of beauty and grandeur.

Those of us who are primarily concerned with curriculum development recognize, as does Mr. Counts, that we must overcome many obstacles, and some of them seem now to be almost insurmountable, if a system of education that will accomplish these broad purposes is to be established and maintained. Heavy demands will be placed not only upon teachers, but also upon all who want young people to be vastly better prepared for the world they will face than we have been prepared to face and cope with our world.

Mr. Counts writes thoughtfully and persuasively. Teachers, administrators, and supervisors will appreciate the care with

Foreword vii

which his argument is documented. Many of them will see more clearly than ever before the close relationship that exists between a civilization and the schools it supports. If one is to be bettered, the other cannot stand still. A constantly changing society requires schools that are experimental—willing to test new methods and materials that give promise of providing boys and girls a better education.

The Horace Mann–Lincoln Institute of School Experimentation is proud to add *Education and American Civilization* to its list of published studies.

STEPHEN M. COREY
Executive Officer

PREFACE
AND ACKNOWLEDGMENTS

This volume represents an effort to meet in the field of education the challenge of totalitarianism in its several forms. It represents an effort to develop a conception of American education which will support the values of free society in the present troubled age as effectively and vigorously as the educational conceptions of the totalitarian states support the purposes of despotism.

The book seeks to achieve this end through an analysis in historical perspective of the broad features of our American civilization, an exploration of the dynamics of industrial society, an examination of the major realities of the contemporary epoch, and an affirmation of the values which should guide us in the rearing of the young in the coming years. It is based upon the assumption that an education always expresses a conception of some living civilization and that a great education must express a great conception of civilization. It is based also on the conviction that our American civilization contains the elements out of which such a conception of civilization can be fashioned. *Education and American Civilization* therefore is essentially a study of the social, cultural, and moral foundations of the program and curriculum of our American common school.

The thing attempted in these pages is extremely ambitious, even pretentious perhaps. I realize fully the greatness of the theme and am keenly aware of the limitations and weaknesses of the treatment. Indeed, I postponed for months sending the manuscript to the press, and now I look forward with many misgivings to the day of publication. But I console myself with the thought that my effort will stimulate others, better qualified, to undertake the task. Moreover, I shall have accomplished my central purpose if I succeed in persuading the members of the profession that those who instruct the younger generation must study our society and civilization in historical and world relations far more seriously and competently than ever before.

My obligations in the preparation of the book are very heavy. First of all I am indebted to our two most profound students of American democracy and two of the greatest teachers of my generation, Charles A. Beard and John Dewey. I am under particularly heavy obligation to Professor Beard. Before his death I discussed at length with him and Mary R. Beard many of the basic positions developed in the work. This of course is not said for the purpose of shifting responsibility for a single sentence to their shoulders or the shoulders of anyone else. I should add perhaps that I have been much influenced in my thinking by several of our younger historians, and particularly by Henry Steele Commager and Merle Curti.

I am indebted beyond measure to my colleagues at Teachers College. I would mention especially President William F. Russell, who has lent me every encouragement through the years in my study of the nature of our democracy, the tendencies of industrial civilization, and the challenge of totalitarian movements. I would mention also Dean Hollis L. Caswell, who first asked me to undertake the preparation of a volume in the series sponsored by the Horace Mann–Lincoln Institute of School Experimentation. I would mention, too, my colleagues in the Department of Social and Philosophical Foundations and especially Professor John L. Childs, with whom I have worked in close association in education and politics for the better part of a generation. And I should not forget the many students who have challenged my thought from year to year respecting all questions both under and over the sun.

Preface and Acknowledgments xi

I am deeply indebted to the members of a committee of the Institute with whom I worked during the years 1944 and 1945 on the social bases of education: Miss Tompsie Baxter, Miss Elmina R. Lucke, and Dr. Frederick J. Rex. I want to thank Professor Stephen M. Corey, Executive Officer of the Institute, and Professor Max R. Brunstetter, Managing Editor of the Bureau of Publications, for reading the manuscript and making many valuable suggestions. I want to thank also my assistant, Mrs. Nucia Lodge, for her indefatigable labors in research and preparation of the manuscript.

The theme of the present volume was first developed in my Kappa Delta Pi Lecture delivered in 1945 and published by The Macmillan Company under the title, *Education and the Promise of America*. I am very grateful to the society for permitting me to make free use of the substance of the lecture. I want to thank Charles Scribner's Sons for permission to use materials from Chapter II, "Natural Endowment," of *The Social Foundations of Education*, which I prepared for the Commission on the Social Studies of the American Historical Association in 1934. I want also to thank *The New Leader* for permission to quote at length from Stefan Zweig's "Europe's Terrible Silence," which appeared in the issue of March 14, 1942.

Finally I wish to make acknowledgments of debt to the following authors and publishing companies for permitting me to quote from the books indicated: Columbia University Press, *The Impact of Science on Society* (1951), by Bertrand Russell. Duell, Sloan and Pearce, *An Autobiography* (1943), by Frank Lloyd Wright. Harcourt, Brace and Company, *North America* (1925), by J. Russell Smith. Harper and Brothers, *Progress and Catastrophe* (1937), by Stanley Casson; and *Machine-Made Leisure* (1932), by Paul T. Frankl. Henry Holt and Company, *A History of Modern Culture*, Vol. I (1930), by Preserved Smith. Roy Publishers, *Freedom and Civilization* (1944), by Bronislaw Malinowski. The Macmillan Company, *New Viewpoints in American History* (1922), by Arthur M. Schlesinger; *The First Freedom* (1946), by Morris L. Ernst; and *The Phantom Public* (1925), by

Walter Lippmann. William Sloane Associates, Publishers, *Human Fertility* (1951), by Robert C. Cook. W. W. Norton and Company, *The Frustration of Science* (1935), by Frederick Soddy, Editor. Yale University Press, *Sketches of Eighteenth Century America* (1925), by St. John de Crèvecoeur.

GEORGE S. COUNTS

New York, January 29, 1952

CONTENTS

Foreword by Stephen M. Corey		*v*
Preface and Acknowledgments		*ix*

Part One
EDUCATION BETWEEN ERAS

1	The Need for a Great Education	3
2	Education and Civilization	22

Part Two
OUR EARLY AMERICAN HERITAGE

3	A Child of the Modern Age	43
4	A Nation of Many Peoples	57
5	A Country of Common People	70
6	A Free Society of Farmers and Tradesmen	87
7	A Rich and Beautiful Land	104

Part Three
TOWARD A NEW CIVILIZATION

8	The Technological Revolution	127
9	New Modes of Livelihood	141
10	New Forms of Communication	156
11	New Vistas of Power	171

	Contents	
12	Old Minds in a New World	185

Part Four
OUR AMERICAN VALUES

13	Values and Choices	207
14	The Hebraic-Christian Ethic	220
15	The Humanistic Spirit	232
16	Science and Scientific Method	244
17	The Rule of Law	259
18	The Democratic Faith	278

Part Five
EDUCATION FOR THE EMERGING INDUSTRIAL AGE

19	The Resources for a Great Education	295
20	Education for Individual Excellence	311
21	Education for a Society of Equals	327
22	Education for a Government of Free Men	344
23	Education for an Economy of Security and Plenty	366
24	Education for a Civilization of Beauty and Grandeur	383
25	Education for an Enduring Civilization	399
26	Education for a World Community	413

Part Six
EDUCATION AND SOCIAL FORCES

27	The American Community	433
28	The American Teacher	451
	Index	475

IF A NATION EXPECTS TO BE IGNORANT AND FREE, IN A STATE OF CIVILIZATION, IT EXPECTS WHAT NEVER WAS AND NEVER WILL BE.

Thomas Jefferson

Part One

EDUCATION BETWEEN ERAS

1

THE NEED FOR A GREAT EDUCATION

1

We live today in deeply troubled times. For a generation now we in America have felt ourselves living in a world increasingly strange and even terrifying. We have known an endless succession of crises at home and abroad. We have watched tragedy compounding tragedy in ever-mounting fury. We have seen our seemingly well-founded hopes ground under the heel of events. The solid verities and certainties of the nineteenth century seem to have vanished. Nothing appears to be secure and enduring. Social institutions, human relations, value systems, and conceptions of life and destiny are in flux. Thoughtful men and women everywhere are anxious and fearful about the future. After a retreat of centuries despotism is on the march again.

We have experienced a great economic disaster at home. At the very moment when our political and industrial leaders confidently predicted an enduring and rising prosperity for an unlimited future under an economic system founded on the laws of nature, we were struck by an economic depression that rocked the foundations of the Republic. The marketing structure collapsed, banks, shops, and factories closed, farms turned backward toward self-sufficiency, wheels of transport stopped turning, lifetime savings were wiped out, twelve to fifteen million workers lost their jobs, the total national income was reduced by half, and rich and poor alike were gripped by fear. In response to the general distress revolutionary doctrines spread through the land and embryonic dictators on European models appeared in America. In spite of heroic measures taken by the federal government the crisis continued in more or less aggravated form down to the opening of the Second World War. This traumatic experience tempered somewhat the traditional optimism of the American democracy.

We have participated in two great wars beyond our borders in a single generation. In both cases the catastrophe was generally unforeseen by our people and found us unprepared both materially and spiritually for the struggle. In both cases we proclaimed our neutrality at the beginning and hoped to stand on the side lines and watch from afar the spectacle of the death grapple of nations. In the first of these wars we saw our young men die by thousands on the battlefields of Europe and in the surrounding seas. In the second we saw them die by tens of thousands in the most distant regions of the earth, on the land, in the air, and in the water, in the prison camps and on the death marches of Germany and Japan. After the end of the first conflict we resolved that never again would we be drawn into a struggle beyond the protecting oceans. Yet, the second war had scarcely started before we found ourselves deeply concerned over the outcome and threw our weight into the scales. In both we contributed without stint of our blood and treasure to the achievement of victory. In both also the might of our arms and industry probably decided the issue of battle. Today we fear the coming of a third war that might well destroy democratic civilization everywhere and push mankind as a whole back toward barbarism.

We have witnessed revolutions and counterrevolutions in both hemispheres. Indeed these violent social convulsions have followed one another so rapidly that only the student would dare attempt to list them. The ancient and autocratic systems of central and eastern Europe collapsed toward the close of the First World War. In Russia a revolution, unsurpassed in depth and scope, destroyed the old regime and proclaimed

The Need for a Great Education 5

itself the spearhead of a world-wide movement dedicated to "the forcible overthrow of all existing social conditions" and the establishment of the reign of socialism throughout the earth—a revolution against private property, the family, the church, and the national state. The response of the great capitalist powers, whether democratic or autocratic, was naturally fearful and hostile. A half-hearted effort was made to destroy the new Soviet state by force of arms. This failing, movements of a counterrevolutionary nature appeared in many countries and developed great strength wherever the revolutionary forces seriously threatened the existing order. Appealing to tradition, supported by privileged elements, and organizing the middle classes, these movements triumphed in Italy, Germany, Spain, and several other countries. Out of the revolutions and counterrevolutions of the period emerged the totalitarian state with its party dictatorship, its regimentation of the mind, its forced labor camps, and its ruthless suppression of all democratic liberties. We have seen millions of oppressed people turn with apparent enthusiasm to despotism as a way out of difficulty and insecurity. Indeed, we have seen frustrated and idealistic youth from our own midst enter the ranks of Soviet espionage and deliberately betray their native land.

We have witnessed a degeneration of morals and a calculated revival of barbarism. In the totalitarian states, whether Fascist or Communist, brute power has been used without mercy and without restraint to break the will of peoples and to convert the individual into an automaton. The glorification of the lie, the refinement of human torture, and the practice of political murder on a vast scale have been developed into powerful instruments of rule. The sadistic impulses of the degenerate have been harnessed to the aims of dictatorship. In the name of race superiority the systematic extermination of a great people has been attempted. It is estimated that in the course of the Second World War the German Nazis put to death five or six million Jews, simply because they were Jews. The horrors of Buchenwald, Dachau, and Auschwitz, though thoroughly documented, remain incredible. A

British parliamentary commission after visiting these camps reported with restraint and discrimination that they constituted the lowest point in moral degradation yet reached by the human race. And since the war the Soviet leaders have "liquidated" several minor nationalities by "resettlement" in other parts of the Union on the charge of having been insufficiently loyal during the war. They have also removed millions from the Baltic states and other territories along the western border. Thus they have followed the example of the Nazis in adding genocide to their arsenal of political weapons. And they seem to have surpassed their wartime adversary in the number of men and women condemned to forced labor.[1]

In the waging of war this process of moral degeneration seems to reach its climax. Our times have seen the development of the conception of total war—war in which there are no noncombatants, in which men, women, and children are all engaged, in which merchant ships are sunk without warning and whole cities are reduced to rubble and lacerated flesh by a deluge of bombs from the sky. Our times have also seen the revival of the conception of unlimited war—war designed so to weaken and mutilate a people that it "may never rise again." To the Nazi dictatorship or the Japanese military caste a war should be decisive in the ultimate sense, in the sense that it should never have to be waged twice, in the sense that ancient Rome concluded her third war with Carthage— *Delenda est Carthago*. The conception of a common humanity is regarded as a form of weakness. Perhaps the greatest tragedy of our tragic age is the fact that the godlike power of the machine, fruit of our highest genius, has been turned to death and destruction. And we are now feverishly engaged in the creation of the "hell-bomb"—a bomb calculated to possess when "perfected" one thousand times the destructive might of the atomic bomb dropped on Hiroshima and Nagasaki. That this suicidal madness of mankind can be halted before the final plunge into the abyss can scarcely be taken for granted today.

[1] See Victor Gollancz, *Our Threatened Values* (London, 1946).

2

We have come to the end of an era.
All peoples are living in a period of most profound social and cultural transition. We in America have come to the end of an age that began with the first settlements along the Atlantic seaboard in the early decades of the seventeenth century. Even the great events that attended first the founding and later the preservation of the Republic were less disturbing and explosive than those that beat upon us today. Both in our domestic affairs and in our relations with the rest of the world we are confronted with new conditions, new dangers, and new possibilities. "The decade of the nineties," writes Henry Steele Commager, "is the watershed of American history"—a watershed between an "America predominantly agricultural" and an "America, predominantly urban and industrial."[2]

With great reluctance and many misgivings we seem to be abandoning our traditional policy of national isolation. Although we were never isolated in any complete sense from the Old World, the great oceans east and west served for almost three centuries as powerful barriers against successful aggression from Europe and Asia. In his Farewell Address in 1796 Washington warned against forming "permanent alliances with any portion of the foreign world" and entangling "our peace and prosperity in the toils of European ambition, rivalship, interest, humor, or caprice." A little more than a generation later Alexis de Tocqueville placed second among the ten "causes" of the success of our democracy "geographical position"—"no neighbors." For a century thereafter we nurtured and cherished the faith that, if we but cultivated our own garden, we could live in safety behind the ramparts provided by nature. As George F. Kennan has said in his thoughtful survey of our foreign policy since 1900, "a half-century ago people in this country had a sense of security vis-à-vis their world environment such as I suppose no people

[2] Henry Steele Commager, *The American Mind* (New Haven, 1950), p. 41.

had ever had since the days of the Roman Empire."[3] But the conquests of space, accompanied by an ever-growing physical integration of the world, have gradually undermined the historical foundations of the policy of isolation. At the end of the nineteenth century, as a phase of the struggle with Spain, we seized by force of arms island territories on the far side of the globe. In 1917 and again in 1941 we were drawn into world conflicts against our hopes and expectations. Our decision in 1945 to join a world organization of nations appears to have put the final seal on the epoch that opened in the early years of the seventeenth century. Today we are exposed to every storm that sweeps the earth.

We have become the first power on the planet. We began our national career one hundred and seventy years ago as a feeble outpost of European civilization. The great military states of the Old World were little concerned over our policies and actions. Our weight in the affairs of nations, except as they might involve the fate of North America, was not seriously regarded. Today we stand before the world as the mightiest state of all history. The total production of American industry equals approximately that of the rest of the world. Our output of munitions of war following Pearl Harbor was fantastic and made us in truth "the arsenal of democracy." Without it the Axis powers would never have been vanquished and the whole earth might have fallen under the domination of military tyranny. Our power is so great that what we do or fail to do will affect profoundly the course of history during the critical years ahead. Without our agriculture millions will die who otherwise would live. Without our trade based on full production the economy of the world will be depressed. Without our technical assistance industrially backward countries will be retarded in their efforts to raise standards of living. Without our vigorous, sustained, and informed support the world organization now in its infancy is certain to perish. Whether we like it or not, we are being cast by history in the role of the foremost guardian of the heritage of human freedom in the present epoch. Unfortu-

[3] George F. Kennan, *American Diplomacy 1900–1950* (Chicago, 1951), p. 3.

The Need for a Great Education 9

nately, our understanding and sense of responsibility still lag behind our strength.[4]

We have conquered the problem of producing goods and services. For the first time in history, here on the continent of North America, man is technically capable of producing in abundance all things necessary to a life of material happiness. This is no longer a matter of speculation and wishful thinking.

Beginning in 1921 with a report entitled *Waste in Industry*, prepared by a committee of the Federated American Engineering Societies, a number of careful studies of the productive capacity of our economy were made by competent scholars during the period between the wars. All of these studies showed that our actual production, even in the most prosperous years, fell far below what was technically possible. It remained for the Second World War, however, to demonstrate the truth of the most optimistic conclusions of the investigators. The opening of the conflict found us still struggling with the depression which had started ten years before. But as orders for war goods poured in, first from foreign governments and then from our own, idle men and machines were put to work, new plants were built, and the production rate rose rapidly to fantastic heights. By 1944, with some twelve million of our most vigorous men and women engaged in the military services, the total production was vastly greater than that of the best peacetime years. Fred M. Vinson, as he wrestled with problems of the post-war economy, observed that the American people face the "predicament" of having to live fifty per cent better than ever before. Man's ancient dream of a world of material abundance is now within our grasp, if we can only solve successfully the social and political problems of peace and distribution. Today our total national income stands at approximately three hundred billion dollars annually.

We are entering a new age in our history and in the history of mankind. The crises, wars, and revolutions of our time, as well as the conquests of space, the advance of the

[4] See Hanson W. Baldwin, *The Price of Power* (New York, 1947).

machine, and the fabulous power of our economy, are for the most part but evidences of the release of mighty new forces that are transforming the very foundations of our existence —science and technology. These new forces, operating in the context of inherited ideas, institutions, and practices, are carrying us swiftly either from one order of civilization to another or to catastrophe. Already they have changed beyond recognition the material bases of our old way of life. We must assume that in the course of time they will affect profoundly our entire civilization, even our moral ideas, our view of the universe, and our conception of human destiny.

Our troubles are due largely to the fact that the times are out-of-joint. We stand between two civilizations—one that is passing away and another that is in birth. We stand between the agrarian and mercantile civilization of our ancestors and a strange and as yet undefined industrial civilization in which our children will live. It was in the former, with its small enterprises, its great distances, its little neighborhoods, its face-to-face relationships, its dependence on human energy, and its economy of scarcity that our social ideas and institutions were molded. Our minds, formed largely in the earlier age, are scarcely equipped to perform the heavy creative, organizing, and managerial labors which the march of events has thrust upon us. We are not yet prepared intellectually and morally to live in an age in which science and technology seem to be moving inexorably from one department of life to another. Our old self-contained agrarian civilization has been annihilated, but the sense of that civilization persists in the minds of our people. As the distinguished English archaeologist, Stanley Casson, observed fifteen years ago in his review of the long human adventure: "When his practical inventiveness ran ahead of his moral consciousness and social organization, then man has equally faced destruction. Perhaps today we are in this stage."[5]

The nature of this new industrial civilization, its imperatives and possibilities, will be treated in later chapters. It

[5] Stanley Casson, *Progress and Catastrophe* (London and New York, 1937), p. 19.

must suffice here to stress the magnitude of the task before us. We of the present and the immediately succeeding generation must decide what elements of our heritage can and should be preserved in the new world that is taking shape in our time. Some of those elements will have to go, simply because they cannot live under the strange conditions of industrial civilization. Others, the product of ignorance, bigotry, and brute power, we would like to abandon and forget. Then there are others, the fruit of centuries of toil and struggle, of thought and aspiration, which are beyond price and constitute the very essence of humane and civilized life. How to preserve these is a major task of our generation. But as we regard our heritage with an appraising eye we must also set our faces resolutely toward the future and grapple fearlessly and imaginatively with the problems of the new age.

The task of coming to terms with the advancing forces of industrial civilization is urgent. Time does not wait. The process of change, shaken by ever-deepening crisis, moves with bewildering speed. Before learning how to live well in our yesterdays we find ourselves thrust ineluctably into our todays and tomorrows. Also, we in America must realize, as we have never realized before, that we do not inhabit the earth alone. For more than a generation now the entire world has been in a deeply disturbed condition. The old order, the order of the eighteenth and nineteenth centuries, is passing away. Powerful revolutionary and counterrevolutionary movements, as we have noted, have been engaged in a ruthless struggle for mastery. The recent war itself was a phase of this struggle. But our troubles continue even though the Axis powers were vanquished six years ago. In fact the whole free world today confronts an adversary far surpassing in potential might the combined strength of Germany, Italy, and Japan, equally aggressive and probably more patient and determined. Also it faces anew the conditions out of which dictatorship came, and will come if those conditions are allowed to persist. In their relations with the East the free peoples of the West are today reaping the bitter harvest of the exploitation of the weak by the strong, for the weak are becoming strong. Unless those who love freedom also love justice and are prepared to move swiftly and surely to correct the mistakes of the past, they may find themselves outmaneuvered by Russian Communism, a resurgent Fascism, or some form of totalitarianism yet to appear. Already in some of the free states of Europe the elections suggest that peoples may follow again the disastrous course of the period between the wars, forsaking the ways of liberty and seeking security in the promises of the extreme "left" or those of the extreme "right."

3

We are challenged today by the rise of "popular despotisms."

Our priceless heritage of individual liberty and our tradition of popular rule through democratic processes are in grave peril. The threat comes from deep-seated troubles throughout the world and from competing conceptions of life and society thrown up by revolutionary and counter-revolutionary movements of the age. Our social and political system, to be sure, aroused from the day of its birth the hostility of the autocracies and despotisms of the Old World. But we generally regarded these adversaries as survivals from the past and destined to be swept aside by the spread of enlightenment and the irresistible struggle for the emancipation of the human race. America was the "haven of refuge" for the oppressed and the "land of the free" for all who could reach her shores. We were certain that history itself was working on our side and that our political ideas in their essence would triumph everywhere. For generations this view was widely shared by exploited classes and idealistic elements of the countries of Europe.

With the opening of the twentieth century those hopes appeared to be on the way to fulfillment. Autocratic and despotic governments were increasingly on the defensive. In the Orient, as well as in the Americas and Europe, monarchs

The Need for a Great Education 13

were being overthrown or shorn of their powers, republican institutions were being established, and popular rights and liberties were being guaranteed by the laws. Human freedom seemed clearly to be on the road to universal victory. Consequently, at least to most Americans, the crumbling of the Romanov, Hapsburg, and Hohenzollern dynasties toward the end of the First World War demonstrated that the conflict had been in reality a "war to make the world safe for democracy." Few indeed foresaw that amid the ruins of these ancient autocracies would arise new despotisms which would far surpass in tyranny the regimes they displaced.

The optimism of the early years of the present century was clearly expressed by J. B. Bury in his *A History of Freedom of Thought*, published in 1913. Near the close of this volume the noted English historian and political philosopher put into words the prevailing sentiment of the wise and good men of his age. "The struggle of reason against authority," he wrote, "has ended in what appears now to be a decisive and permanent victory for liberty. In the most civilized and progressive countries, freedom of discussion is recognized as a fundamental principle."[6] William C. Bullitt looking backward in 1946 pointed to the "early morning atmosphere in which men lived in that age which is separated from today by so few years but by such mountainous and disastrous events." After noting the abolition of human slavery and the general advance of free institutions, he observed: "Mutual trust was so great among civilized nations that passports were not required anywhere in the world except in four backward countries: Russia, Turkey, Bulgaria and Japan. Barriers to international trade were low, and currency restrictions did not exist. Five European nations, France, Belgium, Switzerland, Italy and Greece, indeed, had made their coined monies interchangeable."[7]

At the time, men were living in the afterglow of the hopes of the nineteenth century, and the great convulsions which

---

[6] J. B. Bury, *A History of Freedom of Thought* (London and New York, 1913), pp. 247–248.
[7] William C. Bullitt, *The Great Globe Itself* (New York, 1946), pp. 163, 164.

were to make a shambles of the world lay in the future. The First World War and the Second were scarcely remote possibilities, the term "Bolshevik" was known only to a small circle of revolutionaries, and the word "Fascism" was yet to be coined. Reasonable men could still affirm the faith expressed by Victor Hugo in an address at the Workmen's Congress in Marseilles in 1879: "In the twentieth century war will be dead, the scaffold will be dead, hatred will be dead, royalty will be dead, frontier boundaries will be dead, dogmas will be dead; man will live. He will possess something higher than all these—a great country, the whole earth, and a great hope, the whole heaven. . . . Let us salute it, this beautiful twentieth century which will possess our children, which our children will possess."[8]

When the long-expected Russian revolution broke in March, 1917, the entire free world rejoiced. In those days, before the contemporary totalitarian state had appeared in any one of its several forms, we assumed without question that the Russian people would inevitably establish a regime of popular rule based on constitutional guarantees. Even after the Provisional Government was overthrown and the Constituent Assembly dispersed by force of arms in November, 1917, and January, 1918, few could foresee that the Bolsheviks were destined to continue and even strengthen the harshest traditions of Russian absolutism. We were still comforted by the illusion of our childhood that human liberty was advancing everywhere and that all roads were leading to democracy.

Under the banners of the Marxian doctrines of international revolutionary socialism the Bolsheviks proclaimed that they and they alone were destined to bring salvation to mankind. And on those banners they inscribed the great promises of Marxism which millions in this age crave to hear—the promise of the abolition of the exploitation of man by man through the establishment of socialism, the promise of the abolition of the exploitation of one race or people by another

[8] Frances A. Shaw, *Victor Hugo; His Life and Works*, from the French of Alfred Barbou (Chicago, 1881), p. 191.

The Need for a Great Education 15

through the triumph of the "workers of the world," and the promise of the abolition of war through the overthrow of capitalism and the launching of a universal republic of labor.

Professedly to achieve these goals they established an all-embracing and ruthless dictatorship at home, launched the Third International abroad, declared war on the "system of capitalism" throughout the earth, and proclaimed the imminence of the world revolution. The immediate response in a number of countries, as we have noted, was a counterrevolutionary movement which went by various names—Fascism, National Socialism, Falangism, or some other—and which borrowed heavily from the methods and morals of Bolshevism. The result was the Second World War, which destroyed the counterrevolutionary foes of the Russian Communists and left the "men of the Kremlin" in a vastly strengthened position.

In the meantime, under the impact of domestic and world forces and under the iron dictatorship of Stalin, Communism itself has moved far from its revolutionary professions. Beginning as an international movement with headquarters in Moscow, it has become wholly a Russian movement with branches and agents in other countries. Today it constitutes a strange synthesis of Marxian philosophy, Russian expansionism, Russian absolutism, Russian Messianism, and Russian revolutionary doctrines. In a word, the members of the Soviet oligarchy see the spread of Communism over the earth under the inspired direction of Moscow and through the extension of Russian power. Like the Slavophils of the nineteenth century, they believe that Great Russia is destined to bring salvation to all mankind. And this is to be done under the charismatic leadership of Stalin—the "leader of the toiling masses" of the earth and the "greatest man of all ages." Their unparalleled triumphs during and following the war in extending their dominion in Europe and Asia confirm these men in their doctrines. They are profoundly convinced that, in the words of Molotov, "all roads today lead to Communism." They know that the future belongs to them, "despite all."

We must realize that we are faced with a fact and not a theory. The liberal and democratic forces of the world are under relentless and pitiless attack by a small band of men who within a single generation have extended their sway over approximately one-third of the human race and who believe with the dogmatism of religious conviction that the invincible forces of history are working on their side. Through the All-Union Communist Party, organized like a political army and assisted by the Communist Parties of other countries, the high-command in Moscow rules the Soviet peoples and directs the struggle to vanquish the free nations of the earth. The fact that Stalin and his associates appeal for support in terms of the "great promises" of the revolution still deceives millions in many parts of the world. Yet the evidence is long since conclusive that Russian Communism is profoundly reactionary in essence and is now engaged in an imperialistic drive that dwarfs the imperialisms of the eighteenth and nineteenth centuries. Wherever it goes it destroys the last vestige of individual freedom and subjects men to a tyranny far more terrifying than that of the worst of the tsars. So long as Communism continues on its present aggressive course, free men can breathe easily nowhere in the world.

Bertrand Russell, one of the clearest minds of our time and a close student of the course of Soviet policy since 1917, has recently endeavored to forecast the condition of man following a universal triumph of Soviet power. The glorious achievements in economy, government, education, and science during the past several centuries of Western liberalism and humanism, he writes, "will come to an end." He then proceeds to draw the following picture: "There will be in every part of the world abject poverty, except for a small clique of rulers. There will be despotism and slavery and forced labor. There will be cruelty on a scale never known before. Men of exceptional excellence, whether intellectual or moral, will, with a few exceptions, be extirpated. Mental life will be weighed down by a vast cope of rigid dogma. The bright hopes of our time will be extinguished in a dark night of obscurantism and large-scale torture. It is this issue

The Need for a Great Education   17

which our age has to face."⁹ The picture may be overdrawn. Yet no wise champion of human freedom will assume it to be so and thus still his conscience and set his mind to rest. Rather will he turn to the pages of George Orwell's *Nineteen Eighty-Four*[10] and get a view of what might transpire in the coming years, if the trend of our times should continue.

He might also read the testimony of an American businessman, Robert A. Vogeler, who was arrested in Budapest in 1949, charged with espionage, and subjected to torture and solitary confinement for seventeen months. At the time of his release he was a broken man, incapable of giving a rational account of his experiences. After a period of recuperation in a hospital he thus explained "in low, halting speech" his confession to acts he had never committed: "You can see readily that the incessant questioning, the unremitting pressure, the malnutrition, the copious stimulants, the screaming, shouting, the dead silences, the cold and all the other hardships are designed to force one to say not truth but what they wish to call the truth. The mind, the spirit and the body are attacked over and over again until the will is slowly ground away. The very body is forced into league against one's personality."[11]

4

We face great tasks in the coming years and decades.
We can see clearly now that the winning of the recent war merely gave men another opportunity for removing the conditions out of which war and tyranny came. A new world is being born; a new civilization is being built. This we know. But that the new world and the new civilization will be better than the old is far from certain. All we can be sure of is that we shall have another opportunity to make them so. If we fail, as we did during the period between the wars, a generation hence men

---
[9] *The New York Times*, Magazine Section, Sunday, May 6, 1951, p. 7.
[10] George Orwell, *Nineteen Eighty-Four* (New York, 1949).
[11] *The New York Times*, June 9, 1951, p. 6.

of humane and liberal outlook, if such survive, may look back wistfully to the nineteenth as the most glorious and civilized of all the centuries. The performance of several great labors is clearly imperative.

We must achieve a just and durable peace. The world has become so small and the nations so closely bound together that no single country, however powerful, can stand apart from a general conflict. The fate of each has become linked with the fate of all. War and peace alike have become indivisible. The material and moral costs of war have become unbearable. The conflict recently ended destroyed more than a trillion dollars in goods and services and between forty and fifty million human lives. It also blasted the hopes and maimed the bodies and souls of uncounted multitudes. Another war in a decade or two, after the engines of death now in embryo are fully matured, might well usher in the darkest age of history. Through the United Nations the peoples of the world are taking the first faltering steps toward the creation of a world organization capable of establishing and maintaining peace with justice on the earth. But if this organization is to be successful it must achieve sufficient moral support, military strength, and efficiency of operation to halt even the most powerful aggressor. It must also possess the resources to assist underdeveloped countries in raising their standards of living, achieving economic security, and gaining political independence. The American people, because of their great strength, probably have a heavier responsibility than any other for making this daring venture successful. Possibly the fateful decision to oppose aggression in Korea may prove to be the great divide in human history that marks the transition from the age of war to the age of peace. But even if this should prove to be true, the struggle to build a world community of equal peoples will be long and difficult.

We must fashion at home a stable economy capable of bringing opportunity, security, and well-being to all. That the tyrannies of Europe and the great war itself came in part out of the economic miseries of the people can scarcely be questioned. If we should fail to solve our own economic problems, if we should experience another great depression, comparable in scope and depth to that of the nineteen-thirties, we would encourage the advance of Communism in the world, and we might even witness the raising of the banners of the crooked cross here in America. Whenever millions of ordinary people lose faith in their institutions, experience a deep sense of insecurity and frustration, feel uncertain, anxious, and fearful about the future, the way is open for the rise to power of the contemporary totalitarian dictator. That even our democracy, strong and deeply rooted in our history as it is, would weather another all-embracing economic storm certainly should not be taken for granted.

We must preserve and strengthen the great tradition of political liberty. The importance and urgency of this question can hardly be overemphasized. "Although political freedom is not the only type of freedom in culture," writes the celebrated anthropologist, Bronislaw Malinowski, "yet its absence destroys all other liberties."[12] Fundamental to the achievement of our goal is of course the establishment of a stable economy and the maintenance of full employment and full production. But far more is demanded. We know that full employment and full production of a kind may be accompanied or even achieved by political tyranny. In Russia there has been no general unemployment for many years, and in Germany under Hitler all the people were put to work. Such considerations have led some to contend that in the industrial age a stable economy can be established only by dictatorship and that widespread economic insecurity is a necessary condition of political liberty. This of course is a thoroughly unenlightened position and, if supported indefinitely, is certain to lead to disaster. Indeed, it is a proposal to surrender before the battle. The experience of our times shows that if men are forced to choose between jobs and political liberty, many will choose jobs, or even the promise of jobs. The historic task of our people in the present age is to demonstrate that economic stability can be achieved under a regime of political liberty. Nothing less than the fate of

[12] Bronislaw Malinowski, *Freedom and Civilization* (New York, 1944), p. 15.

our democracy hangs in the balance. We must therefore be always on our guard against every proposal either to achieve economic stability or to protect political liberty by resort to totalitarian methods.

We must extend the benefits of our democracy to all of our people. In our origins we are a country of many races, nations, and religions. To our shores have come immigrants from all the continents and from many of the islands of the sea. We know that some of these ethnic groups, particularly the Indians, the Negroes, the Jews, the Orientals, and recent arrivals generally, live under severe disabilities. Some of them are the objects of prejudice, hatred, contempt, and discrimination. To the extent that this condition exists we are weakened both at home and abroad, our full human resources are not developed, and the political adventurer will be able to divide and conquer. Also we shall be unable to stand before the nations and fight in good conscience for the principles of justice in the world. To the oppressed and underprivileged, the colored and colonial peoples beyond our borders, our actions in our own country will overwhelm our words in international councils. Still more important perhaps is the influence of our behavior on ourselves. As long as we practice the doctrine of racial, national, or religious superiority, our democracy will be corrupted at the core. We shall know in our hearts that we are false to our professions.

We must strive to improve the quality of living in America. Peace and work, liberty and equality are vastly important today, as always. But they fail to comprehend the full task before us. In a sense they provide for the most part the conditions for the achievement of a rich and good life for the individual, for the development of a civilization of beauty and grandeur. It would be one of the tragedies of history if the mastery of the art of producing and exchanging goods should be attended by a degradation of the art of living. Our economic conquests should provide the material foundation for the flowering of the human spirit in the simple relationships of life, in the conduct of our common affairs, in the architecture of community and nation, in the realm of science and thought, and in all the great arts of expression and communication. Only with such a generous and humanistic conception will our democracy fulfill itself.

5

We must develop an education equal to these great tasks.
That such tasks cannot be accomplished by education alone is of course readily granted. Yet it is equally evident that they will never be accomplished without the assistance which organized education can provide. The time calls for greatness in every department of life. It calls for the highest qualities of character in our leadership and in ourselves as a people. It calls for understanding, for courage, for wisdom, for tolerance and charity on the part of all groups and classes. It calls upon us to display in the waging of peace the resourcefulness, the energy, the steadfastness, the devotion to the common good that enabled us with our valiant associates among the United Nations to wage and win the most terrible and destructive of wars. It calls for a militant faith in democracy and human freedom that surpasses in its power the faith of any totalitarian system. It calls upon us to eschew alike the moods of panic and complacency and to live on a higher plane of understanding and conscience than ever before in our history. All of this means that the present age calls for a great education, for an education liberally and nobly conceived, for an education directed toward the accomplishment of the heavy tasks before us, for an education that expresses boldly and imaginatively the full promise and the full strength of America in her historical and world setting.

2

EDUCATION AND CIVILIZATION

1

We have great faith in the power and beneficence of education.

From early times we have identified education with the advance of civilization. During colonial days, even as we struggled to survive in a strange land, we nurtured this faith. The founders of the Republic, under the influence of the revolutionary thought of the age in both Europe and America, believed that the strength of the new nation would depend on the spread of learning and enlightenment. "If the condition of man is to be progressively ameliorated, as we fondly hope and believe," wrote Thomas Jefferson, father of American democracy, in 1818, "education is to be the chief instrument in effecting it." The great champions of popular liberty throughout our national history have generally insisted that the survival of free institutions requires an educated people. Horace Mann, father of the common school, expressed the sentiments of generations of Americans when he said: "The Common School is the greatest discovery ever made by man." When confronted with difficult personal or social problems in the present critical epoch, we are inclined to turn to education as an unfailing solution. And today American educators would carry this faith round the globe through UNESCO. If illuminated with understanding and applied with wisdom, it should constitute a powerful resource in the current struggle for a free and peaceful world.

Students of our civilization, both native and foreign, have remarked this faith. William Graham Sumner once referred to it as a "superstition of the age."[1] Clark Wissler included "mass education" among the three "dominant characteristics of our culture."[2] The great Frenchman, Alexis de Tocqueville, perhaps the most brilliant and penetrating student of our institutions from beyond the Atlantic, observed in 1831 that "the universal and sincere faith that they profess here in the efficaciousness of education seems to me one of the most remarkable features of America."[3] Although he did not share fully this faith himself, he did list the "diffusion of *useful* education" among ten factors contributing to the success of democracy in America a hundred and twenty years ago.

Our historic faith in education has been translated into vigorous and sustained action. In 1837 Francis J. Grund, a Bohemian-born and Austrian-educated American writer, observed that "with the exception of Protestant Germany, there is no country in which so much has been done for the education of children, as in the United States of America."[4] During the succeeding century we developed a comprehensive system of public schools which has challenged and influenced the educational thought and practice of the Old World. In our justly celebrated "educational ladder" we repudiated the European aristocratic idea of separate schools for the "classes" and the "masses" and established the principle of a single educational system for all the people. Reaching from the kindergarten to the graduate and professional faculties of the university and designed to shatter the time-honored social barriers to advanced training, it is one of the finest and most distinctive expressions of our democracy. Although the measures adopted have by no means overcome differences in family income and circumstance or fully equalized educational opportunities at the higher levels, our secondary schools and

[1] William Graham Sumner, *Folkways* (Boston, 1906), p. 629.
[2] Clark Wissler, *Man and Culture* (New York, 1923), p. 5.
[3] George Wilson Pierson, *Tocqueville and Beaumont in America* (New York, 1938), p. 453.
[4] Francis J. Grund, *The Americans, in Their Moral, Social, and Political Relations* (Boston, 1837), p. 124.

colleges enroll more young people from fourteen to twenty-two years of age than the corresponding institutions of all the rest of the world. Moreover, wherever the system of rigid social classes is rejected our American "educational ladder" is welcomed. The contribution to our democracy of this vast network of schools can scarcely be overemphasized. If they were to be closed for a generation, our entire social system would collapse and we would be forced back to some relatively primitive and simple mode of life. The war demonstrated beyond question the high quality of the work of the schools. The criticism of our education which was so widespread and vocal during the early months of the struggle, it is interesting to note, practically disappeared before the day of military victory. It disappeared because our young people on both home and battle fronts gave an extraordinarily good account of themselves. Though not prepared for the great ordeal through which they were destined to pass, they exhibited an adaptability, a capacity for learning and understanding, a power to endure and face hardship and danger unsurpassed by any earlier American generation. Nothing said anywhere in this volume, therefore, should be interpreted as a general condemnation of our educational system or of our faith in education. Our schools, with all their deficiencies, constitute one of the glories of our Republic.

2

Our faith in education has been uncritical and immature.
As a people we have rarely, if ever, inquired deeply into the social, moral, and cultural foundations of education. We have failed to give sufficient thought to the diversity of educational conceptions in history and the contemporary world. We have equated education with enlightenment and even book learning. We have assumed it to be something that goes on more or less naturally in the school and is good in any quantity for the ills

besetting mankind. We have assumed further that in essence it is a single thing, everywhere the same, governed by its own laws, feared by despotisms, and loved by free peoples. We have tended to identify it with democracy and human progress, not sensing clearly and positively that there is an appropriate form of education for every society or civilization and that a form which is suited to one may destroy another. Long ago we could have read and pondered with profit the sage observation of Montesquieu "that the laws of education ought to be in relation to the principles of government."[5]

The failure on the part of the American people to realize fully that their great experiment in popular rule demanded a peculiar kind of education alarmed a distinguished Scotch scholar and traveler, George Combe, who came to the United States in the autumn of 1838 and remained with us for more than a year and a half, lecturing in almost every community of any size in the country. He was a devoted friend of our growing democracy and wished us well. He was one of the few visitors from Europe who were interested in both our political system and our educational program. He saw clearly that such a system, if it was to prosper, required "a vastly improved education to render" the people "equal to the faithful and successful discharge of the important duties committed to them by the institutions of the States and of the Federal Government." He referred again and again to the deficiencies in our education. "I have seen men of sense and understanding," he wrote, "regard my views as obviously Utopian and absurd, when I ventured to express the opinion that both the quantity and quality of instruction communicated in the common schools of the United States, and even in Boston, is fitted much more for a government like that of Austria, than for that of the United States!"[6] He knew Horace Mann well and felt that even this great educational leader failed to grasp the essence of the problem. While

---
[5] Charles de Secondat Montesquieu, *The Spirit of Laws*, J. V. Prichard, Ed. (London, 1902), Vol. I, p. 31.
[6] George Combe, *Notes on the United States of North America* (Edinburgh, 1841), Vol. III, p. 418, Vol. I, p. 162.

our education has been greatly increased in quantity and improved in quality since George Combe's sojourn among us, it is unlikely that, in view of the profound changes in our society and civilization, he would appreciably soften his indictment if he were to visit us today.

Our uncritical attitude may have had a certain justification in the nineteenth century when, with a single exception, despotic states opposed the founding of schools in order "to keep their people in ignorance." The case of Prussia was conveniently disposed of as "the exception that proves the rule." But the rise of the contemporary totalitarian systems, of the "popular despotisms" of the twentieth century, has made imperative a critical examination of our historic conceptions. These systems have equaled or surpassed the democracies in their devotion to and support of organized education. We should know now that literacy, earlier regarded as a reliable index of enlightenment, may be an instrument through which a controlled press may enslave a whole people. We should know also that the level of civilization cannot be measured by the number of schools and other agencies for teaching the young established and maintained by a society. Germany under the Nazis and Japan under the military caste were among the most literate and well-schooled lands on the face of the earth. Our traditional faith in education as a liberator of mankind is justified only if education is carefully and effectively directed toward such a purpose.

3

Education may be the handmaiden of freedom or tyranny.
An unvarnished account of the role of organized education in history from the age of pre-literate man to the middle of the twentieth century fails utterly to support our traditional faith in the general beneficence of schools and other agencies for the rearing of the young. The period between the great wars of our generation is particularly illuminating in this respect. The record

should teach us that only an education devised to serve beneficent ends can ever be beneficent.

In *The Outline of History*, published in 1920, H. G. Wells, one of the prophets of our time, declared that "human history becomes more and more a race between education and catastrophe."[7] During the nineteen-twenties this statement was probably quoted more widely with approval by American educators than any other. It was clearly in accord with our traditional faith. Early in 1939 Wells observed that catastrophe was "well on its way," that education seemed "unable to get started," that indeed it had not even "readjusted itself to start." He concluded with the dismal thought that "the race may, after all, prove a walk-over for disaster."[8]

We know today that catastrophe triumphed, and with terrifying swiftness. Yet that it was a race between education and catastrophe is true only with qualifications, as Mr. Wells himself perhaps would have been among the first to admit. The years between the wars witnessed an unprecedented expansion of organized education in the world, of schools and colleges and other agencies for informing and molding the mind. In fact, never before had the problem of rearing the young and instructing the old received so much attention from the heads of government and the leaders of society. Here in the United States the number of students attending secondary schools increased from 2,500,000 in 1920 to 6,925,000 in 1940, while the enrollment in higher schools advanced from 750,000 to 1,800,000. During the same period Soviet Russia probably directed a larger *proportion* of the total national income to the support of education than any other country in history. The number of young and old attending schools and classes of all grades and types advanced from eight or nine millions to probably thirty-five or forty millions. Following the Revolution and particularly after launching the First Five-Year Plan in 1928 the Soviet leaders conducted the most comprehensive campaign ever attempted to wipe out illiteracy. And the entire cultural apparatus, including the press,

[7] H. G. Wells, *The Outline of History* (New York, 1920), p. 608.
[8] H. G. Wells, *The Fate of Man* (New York, 1939), p. 84.

the radio, the theater, the movie, and even the circus, was directed toward the achievement of educational purposes. The Axis powers—Germany, Italy, and Japan—spent enormous sums on education and gave as close attention to shaping the minds of children and youth as to the reconstruction of the economy and the building of the armed forces. In many other countries it was an era of educational expansion.

The fact is that the race was not between education and catastrophe. To a very large degree education was actually the handmaiden or midwife of catastrophe. This was obviously and avowedly true in the case of the totalitarian states. Children were taught in Italy that the time had come to restore the Roman Empire, that "it is better to live a day as a lion than a thousand years as a lamb"; in Germany that the Nordic race is immeasurably superior to all others, that the soil of the Ukraine, the minerals of the Urals, and the forests of Siberia should really belong to the Third Reich, that only in war does man fulfill his highest destiny; in Japan that the Japanese are the chosen people of God, that they should rightly covet the orange groves of California, that death in battle for the glory of the Son of Heaven is the most exalted purpose in life. In the Soviet Union the schools were employed to foster the class struggle, to misrepresent the social institutions of other nations, and to propagate the doctrine that Russia was the spearhead of a world revolution which in time would spread to all countries and overthrow the existing order everywhere. At the same time no free society anywhere confronted the problem boldly and imaginatively. In the United States, educational agencies, besides teaching by example, if not by precept, the superiority of the white peoples and the sanctity of the system of private capitalism, were busily engaged in preparing the young to struggle for individual material success and to live in a world that had passed away. Throughout the earth education, either deliberately or unwittingly, helped to bring upon mankind the disasters that all but destroyed the best in our civilization. At the very least, it was not designed, either in conception or in practice, to oppose the swift advance of catastrophe.

We know today, if we have learned the lesson of the immediate past, that organized education may or may not serve the cause of human progress. In fact, we know that it may serve any cause, that it may serve tyranny as well as freedom, ignorance as well as enlightenment, falsehood as well as truth, war as well as peace, death as well as life. It may lead men and women to think they are free even as it rivets upon them the chains of bondage. Education is indeed a force of great power, but whether it is good or bad depends, not on the laws of learning, but on the conception of life or civilization which it expresses.

4

Current proposals for educational reform are inadequate.

Our great interest in education has stimulated a vast amount of discussion, research, and experimentation throughout the period of our history as a nation. But because of our general and persistent failure to probe deeply into the nature of education as a moral and social undertaking, much of this activity has been relatively futile. Although we have developed a good education, an education of which we may be rightly proud, we have not developed a truly great education, an education which confronts the realities of the age, expresses the best in our heritage, and takes full advantage of our prospects. In education we have lived below the possibilities of our civilization.

During the current century, with the establishment of numerous teachers colleges and departments of education in our universities, we have devoted an enormous amount of energy to the improvement of education. Our literature, both lay and professional, is full of discussions of what is wrong with the school and of proposals to correct its weaknesses. The shelves of our libraries groan under the weight of educational reports, surveys, and studies. New theories and experiments follow one another in an endless stream. This activity is by no means all lost motion; it has undoubtedly resulted in very considerable improvement in the conduct of the school. Yet most of it deals with either the surface or the mechanics of the problem. Indeed, some of the most widely and hotly discussed proposals for reform during our generation are little more than nostrums which largely ignore the basic problem of all educational thought—the problem of the relation of education to the nature and fortunes of our civilization in its historical and world setting. Three such proposals have been prominently before us for some time.

The first proposal accepts the substance of the traditional program and concentrates on the concept of mechanical efficiency. The principles and philosophy of mass production, one of the truly magnificent products of American genius in the field of industry, are applied to the rearing of the young. The school system is regarded as a gigantic automobile assembly line which at the upper levels divides and subdivides in terms of desired models. It takes in the children as raw material at one end, passes them on from one teacher or workman to another, and finally turns them out as finished products, each leaving the school or factory freshly painted, under his own power, and hitting on all cylinders. Vast attention is of course given to the perfection of the machinery of education, to the integration of parts, and to the elimination of friction, to the improvement of buildings and equipment, to the standardization of procedures, to the invention of pedagogical gadgets, to the construction of tests and rating scales for both pupils and teachers, and to the keeping of records of all actions and transactions. Never in the history of education has so much paper been used to so little purpose.

This drive for mechanical efficiency has been unfortunate, not because efficiency is not desirable. The contrary is clearly the case. But efficiency is secondary to the ends that are to be served. It seems probable that the transference to education of a conception of operation developed in relation to the production of material things is a fundamental mistake. Unfortunately, moreover, many of the best minds of the profession have been engaged in the study of the mechanics of education at a time when the consideration of its substance has been

Education and Civilization 31

imperative. Primary concentration on school efficiency during a period of cultural crisis and transformation is both a form of escape and a way of compounding the troubles of the age.

The second proposal seeks guidance in the interests and problems of children. The presumption here seems to be that the child achieves maturity through a process of spontaneous generation or unfoldment which the adult world through its educational agencies should merely guard and nourish. According to this view the child, and not the teacher or the school, should play the decisive role in shaping both the processes and the ends of education. The interests and problems of boys and girls are assumed to constitute a more trustworthy guide than the experience and wisdom of their elders. It is argued, moreover, that any positive interference by members of the older generation is a form of imposition or indoctrination and is certain to lead to frustration. Here undoubtedly is the most romantic interpretation of human nature since Rousseau.

In the proposal, however, there is an important insight. It recognizes the psychological truth that interest is a condition of effective and economical learning. The immediate concerns of the young therefore should always play a large role in education. Like the learning process and the "laws of the organism" generally, they provide the limits within which the teacher must operate. But those limits are known to be extremely wide. We must assume, if we are faithful to the findings of science, that children in their biological inheritance are essentially the same in all times and places, among all races and peoples, among all groups and classes. Yet their interests vary greatly from epoch to epoch and from society to society. Also they are extraordinarily fluid. The interest that a child brings to school in the morning may be the result of the casual conversation of parents at home, of a radio program devised to sell a hair tonic, of a moving picture produced with an eye on the box office, or of some incident observed in the street or on the highway. The responsibility of the school is, not to follow the interests of the young, but rather to assist in arousing and building worthy and fruitful interests.

It should be recognized also that this proposal contains a great moral affirmation. In conformity with the democratic ethic, it affirms that the child is a person and that his personality should always be treated with respect and regarded as precious. The historical record of the treatment of the young by their elders is full of horrors. The liberation of boys and girls from the reign of adult tyranny and ignorance is one of the marks of a high civilization. Yet respect for the personality of the child is expressed most fully in an educational program designed to develop a mature personality deserving respect. "We see quite clearly," writes Bronislaw Malinowski, "why the freedom of the child, in the sense of letting him do what he wishes and as he likes, is unreal. In the interest of his own organism he has constantly to be trammeled in education from acts which are biologically dangerous, or which are culturally useless. His whims, his fits of idleness or disobedience must be gradually curtailed, formed, and translated into culturally relevant choices. There is also no freedom in action except within the context of organized human groups."[9]

The third proposal finds the solution of the educational problem in the study of the "one hundred great books" at the college level and in preparation for their study in the lower schools. It must be admitted at once that from the standpoint of the teacher this is the most attractive proposal now current. It is the ideal answer of the pedagogue to the truly vexing problems confronting education. In the first place, it would give him a virtual monopoly over a special body of knowledge. He would have no competitors. If he could only convince the other members of society of the worth of this knowledge, he would be in the enviable position of a long line of ancestors reaching back to the shaman and the medicine man of primitive society. In the second place, once having mastered the "great books" he could pursue his calling for the rest of his life without being disturbed by the issues

[9] Bronislaw Malinowski, *Freedom and Civilization* (New York, 1944), p. 145.

of depression and prosperity, of war and peace, of tyranny and freedom, of the future of civilization. He could withdraw from the world and dwell all his years in a scholastic paradise. He could be fairly sure, moreover, that only two or three books would be added in his lifetime, that their status would be uncertain for at least a century, and that anyway they could not equal those written by the "ancients" long ago.

The basic argument of the proposal seems to be that education is essentially a process of mental training, that the great literary classics are the finest product of the human mind, and that therefore they are the best tools for the development of the mind. As a matter of fact, education is far more than mental training: it is first of all a process of inducting the young into the ways, privileges, and responsibilities of a given society. Also, these classics, precious as they are, cannot be said without qualification to be the finest products of the human mind: they scarcely rank above a great living civilization, a system of democratic government, or even a fine person who possibly never read a single one of them. Likewise, that they are the best tools for the development of the mind is hardly supported either by the history of education or by psychological investigation. Experience suggests rather that this is the surest road man has yet discovered to formalism, sterility, and death in education. Although the proposal properly directs attention to certain sublime achievements of the mind of man, emphasizes the processes of thought and reflection, and stresses enduring and universal elements in the human heritage, it is fundamentally a manifestation of academic nostalgia. It constitutes an attempt to retire, without sacrifice of glory, from the present troubled age.

5

Education always expresses a conception of civilization.
Education can never be a purely autonomous process, independent of time and place and conducted according to its own laws. It is as much

an integral part of a civilization as an economic or a political system. The very way in which education is conceived, whether its purpose is to free or enslave the mind, is an expression of the civilization which it serves. The great differences in educational philosophy and practice from society to society are due primarily to differences in culture and civilization. Although all educational programs in the world today, including our own, should embrace the conception of a common humanity, no such program as a whole should be regarded as an article of export either with or without the support of dollars or machine guns.

Our American education has always expressed an interpretation of our civilization. Many foreign visitors from Alexis de Tocqueville to D. W. Brogan have dwelt at length on this fact. "There is probably no better place than a school-room," wrote Francis J. Grund more than a century ago, "to judge of the character of a people." He then proceeded to contrast American and German education as follows: "Who, upon entering an American school-room, and witnessing the continual exercises in reading and speaking, or listening to the subject of their discourses, and watching the behavior of the pupils towards each other and their teacher, could, for a moment, doubt his being amongst a congregation of young republicans? And who, on entering a German academy, would not be struck with the principle of authority and silence, which reflects the history of Germany for the last half dozen centuries? What difficulty has not an American teacher to maintain order amongst a dozen unruly little urchins; while a German rules over two hundred pupils in a class with all the ease and tranquillity of an Eastern monarch?" He concludes his discussion with the warning directed beyond the Atlantic that "it would only be necessary to conduct some doubting European politician to an American school-room, to convince him at once that there is no immediate prospect of transferring royalty to the shores of the New World."[10]

Sir Charles Lyell, lamenting the undisciplined character of American children, made a like observation: "Many young

[10] Grund, *op. cit.*, pp. 133–134.

Americans have been sent to school in Switzerland, and I have heard their teachers, who found them less manageable than English or Swiss boys, maintain that they must all of them have some dash of wild Indian blood in their veins. Englishmen, on the other hand, sometimes attribute the same character to republican institutions."[11]

Our education today expresses a conception of our civilization. This it does in spite of our heavy borrowings from other times and places, in spite of the lag behind the movement of events and conditions. It expresses a conception of our civilization, however partial or limited, in every part of its program—in its controlling purposes and in the extension or limitation of opportunities, in the architecture of the school and in the subjects of study, in the methods of instruction and in the forms of motivation, in the activities of the pupils and in their social relations, in the status of the teacher, in the patterns of administration, and in the relations of the school to the local community and the state. In similar fashion the education of every other country is seen to be a creature of its civilization. The more the civilization differs from our own the more obvious is this relationship.

It must be emphasized, however, that organized and deliberate education does not reflect a civilization. Nor is it derived automatically through a process of assembling and analyzing data. Always at the point where an educational program comes into being definite choices are made among many possibilities. And these choices are made, not by the gods or the laws of nature, but by men and women working both individually and collectively—by men and women who often do not quite know what they are doing—by men and women who are moved by all of those forces and considerations that move them in other realms of conduct, by their knowledge and understanding, their hopes and fears, their purposes and loyalties, their views of the world and human destiny. Presumably a given society at any time, therefore, might formulate and adopt any one of a number of educa-

[11] Charles Lyell, *A Second Visit to the United States of North America* (New York, 1849), Vol. II, p. 169.

tional conceptions or programs, each of which would obviously be an expression of a conception of its civilization. But each would also be stamped by the special qualities of the men and women who framed it. These men and women in turn would be authentic, though not exclusively authentic, products of their civilization.

The formulation of an educational program is thus a creative act, or rather a long series of complex creative acts. It is a threefold process embracing analysis, selection, and synthesis. It always involves choice among possibilities, and even decision as to what is possible. It likewise involves the affirmation of values and the framing of both individual and social purposes. Inevitably education conveys to the young responses to the most profound questions of life—questions of truth and falsehood, of beauty and ugliness, of good and evil. These affirmations may be expressed in what an education fails to do as well as in what it does, in what it rejects as well as in what it adopts. In its organized phases it is deliberately designed to make of both individual and society something which otherwise they would not and could not become. The launching of an educational undertaking is therefore a very serious business. It is one of the most vital and responsible forms of statesmanship. It throws whatever power it represents to the support of one rather than another conception of civilization. And in so doing it supports one rather than another conception of man.

6

A great education always expresses a great conception of civilization.

There is no quick and easy road to a great education. There is no simple device or formula for the achievement of this goal. Such an education cannot be derived from a study of the process itself, nor can it be found in the interests of children or in any number of "great books." It can come only from a bold and creative confronting of the nature, the values, the conditions, and the potentialities of a civilization. An education can rise no higher than the conception of civilization that pervades it, gives it substance, and determines its purpose and direction.

At this point the democracies are challenged by the totalitarian states and movements of our time. In each case the leadership has formulated a conception of life and destiny of great power and appeal. That the champions of human freedom cannot accept any one of them and must in fact repudiate them all is of course taken for granted. The Fascist conception of a master race or people destined to rule the world under a divinely appointed leader is too horrifying to contemplate. Likewise the Communist conception of a revolutionary elite dedicated to the task of liberating all oppressed peoples, through the medium of dictatorship and violence, terror and fraud, cannot satisfy us. But we should realize before it is too late that the totalitarian conceptions have shown themselves in our time to possess vast power to arouse and enlist the energies and loyalties of the young. If the democracies are to triumph in this struggle for the minds and hearts of men, they will be compelled to derive from their civilizations conceptions of equal power.

At no time in our history have we as a people recognized clearly the obvious and fundamental truth that a great education for America must express a great and authentic conception of our civilization. Individuals now and then, to be sure, have caught a glimpse of this truth. It was grasped most generally perhaps in the heroic period of our national history, in the later years of the eighteenth century that marked the launching of the Republic. The American Philosophical Society, founded in 1743 and led successively by Benjamin Franklin, David Rittenhouse, and Thomas Jefferson, offered a prize of one hundred dollars in 1796 for the best essay outlining a "System of liberal Education and literary instruction, adapted to the genius of the Government of the United States."[12] Some of the best minds in the country

[12] Samuel Knox, *An Essay on the Best System of Liberal Education, Adapted to the Genius of the Government of the United States* (Baltimore, 1799), p. 45.

took part in the contest. The essays presented were fresh and original, obviously reflecting a consciousness of the historical significance of our bold venture in popular government. Unfortunately, though they constituted one of the high points in the history of educational thought in America, they seem to have had little effect on the practices of the period.[13]

During the nineteenth century the idea of the development of an education expressing a great conception of our civilization appeared from time to time.[14] But curiously enough, except for an occasional native social radical, the proposals came generally either from foreign travelers or from naturalized American citizens, probably because they could see the novel and challenging features of our institutions more clearly than those who were familiar with them from birth. Of the visitors from abroad, as we have noted, George Combe was most articulate. Of American citizens by choice Francis J. Grund and Francis Lieber, both of German origin, were outstanding. But in the middle of the century a Connecticut-born educator, Edward D. Mansfield, author and public servant, in his *American Education* advanced something of the argument of the present volume. Here is the substance of his thought:

If America has presented any thing new to the world, it is a new form of society; if she has any thing worthy to preserve, it is the principles upon which that society is instituted: hence it is not a Grecian or a Roman education we need—it is not one conceived in China, Persia, or France. On the contrary, it must have all the characteristics of the American mind, fresh, original, vigorous, enterprising; embarrassed by no artificial barriers, and looking to a final conquest over the last obstacles to the progress of human improvement.[15]

In the present century, amidst a vast amount of irrelevant, superficial, and escapist educational discussion, research, and experimentation, the question of the relation of education to

[13] See Allen Oscar Hansen, *Liberalism and American Education in the Eighteenth Century* (New York, 1926).
[14] See Lawrence A. Cremin, *The American Common School* (New York, 1951).
[15] Edward D. Mansfield, *American Education* (New York, 1851), p. 60.

civilization has slowly forced its way into the arena. More than a generation ago, in 1899, John Dewey published his *School and Society*. From this volume and subsequent works by the same author and from the studies of American civilization by Charles A. Beard and others, there stems a vigorous movement for educational reform and reconstruction. Increasingly attention has been given to the role of the community and the culture in the educational process, to the importance of relating the school and all educational agencies to the ongoing life of society. And in more recent years, probably because of the crisis facing mankind and free institutions, we have become more and more conscious of the value and meaning of democracy for education. But unfortunately much of our discussion has tended either toward the abstract and the universal or toward the immediate and the local. At its best our approach has been incomplete and partial. The time has arrived to relate our thought about education to the whole sweep and substance of our American civilization—its history, its finest traditions, its present condition, and its promise.

7

We must proceed without delay to develop a great conception of our civilization.
 The age now unfolding, to repeat, is the most critical age of our history. We face deep troubles at home, powerful revolutions and counterrevolutions abroad, unprecedented responsibilities in the world, a future of almost limitless possibilities for good and evil. In the decades ahead our democracy may be transformed into some form of totalitarian despotism or it may march from triumph to triumph and fulfill gloriously and nobly the historic promise of America.

Our first responsibility as educators is to formulate on the foundations of fact a living and challenging conception of American civilization. We must ask ourselves in all soberness what is to be the course of our democracy. Only when we have answered this question, and answered it magnificently and powerfully, will we be in a position to draw the broad outlines of a great education for our people in the coming years. If we can find no answer, or if we find a mean and feeble answer, our education, however efficiently it may be conducted, will at best be mediocre and uninspired. And if we find a narrow, exclusive, and bigoted answer, the people of the world may come to regard the development of America into the mightiest power of the earth as one of the foremost tragedies of history. We must fashion a conception of civilization that will respect the rights of all nations and champion the cause of human liberty at home and before the world. Such a conception should provide the source of an education for the American people that would prepare them to discharge with honor and strength the heavy responsibilities which history has placed firmly on their shoulders.

We shall begin this task in the present volume with a broad inquiry into the historical and geographical bases of our civilization. Without getting lost in details, we shall strive to set forth the great and profoundly characteristic strands of our heritage which seem to have meaning for the emerging age. The resulting synthesis will of course embrace elements of faith and affirmation as well as elements of fact.

Part Two

OUR

EARLY

AMERICAN

HERITAGE

3

A CHILD OF THE MODERN AGE

1

Every people is influenced profoundly by its heritage. What a people can or cannot do, even what it may dream, is always conditioned and limited by its traditions. Although vast changes are coming in all contemporary societies, those changes will inevitably be affected deeply by the past of each. This truth has been demonstrated on a gigantic scale in our time. The Bolshevik Revolution, probably the most radical and deliberately conceived effort of all ages to break the continuum of history, has become more Russian with every passing year. Launched in the name of a body of social doctrine developed in western Europe and led chiefly by men and women who had lived for many years in foreign lands, it moved swiftly under the direction of powerful and deep-running currents of Russian history and civilization. Today, carrying the banners of freedom and democracy, it seeks to fasten on the world the absolutism of ancient Muscovy. In contrast, the British people in the war just concluded maintained their political liberties during the darkest hours of the conflict when even their friends throughout the world scarcely dared hope they would survive. And now, as they proceed to modify profoundly the institution of private property, they cling tenaciously to these liberties.

Fortunate is a people during these troubled times whose history records centuries of struggle for individual liberty, whose political heritage includes the Great Charter, the English Bill of Rights, the Declaration of Independence, the Federal Constitution, and the Gettysburg Address. Fortunate indeed is a people whose dearest traditions proclaim that "to no one will we sell, to no one will we refuse or delay, right or justice," that "all men are created equal," that "government of the people, by the people, for the people, shall not perish from the earth." While a tradition may bind and restrain, it may also free and inspire. Even though a great tradition of human liberation may be violated in practice, it places a powerful weapon in the hands of those who in any generation would battle for "right or justice."

2

America has a unique and glorious heritage. Although every country or people has its own past in which it naturally feels pride, we know that our history has followed a most unusual course. This land that became America was settled more swiftly than any other; and the great migrations hither were unlike the migrations of other times. They were marked by the deliberate choice of individuals and families to move to a happier sphere where life would be freer and richer. Moreover, as the decades passed into generations, America came to represent something distinctive in the long human struggle. She came to symbolize certain ideas, certain values, and a certain way of life which had more than national significance. We can say this without depreciating the heritages of other peoples or voicing the bigotry of narrow nationalism, for America was built by the labors of the sons and daughters of many races and nations. "Every people of Europe," wrote Francis J. Grund in 1837 with pardonable exaggeration, "is represented in the United States; every tongue is spoken in the vast domain of freedom; the history of every nation terminates in that of America." [1]

[1] Francis J. Grund, *The Americans, in Their Moral, Social, and Political Relations* (Boston, 1837), p. 108.

A Child of the Modern Age   45

Ever since we embarked on our revolutionary experiment in popular rule we have been the source of hope to the oppressed classes of the earth. Washington in his first inaugural put this hope into words which were heard beyond the Atlantic. "The preservation of the sacred fire of liberty and the destiny of the republican model of government," he said, "are justly considered as *deeply*, perhaps as *finally* staked, on the experiment intrusted to the hands of the American people." A generation later Daniel Webster in his Bunker Hill Oration reaffirmed the faith of the Father of the Republic: "If, in our case, the representative system ultimately fail, popular governments must be pronounced impossible. No combination of circumstances more favorable to the experiment can ever be expected to occur. The last hopes of mankind, therefore, rest with us; and if it should be proclaimed that our example had become an argument against the experiment, the knell of popular liberty would be sounded throughout the earth." In rallying his people for the supreme effort in the darkest days of civil struggle Lincoln, the Great Emancipator, spoke of the American Union as "the last best hope of earth." A few years later, while the memories of fratricidal strife were still fresh, Longfellow gave immortal expression to this sentiment in his *The Building of the Ship:* "Humanity with all its fears, with all the hopes of future years, is hanging breathless on thy fate!" And even Karl Marx, joint author of the Communist Manifesto, unsentimental and tough-minded apostle of world revolution, suggested in 1872 that in England, Holland, and the United States "the workers may hope to secure their ends by peaceful means."

Whatever our present merits, whatever our future may hold, we possess a glorious heritage. Although the great peoples of Europe and Asia have far longer records of achievement, the story of the rise of the American democracy within a few generations from the status of a European colony to a position of unsurpassed power in the world is one of the truly great epics of history. We of course have known the agony of internal conflict, and we have often been false to our finest traditions. We have sometimes stoned our prophets, nourished barbarous prejudices, winked at injustice, practiced shameless bigotry, condoned corruption in high places, neglected the general welfare, worshiped the "bitch goddess of material success," waged wars of aggression, and tolerated the most callous exploitation of man by man. Yet as a people we do not celebrate these things. On the contrary, we deplore them and would expunge them from the record. We cherish as the true expression of our genius our incomparable declarations of human rights, our achievements in the realm of popular rule, our conquests of natural forces, and our many struggles at home and abroad for liberty and justice. Ours has been a peculiarly happy and favored land, a land of opportunity and hope, a land of vast horizons and unlimited promise. Ours has also been a sheltered land. Never have we felt the iron heel of the conqueror; nor have we ever seen our republic swept from border to border by the fire and sword of foreign armies.

To outline this heritage in a few chapters is obviously impossible. A complete and exhaustive presentation, moreover, would not serve the purposes of the present volume. The treatment here is frankly and deliberatively selective—selective, within the limits of truth, of the best in our history. It is an interpretation of our past and of ourselves conceived in terms of the great patterns of our civilization and designed to guide and shape the education of our children, to guide and shape our course through these troubled times, to guide and shape our long future. Its veracity and worth must be left to the judgment of the American people. If they should reject it, no amount of scholarship could breathe into it the breath of life.

3

America was discovered, settled, and developed in the modern age. In comparison with the countries of the Old World, if we leave out of account the original inhabitants of

North America, our history is brief. Our beginnings are not lost in the mists of the past. From the first settlements of Europeans the record is relatively full and clear. "America is the only country," observed Tocqueville, "in which it has been possible to witness the natural and tranquil growth of society, and where the influence exercised on the future condition of states by their origin is clearly distinguishable."[2] The word "only" would of course have to be removed from such a statement today.

Our country was born and grew to early maturity during one of the great revolutionary periods of history, during a time when Western man had struck his tents and was once more on the march. This fact is of vast significance to those who would understand America. The early and formative years are probably as critical in the life of a nation as in the life of an individual. If our land had been settled earlier, when the social system and the world outlook of mediaeval Europe were in full flower, our history undoubtedly would have followed a vastly different course. We could then have brought to the New World only the institutions and ideas of the feudal age. This is of course precisely what happened in those settlements made by peoples who had lagged behind the English in the movement of political history. Unquestionably, for good or for ill, the special characteristics of the modern age have left their stamp on our civilization.

The discovery and settlement of America were an expression of the spirit of this great age. The movement across the unknown and forbidding waters of the Atlantic required spiritual qualities, practical interests, and physical means which for the most part were lacking in the Middle Ages. The few voyages to the coasts of America prior to Columbus of which we have record, and there were doubtless others, led to no lasting settlements. The civilization of Europe had to move into a creative and revolutionary phase before the exploration and conquest of the New World could enter the realm of practicality. Certain of the colonies were actually the achievements of novel forms of economic enterprise that

[2] Alexis de Tocqueville, *Democracy in America* (New York, 1898), Vol. I, p. 32.

marked the passing of the old order. In a very genuine sense, therefore, the launching of American civilization was an aspect of a great social convulsion and a spiritual awakening which were sweeping through the countries of western Europe in the early modern period. It was the outward thrust of these new forces.

4

The modern age extended the physical and intellectual horizons of Western man.

The rich heritage of the ancient world, lost or little understood for centuries, was rediscovered in its fullness. Also, the learning of the Arabs, embracing geography, astronomy, mathematics, medicine, physiology, surgery, pharmacy, architecture, and philosophy, entered the thought of European peoples. As a consequence the realization gradually dawned upon them that men in other times and other places had liberated themselves from authoritarian dogmas, explored freely the realms of art and nature, lived lives of richness and beauty, and focused their minds on the temporal world of sense. The result was an intellectual revolt which, originating in Italy, the cultural center of the period, gradually moved north and west, adapting itself to differing conditions, affecting profoundly many phases of life, and fostering a secular outlook on the world.

Old institutions of learning were imbued with the new spirit and new schools and universities spread over Europe. Both the purpose and the content of education were changed. Particularly in Italy the goals of life were defined in terms of the development of a free moral personality, and the conception of liberal education as developed by the ancient Greeks was revived. "We call those studies *liberal*," wrote Petrus Vergerius, an educator of the period, "which are worthy of a free man; those studies by which we attain and practice virtue and wisdom; that education which calls forth, trains, and develops those highest gifts of body and of mind

A Child of the Modern Age

which ennoble men, and which are rightly judged to rank next in dignity to virtue only."[3] In the fourteenth, fifteenth, and sixteenth centuries the secondary school, under divers names, appeared in the major countries of western Europe. At the same time universities devoted to the study of both the ancient classics and modern subjects were founded. Out of these beginnings came eventually the great school systems and intellectual achievements of the modern world.

Science pushed back the boundaries of human knowledge. Western man witnessed the rebirth of objective inquiry and the renewal of bold speculation concerning the nature of both man and the universe in which he dwells. Abandoning the appeal to authority and the method of disputation as a source of knowledge, men turned to observation and experimentation, first in the field of astronomy and then successively in the realms of physics, chemistry, biology, and physiology. The result was a new heaven and a new earth and a new conception of man. "Of all the elements of modern culture," writes Preserved Smith, "as of all the forces moulding modern life, science has been the greatest. It can be shown that all other changes in society are largely dependent upon this. Thought, philosophy, religion, art, education, laws, morals, economic institutions, are to a great extent dependent upon the progress of science. Not only does science alter technique in the production of wealth, but it alters man's view of the world in which he lives. The world-view is perhaps the decisive factor in moulding life and civilization."[4] Pre-eminently the modern age is the age of science.

Geographical exploration doubled the size of the known world and established the rotundity of the earth. It also opened up new sources of wealth, stimulated commerce and travel, revealed strange peoples and cultures, and banished many ancient fears. Spurred by the material rewards of trade and the thirst for gold and precious stones, the love of adventure and the desire for knowledge, the rivalries of

[3] William Harrison Woodward, *Vittorino da Feltre and Other Humanist Educators* (Cambridge, 1921), p. 102.
[4] Preserved Smith, *A History of Modern Culture* (New York, 1930), Vol. I, p. 17.

princes and the commands of the Church, men of unsurpassed daring sailed in frail ships from the ports of Italy, Spain, Portugal, France, Holland, and England out into the unknown. In 1486 Bartholomeu Diaz explored the waters of the Cape of Good Hope; in 1497 Vasco da Gama sailed on to Calicut by the same route; in 1492 Christopher Columbus discovered America; in 1519 a fleet, commanded by Ferdinand Magellan, set out on a voyage which resulted in the circumnavigation of the globe and the empirical demonstration that the earth is round. Thereafter European peoples moved out from their cramped quarters to establish in the course of time their rule over practically all lands and seas. The impact of these explorations, discoveries, and conquests on the mind of Western man was beyond all calculation.

5

The modern age brought hope for a better life to the common man.

New inventions and the advance of practical knowledge increased man's dominion over nature and heralded the progressive amelioration of the lot of common people. The compass made possible the glorious age of exploration, the printing press promised the democratization of the world of learning, and the firearm undermined the power of the armored knight on his horse and the structure of the social order of which he was the symbol. The spirit of optimism generated by man's successful grappling with the forces of nature is well expressed in the following extract from an article which appeared in the *Virginia Gazette* in 1737:

The World, but a few Ages since, was in a very poor Condition, as to Trade, and Navigation. Nor, indeed, were they much better in other Matters of useful Knowledge. It was a Green-headed Time, every useful Improvement was hid from them; they had neither look'd into Heaven nor Earth; into the Sea, nor Land, as has been

A Child of the Modern Age

done since. They had Philosophy without Experiment; Mathematics without Instruments; Geometry without Scale; Astronomy without Demonstration. . . . They went to Sea without Compass; and sail'd without the Needle. They view'd the Stars without Telescopes; and measured Latitude without Observation. . . . They had Surgery without Anatomy, and Physicians without the Materia Medica. . . . As for Geographic Discoveries, they had neither seen the North Cape, nor the Cape of Good Hope. . . . As they were ignorant of Places, so of Things also; so vast are the Improvements of Sciences, that all our Knowledge of Mathematics, of Nature, of the brightest Part of humane Wisdom, had their Admission among us within the last two Centuries. . . . The World is now daily increasing in experimental Knowledge, and let no Man flatter the Age, with pretending we are arrived to a Perfection of Discoveries.[5]

New conceptions of human worth and destiny challenged traditional authority in both church and state. The Protestant Reformation which swept over northern Europe in the sixteenth century and shaped profoundly the thought of colonial America weakened the power of the priesthood and theoretically placed responsibility on the individual for the salvation of his own soul. Also, by disrupting the unity of the Western church, encouraging the growth of national religious movements, and fostering the multiplication of sects, particularly among the English-speaking peoples, it weakened ecclesiastical control over the human mind and stimulated men to think their own thoughts.

In seventeenth century England John Locke laid the intellectual foundations of popular rule. He denied the ancient dogma of the divinity of kings, placed sovereignty squarely in the hands of the people, and defended the right of rebellion. To him the guarding of individual liberty against every form of encroachment by pope or king, by minority or majority, was one of the chief obligations of government. It is not surprising that he was "The Great Mr. Locke" to the founding fathers of our Republic and that much of his thought was written into the Federal Constitution.

[5] Quoted in James Truslow Adams, *Provincial Society 1690–1763* (New York, 1928), p. 273.

In the eighteenth century the leadership in thought crossed the Channel to France. A galaxy of brilliant minds, with great gifts of expression, so dominated the age that it has come to be called after them and their work—the Age of Enlightenment. They proclaimed the coming victory of naturalism over supernaturalism, of science over theology, of human reason over established authority. Voltaire attacked the traditional dogmas of church and state as barriers to human advance. Montesquieu saw government, not as unchanging and sanctified by divine will, but as an expression of a people living in a particular time and place. Diderot and d'Alembert edited the great Encyclopedia which, they hoped, would bring the best of scientific and practical knowledge to many people and arouse enthusiasm for reform and improvement. Rousseau popularized the political ideas of Locke, defending with the power of genius the doctrine that only the freely expressed will of the people can render any government legitimate. Condorcet, in his *Historical Sketch of the Progress of the Human Mind*, clothed with vast learning and philosophic grasp the idea of human progress and the perfectibility of man and his institutions. These men, and others like them, prepared the way for the French Revolution and other revolutions to follow in the nineteenth century.

6

The modern age brought social revolution.

The twelfth and thirteenth centuries marked the emergence of social forces within the general framework of existing institutions which were destined eventually to destroy feudal society. Towns and cities, centers of industry and trade, were appearing in all the countries of western Europe. In these centers, peopled by men and women who had escaped from the land, a new social class of artisans and merchants, champions of economic and political liberty, grew in numbers and resources from generation to generation. In time they became the Third Estate and achieved sufficient power to challenge the existing order, not by direct assault but by supporting the king against the nobility or the nobility against the king. It was to this growing class of urban dwellers, rather than to the serfs on the land, that the new doctrines of individual rights and freedom were first addressed.

In England, politically the most advanced of the countries of Europe, the revolutionary struggle to overthrow the feudal order began toward the end of the sixteenth century and was carried on with varying fortunes and by diverse means for a hundred years. Involving the beheading of a king and the establishment of a popular dictatorship, it culminated in the signing of the Declaration of Rights by William and Mary in 1689. In France the revolution, in its political phase, broke with great violence a century later. Under the banner of liberty, equality, and fraternity the revolutionists overthrew the ancient regime, proclaimed the rule of reason, inaugurated a reign of terror, turned back to a dictatorship under Napoleon, and soaked Europe in blood for twenty years. These great revolutions, terrifying though they were, marked a phase of the rise of the common man to power and the establishment of popular governments in many countries.

The so-called revolutions of our time, with their concentration of all power in the hands of a party oligarchy or a divinely anointed dictator, are essentially counterrevolutionary in character. They proclaim and enforce with all the instruments for social control devised by science and technology the basic principle that the people cannot and should not rule themselves.

7

The spirit of the new age found an easier birth in North America.

This new land was discovered and settled as the social system and the intellectual outlook of the Middle Ages were disintegrating. It was settled, moreover, largely by people who in their national, religious, and class origins were most closely identified with the new forces. It was settled chiefly in the early days by Englishmen, and by poor, young, adventurous, dissenting, and even outcast Englishmen—a people who was already engaged in a sustained struggle for individual and political liberty—a people who at the time was in the vanguard of the march toward popular government. From the beginning America was also a haven of refuge for men and women of many nations fleeing the oppressions and tyrannies of feudal institutions. The whole continent was a virgin seed-bed for the "dangerous thoughts" then agitating the Old World.

Here in America were no vested rights and interests deeply and firmly rooted in law and custom. Here were no great landed estates that had been passed from father to son for generations and centuries. Here were few noble lords, of either church or state, who by armed retainers or by "motto and blazon" imposed their will upon the "inferior orders." Here were few prisons and dungeons and torture chambers for breaking the bodies and spirits of dissenters and rebels. Here, with rich and unoccupied land ever beckoning, men and women of European origin craving freedom could not be held long in bondage. In remarkable measure, therefore, those who came to America were able to cast off the fetters of the past and make a fresh start in building a freer and better way of life. Although attempts were made to establish feudal ideas and institutions in America, these attempts were never really successful. "America was opened after the feudal mischief was spent," wrote Ralph Waldo Emerson in 1878, "and so the people made a good start. We began well. No inquisition here, no kings, no nobles, no dominant church. Here heresy has lost its terrors."[6] Even to this day the term "feudal" carries a stench to the nostrils of our people. The fact that the present class structure of American society has little support in feudal attitudes and outlooks surviving from the pre-capitalistic age is a source of great strength to our

[6] Ralph Waldo Emerson, "The Fortune of the Republic," *Emerson's Complete Works* (Cabot edition, Boston, 1878), Vol. XI, pp. 410–411.

A Child of the Modern Age 55

democracy. As late as 1888, in a period marked by bitter struggles between capital and labor, James Bryce, a close student of our institutions, could say: "Classes are not prime factors in American politics or in the formation of native political opinion."[7] And in 1951, George Meany, Secretary-Treasurer of the American Federation of Labor, declared: "American society has always been dynamic, flexible and progressive. It has never been feudalistic."

The powerful movements for intellectual and political liberation, which swept the Old World during the sixteenth, seventeenth, and eighteenth centuries, were given a friendly reception in America. A distinguished French historian has said that the ideas of the Enlightenment took deeper root here than in France. Of these ideas, perhaps the most revolutionary was that of human progress and the indefinite perfectibility of man and his institutions. This idea found its natural home in America. The proposition that the future can be better than the past is an essential and distinctive part of our heritage. Although it may foster an irrational optimism and may be narrowly interpreted as material or mechanical advance, it is one of the great liberating ideas of history. Even our most conservative interests always claim to be battling in the name of progress.

The American Revolution itself was a vigorous affirmation of the spirit of the modern age. Deriving its philosophy in part from English and French sources and in part from the life conditions of the New World, this revolution not only launched the most far-flung and successful experiment in popular government in history but also reacted powerfully on the social ideas and institutions of the rest of the world. It helped mightily to explode the age-old doctrine of the divinity of kings and aristocracies and encouraged people to revolt against their inherited and self-appointed masters. It caused tyrants to sit uneasily on their thrones and members of privileged orders to worry about their privileges. Our revolution served as a great sounding board to send certain ideas of the modern age around the world.

[7] James Bryce, *The American Commonwealth* (London, 1888), Vol. II, p. 309.

As the Republic proceeded successfully on its course, it became a subject of discussion and controversy everywhere. Increasingly it aroused the fears of ruling classes, the hopes of the oppressed, and the interest of all. Generation after generation visitors from the Old World came to our shores in an endless stream—some to abuse, some to praise, some simply to learn. Millions came so that they and their children might live among us and join their blood and fortunes with ours forever. But that is another story. The fact to remember is that the spirit of daring and adventure, the faith in man and his powers, and the promise of a better world which characterize the modern age constitute a distinctive and priceless element in our heritage. To abandon these things, to become timid in the face of difficulties, to retreat from reason into the arms of authority, to grow fearful of the future, to cling blindly to the old, would be to betray the genius of American history.

4

A NATION OF

MANY PEOPLES

1

Only people build a civilization.
          The first resource of any society is its people. The true wealth of a country, it has been said, lies in its men and women. The riches of physical nature, of climate, soil, water, forests, and minerals, are of course important. Men have fought for them and over them in every age. Yet, within broad limits, the qualities of the people who inhabit a land constitute the critical factor in the development of a civilization. History provides many examples of high standards of living and high cultural achievements in relatively harsh and barren regions. History records no instance of such achievements by a people lacking in vigor and inventiveness. A wise society therefore will give every attention to the guarding and development of its human resources.

How the people of a country are regarded in the customs, the mores, the laws, and the institutions of society must always be a major concern of both statesmanship and education. We have witnessed and are witnessing in our time the demonstration on a colossal scale of the crucial character of this question. The German Nazis, with their arrogant doctrine of unlimited Nordic superiority, brought untold misery and tragedy to mankind, failed utterly to win the peoples of Europe to their "new order," and suffered the most terrible and decisive defeat of modern times. And the Japanese conquerors might have rallied the peoples of eastern Asia and the western Pacific to their banners, if they had regarded and treated them as equals. On the other hand, the proclamation by the Soviets of the principle of equality of races and nations, spurious though it is, constitutes a powerful weapon in the Communist struggle for the loyalties of the colored and colonial peoples of the world. The pages of history, moreover, are filled with examples of evil results flowing from the exploitation of man by man, of people by people, of race by race.

One of our major tasks in America during the coming generation is the development of a conception of our people that will endure every strain. Because of the composition of our population, the legacy from slavery and colonialism, and certain political tendencies in the contemporary world this task takes on a terrible urgency. We learned long ago that in union there is strength. This truth is as applicable to the elements composing our population as to the political divisions comprising our country. The fortunes of free institutions on this continent and the role of America among the nations of the world will be deeply affected by the policies we pursue in this area.

2

America was populated over a period of more than three centuries by the greatest migration of history.

In all not far from forty million people were involved in this movement. During the one hundred years preceding the attack on Pearl Harbor approximately thirty-eight million men, women, and children crossed the great oceans east and west and the borders north and south to make their homes in the United States. In terms of numbers and distances the migrations of all other times and places dwindle into relative insignificance. These immigrants and their descendants, from Jamestown down to the last boat entering an American port, have made, are making, and will make the American people. By their toil and creative energies, their hopes and ambitions, they have built our country and our civilization.

This migration also was a movement of many and diverse peoples—diverse in race, religion, language, and every aspect of culture. When traveling through Pennsylvania in 1778, Thomas Anburey, an officer in the British army, voiced the observation of innumerable foreign visitors in these words: "You meet with people of almost every different persuasion of religion that exists; in short, the diversity of religions, nations, and languages here is astonishing, at the same time, the harmony they live in is no less edifying."[1] Year after year, generation after generation, century after century, they came to this land of hope and promise from almost every clime and region, from all the continents and most of the great islands of the sea. As a consequence a considerable percentage of our people have always been foreign-born. Even today after a quarter of a century of increasingly rigorous restriction not far from ten per cent were born in other lands. Thus throughout her history America has been the scene of a most extraordinary mingling and clashing of classes, religions, nationalities, and races.

At the time of the discovery by Europeans, America was sparsely inhabited by a brave and vigorous native population living in a primitive stage of culture and probably derived originally from Asiatic sources. Although these people fought a bloody and losing battle with the white man as he pushed his way inexorably across the continent from the Atlantic to the Pacific, they have left their mark upon us and have influenced our life and civilization. They have enriched our language, added much to our agricultural economy, modified our modes of warfare, and affected in some measure our moral and political ideas. Also they have contributed more than is commonly believed to the formation of the American stock.

The earlier migrations from the Old World were largely

[1] Thomas Anburey, *Travel Through the Interior Parts of America* (London, 1791), Vol. II, p. 254.

of Anglo-Saxon origin—people from England, Wales, and Scotland. But included among the first settlers were members of other races and nationalities, notably Negroes, Dutch, Swedes, French, Spaniards, Irish, and Germans. It was the British elements, however, that dominated the migrations down to the end of the colonial period and even into the early decades of the nineteenth century. It has been estimated that in 1790, at the time of the launching of the Republic, 66 per cent of the population were descended from English and Welsh stock. Next came the Negroes with 19 per cent, followed by the Scotch with 6, the Germans with 5, the Dutch with 2, the Irish with 1.5, and the French with .5.[2]

As the nineteenth century advanced and gave way to the twentieth, the source of the migration shifted again and again. Although immigrants continued to come from Protestant Britain, in the eighteen-forties they came in a great flood first from Catholic Ireland and then from Germany. Subsequently there were migrations, great or small, from Scandinavia, from Italy, from all the countries of central and eastern Europe, and even from China, Japan, India, and the Philippines. Also many people entered the United States from Canada and Mexico. These later migrations, moreover, not only brought new national and racial elements to America; they also brought new religious sects and faiths. To the originally preponderant Protestant population they added many Jews, Roman Catholics, and Greek Catholics, and some Mohammedans, Buddhists, and others. Alexis de Tocqueville, viewing this mingling of peoples in 1831, remarked that "the whole continent, in short, seemed prepared to be the abode of a great nation yet unborn."[3] Although four generations have passed since these words were written, generations marked by the disappearance of many ancient cleavages, the advance of the process of cultural integration, and the growth of national consciousness, few informed persons would say that the period of gestation is over.

[2] Percentages derived from Samuel P. Orth, *Our Foreigners* (New Haven, 1920), p. 29.
[3] Alexis de Tocqueville, *Democracy in America* (New York, 1898), Vol. I, p. 29.

3

The great migration compelled the development of a new civilization.
All immigrants to a new and strange land leave many of their possessions, material and spiritual, behind them. They can of course bring in limited measure, if they are fortunate, their clothes, tools, and domestic animals; but they cannot bring their climate, forests, and fields, their ancient castles, cathedrals, and monuments. They can bring their language, their ideas, their memories, and some of their institutions; but they cannot bring their entire social structure, their community organization, or even their history in its fullness. Moreover, many elements of a civilization which may be transported from the old home to the new are sooner or later abandoned because they are unsuited to the new circumstances. The early colonists found heavy armor a handicap in battling the agile Indian in the forest; and they soon learned that the feudal system of land tenure could hardly be maintained in a country with boundless frontiers. "The Europeans, on coming to America," Tocqueville wrote, "left behind them, in large part, the traditions of the past, the institutions and customs of their fatherland, they built a society which has analogies with those of Europe, but which at bottom is radically different."[4] A premium was consequently placed on inventiveness, resourcefulness, and adaptability.

The migration to America, in comparison with earlier movements of peoples, was unique in several respects. It was quite unlike the exodus of the ancient Hebrews from the land of Egypt or the incursions of the Germans into the Roman Empire. It was a migration, not of clans or tribes or nations, wandering away from the homeland and adjusting themselves to slowly changing surroundings, but rather of individuals and families forsaking by deliberate resolve their place of birth and moving by modern means of locomotion

[4] George Wilson Pierson, *Tocqueville and Beaumont in America* (New York, 1938), p. 568.

to a strange and distant country. A fully functioning group, composed of both sexes and all ages, ranks, and occupations, can be far more successful in transporting its civilization to a new land than isolated individuals and families with their limited and partial command of the culture. This fact also forced the immigrants to America to improvise and build anew.

The migration to America was recruited largely from the underprivileged classes of the Old World. As two British investigators have recently observed, "very little of the English class structure was transported to North America with the Anglo-Saxon stock which originally colonized the territory."[5] In any complex society civilization is developed and transmitted from generation to generation, not by one class or group, but by all. Clearly the underprivileged Englishmen who came to America in the seventeenth and eighteenth centuries could bring with them only what they possessed. They could not bring the accomplishments, the social outlooks, the virtues and vices of the ruling and favored classes. The same may be said of the later migrations from other countries. Our alleged absorption in material things, vulgarity in recreations, crudeness of manners, and neglect of the aristocratic arts, so frequently the subject of adverse comment by foreign travelers, were doubtless due in part, in so far as they had substance, to the selective character of the migration. At any rate, there were probably large empty spaces in the civilization which our ancestors brought to America—spaces which they proceeded to fill as best they could.

The migration also, as we have noted, brought the most diverse and conflicting cultural patterns. It brought different languages and traditions, different modes of dress and livelihood, different political conceptions and practices, different sex and family customs, different moral and religious ideas and values. The immigrants, moreover, were derived from peoples beyond the Atlantic who had fought one another on innumerable battlefields for centuries and had come to re-

[5] Roy Lewis and Angus Maude, *The English Middle Classes* (New York, 1950), p. vii.

A Nation of Many Peoples 63

gard one another with suspicion, fear, hatred, and contempt. That this vast and persistent diversity failed to wreck the entire enterprise of building a new society on this continent is one of the miracles of the ages. It did of course create dissension and increased the difficulties attending the adjustment to new conditions of life. But it also enlarged our conception of democracy, fostered tolerance of differences, erased many ancient prejudices, enriched our stock of ideas, and forced the contriving of new ways of living. Our civilization is undoubtedly far different from what it would have been if the migration had come from a single source.

The great migration continued westward across the continent for almost three centuries. As the young and adventurous of generation after generation moved beyond the reach of tidewater, crossed the eastern mountains, took possession of the Mississippi valley, traversed the great plains, and advanced over the Rockies, the American deserts, and the coast ranges to the waters of the Pacific, the process of adaptation continued. Tocqueville waxed romantic as he contemplated these pioneers. "They are founding in the valleys of the Mississippi," he said, "a new society which has no analogy with the past and is connected to Europe only in language. It's here one must come to judge the most singular state of affairs that has doubtless existed under the sun. A people absolutely without precedents, without traditions, without habits, without dominating ideas even, opening for itself without hesitation a new path in civil, political, and criminal legislation; never casting its eyes about to consult the wisdom of other peoples or the memory of the past; but cutting out its institutions, like its roads, in the midst of the forests. . . ."[6] There is of course exaggeration in these words. Tocqueville himself emphasized again and again in his account of our institutions the persisting and pervasive influence of the English heritage. Yet the fact remains that the farther we proceeded on our westward journey, the more American we became. "Europe stretches to the Alleghenies," said Emerson; "America lies beyond."

[6] Pierson, *op. cit.*, p. 568.

4

The great migration is over. Although immigrants will continue, perhaps for generations, to come to our shores in considerable numbers, the American people are here. The future of our country, the destiny of our civilization, is essentially in the keeping of ourselves and our children forever. The talents, actual and potential, of all the many elements composing our population constitute the total of our human resources for the long future. It is well for us to take stock and to formulate a conception of our people for the tasks that lie ahead.

America is no longer an Anglo-Saxon Protestant country, as she was at the time of the founding of the Republic. This is one of the stubborn facts of our society. It has been estimated that the contribution of England and Wales to the formation of the American people amounts to approximately 34 per cent. The corresponding percentages for the other major national and racial groups are as follows: German, 15; Negro, 10; Irish, 10; Scotch, 7; and French, Italian, and Polish, something less than 4 each. All the others, embracing a vast number of peoples, provide the remaining twelve per cent.[7] In 1950, according to the *Yearbook of American Churches*, there were 265 different religious bodies in continental United States, the largest being the Roman Catholic with an approximate membership of 28,000,000 persons. All Protestant sects combined provided an estimated total of 49,000,000. The Jewish congregation amounted to 5,000,000 and the Eastern Orthodox to about 1,000,000. This means that not far from one-half of the people of the country were unaffiliated with any church. It seems probable that in their antecedents they were largely Protestant.

These diverse peoples, living and working together, are creating a new nation whose cultural and biological roots

---

[7] Percentages derived from Joseph A. Hill, "Composition of the American Population by Race and Country of Origin," *The Annals of the American Academy of Political and Social Science* (Philadelphia, 1936), Vol. 188, pp. 177–184.

A Nation of Many Peoples

reach back to most of the countries of the earth and to most of the races of mankind. Some came early; some came late; the vast majority came because they wanted to come. Some came to escape oppression, some to avoid the jail or the rope, some to find adventure, some to make their fortunes, some to enjoy the liberties of the new land: they came from many motives. All, except those who were dragged into bondage, taken by force from their native lands, or sentenced to penal colonies, came voluntarily to better their condition. Almost uniquely among the great nations of history, we descend from men and women who deliberately chose to live, not in the land of their fathers, but in the land of their children. All of us, except a small minority who have sought to live as parasites by their wits or the wits of their parents, have helped to build America.[8]

Every one of these peoples has made its special contribution to the common undertaking. To assess the value of each is of course impossible. We are fortunate perhaps that British elements dominated the colonial migration and played the major role in laying the foundations of our civilization. Although they had their weaknesses, they were probably on the whole the most advanced people of the time in the realm of social philosophy. They gave us their language and through their language their literature and thought. More than any other national group they gave us our political ideas and institutions, our conception of individual rights, and our love of freedom. A recent "anthology of the world's greatest poetic expressions in the struggle for political liberty" reveals in some measure the great debt which mankind owes to this people. Out of a total of 800 pages Britain, with the other members of the British Commonwealth of Nations, excluding India, contributes 332. The American contribution of 216 pages is unquestionably an expression of the vitality of the great tradition of human freedom developed through the centuries by the "mother of parliaments."[9]

---

[8] See Carl Wittke, *We Who Built America* (New York, 1940).
[9] William Rose Benét and Norman Cousins, *The Poetry of Freedom* (New York, 1945).

Yet the contribution of the British to our conception of liberty can be overrated. Many who came to America from other lands came because they loved freedom, because they had fought against tyranny at home and lost. Every popular revolt in the Old World that failed, and there were many, sent its contingent of rebels and dissenters to America. "Driven from every other corner of the earth," declared Samuel Adams in a speech in Philadelphia in 1776, "freedom of thought and the right of private judgment in matters of conscience direct their course to this happy country as their last asylum." Of the fifty-six signers of the Declaration of Independence, eighteen bore non-English names—a proportion far higher than the representation of other nationalities in the general population. "It was the genius of liberty," declared Francis J. Grund, "which gave America a national elevation; and it is to this genius, therefore, we must look for national productions. It is the bond of union, the confession, the religion, the life of Americans; it is that which distinguishes them above all other nations in the world."[10] And Grund was of German origin.

If the British laid the foundations of our civilization, all other elements have certainly helped to build the superstructure. Who can measure the toil and sorrow, the sweat and tears, that the Negroes have given to our common country, in the cotton fields, on the docks and wharfs, on the highways and rivers, wherever hard labor has been required? And who can measure the contribution of the Scotch-Irish and Scandinavians to the pushing back of our frontier, of the southern Irish to the construction of our canals and railroads, of the Germans to the development of our agriculture, of the Slavs and Italians to the building of our cities and industries? And it was not the English alone who created our intellectual and artistic heritage. A large proportion of our novelists, artists, poets, and scholars come from either mixed or other strains. Our most significant contribution to the folk music of the world is an expression of Negro genius. In the sciences

[10] Francis J. Grund, *The Americans, in Their Moral, Social, and Political Relations* (Boston, 1837), p. 107.

A Nation of Many Peoples

and the arts we owe much to the French, the Germans, the Italians, the Slavs, and the Jews. Twenty-five hundred of the thirty thousand men and women included in *Who's Who in America* for 1940 were foreign-born. The refugees from the European continent from 1933 to 1945 included twelve Nobel prize winners, over two hundred persons listed in *American Men of Science*, more than seven hundred sculptors and artists, and many hundreds of authors, editors, and journalists.[11] Our civilization is undoubtedly richer, more varied and colorful, than it would have been if our population had remained Anglo-Saxon.

This attempt to build a new nation out of elements from most of the races and peoples of the world is one of the greatest experiments in history. In the long run it may equal in significance our experiment in popular government. Under the fundamental law of the land all of our present inhabitants, whatever their origin or time of arrival, whatever their race or creed, are entitled to all the rights, privileges, and responsibilities constituting the American birthright. No one of the many elements composing our nation, not even the Anglo-Saxon, can properly claim to be the "true Americans" or to be entitled to preferred treatment. The Federal Constitution makes no distinctions in citizenship. "All persons born or naturalized in the United States," declares the Fourteenth Amendment, "are citizens of the United States and of the State wherein they reside." It declares further that "no State shall . . . deny to any person within its jurisdiction the equal protection of the laws." This statute is supported by our moral professions and our religious tenets.

Yet America today, as in the past, is a land of unequal peoples. Whatever law or precept may say, this is the reality. Recent immigrants, particularly if they come from a new source, have always been the victims of discrimination and exploitation. This was almost as true of the Scotch-Irish in the eighteenth century as of the Slavs in the twentieth. Immigrants of the Roman Catholic faith were long feared and

[11] Maurice R. Davie, *Refugees in America* (New York, 1947), pp. 324, 334, 432, 435-440.

hated by their Protestant neighbors. Today in many parts of the country the relations between the two groups are marked by suspicion and prejudice. And the Jew has often found that apparently the provisions of the Declaration of Independence are not meant for him. Even the Indian has always been made to feel himself an alien in the land of his fathers.

The Negro, however, has been the object of the most severe, lasting, and bitter discrimination. From 1619, when the first Negroes were landed at Jamestown, down to the Emancipation Proclamation in 1863, the Negro was generally a slave. Thereafter he has been struggling with only limited success to surmount the many disabilities under which he lives and suffers. His perpetual exclusion from full democratic rights and liberties in many parts of the country is the first shame of America. The fact has been remarked by intelligent foreign visitors in every generation from Crèvecoeur in the middle of the seventeenth century to D. W. Brogan in 1944. Gunnar Myrdal, a distinguished Swedish social scientist, after the most exhaustive study of the question ever attempted, says in italics: *"The simple fact is that an educational offensive against racial intolerance, going deeper than the reiteration of the 'glittering generalities' in the nation's political creed, has never seriously been attempted in America."*[12]

5

We must decide who are the American people.

The preamble to our Constitution begins with the words: "We, the people of the United States." It is time that we faced squarely the question of what these words mean. Do they mean all of us or just some of us? If they mean the latter, on what basis will the selection be made? We know that neither genius, love of country, nor loyalty to the cause of human liberty and justice follows the line of color, national origin, or religious belief. If these words mean all of us, then we have much work to do.

[12] Gunnar Myrdal, *An American Dilemma* (New York, 1944), Vol. I, p. 49.

But in doing it we shall be fulfilling the promise of America. We shall be preserving and strengthening that great heritage of good will throughout the world which we built up during earlier generations and which is one of our most precious possessions. We shall be preparing ourselves morally for the heavy responsibilities of leadership among the nations which our vast physical might has thrust upon us. Also we shall be making the most of our richest resource—the diverse talents of our people. Let us hope that we have the wit and the wisdom to meet this challenge.

5

A COUNTRY OF COMMON PEOPLE

1

America was settled by common people.

From beginning to end the great migration was essentially a migration of common people. This of course does not mean that no men and women of talent and personal distinction came to America from the Old World during these three and a half centuries. The contrary is clearly the case. Indeed it would seem highly probable, as we shall argue later, that the millions of common people who elected to cross the oceans were beyond or outside the ordinary in some way. They were common only in the sense that they made no pretensions to social rank or superiority. They neither possessed nor craved the support of the artificial insignia of class and caste. To this of course there were many individual exceptions, but the exceptions were generally unsuccessful in the attempt to transport their conceptions of social relations to the New World. Even today, in spite of wide differences in material possessions, the historic mores are strong and will doubtless continue to prevail. As the average citizen feels no embarrassment in accepting an invitation to dine at the White House, so he bitterly resents affectation of superiority on the part of the president of the Republic, the head of a great corporation, or anybody else. Here is one of the most distinctive and precious elements of our heritage, and an essential component in the moral foundations of democracy.

2

America was settled mainly by the poor, the oppressed, and the persecuted of Europe.
The records show clearly that for the most part only the "middling and lower orders" of the Old World came to the New. Indeed in large measure it was the very poor who migrated. According to the Beards, "it seems probable that at least one-half the immigrants into America before the Revolution, certainly outside New England, were either indentured servants or Negro slaves."[1] Arthur M. Schlesinger places the estimate even higher: "Perhaps one-half of all the white immigrants during the larger part of the colonial period were unable to pay their expenses. They came 'indentured' and were auctioned off for a period of service by the ship captains in payment for their transportation. Still another element of the population, perhaps one-fifth of the whole in the eighteenth century, consisted of Guinea negroes."[2] This same writer also says, "it has been estimated that as many as fifty thousand criminals were sent to the thirteen colonies by Great Britain." Besides such figures we should place the fact that "the great English Puritan migration did not exceed twenty thousand."

Richard B. Morris concludes, after a comprehensive review of the evidence, that the above estimates "must be considered very conservative." He states further that "the institution of the redemptioner provided the principal means of populating the American colonies by European settlers." He found that eighty-seven per cent of the emigrants departing from the port of London for the colonies during a two-year period just prior to the War for Independence "went over as indentured servants." And Entry Books of the Port of Annapolis for the years 1746-75 record the arrival of "2,142 German and Irish passengers, 9,035 indentured servants,

---
[1] Charles A. Beard and Mary R. Beard, *The Rise of American Civilization* (New York, 1927), Vol. I, p. 103.
[2] Arthur Meier Schlesinger, *New Viewpoints in American History* (New York, 1928), p. 4.

8,846 convicts, and 3,324 Negroes." Morris adds that many of the passengers "were doubtless bound for their passage."[3]

Members of privileged orders rarely migrate. In the very nature of the case such people remain at home, unless they are able to surmount the infirmities of their class, unless they are moved by love of adventure or devotion to ideals, or unless they lose their privileges. Individuals from each of these categories came to America in every age to play a distinguished role in the development of the country. Among religious and political dissenters were sometimes men of property who placed their convictions above material goods —English Puritans and French Huguenots in the seventeenth century, German, Hungarian, and Italian democrats in the nineteenth. Also, following the success of popular revolts in Europe members of former ruling classes in limited numbers crossed the Atlantic—a few English Cavaliers after 1649, a few French aristocrats after 1789, and a few Russian landlords and Georgian princes after 1917. But as a general rule the privileged stay with their privileges. "The happy and the powerful," said Tocqueville, "do not go into exile."

Migration is always painful and hazardous. To leave home, to leave the land where one is born and where one's ancestors lie buried, requires powerful motivation. This is particularly true if life in the new country is lacking in accustomed comforts, if the language, customs, and institutions there are strange, and if the journey thither is long and perilous. Certainly, for many generations the comforts associated with European aristocracy were absent and the whole way of life was barren of the supports of gentility. As to the voyage across the Atlantic in the seventeenth and eighteenth centuries, it "taxed the resources and the fortitude of even the most venturesome and courageous." In the sailing vessels of the time, subject to the caprice of wind and wave, the journey required from five weeks to six months. "During the voyage," wrote Gottlieb Mittelberger, a German music teacher who traversed the ocean in 1750, "there is on board these ships

[3] Richard B. Morris, *Government and Labor in Early America* (New York, 1946), pp. 315–316.

terrible misery, stench, fumes, horror, vomiting, many kinds of sea-sickness, fever, dysentery, headache, heat, constipation, boils, scurvy, cancer, mouth-rot, and the like, all of which come from old and sharply salted food and meat, also from very bad and foul water, so that many die miserably."[4] The death rate on these voyages, particularly for the very young, the feeble, and the old, was extremely high, often above twenty-five per cent. And many a ship went down at sea.

America was indeed a land of opportunity. But it must be remembered that opportunity is always relative. What is opportunity for the poor may be deprivation for the rich. And to the privileged classes of the Old World, America was rarely a land of opportunity, at least not until these latter days when in the marriage market fortunes may be purchased with badly worn titles and pedigrees. Benjamin Franklin stated the case very succinctly shortly after the Revolution in a letter to the English press, entitled: "To Those Who Would Remove to America":

It cannot be worth any man's while, who has a means of living at home, to expatriate himself, in hopes of obtaining a profitable civil office in America. . . . Much less is it advisable for a person to go thither, who has no other quality to recommend him but his birth. In Europe it has indeed its value; but it is a commodity that cannot be carried to a worse market than that of America, where people do not inquire concerning a stranger, *What is he?* but, *What can he do?*[5]

To the poor America was a land of opportunity—of opportunity to work and work hard to improve their condition. "What attachment," wrote Crèvecoeur in the middle of the eighteenth century, "can a poor European emigrant have for a country where he had nothing? The knowledge of the language, the love of a few kindred as poor as himself, were the only cords that tied him: his country is now that which gives him land, bread, protection, and consequence: *Ubi panis ibi*

[4] Gottlieb Mittelberger's *Journey to Pennsylvania in the Year 1750 and Return to Germany in the Year 1754* (Philadelphia, 1898), p. 20.
[5] Jared Sparks, *The Works of Benjamin Franklin* (Boston, 1836), Vol. II, p. 469.

patria, is the motto of all emigrants."[6] To be sure, many were dragged to America as slaves or as bondsmen. Others, convicted of crime under the harsh laws of the age, were sent by force to penal colonies on this side of the Atlantic. But it should be remembered that as late as 1800 the British criminal code listed about two hundred capital offenses, branding and mutilation were common punishments, and men were imprisoned for trivial debts. Also throughout our entire history many men, women, and children were persuaded by false representations to come to America by employers, steamship companies, and others seeking profit from the miseries of the Old World and the promise of the New. Yet the vast majority of the immigrants came to America voluntarily and with some knowledge of the nature and conditions of the venture.

In the course of time, consequently, there developed a glorious tradition about our country. America became a haven of refuge for the oppressed and downtrodden, a land of opportunity for the poor, the underprivileged, and the disposssesed, a promise of redemption for the outcast, the criminal, and the damned of the earth. The substance of this tradition, expressed in the poetry of Emma Lazarus, is inscribed on the base of the Statue of Liberty:

> "Keep, ancient lands, your storied pomp!" cries she
> With silent lips. "Give me your tired, your poor,
> Your huddled masses yearning to breathe free,
> The wretched refuse of your teeming shore.
> Send these, the homeless, tempest-tost to me.
> I lift my lamp beside the golden door!"

That America was settled by common people is in the record. It is equally in the record, however, that all of the common people, all of the oppressed and downtrodden, all of the poor and underprivileged of the Old World did not migrate to the New. Those who came must have been in some way exceptional. Doubtless many who represented the established order regarded them with proper upperclass or aristocratic

[6] J. Hector St. John de Crèvecoeur, *Letters from an American Farmer* (New York, 1904); p. 54.

A Country of Common People

contempt. This view was expressed without restraint in 1777 by Nicholas Cresswell, the son of a modest English landholder in Derbyshire, who came to America to seek his fortune in 1774. He characterized the revolutionary army as "a ragged Banditti of undisciplined people, the scum and refuse of all nations on earth." Washington, he said, "was second son of a creditable Virginia Tobacco Planter (which I suppose may, in point of rank, be equal to the better sort of Yeomanry in England)."[7]

This view of the emigrant was also expressed with unstrained eloquence in 1798 by Timothy Dwight, President of Yale College and stout defender of property, church, and state in Connecticut. He thus describes those who composed the first wave of the great westward migrations from the older settlements, those who made the first clearings in the forest:

These men cannot live in regular society. They are too idle; too talkative; too passionate; too prodigal; and too shiftless; to acquire either property or character. They are impatient of the restraints of law, religion, and morality; grumble about the taxes, by which Rulers, Ministers, and School-masters, are supported; and complain incessantly, as well as bitterly, of the extortions of mechanics, farmers, merchants, and physicians; to whom they are always indebted. At the same time, they are usually possessed, in their own view, of uncommon wisdom; understand medical science, politics, and religion, better than those, who have studied them through life; and, although they manage their own concerns worse than any other men, feel perfectly satisfied, that they could manage those of the nation far better than the agents, to whom they are committed by the public. After displaying their own talents, and worth; after censuring the weakness, and wickedness, of their superiours; after exposing the injustice of the community in neglecting to invest persons of such merit with public offices; in many an eloquent harangue, uttered by many a kitchen fire, in every blacksmith's shop, and in every corner of the streets; and finding all their efforts vain; they become at length discouraged: and under the pressure of poverty, the fear of a gaol, and the consciousness of public contempt, leave their native places, and betake themselves to the wilderness.[8]

[7] *The Journal of Nicholas Cresswell, 1774–1777* (New York, 1928), p. 252.
[8] Timothy Dwight, *Travels; in New-England and New-York* (New-Haven, 1821), Vol. II, p. 459.

Among the emigrants from Europe there were probably many to whom this description might apply. But it should be remembered that Timothy Dwight had little respect for common people who refused to accept their "station" in life and obey the commands of their "betters." Both those who came to America and those who continued the migration toward the Pacific must have had positive as well as negative qualities. We know that they were relatively youthful and adventurous. Also they must have longed to be free; they must have rebelled against poverty and oppression; they must have had unusual faith in themselves; they must have had greater energy and daring than their brothers and sisters and neighbors whom they left behind. On the other hand, it seems probable that not a few courageous souls chose to remain at home and fight "to make Old England free." The fact remains, however, that in a very special and unique sense America has been the home of people scornful of social rank. In this land all men became "gentlemen" and all women "ladies." Also Smith, Taylor, Shoemaker, Carpenter, and Shepherd, and their counterparts in other languages, became surnames of dignity.

3

The story of the rise of these common people to power and dignity in America is one of the most inspiring in history.

Those who established the early settlements were generally without property, without equal civic rights, without formal education in the country of birth. In many cases they were either just emerging or not far removed from serfdom. Here in America they gradually cast off the weight of centuries of oppression, rose to their feet, looked their former masters in the eye, and became free men and women. Given opportunities denied them in the older societies, they achieved confidence in themselves, grew to higher moral stature, and developed a new conception of their own worth, nature, and powers. It is even reported by aristocratic visitors from the other side of the Atlantic that they often became "downright impudent and disrespectful." Unquestionably, as we shall note later, they lost many of those qualities which the master finds so pleasing and charming in the servant. This spiritual transformation was graphically described by Crèvecoeur, the original discoverer of the role of the frontier in American history:

In this great American asylum, the poor of Europe have by some means met together, and in consequence of various causes; to what purpose should they ask one another what countrymen they are? Alas, two thirds of them had no country. Can a wretch who wanders about, who works and starves, whose life is a continual scene of sore affliction or pinching penury; can that man call England or any other kingdom his country? A country that had no bread for him, whose fields procured him no harvest, who met with nothing but the frowns of the rich, the severity of the laws, with jails and punishments; who owned not a single foot of the extensive surface of this planet? No! urged by a variety of motives, here they came. Every thing has tended to regenerate them; new laws, a new mode of living, a new social system; here they are become men: in Europe they were as so many useless plants, wanting vegetative mould, and refreshing showers; they withered, and were mowed down by want, hunger, and war; but now by the power of transplantation, like all other plants they have taken root and flourished! Formerly they were not numbered in any civil lists of their country, except in those of the poor; here they rank as citizens. By what invisible power has this surprising metamorphosis been performed? By that of the laws and that of their industry. The laws, the indulgent laws, protect them as they arrive, stamping on them the symbol of adoption; they receive ample rewards for their labours; these accumulated rewards procure them lands; those lands confer on them the title of freemen, and to that title every benefit is affixed which men can possibly require. This is the great operation daily performed by our laws.[9]

In America the poor and underprivileged, recruited from the powerless classes of Europe, stormed the citadels of power.

[9] Crèvecoeur, *op. cit.*, pp. 52–53.

The significance of this achievement is rarely grasped in its fullness because the role of power in shaping the fortunes of democracy and aristocracy, of freedom and despotism, is little understood. Yet the rise of the totalitarian states during the past generation has demonstrated the truth of Lord Acton's famous aphorism: "Power tends to corrupt and absolute power corrupts absolutely."[10] We are also beginning to see what Thucydides meant when he said more than two thousand years ago: "We both alike know that into the discussion of human affairs the question of justice only enters where the pressure of necessity is equal, and that the powerful exact what they can, and the weak grant what they must." In the course of the generations the common people of America sought with striking success to conquer power in its several forms.

First of all, more or less through the accidents of history, they gained possession of the power to take life. This is the most elemental form of power, the court of last resort in any dispute, as the tyrants of the past and Hitler and Stalin in our time have clearly taught us. Through a strange combination of circumstances in America during the seventeenth and eighteenth centuries this power passed literally into the hands of the people. The invention of firearms and the conditions of life on the new continent were chiefly responsible. The colonist or settler was often dependent on game for food and had to rely on himself to defend his property and his family from the Indians. In contrast with the countries of Europe, hunting was "free" in America. As a consequence the common man gradually perfected the most accurate and deadly weapon known to history at the time. It was sometimes called the "Pennsylvania rifle" because it was developed in that colony by immigrant German gunsmiths, sometimes the "squirrel rifle" because a man expert in its use could bring down the elusive squirrel hiding behind the limb of a tree, and sometimes the "long rifle" simply because it was long. This weapon was an important factor in the winning of inde-

[10] John Emerich Edward Dalberg-Acton, *Essays on Freedom and Power* (Boston, 1948), p. 364.

pendence. In spite of the inferior training and discipline of the Revolutionary armies, though only a portion of the soldiers were armed with the rifle, the English lost more men than the Americans. In 1821 Fanny Wright was merely repeating the observation of many foreign visitors who had preceded her when she reported that the ordinary American was "not only regularly trained" to the musket "as a man, but practiced as a boy."

The generation of the founding fathers realized the importance of keeping military power in the hands of the people. They abolished the military caste, made the military subordinate to the civil authority, and thus erected one of the most powerful defenses of liberty in the political history of the human race. Also they inserted as the second article in the Bill of Rights the provision that "the right of the people to keep and bear arms shall not be infringed." With the improvement of weapons and the westward migration of our people the idea seems to have developed that the principle of equality rested in some measure on the firearm. The following couplet, it is said, may be found on some old Colt revolvers: "Be not afraid of any man, no matter what his size. When danger threatens, call on me, and I will equalize." Sometimes the thought was expressed thus: "It wasn't God or the Declaration of Independence that made all men free and equal; it was Colonel Sam'l Colt." Another variant was: "All men are not born equal—Sam'l Colt made 'em that way." Certainly on the frontier pretensions of social superiority were not easily sustained.

Second, the common people of America achieved a large measure of economic power. The importance of this conquest can scarcely be overemphasized. When Daniel Webster declared at the Massachusetts Constitutional Convention in 1820 that "in the absence of military force, political power naturally and necessarily goes into the hands which hold the property," he was merely repeating an observation as old as Aristotle. Almost two centuries earlier James Harrington, to whom the founding fathers were greatly indebted, made an almost identical statement. "If the people," he said, "hold three parts in four of the territory, it is plain there can neither be any single person nor nobility able to dispute the government with them; in this case, therefore, *except force be interposed*, they govern themselves."

Although efforts were made in the seventeenth century to introduce into the colonies the feudal system of land tenure, they were attended by little success. Land was too abundant. Very early, therefore, the practice of freehold became the dominant pattern of the rural economy. The common man thus won the right to dispose of his own labor, acquired title to land and the tools of production, learned to manage his farm or shop in his own interest, and attained a large measure of economic freedom and security. As a result, according to J. Franklin Jameson, "America stood committed to economic democracy" long before she "came to be marked by political institutions of a democratic type."[11] This fact so impressed Tocqueville that he began his introduction to his great work on *Democracy in America* with a reference, not to politics, but to economics. "Amongst the novel objects that attracted my attention during my stay in the United States," he wrote, "nothing struck me more forcibly than the general equality of condition among the people. I readily discovered the prodigious influence which this primary fact exercises on the whole course of society; it gives a peculiar direction to public opinion, and a peculiar tenor to the laws; it imparts new maxims to the governing authorities, and peculiar habits to the governed."[12]

Third, the common people of America achieved a large measure of political power. They won the right to choose their rulers and to frame their political institutions. They gradually extended the privilege of suffrage, assumed responsibility for legislation, formulated a bill of civil liberties, and created a "government of the people, by the people, and for the people."

Perhaps their supreme achievement, and the achievement

[11] J. Franklin Jameson, *The American Revolution Considered as a Social Movement* (Princeton, 1926), p. 41.
[12] Alexis de Tocqueville, *Democracy in America* (New York, 1898), Vol. I, p. 1.

A Country of Common People

with which they have become peculiarly identified in the world, was the establishment of a system of democratic constitutional government. As they struggled for independence from the mother country they carried through a uniquely successful political revolution. Building on the ancient traditions of human freedom, the heritage of English liberalism, and the experience in self-government gained during the colonial period, they struck out boldly along new paths. They resolutely refused to follow the classical revolutionary pattern of the Old World with its cycle from tyranny through popular revolt and military triumph back to tyranny. They broke through this cycle and moved from victory on the battlefield to a novel and daring venture in statecraft.

Led by a company of men of unsurpassed courage, inventiveness, and wisdom, the American people consolidated the gains of the Revolution and framed a great charter of political rights and duties, of political processes and institutions designed to achieve justice, change, and stability under a regime of law. In spite of the heavy strains put upon it by the extraordinary growth of the nation and the radical transformation of life conditions, this charter has endured for more than a century and a half. Its authors hoped that it would make possible fundamental changes in economy and even government itself by peaceful and rational means. "And it is the glory of our republican government," wrote John McCulloch in the third edition of the first history of the United States prepared for use in the schools, "that the people have the supreme controul; and that when they apprehend their rulers err, they can effect a change of measures at the periods of election, without tumult, or the hazard of a revolution."[13] This is the central article of the American political faith and the basic element in the American way of life.

Fourth, the common people of America won the right to knowledge. In 1798 a Massachusetts farmer, who had attended school less than six months in his life, completed a manuscript on the foundations of political freedom. Though

---

[13] John McCulloch, *A Concise History of the United States, from the Discovery of America, till 1807* (Third edition, Philadelphia, 1807), pp. 205–206.

his spelling was bad and his grammar worse, he attacked the problem with rare insight. He had been a soldier in the Revolutionary army and had watched with a sense of destiny the establishment of the Republic. He knew that popular governments had been attempted before in human history and that sooner or later they had failed. The fact greatly disturbed him and drove him to search for the key of liberty. Influenced no doubt by the currents of liberal thought then flowing on both sides of the Atlantic, he came to the conclusion that free governments had failed because of the ignorance of the people, that "therefore the ondly Remidi is knowledge." He then proceeded to outline what he called the "knowledge nesecary for a freeman."[14]

The proposition that knowledge is the sole key of liberty can scarcely be defended. Undoubtedly there are other keys. Yet this relatively untutored farmer who had never been fifty miles from where he "was born in no direction" and "always followed hard labour for a living" was profoundly right in his emphasis on knowledge. The common people of America struggled through the seventeenth, eighteenth, and nineteenth centuries to establish the rights and the institutions through which they might gain understanding of their world and equip themselves to defend their true interests. They fought for the right to speak and to think, to assemble and petition; they fought for a free press and for public schools. Some of these rights they wrote into the fundamental law of the land.

Fifth, the common people of America won the right to freedom of conscience, to worship as they pleased. One of the most powerful instruments for controlling the mind of a people is an established church, whether Eastern Orthodox, Roman Catholic, or Protestant, whether Fascist, Nazi, Communist, or some other. The struggle to abolish this feature of the feudal system was long and bitter. It began with the opening of the modern period in Europe and was carried to America by the settlers. State or preferred churches were established everywhere, although the laws were far more

[14] William Manning, *The Key of Libberty* (Billerica, Mass., 1922), pp. 60–61.

A Country of Common People

lenient or less rigorously enforced in some colonies than in others. The trend toward religious tolerance and freedom gradually made progress in the new land, hastened certainly by the presence in the same community of several or even many different sects. It triumphed on a national scale in the first provision of the *first* article of the federal Bill of Rights, which declares that "Congress shall make no law respecting an establishment of religion, or prohibiting the free exercise thereof." The legal battle, however, was not completely won in the states until the "optional title system" was abolished in Massachusetts in 1833. And thereafter the struggle against religious dogma and bigotry has continued down to the present day.

4

The common people of America proclaimed the principle of human equality.

They conducted a general assault on the entire system of class and caste. They abolished the laws of primogeniture and entail. They nurtured the doctrine that the individual, regardless of ancestry or previous condition, should be judged only by his own industry, talents, and character and that he might properly aspire to the highest positions in the economic, political, and cultural life of the nation. Moreover, since they worked, and usually worked hard, for a living, they succeeded in giving to labor in its various useful forms a dignity and a status not to be found in the societies of the Old World. In the words of Francis J. Grund, they attacked successfully the Old World doctrine that "labor is incompatible with respectability, and that the highest title to respect is the having *inherited* a fortune."[15] Also in very considerable measure they pricked the ancient bubble of the innate superiority of the man of family and rank. The professed aristocrat, stripped of the artificial supports of tradition, dress, and manner, was often found to

[15] Francis J. Grund, *The Americans, in Their Moral, Social, and Political Relations* (Boston, 1837), p. 157.

be quite an ordinary person. Indeed on the frontier he frequently revealed himself to be without discernible resources or talents. Here, therefore, the very idea of a social class, endowed with special rights and privileges, tended to become repulsive and un-American.

The American descendants of the poor of Europe, particularly in the west, developed a militant and aggressive spirit of equality. They became fiercely resentful of every assertion or assumption of social superiority. This spirit was particularly manifest in the status and attitudes of persons engaged in manual labor or in personal service of various kinds. The condition and behavior of these people were a source of perennial interest and comment by foreign travelers during the latter part of the eighteenth and the first half of the nineteenth century. Many visitors from Europe noted that an American, regardless of his occupation, expected to be treated as a man, as a first-class citizen of the Republic. They were astonished to see farmers and mechanics ride in the same conveyances, sit at the same tables, and participate in the same conversations with eminent lawyers and even judges of the Supreme Court. They were still more astonished when they saw "servants" sitting down to dinner with their "masters." But they were probably most astonished at the sight of a president of the United States signing himself in a letter to a "butcher" or a "hat-maker" as "Your humble servant."

Aristocratic visitors from beyond the Atlantic who brought to America the European conception of class relations invariably had many unpleasant and harrowing experiences. One commented on the "want of common civility" on the part of "the lower classes of people in America"; another noted with sorrow that "the lower classes of people will return rude and impertinent answers to questions couched in the most civil terms"; yet another bewailed the fact that servants responded very sluggishly to the "ringing of bells," to the "thumping of the floor," or to "the rapping of the plate with your knife." Naturally such visitors carried back to Europe a very unfavorable impression of American society and were certain that the Republic could not long endure.

Other visitors, however, recognized the emergence of a new form of society in which the ordinary man had achieved a new sense of dignity and worth. One said that he had observed none of "that species of hauteur which one class of society in some countries show in their intercourse with the other"; another remarked that in America a man "will not wear a *livery*, any more than he will wear a halter round his neck"; and another reported that "there are few native Americans who would submit to the degradation of wearing a livery, or any other badge of servitude," and thus "becoming a man's man." In 1845 Sir Charles Lyell advised his friends in England that if they should ever "venture on the experiment" of traveling in America, "they had better not take with them an English maid-servant, unless they are prepared for her being transformed into an equal."[16] In 1861 Anthony Trollope, after referring to the uncouth manners and the tobacco-spitting propensities of the people on the western frontiers, speaks of "a certain manliness of the men, which gives them a dignity of their own." And the investigator today could probably find in some "backward" parts of America men and women who would refuse indignantly to accept gratuities for services rendered.

Although the principle of equality has always been limited in its application, it has been more generally respected and honored in America than in any other major country of history. It is one of the most precious elements of our heritage. Down through the generations we have waged an unceasing struggle against privilege and aristocracy.

5

The story of the common people who built America is still unfinished.

What they will do in the strangely complex and dynamic industrial order which is sweeping the

[16] Charles Lyell, *A Second Visit to the United States of North America* (New York, 1849), Vol. II, p. 167.

world, no one can say. That great trials and hazards throng the pathway to the future is evident. Yet this much is in the record: American civilization, whatever its merits or faults, is a monument to the powers resident in common people—in those millions of common people who in the course of more than three centuries came to this land and made it their home. Faith in America has always been faith in common people—in common people capable of producing leaders of virtue and talent from their own ranks. If the age of the common man is in truth opening throughout the world, as some prophets are proclaiming, we should be well prepared by our history to play a great and significant role in this new age.

6

A FREE SOCIETY OF FARMERS AND TRADESMEN

1

The America of the founding fathers and the early decades of the Republic was a pre-industrial society of farmers and tradesmen.

There were no cities as we understand the term today. The largest center of population at the beginning of the nineteenth century contained less than fifty thousand inhabitants. There were no buildings above three or four stories, no apartment houses, no great factories or department stores. The wood-burning stove and the sulphur match had not yet displaced the fireplace and flint and steel. Fields were cultivated with the hoe and the wooden plow, crops were harvested with the hand and the sickle. Mining was in its infancy and forests were regarded, not as a source of wealth, but as a powerful barrier opposing the advance of agriculture. Even hunting, fishing, and trapping made important contributions to the larder and the wardrobe of many an American family. Commerce was limited to the itinerant peddler and widely scattered towns and trading posts. The rearing of the young was largely incidental to the life of family and neighborhood. It was a simple and loosely organized society.

The development and application to the economy of the basic sciences of physics and chemistry, of astronomy and geology, of biology and physiology, lay for the most part in the future. Engineering, manufacture, agriculture, home economics, medicine, and surgery rested on empirical foundations. Men knew little about metallurgy or machine construction, still less about metal alloys, drugs, and mineral fertilizers, and nothing about plastics, calories, vitamins, and antibiotics. There were no railroads, nor even canals, and few highways capable of withstanding frost and sun and rain. There were no steamboats, trolley cars, automobiles, or airplanes; there was neither telegraph, telephone, nor radio, neither rotary press nor moving picture. Steam and combustion engines and electric motors were still to come. The vacuum tube, radar, and television were inconceivable. Men waged war without machine guns or rifled cannon, without armored ships or submarines, without tanks or airplanes, without the atomic bomb. In terms of the ordinary ways of life it was a pre-scientific age.

2

America was predominantly a land of families and rural neighborhoods.

During the colonial period a form of social organization emerged under which, according to James Truslow Adams, "a widely scattered and mainly agricultural population" led "a hard-working, narrow, parochial and sometimes dangerous existence in solitary farms, tiny hamlets, or at most in what would now be considered small villages."[1] The emphasis here should be placed on the "solitary farms." Unlike the inhabitants of the Old World, the American people, after they had established themselves in the new land, lived in more or less isolated rural households rather than in villages. Peter Kalm, a Swedish "professor of Oecon-

[1] James Truslow Adams, *Provincial Society 1690-1763* (New York, 1928), p. 23.

A Free Society of Farmers and Tradesmen

omy," noted this distinctive feature of American social organization in the middle of the eighteenth century. "The farms are most of them single," he wrote from New Jersey in 1748, "and you seldom meet with even two together, except in towns, or places which are intended for towns; therefore there are but few villages. Each farm has its corn-fields, its woods, its pastures and meadows."[2] The role of the family in our history consequently assumes a special significance. Frederick Jackson Turner was not exaggerating when he said that the family was the vehicle for carrying European civilization across the North American continent. That it was supported by the rural neighborhood is of course recognized. But in its operations it bore little resemblance to the family of today.

The rural household was relatively self-sufficient. Most of the activities necessary to sustain life were carried on in the home by the members of the family. As a result the farmer was far more than a farmer. He not only tended fields and flocks, but also practiced a vast array of arts long since forgotten by the cultivator of the soil. "The philosopher's stone of an American farmer," wrote Crèvecoeur, "is to do everything within his own family."[3] With his sons he was at the same time a tiller of the soil and "a jack of all trades"—a butcher, a tanner, a cobbler, a carpenter, a mechanic, a mason, and even a hunter, a fisherman, and a trapper. Likewise, his wife was far more than a "house-keeper" in the contemporary sense. With her daughters she was skilled in all the arts associated with the curing of foods and the preparation of clothing from the raw fiber to the finished article. The rural household was almost an entire economy in itself. Tench Coxe, Assistant Secretary of the Treasury under Alexander Hamilton, characterized this condition as a "union of manufactures and farming."[4] Horace Bushnell, describing in 1851 the "age of homespun" in which he was born, said that

---

[2] Peter Kalm, *Travels into North America* (London, 1771), Vol. II, p. 25.

[3] J. Hector St. John de Crèvecoeur, *Sketches of Eighteenth Century America* (New Haven, 1925), p. 104.

[4] Tench Coxe, *A View of the United States of America* (Philadelphia, 1794), p. 442.

"the house was a factory on the farm, the farm a grower and producer for the house."[5] One phase of this self-sufficiency, as it appeared in Suffolk County, New York, toward the close of the eighteenth century, was graphically reported by Henry P. Hedges two generations ago:

> From his feet to his head the farmer stood in vestment produced on his own farm. The leather of his shoes came from the hides of his own cattle. The linen and woolen that he wore were products that he raised. The farmer's wife or daughter braided and sewed the straw hat on his head. His fur cap was made from the skin of a fox he shot. The feathers of wild fowl in the bed whereon he rested his weary frame by night were the results acquired in his shooting. The pillow-cases, sheets and blankets, the comfortables, quilts and counterpanes, the towels and table cloth, were home made. His harness and lines he cut from hides grown on his farm. Everything about his ox yoke except staple and ring he made. His whip, his ox gad, his flail, axe, hoe and forkhandle, were his own work. How little he bought, and how much he contrived to supply his wants by home manufacture would astonish this generation.[6]

The self-sufficiency of the rural household went far beyond the borders of the economy. The family was immediately responsible for the physical care of its members from the cradle to the grave. It nurtured the young, tended the sick, and watched over the aged. It was the major educational agency, transmitting to the young its cultural possessions, its useful skills and knowledges, its moral principles and conceptions, its outlook upon the world. It supervised the precious hours of relief from back-breaking toil and with the assistance of the surrounding community organized the recreational interest. Before the day of commercial amusements it filled the limited leisure time with simple, often crude and rough, entertainment, closely associated with the economic, religious, and political life. In many a family, too, various forms of religious worship, Bible reading and prayers, were a part of the daily routine.

[5] Horace Bushnell, "The Age of Homespun," in *Work and Play* (New York, 1864), p. 392.
[6] Henry P. Hedges, "Development of Agriculture in Suffolk County," in *Bi-Centennial History of Suffolk County* (Babylon, N. Y., 1885), p. 42.

The rural neighborhood was a community of families. Everywhere, but particularly on the frontier, these families were closely bound together in a common venture for survival. Misfortune, danger, and even death lurked around many a corner. The basic institutions of school and church were joint undertakings. Also there were many economic burdens to be borne which surpassed the strength of a single family or which might be carried more easily or pleasantly by group or cooperative action. This propensity for mutual aid, for festivals, frolics, and bees, as they were called, was especially remarked by foreign travelers. The Marquis de Chastellux, a member of the French Academy and a general in the French armies serving the American cause during the last years of the War for Independence, gave an account of the establishment of a new settlement in the wilderness—a process which he said he had "observed a hundred times." The following observation he set down in his journal under the date of 1780 at Farmington, Connecticut:

I shall be asked, perhaps, how one man, or one family can be so quickly lodged? I answer, that in America a man is never alone, never an isolated being. The neighbours, for they are every where to be found, make it a point of hospitality to aid the new farmer. A cask of cyder drunk in common, and with gaity, or a gallon of rum, are the only recompense for these services. Such are the means by which North America, which one hundred years ago was nothing but a vast forest, is peopled with three millions of inhabitants.[7]

John Bradbury, a British naturalist, whose scientific studies took him into the Mississippi and Missouri valleys beginning in 1809, was much interested in this feature of American rural life. "This combination of labour in numbers, for the benefit of one individual," he wrote, "is not confined to the new comer only, it occurs frequently in the course of a year amongst the *old settlers*, with whom it is a continued bond of amity and social intercourse, and in no part of the world is *good neighbourship* found in greater perfection than in the

[7] François Jean de Chastellux, *Travels in North-America, in the Years 1780, 1781, and 1782* (Dublin, 1787), Vol. I, p. 47.

western territory, or in America generally."[8] John Woods, an English traveler to Illinois in 1820–21, drew a sharp contrast between an English and an American settlement in that territory. Whereas the English settlers were strongly individualistic, he said, the "Americans seldom do anything without having" a frolic. "Thus, they have husking, reaping, rolling frolics, &c. &c. Among the females, they have picking, sewing, and quilting frolics."[9] Tocqueville observed that "when an American asks for the cooperation of his fellow-citizens, it is seldom refused." In many matters such action was a condition of survival under the hard conditions of life generally prevailing.

All relations among people were comparatively personal, intimate, and enduring. The neighborhoods were small and neighbors saw one another face to face. Although there was a vast amount of movement of population, far more than in any other society of the age, people played as children, grew to maturity, passed through middle age, and grew old together. As a consequence, they knew one another, as they do not and cannot today in the vast reaches of industrial society. The true character of an individual lay exposed to inspection through his behavior over a long period of time. Neither virtues nor vices could be easily concealed. The process of synthetic fabrication of reputations, so common in our time, was not possible. Actions quickly received their proper rewards and punishments, according to the code. Even the stranger was regarded, neither as a part of the landscape nor as an object for exploitation, but above all as a human being filled with interesting information, sentiments, and ideas. Economic transactions, moreover, were not merely business deals involving the exchange of goods or services, but actions between people, actions suffused with personal values and subject to moral judgment. In the rural neighborhood, de-

[8] John Bradbury, "Travels in the Interior of America in the Years 1809, 1810, and 1811," in R. G. Thwaites, *Early Western Travels* (Cleveland, 1904), Vol. V, p. 283.
[9] John Woods, "Two Years' Residence in the Settlement on the English Prairie, in the Illinois Country, United States," in R. G. Thwaites, *Early Western Travels* (Cleveland, 1904), Vol. X, p. 300.

A Free Society of Farmers and Tradesmen 93

spite its many limitations and hardships, the individual enjoyed a sense of status and security which industrial civilization as yet has not provided. Here is a major challenge from the agrarian age.

3

The economy was based on individual and family enterprise.

As the foregoing analysis discloses, the individual farmer with his family, supported when occasion demanded by the neighborhood, was the basic economic reality. He asked and received very little assistance from government. Nor did he combine with those of like interest to exact a larger share of the national income from the community. His struggle for the most part was not with his fellow men but with the elements. This economy had a number of distinguishing characteristics.

Private property in land and the tools of production was the basic institution. For the establishment of this institution in the law the colonists fought without ceasing from generation to generation. The success of this struggle laid the economic foundations for the development of American democracy and political liberty. Because of the abundance of land it was not excessively difficult to obtain title to a small farm. And since the tools of production were extremely simple and inexpensive, mostly made of wood, their acquisition was not too arduous. Indeed, with a few bits of iron the "jack of all trades" could make most of them. The right to private property under the conditions of time and place therefore guaranteed to the individual of industry an unprecedented opportunity to achieve limited economic success. Crèvecoeur tells the story of a man who reached our shores "stark naked," found clothes and friends, settled at Maraneck, married a wife, and "left a good farm" to each of his several sons. The right to private property also practically guaranteed the right to work.

The market was but feebly developed. People produced for themselves and for their neighbors. There was little exchange and very little money. A single household saw only a few tens of dollars in the course of the year and financial transactions were strange and unfamiliar events. The wares to be found in the trading posts were limited in quantity and variety—largely iron and metal goods of various kinds, earthenware, simple drugs, salt, sugar, ginger, tobacco, and fine cloth. In his study of rural economy in New England at the beginning of the nineteenth century, a region particularly favorable for trade, Percy Wells Bidwell concludes that in the states of Connecticut, Rhode Island, and Massachusetts "one-fifth to one-fourth of the total population" was the "maximum number to whom the market, such as it was, was at all accessible. The remaining portion of the agricultural population was almost entirely isolated from commercial relations with the outside world."[10] The same writer, moreover, states that "of manufactures," that is, of "articles produced for a wide market . . . we may say that there were practically none in New England in 1810."[11] One can easily imagine the condition of trade in those regions of the country less well endowed with waterways.

The condition of the market reflected the primitive character of the means of communication. In comparison with the Old World the country was sparsely inhabited and the distances were vast. It was this fact that compelled the overwhelming majority of our people to live in relatively isolated families and neighborhoods. Except for a few turnpikes connecting some of the larger towns in the east, America was practically without highways in the contemporary sense. Settlements were connected only by trails and ungraded roads cut through the wilderness, with stumps often standing and made almost impassable by mud-holes during the rainy or thawing seasons.

The physical hardships associated with travel were a sub-

---

[10] Percy Wells Bidwell, *Rural Economy in New England at the Beginning of the Nineteenth Century* (New Haven, 1916), p. 318.
[11] *Ibid.*, p. 275.

ject of endless comment by foreign visitors and doubtless goaded many of them to speak contemptuously of the level of civilization in America. And it should be realized that they probably experienced only the best of our roads and the most comfortable of our conveyances. The Irishman, Isaac Weld, traveling through Maryland in 1795, described an old American custom which was reported again and again during the next fifty years. "The driver," he said, "frequently had to call to the passengers in the stage, to lean out of the carriage first at one side, then at the other, to prevent it from oversetting in the deep ruts with which the road abounds: 'Now, gentlemen, to the right'; upon which the passengers all stretched their bodies half way out of the carriage to balance it on that side: 'Now, gentlemen, to the left,' and so on. This was found absolutely necessary at least a dozen times in half the number of miles."[12] In 1846 Sir Charles Lyell reports precisely the same experience from Georgia. Often male passengers were asked to get out and walk over a particularly muddy stretch of road or even to assist the driver by using rails to "pry the coach out of the ruts." Between Philadelphia and Baltimore in 1797, according to *The American Annual Register* for that year, "chasms to the depth of six, eight, or ten feet occur at numerous intervals." Obviously passage over such roads was hazardous as well as unpleasant: "Coaches are overturned, passengers killed, and horses destroyed by the overwork put upon them."[13]

Such primitive means of communication obviously made extensive trade impossible. Going to market except on horseback was limited largely to certain favorable seasons. Commerce was confined also to the most necessary and precious articles. The French botanist, François A. Michaux, wrote from Kentucky in 1802 "that there is not a single species of colonial produce in Kentucky, except ginseng that will bear the expense of carriage by land from that state to Philadel-

[12] Isaac Weld, Jr., *Travels Through the States of North America and the Provinces of Upper and Lower Canada During the Years 1795, 1796, and 1797* (London, 1799), Vol. I, pp. 37–38.
[13] Quoted in Seymour Dunbar, *A History of Travel in America* (Indianapolis, 1915), Vol. I, p. 191.

phia."[14] It has been estimated that in the early years of the nineteenth century the cost of land carriage in the western regions ranged from a cent to a cent and a half per mile for one hundred pounds. "At such rates," say Percy Wells Bidwell and John I. Falconer, "corn could not stand the expense of moving 20 miles, even though produced at no cost, and wheat could not be profitably transported by land more than 50 or 75 miles."[15] Before the completion of the Erie canal "the expense of transportation from Buffalo to New York was stated at $100 per ton, and the ordinary length of passage *twenty days*; so that, upon the very route through which the heaviest and cheapest products of the West are now sent to market, the cost of transportation equalled nearly *three* times the market value of wheat in New York; *six* times the value of corn; *twelve* times the value of oats; and far exceeded the value of most kinds of cured provisions."[16] Clearly the development of the market and the differentiation of labor awaited the radical improvement of the means of communication.

Most people pursued the same occupations. To be sure, there were distinctions according to age and sex. But beyond this there was little occupational differentiation among the inhabitants of rural America, even in the villages and the smaller centers of population. Percy Wells Bidwell, in his study of New England in the early years of the Republic, looked for division of labor in the towns and found little. After "taking up successively the representatives of what we now call the professional class, the business men and the artisans," he concluded "that with the usual exception of the minister" they "all held farms which provided their food as well as other necessities of life." "We may think, then, of this whole group of persons," he continued, "as standing on

[14] François A. Michaux, *Voyage à l'Ouest des Monts Alléghanys* (Paris, 1808), p. 138.
[15] Percy Wells Bidwell and John I. Falconer, *History of Agriculture in the Northern United States 1620–1860* (Washington, 1925), p. 181.
[16] Israel D. Andrews, *Report on the Trade and Commerce of the British North American Colonies, and upon the Trade of the Great Lakes and Rivers* (Washington, 1854), p. 234.

the borderline between agriculture and a specialized nonagricultural occupation. They were at times doctors, lawyers, inn keepers or storekeepers, fullers, carpenters, or tanners, but most of the time plain farmers. Thus we can see that the distinction between various occupations which we had set up for purposes of analysis tends to vanish. The broad outlines of a future division of employments were marked out, but the process of separation was as yet hardly begun."[17] Evidence is at hand, moreover, that even the minister was not wholly an exception to the general rule. Not infrequently he was "borne down with the fatigues of manual labor."

Foreign travelers often remarked the lack of occupational and class divisions. One speaks of a tavern-keeper at Millston River, New Jersey, in 1783, who was also a "weaver, a shoemaker, a furrier, a wheelwright, a farmer, a gardener." Another in 1797 at Columbia, Ohio, tells of an acquaintance who "supported the characters of a merchant, a farmer, and a parson" and then observes that such versatility "is a thing not very uncommon to be met with." Another reports that "in the country parts of Pennsylvania" about this same time judges "are no more than plain farmers, who from their infancy have been accustomed to little else than following the plough." Yet another, while traveling in Vermont a few years later, notes with amazement that "of the judges, at present on the bench of the supreme court, only one was bred to the law. Of the others, one, at the present time, finds leisure, in the vacations, to drive a team between Rutland and Troy." The fact that our people lived and labored in much the same way must have been a powerful factor in fostering the conception of equality.

Most people worked for themselves. Moreover, because of the high degree of self-sufficiency of the rural household, the individual farmer achieved a kind of independence that has been extremely rare in history. As John Melish, a Glasgow manufacturer who visited America several times between 1806 and 1811, somewhat lyrically observed, he could "stand

[17] Percy Wells Bidwell, *Rural Economy in New England at the Beginning of the Nineteenth Century* (New Haven, 1916), pp. 266–267.

erect on the middle of his farm, and say, 'This ground is mine: from the highest canopy of heaven, down to the lowest depths, I can claim all that I can get possession of within these bounds; fowls of the air, fish of the sea, and all that pass through the same.' And, having a full share of consequence in the political scale, his equal rights are guaranteed to him. None dare encroach upon him; he can sit under his own vine, and under his own fig-tree, and none to make him afraid."[18]

It was these self-sufficient farmers on whom Thomas Jefferson erected his political philosophy and whom he had in mind when he declared that "those who labor in the earth are the chosen people of God." And Alexander Hamilton recognized the same economic foundation of personal integrity and independence in his powerful argument in favor of a fixed provision for the support of federal judges. "In the general course of human nature," he said in the seventy-ninth number of *The Federalist*, "*a power over a man's subsistence amounts to a power over his will.*" Our great tradition of political liberty and individual rights must have been derived in very considerable measure from the fact that for generations most of our people worked for themselves and held in their own hands the means of livelihood.

Human energy was the chief source of power. In this respect the American people down to the days of Jackson were not far removed from the men who built the pyramids of Egypt, the palaces of Cambodia, or the temples of Peru. Although during the intervening centuries some progress had been made in the harnessing of the energies of ox and horse and the natural forces of wind and water, the advance was not revolutionary in character. Like the inhabitants of the ancient empires, the people who settled America and founded our Republic cut down the forests, tilled the soil, harvested their crops, built their dwellings, fabricated their tools and utensils, constructed their bridges and highways, and moved from place to place largely under power derived from human muscle. This of course meant that life, even on this fabu-

---

[18] John Melish, *Travels in the United States of America* (Philadelphia, 1812), Vol. II, pp. 357–358.

lously rich continent during the pre-industrial age, was always marked by severe and unremitting toil for both sexes and all ages above the years of infancy. It meant also that the great masses of people had to be satisfied with the barest necessities of life. Comforts and leisure were and could be the lot of only a favored few.

Another form of economy was rising even in the early colonial period. This economy shared with the economy of the rural household the institution of private property in the tools of production. But from that point there was little resemblance. It emerged in the towns of mediaeval Europe, developed increasing power from generation to generation, and came to the New World with the earliest settlements. It was associated at first primarily with the lending of money, the conduct of trade, and the accumulation of wealth through the purchase and sale of goods. Later it moved into the spheres of manufacturing, mining, lumbering, construction, communication, and even agriculture. In early America it ruled the trading posts and markets of the towns. Its spirit is clearly expressed in a letter addressed by Benjamin Franklin to a young friend in 1748 on the general subject of getting rich. The substance of the letter is set down in a series of admonitions: "Remember, that time is money. . . . Remember, that credit is money. . . . Remember, that money is of the prolific, generating nature. . . . Remember, that six pounds a year is but a groat a day. . . . Remember this saying, *The good paymaster is lord of another man's purse.*" In conclusion he observes that "the way to wealth, if you desire it, is as plain as the way to market."[19] This economic individualism of the merchant or the enterpriser gradually invaded and eventually conquered the domain of the self-sufficient farmer. "We may trace the conflict between the capitalist and the democratic pioneer," writes Frederick Jackson Turner, "from the earliest colonial days." We know of course that the capitalist triumphed and in triumphing built the present industrial order and ushered in a new age.

[19] Jared Sparks, *The Works of Benjamin Franklin* (Boston, 1836), Vol. II, pp. 87–89.

4

Government played a minor and limited role in early America.

The generation that founded the Republic feared government. Popular opposition to the Federal Constitution, even with its limitations on the national authority and its system of checks and balances, was intense. This deep-seated fear on the part of our people grew out of their knowledge of despotism in Europe and their long struggle with royal governors and representatives of the English crown. They did not want to exchange a tyranny in distant London for a tyranny nearer home in Philadelphia or Washington. Thomas Paine was but expressing a common sentiment when he wrote: "Government, even in its best state, is but a necessary evil; in its worst state, an intolerable one." Thomas Jefferson, peerless champion of human liberty and father of American democracy, in similar vein declared that a "very energetic government" is "always oppressive" and that people who live without government "enjoy in their general mass an infinitely greater degree of happiness than those who live under the European governments." Grover Cleveland was speaking in this tradition in 1887 when he vetoed the "Texas Seed Bill" with these words: "Though the people support the Government, the Government should not support the people." Throughout a large part of their history the American people subscribed in both theory and practice to the view that the true function of government is to "restrain men from injuring one another," and to "leave them otherwise free to regulate their own pursuits of industry and improvement."

In actuality during the period of the simple agrarian economy, both state and federal government had but little to do beyond regulating foreign trade, fostering manufacture, defending the nation from external aggression, and protecting the individual in the exercise of his constitutional rights. The family or the neighborhood was able to take care of itself. Because of the great distances and the primitive condition of

A Free Society of Farmers and Tradesmen 101

communication, moreover, the federal authority in particular was very far away. And as the people moved across the continent, they often advanced ahead of government, took the law into their own hands, and built their political institutions. This led to the development of a tradition of lawlessness which remains with us to this day. It also nurtured the idea that the people themselves are the ultimate authority in the affairs of state. This conception is the foundation of political liberty. To maintain it in the emerging age will be difficult.

5

Education was largely unorganized.

On the farm and on the frontier there was comparatively little demand for those forms of learning associated with the traditional school. Society was still in very considerable degree in the pre-literate stage. Given the level of practical techniques then prevailing, reading, writing, and arithmetic were far less important in achieving success than the knowledges and skills demanded in the many occupations which filled the life of the farmer or the frontiersman.

This does not mean, however, that the young received no education. As a matter of fact, they received a most rigorous education, an education superior in many ways to that which they receive today. Certainly it was far more closely linked with life than anything to be found in even the most modern school. It was in the family that the individual received the major part of his vocational, civic, and moral training. Almost from the time he was able to walk about the house or yard, he was expected to assist in guarding family interests and promoting family welfare. And as he grew in strength and understanding new responsibilities were placed upon his shoulders. The boy performed innumerable chores having to do with the supply of fuel and water, the care of animals, the tilling of the fields, the harvesting of crops, and the practice of the mechanical arts; the girl helped to prepare the meals, wash the dishes, do the laundry, preserve fruits, vegetables, and meats, look after the needs of younger children, and perform the diverse industrial activities carried on in the home in the age of homespun. Gradually, as the youngster matured, and as a part of the process of maturing, he acquired all the occupational skills and knowledges appropriate to the sex. There was no problem of providing "work experience." At the same time, as he labored and played and lived in the family circle, he received civic and moral training. While this education inevitably reflected the cultural and ethical standards of the home, it was marked by a quality of genuineness that is rarely found in the school. It was intimately related to life. Indeed, it was an integral part of the process of living. Percy Wells Bidwell thus appraises the practices of rural New England at the beginning of the nineteenth century:

In its educative effects the self-sufficient household produced certain results which the more formal training of our modern homes and schools has never been able to approximate. In the first place, it inculcated habits of self-reliance and an ability to bear responsibility. In large families where the various tasks of the house and farm were apportioned to each member of the family according to his strength and ability, even the little children were taught early that for the performance of their particular tasks they were to be strictly accountable. It was a hard discipline often, and perhaps it developed too early a serious way of taking life, but under proper control it evolved a race of men strong and independent.[20]

The family, however, was not the only educational agency of pre-industrial society. The youngster grew up in the rural neighborhood and participated, according to his level of maturity, in the many activities of the community. He took part eagerly in picnics and socials, in frolics and bees and festivals, in hunting and fishing parties, in holiday celebrations and sporting contests. The church, with its ancient traditions, its organized services, its camp meetings, and its sacred ceremonies marking and solemnizing the great crises of birth, marriage, and death, occupied a central position in

[20] Bidwell, *op. cit.*, p. 378.

the moral life of the people. The district school, weak though it was, challenged the authority of parents at some points and served to foster relationships beyond the family circle. Even the press sent occasional books, magazines, and newspapers into an occasional home. Yet the fact remains that for the most part education was carried on without the directing influence of formal agencies. The individual received his education primarily as a by-product of genuine participation in the life of family and neighborhood.

6

The simple society of farmers and tradesmen has been swept away.

Our old way of life, the way of life in which the young Republic was nurtured, is gone, and gone forever, even though much of the spirit which it engendered remains. One can scarcely contemplate this fact without a feeling of melancholy. If there was much in this early society that we would be happy to leave to history—the bitter toil, the lack of refinement, and the crudeness of manners, there was also much that we would like to preserve as the essence of American character. The life on the frontier and on the farm bred in our people a sturdy and self-reliant quality, an inventive and resourceful mind, a sense of individual worth and integrity, an abhorrence of show and pretense, a fierce assertion of human equality, a deep love of personal freedom. Let us hope that in the new civilization which is unfolding, we shall be able to preserve some of these traits. But "be the issue as it may," as Horace Bushnell said in the infancy of the industrial age a century ago, "it has come; it is already a fact, and the consequences must follow."

7

A RICH AND BEAUTIFUL LAND

1

Every civilization must have a geographical base or home. It must be located somewhere on the surface of the earth. And as man ever strives to bend the forces of nature to his will, so those forces invariably leave their stamp on him and his institutions. Although he has been able through increase of understanding and progress of invention to extend his sway over the entire earth and to live under the most diverse conditions of climate and soil, he has never achieved independence from the molding influence of geography. At any particular level of the practical arts, moreover, nature sets limits which man cannot surmount. We do not look for the highest cultural achievements in the deserts, in the frozen places, or in the torrid regions of the earth. Neither do we find a maritime civilization on the central plains of a great continent, an agricultural civilization on an arid steppe, or an industrial civilization in a region devoid of mineral deposits. The fortunes of a people are strongly conditioned by the spot it has chosen for its habitation.

America was and is a fabulously rich land. At the time of Jamestown and Plymouth it was rich for almost every level of human culture. It was rich for the savage with his bow and arrow and his dependence on the wild and uncultivated bounty of nature; it was rich for the most advanced form of civilized existence. We know that for any particular type of

A Rich and Beautiful Land 105

civilization some spots on the earth are far more choice than others. The people who settled America found themselves possessing in generous proportions one of those choice spots. In this respect we stand even today, after generations of heedless waste and exploitation, among the most favored of the nations. This land of ours was and is almost uniquely rich in those resources of climate, soil, flora, fauna, minerals, and energy resources necessary to the development of a great, progressive, and enduring civilization in the industrial age.

2

At the time of the first settlements America was rich in the resources of climate and soil.

The colonists found the climate favorable to a high release of human energy and to the growth of an extraordinary variety of plants and animals. Indeed, America possesses one of the largest, if not the largest, of the most favored climatic regions of the earth. On the basis of an extended inquiry into climatic conditions affecting the release of human energy, Ellsworth Huntington divided the land surface of the globe into five zones. In the highest zone, which comprises only those areas where the factors of temperature, humidity, and variability are most conducive to physical and mental vigor, he placed but two regions of any magnitude. One embraces practically the whole of western and northwestern Europe, including the British Isles; the other lies in North America and is bounded by a line that starts on the northern bank of the mouth of the St. Lawrence, follows this river to the region of the Great Lakes, moves westward and a trifle northerly to the Rocky Mountains, turns back to the southeast and then south into Colorado, bends sharply eastward through Kansas, Missouri, and Illinois, and finally cuts the Atlantic shore line on the Virginia coast. Moreover, except for a narrow strip in the extreme south extending from coast to coast, the rest of the country lies in Huntington's first or second zone.[1]

[1] Ellsworth Huntington, *Civilization and Climate* (New Haven, 1915), *passim*.

The range of climate to be found within our borders is in itself a valuable resource. The fact that the country contains large areas peculiarly suited to human life does not mean uniformity of conditions. On the contrary, as Huntington has pointed out, variability of temperature and atmosphere is a crucial factor in promoting physical and mental vigor. One of the most striking features of American climate is its changeableness. But aside from its beneficent effect on health and vitality, this factor of variability possesses other merits. It means that, within certain broad limits, climate is of the moment and the locality. As a consequence, the country never has experienced and probably never will experience a famine of the type that periodically for centuries has swept over parts of Europe and Asia and exacted its toll of millions of human lives. The United States has its droughts and floods, to be sure, but such catastrophes are never widespread or long-sustained. As an eminent geographer has said, "While New Jersey burns, Virginia is sometimes too wet, and the plenty of one locality can supply the shortage of the other. Further than this, the drought east of the 100th meridian rarely if ever covers a whole season. Thus April and May may be dry, injuring the hay, but June and July may be wet, injuring the wheat but making good corn and pasture."[2]

The range of climate from region to region is also very wide. In a country of three million square miles, with its eastern and western shores lapped by the waves of two great oceans, with its exposure on the north to the unbroken sweep of arctic winds and its penetration on the south by the warm waters of a subtropical gulf, with its low-lying Appalachian range in the east and its snow-capped Cordilleras in the west, with its great rivers and lakes, its forests, prairies, plains, and plateaus—in such a country great diversity of climate is inevitable. Although the land is comparatively well watered, the average annual precipitation being twenty inches or more for the entire eastern half of the country, the figure may range from two or three inches in Death Valley to 120 in the Olympic Mountains. Much of the eastern United States en-

[2] J. Russell Smith, *North America* (New York, 1925), pp. 17–18.

joys a yearly rainfall of over fifty inches, while precipitation is generally deficient from central Kansas to the region of the Pacific coast. Snow falls throughout the country, with the possible exception of certain districts in the extreme south. Wide variations likewise occur in the degree of humidity, the prevalence of fog, and the frequency and intensity of atmospheric changes. To America nature has given climates in great variety. And this perhaps is our one great natural resource, apart from the air we breathe, which for the most part has escaped the ravages of human exploitation.

The soil in vast regions is highly fertile. So rich is the soil and so varied is the climate that few indeed are the products of garden, field, orchard, and pasture, useful or pleasing to man, that cannot be grown somewhere in the country. Although for various reasons only two-fifths of the total area are adapted to farming, the American nation possesses more than its proportionate share of the soil resources of the world. Five-sixths of the land surface of the globe cannot be cultivated at the present level of technology; and almost one-fourth of the arable land lying within the temperate zones is in the United States. Probably no other single country possesses on a similar scale such a happy union of climate and soil; and the region bounded by the Great Lakes, the Gulf of Mexico, the Atlantic Ocean, and the Rocky Mountains has been called "the choicest large block of homeland in all the world, with the possible exception of western Europe." Dominating this huge block of land is the basin of the Mississippi. Lying between the eastern and western mountains, embracing an area larger than the whole of India, and prepared through the ages to become one of the great granaries of the world, this wide expanse of fertile soil is truly one of the favored spots of the earth for the human race. "The valley of the Mississippi," said Tocqueville, "is, upon the whole, the most magnificent dwelling-place prepared by God for man's abode."[3]

The Mississippi basin, however, is not the only important

[3] Alexis de Tocqueville, *Democracy in America* (New York, 1898), Vol. I, p. 22.

block of arable land in the United States. Mention should be made of the Atlantic and Gulf Coastal plains, of the renowned Appalachian Valley reaching from Alabama to the Gulf of St. Lawrence, of the Sacramento and San Joaquin rivers, of the valleys of the Connecticut, the Rio Grande, the Red, the Columbia, the Willamette, and Puget Sound, and of the many other valleys, basins, plains, and plateaus that literally dot the intermontane regions and add variety and wealth to the soil resources of the nation.

The favorable union of climate and soil brought forth wild plant and animal life in great abundance. The indigenous plants have been estimated at five thousand species; wild fruits, nuts, and edible roots grew in great profusion; and nutrient grasses covered the forest glades everywhere, the prairies of the Mississippi basin, the High Plains of the Rocky Mountain region, and occasional open districts both east and west. But it was the seemingly boundless forests that impressed so many early visitors to America. No less than 120 native species of timber trees grew in sufficient quantities to be of commercial importance. In their primeval state these forests were unsurpassed anywhere in the world and covered an area of 850,000,000 acres. Although the country was by no means one vast woodland, few large areas east of central Kansas and Nebraska were wholly treeless. Even in the drier regions to the west, cottonwoods and willows grew along the streams and rivers. Beyond the plains were the great coniferous forests of mountain slope and valley.

In their primeval state the waters and forests and grasslands of the continent teemed with animal life. The rich variety of fish and beast and bird made it the paradise of the angler, the huntsman, the trapper, and the naturalist. Songbirds in both bright and somber plumage cast a peaceful mantle over "nature red in tooth and claw" and brought color and music to wood and thicket and tuft of grass. Squirrels and rabbits, quail and grouse, ducks and geese in appropriate season were to be found wherever conditions were suitable. The wild turkey ranged from Mexico to Canada and from the Atlantic to the Pacific; the white heron in great flocks

A Rich and Beautiful Land 109

fed in the shallow and sheltered waters of Florida and the Gulf Coast; and the passenger pigeon darkened the sun in its migratory flights and roosted by the million in the hardwood forests of the Mississippi basin. The deer and the elk were widely distributed; the moose inhabited the northeastern forests; the pronghorn fed on the grasses of the western plains; the mountain sheep made its home in the high Cordilleras; and, most majestic of all, the American bison in countless herds roamed over plain and prairie and grassland and with his sharp hoofs cut deep trails through forest and mountain pass. Fur-bearing animals—muskrat, mink, beaver, marten, otter, wolf, panther, and bear—were present wherever other forms of animal life were to be found. And the streams, the rivers, the lakes, and the seas of this land were full of fish.

3

At the time of the first settlements America was rich in mineral resources.

According to C. K. Leith,[4] approximately forty per cent of the mineral reserves of the earth were located within the borders of the United States.[5] "It is the only country in the world," he says, "possessing adequate quantities of nearly all the principal industrial minerals." He also states that nowhere else, regardless of national boundaries, were these minerals grouped so favorably for human use.

Of the metals, iron is easily the most important. And with respect to this metal the United States was the most richly endowed among the nations, possessing approximately twenty-five per cent of the world's resources. According to estimates made in 1910 including all grades of ore, the actual original reserves amounted to more than 4,000,000,000 and the potential reserves to 75,000,000,000 tons. Of the ten or

[4] C. K. Leith, *World Minerals and World Politics* (New York, 1931), p. 48.
[5] Later discoveries, and discoveries yet to be made, probably make necessary the downward revision of this statement.

twelve major iron deposits of the earth two were found in the United States—one in the region of Lake Superior and the other in Alabama. The former reserves included the "incomparable Mesabi Range of Minnesota," the richest and most easily mined deposits in the world, "where vast pockets of soft rich ore can be worked in open cuts with steam and electric shovels." The Alabama region was unique among the iron centers of the earth because of the presence in the same locality of rich stores of iron ore, coal, and lime. The United States also contained other important stores of iron. The Great Valley of the Appalachians held significant reserves from Alabama to Lake Champlain. Then there were the relatively accessible supplementary deposits of Cuba and Newfoundland. And the United States is somewhat nearer than Europe to the mines of Venezuela and Brazil.

In the case of the nonferrous metals the country was also unusually well supplied. The deposits of copper, by far the most valuable of these metals, were extremely rich and extensive. In North Michigan the ores were originally the richest in the world; in Butte, Montana, nature conspired by means of molten lava to concentrate great stores of copper; and in Utah large reserves of proven ore have been found. The metal was also present in considerable quantities in Arizona and Alaska. Lead was relatively abundant in Virginia, Wisconsin, Colorado, Idaho, and Utah; zinc in Missouri, Oklahoma, Kansas, and New Jersey; and bauxite in Arkansas, Alabama, Mississippi, and Georgia. Large deposits of molybdenum were discovered in Colorado, and great reserves of silver in the Rocky Mountain region. In California and Alaska the American people were given their full share of the gold of the world.

However, in spite of its general richness and in terms of the needs of industrial civilization, the country suffered from certain deficiencies among the minor metals. According to present knowledge the supplies of nickel, tin, manganese, platinum, chromium, mercury, antimony, cobalt, bismuth, tungsten, vanadium, and radium were more limited. For these metals the United States apparently was destined from

A Rich and Beautiful Land

the beginning to be more or less dependent on other districts of the world.

In the sphere of nonmetallic minerals America was also strangely fortunate. Sulphur, the most important of these minerals for industry, was found in huge masses in the salt domes of the Louisiana and Texas coasts. Here by all odds were the biggest deposits of sulphur yet discovered in the world. The reserves of phosphates in the western states, the greatest of the commercial fertilizers, were the largest on record. Additional deposits of this valuable mineral are found in Florida and Tennessee. Recent discoveries of potash in the Permian rocks of the Southwest, a resource in which the country was long thought deficient, may make the United States independent of other nations. This land was also well supplied with feldspar, asphalt, sheet mica, and the important building materials—cement rock, brick clay, sand, slate, building stone, lime, and gypsum. The deficiencies included cryolite, asbestos, barite, magnesite, talc, graphite, fluor spar, nitrate of soda, and the better grades of China clay.

4

At the time of the early settlements America was rich in energy resources. Indeed, these resources were unrivaled in both quantity and quality. Although a fertile soil, acted upon by wind and rain and frost and the rays of the sun, is a matchless fountain of energy, attention will be directed here to those other sources of energy on which industrial society increasingly rests and from which comes the motive power to quicken the tools and machines of man's contriving. Of these the most important, prior to the full development of atomic energy, are coal, petroleum, gas, and water. The first three are the product of aeons of time and consequently when once used are gone forever. The fourth is perpetually renewed and may be expected to continue in undiminished strength for ages, and perhaps as long as the world endures.

Concentration of so large a part of the coal reserves of the earth within the borders of the United States is one of those strange tricks which nature has played upon mankind. Approximately one-half of the known coal of the world was deposited in the region bounded by the Atlantic and Pacific and by the Great Lakes and the Gulf of Mexico. These truly fabulous stores have been estimated at somewhere between two and three-quarters and three and one-quarter trillion metric tons and are widely distributed over the country. America possesses several great coal fields, any one of which would seem to be a just share of the world's supplies for a single nation. The first underlies the Allegheny Plateau and extends from Alabama almost to the northern boundary of Pennsylvania. Because this same district was endowed with rich supplies of petroleum and natural gas, it has been called "the powerhouse of the richest nation in the world." But this land has other powerhouses in the Middlewest, in the Northwest, in the southern Rockies, in the Gulf states, along the Pacific coast, and in Alaska.

These incomparable stores of coal were supplemented by exceptionally rich reserves of petroleum and natural gas. While any estimate of America's share of the world's endowment of these fluid fuels would be extremely untrustworthy, because of the incompleteness of the data, the United States unquestionably was accorded an extremely favored position among the nations. Rich and extensive oil fields have been found in many parts of the country—the Allegheny Plateau, the Ohio Valley, Oklahoma and Kansas, central and north Texas, the Gulf Coast, Wyoming, and California. The amount of petroleum in the natural reservoirs of these fields, originally, has been estimated at approximately 40,000,000,000 barrels. Then there are the oil-bearing shales of Kentucky and the central Rocky Mountain region which probably contain several times the oil of the reservoirs. Of natural gas, a truly peerless fuel, the United States was equally well endowed. Being associated with oil, where the strata have not been disturbed, it has approximately the same geographical distribution as petroleum.

A Rich and Beautiful Land 113

Water, as it flows down to the sea, provides another great source of energy. Since the power of river and stream may be used perpetually and never be consumed, a peculiar significance attaches to its development. The extent of this resource, however, is not unlimited, as so many seem to believe, but clearly depends on rainfall and land elevation. In both these respects the United States is well situated, although somewhat less so than parts of Africa and Europe: rainfall is relatively abundant over wide areas, and two great mountain systems, as well as numerous smaller ranges and isolated units of rugged terrain, give the country an average elevation of more than 3000 feet. The fact that the heavier precipitation occurs in the regions of lower altitude is unfortunate. Yet according to the conservative estimates of the United States Geological Survey, the rivers and streams of the United States are capable of developing 38,000,000 horsepower. And through the construction of storage dams this amount might be greatly increased and perhaps even multiplied several fold. The full development of the water power of the country would proportionately lengthen the life of the coal, oil, and gas reserves of the nation.

With the advent of the atomic age a relatively rare element, formerly regarded of little utility, has become one of the most precious of metals—uranium. Although the United States does not appear to be exceptionally rich in this resource, it does possess one of the four most important known reserves in the world. Uranium is widely distributed through the Colorado Plateau in the states of Colorado, Utah, Arizona, and New Mexico. Deposits have also been discovered in one form or another in Idaho, Montana, Wyoming, Tennessee, and Florida; and promising leads have been found in other places. Outside the borders of the country the major sources of uranium are Northwest Canada, the Belgian Congo, and the Erz Mountains of Czechoslovakia and East Germany. Recent explorations suggest that the Canadian deposits, extending from Great Bear Lake southward through Great Slave Lake and Lake Athabaska and eastward along the northern shores of Lake Superior, are among the richest in the world, rivaling those of the Belgian Congo.[6] It would seem, therefore, that this land is not badly situated for the development and utilization of atomic energy.

5

At the time of the first settlements America was a beautiful land.

As a forest draping slope and stream is more than timber for the mill, as a river winding among the hills is more than power for industry, as a mountain range pushing its snowy peaks into the clouds is more than ore for the smelting furnace, as an orchard in blossom in the springtime is more than fruit for the cannery in the autumn, or as a field of ripened wheat waving and billowing in the breeze is more than grain for the oven; so this land with its "rocks and rills," its "woods and templed hills," is more than the source of our livelihood. It is our home, our dwelling place forever—the place where we are born and grow up, where we live and love, work and play, grow old and die. And it was a beautiful place as it came from the hand of nature—beautiful in the grandeur and majesty of its great distances and proportions, in the contours and settings of its brooks and rivers, its ponds, lakes, and seas, in the lines and shades of its valleys, hills and mountains, in the rhythms of its calms and storms, of its days and seasons. Fortunate indeed were the people who crossed the oceans to possess it.

The fertility of the soil, the abundance of the vegetation, the number of the lakes and streams, the irregularity of the topography in many regions would in themselves make this a beautiful land. But of equal significance is the factor of variety that characterizes every manifestation of nature. Within the borders of the United States may be found almost any type of landscape that the temperate zones of the earth can fashion: from the perpetual verdure of Florida and south-

[6] See Paul F. Kerr, "The Earth's Uranium," *Scientific American*, May, 1951, pp. 17-21.

A Rich and Beautiful Land 115

ern California to the everlasting snows of the Rockies, from the low-lying shores of the Gulf region to the lofty summits of the High Sierra, from the rugged coastline of the north Pacific to the gently sloping beaches of the south Atlantic, from the soft contours of the hills and valleys of New England to the titanic peaks and deep gorges of the western ranges. And within this massive frame of nature may be found the narrow pastures of the eastern seaboard and the broad prairies of the Middlewest, the short grass of the Great Plains and the towering sequoia of the Calaveras grove, the burning sands of the Mojave and the dripping swamps of the Everglades, the gentle flow of the Hudson and the rushing cataracts of the Niagara, the gray fogs of Puget Sound and the brilliant colors of the "Great American Desert," the canebrakes of the lower Mississippi and the solid carpets of Alpine flowers in the upland parks of Montana.

Among our treasures are some very special works of nature's art: the falls of the Niagara, where for ages the waters of Lake Erie have plunged over a one-hundred-and-sixty-foot precipice on their journey to the sea; the Mammoth Cave of Kentucky, whose Stygian chambers extending for miles through limestone strata are everywhere adorned with beautiful and fantastic formations; the charmed valley of the Yosemite, which shelters a grove of the giant sequoia, nourishes a luxuriant growth of trees, shrubs, and grasses, and in a matchless setting of rock and foliage and flower drops its waters in three successive falls to a river bed 2500 feet below; the basin of the Yellowstone with its more than 100 geysers, its 4000 springs of every description, its great canyon, lakes, streams, and waterfalls, its rich stocks of fish, bird, and beast, and its generally unrivaled position as the child of nature's most whimsical moods; and finally the Grand Canyon of the Colorado whose two-hundred-mile gorge cleaves through the high plateaus of Utah and Arizona to a depth of 2000 to 5000 feet, whose bastions, towers, cliffs, and terraces, marked by red, white, green, brown, and black strata, rise in fantastic but always impressive compositions, and whose immensity so moved Coronado, the first white man to behold it, that he reported banks reaching "three to four leagues into the air" and broken "into pinnacles higher than the tower of the Cathedral of Seville."

But far more precious than those rare spectacles of nature, however beautiful and picturesque they may be, are the scenes amid which the great masses of people must live. Few indeed are the regions in the United States, where life is tolerable, that are altogether lacking in charm. The eastern portion of the country, dominated by the Appalachian highlands from the Gulf of the St. Lawrence to Georgia and Alabama, is one of the most beautiful parts of the earth. In New England the Berkshires, the Green Mountains, and the White Mountains; in New York the Adirondacks and the Catskills; and in the regions to the southwest the Poconos, the Blue Ridge, the Black Mountains, the Great Smokies, and the parallel ranges of the Alleghenies, give character and variety to the landscape. In the northeast the country is studded with innumerable lakes of glacial origin; and, because of the abundant rainfall, the entire Appalachian country is traversed by streams and rivers. The Hudson, flowing between its high and heavily wooded valley walls, has few rivals among the rivers of the world.

The beauty of this part of the United States is greatly enhanced by the luxuriance of the vegetation. Everywhere in summer, except on the rocky summits of the White Mountains of New Hampshire, the land is draped from highest peak to water's edge with a green mantle of forest. In the north and the south the dominant tone derives from the dark needles of the conifers; in the middle regions, from the lighter foliage of the hardwoods which in the autumn assumes the most brilliant hues of red and yellow and orange. In much of this region, moreover, the land is blanketed with a covering of flowers which changes its color and pattern from season to season; and in many places the slopes of the Alleghenies are clothed in a thick growth of azalea, rhododendron, and mountain laurel, which in May, June, and July burst into blossom and bathe the entire landscape with their loveliness.

A Rich and Beautiful Land

Originally these forests reached far beyond the Appalachian highlands. In changing form, responding to differences in soil and climate, they draped the valleys of the Ohio and the Mississippi, covered half of Texas and Oklahoma, embraced practically the whole of Missouri and Wisconsin and the major part of Illinois and Minnesota, and extended long fingers up the watercourses into the prairies of Kansas, Nebraska, and Iowa. Beyond the forests lay the vast reaches of the plains with their spring blanket of flowers and their cloak of long and short grasses, pierced here and there by clumps of willow and cottonwood. While this region may convey an impression of unbroken monotony to the casual traveler, to those who have come to know it by long residence the open sky, the great distances, the heroic mold of the landscape, the soft colors of dawn and sunset, the untempered fury of storm and blizzard, the direct exposure to the clashing of the elements, hold an ineffable charm.

Out of the plains rise the eastern outposts of the Cordilleras, a system of mountain ranges that reaches from central Colorado to the Pacific, passes northward into Canada and Alaska to the borders of the Arctic and sweeps southward through the tropics and on to the tip of South America and Tierra Del Fuego to plunge beneath the chill waters of the Southern Ocean. Within the United States this system includes numerous rugged ranges, steep-walled canyons, sheltered valleys, and intermontane plains and plateaus. Here is one of the great natural playgrounds of the continent, partitioned by the barren majesty of the Rocky Mountains, the awe-inspiring grandeur of the Sierra Nevada, and the forest-clad ridges of the Cascade and Coast Ranges. To describe the natural beauty of this vast empire of forest and flower and mountain and gorge is impossible. Even the "Great American Desert" lying between the Rockies and the Sierra is a land of bewitching beauty—a region of riotous coloring, of brown and yellow and tawny reds tinted with blacks and grays, where "the brilliant colors of midday turn to violet in the softer lights of dawn or sunset." Beyond the Coast Range the continent falls rapidly and, in many places, precipitously into the Pacific. In the Northwest, from Washington to the Gulf of Alaska, the union of land and water conveys a sense of the everlasting power of nature. Deep fiords, flanked by cliffs 2000 to 5000 feet high, cut great gashes into the coast line, mountain walls rise in silent might out of the ocean, and ageless glaciers pour immense ice streams down the valleys to the sea. And thus our rich and beautiful land dips beneath the waves of the western waters.

6

This favored land has left its mark on us and our institutions.

Above all it provided almost ideal conditions for our great experiment in popular rule and human freedom. After the achievement of independence and the consolidation of the several colonies into a single state, America occupied for generations a uniquely sheltered position among the nations, far removed from the quarrels, the wars, and the aggressions of the Old World. The expanse of oceans on either side gave to our people a sense of security and a guaranty of relatively peaceful development. Safe behind her powerful natural ramparts, America was almost a world by herself— a great fortress for common people set in the western seas and guarded by their waters—a "city of refuge" to which the hunted and the persecuted might repair. "The Americans," said Tocqueville, "have no neighbors, and consequently they have no great wars."[7] They were allowed, therefore, to escape the burden of a great military establishment and that most formidable scourge of republics—military glory.

It was this rich land, administered under relatively just laws and free institutions, that, like a powerful magnet, drew the peoples of the earth to our shores and then beckoned them onward by ever brighter prospects toward the western sun. But it did far more than attract them. It helped to develop

[7] Tocqueville, *op. cit.*, Vol. I, p. 369.

in them new traits—traits which have come to be regarded as American. On arriving the immigrant begins to slough off the limited outlook of the Old World. As Crèvecoeur observed, "he very suddenly alters his scale; two hundred miles formerly appeared a very great distance, it is now but a trifle; he no sooner breathes our air than he forms schemes, and embarks in designs he never would have thought of in his own country."[8]

He develops a hopeful, progressive, and venturesome spirit. Urged on by the opportunities for personal advancement about him, he turns from the past and the present to the future. "Not distances alone," wrote Francis Lieber, a brilliant young German who came to America in 1821 and remained to become a distinguished citizen, "are measured here by a standard different from that of other countries; time, too, receives a different value, but it is measured by a smaller standard than in Europe. An American wants to perform within a year what others do within a much longer period. Ten years in America are like a century in Spain."[9] Francis J. Grund put the case even more powerfully: "I will now add that the Americans *love* their country, not, indeed, *as it is*, but *as it will be*. They do not love the land of their fathers; but they are sincerely attached to that which their children are destined to inherit. They live in the future, and *make* their country as they go on."[10] For almost three centuries, as we moved westward with the advancing frontiers, we were under the spell of a land that seemed almost boundless in extent and exhaustless in resources. That experience contributed mightily to make us what we are. Its liberating power was expressed long ago by William Blake:

> Why should I care for the men of Thames,
> Or the cheating waves of charter'd streams;
> Or shrink at the little blasts of fear
> That the hireling blows into my ear?

[8] J. Hector St. John de Crèvecoeur, *Letters from an American Farmer* (New York, 1904), p. 76.
[9] Francis Lieber, *The Stranger in America* (London, 1835), Vol. II, p. 186.
[10] Francis J. Grund, *The Americans, in Their Moral, Social, and Political Relations* (Boston, 1837), p. 151.

Tho' born on the cheating banks of Thames,
Tho' his waters bathed my infant limbs,
The Ohio shall wash his stains from me:
I was born a slave, but I go to be free!

7

We have left our mark on this favored land.

As we look about today we are reminded of the parable of the prodigal son. Our heritage from nature is not what it was when the first settlers landed on the Atlantic shores. We have wasted much of our substance in careless, if not riotous, living. We began this orgy of spoliation in the colonial period and have continued it with the ever-increasing power of technology down practically to the present moment. In 1748 Peter Kalm, saddened by our treatment of soil and forest, spoke of our "gross mistakes and carelessness for futurity." A half-century later Francis Baily, President of the Royal Astronomical Society, told of having often seen great oaks, measuring "near four feet diameter at the bottom" and possessing a "straight trunk *without a single branch* for seventy feet . . . cut down . . . for the sake of killing a poor bear" or "set on fire merely to dislodge a paltry raccoon!"[11]

We have attacked the plant and animal life of this land without mercy or prudence. We have destroyed utterly the white heron and the passenger pigeon, almost exterminated the bison, and have brought close to extinction many valuable species of game, fish, and fowl. We have reduced our forests to a fraction of what they were and are still cutting trees faster than they are growing. To be sure, for some time now we have been moving toward a program of conservation, but we are still scarcely embarked seriously on the journey.

We have treated our soil as if we were merely sojourners in the land and were destined to move ever westward to

---

[11] Francis Baily, *Journal of a Tour in Unsettled Parts of North America in 1796 & 1797* (London, 1856), p. 214.

A Rich and Beautiful Land   121

greener and greener pastures. "Soil washing and blowing during the past three centuries," writes J. Frederic Dewhurst, "have destroyed or severely impoverished 282 million acres and damaged 775 million more acres."[12] Much of the best soil in America in 1607 is now on the bottoms of our lakes, in the Gulf of Mexico, and beneath the waters of the Atlantic and Pacific oceans.

In the exploitation of our mineral resources we have perhaps shown equal indifference toward the future. According to a survey of the situation in 1943, "at prewar rates of production the known copper supplies of the United States would last about 30 years; the zinc deposits, 20 years; the known oil, less than 20 years . . . the Lake Superior iron ores of present commercial grades, 30 years."[13] It seems that "supplies of most of our high-grade metallic ores" are "likely to become deficient in one or two decades."[14] On the other hand, of coal there is enough for centuries, and of the more important nonmetallic minerals there is relative abundance. The favorable situation here, however, is attributed not to our wise policies but to the bounty of nature.

As to our heritage of natural beauty, our record is not much better. We have established some national and state forests, parks, and playgrounds. But for the most part aesthetic interests have had to give way to "practical," that is to say, to immediate business, financial, and economic considerations. Onetime beautiful forests have been converted into hideous graveyards, charming streams and lakes have been filled with debris and silt, lovely hills have been blackened and disfigured by the offal of our mines. We have burned and slashed and rooted our way across this wonderful land. And most of our own handiwork has lacked beauty, much of it has been coarse and ugly. Except for some of the smaller and older communities in the East and the Far West, our villages, towns, and cities are without charm or elegance,

[12] J. Frederic Dewhurst and Associates, *America's Needs and Resources* (New York, 1947), p. 431.
[13] C. K. Leith, J. W. Furness, and Cleona Lewis, *World Minerals and World Peace* (Washington, 1943), p. 89.
[14] Dewhurst and Associates, *op. cit.*, p. 574.

some of them are monstrosities. Our railroads and highways have been built with little regard for appearance. As yet we have developed no conception of our material civilization equal in beauty and grandeur to the land which nature gave us.

Yet America remains today a marvelously rich and beautiful land, a land capable under wise management of sustaining a great civilization for ages to come. Science and technology may rescue a profligate people. If we so resolve, we can rebuild our soil, restore our forests, and utilize oil shales and low-grade ores which exist in great abundance and which have scarcely been touched. Through the advance and application of knowledge we can perhaps vastly extend the range of useful materials. This we are now doing on a revolutionary scale in the case of uranium. And who will say that the release and harnessing of atomic energy may not move to elements existing in far greater abundance? The time is apparently not too distant, maybe ten, twenty, or thirty years, when the energy base of human civilization will be raised to a new order of magnitude.

It seems, too, that the saga of the pioneer in a very literal sense is not finished. We know now that the geographical frontier can be pushed back along our entire shore line into the waters of the Atlantic, the Gulf, and the Pacific. Members of the staff of the United States Military Academy have estimated that "the continental shelf off the United States includes an area approximating 30% of the total area of the United States."[15] According to these students, "the vast reservoir of the oceans and the ocean beds may hold the key to almost unlimited reserves of many materials." We seem to be approaching the age when man will move from fishing to mariculture, from the gathering of the wild fruits of the waters to the farming of the seas.

In spite of the promises of science and technology, however, the time has come for a sober accounting of our rela-

---

[15] Associates in International Relations, Department of Social Sciences, United States Military Academy, *Raw Materials in War and Peace* (West Point, 1947), p. 18.

tions to this rich and beautiful land. We need to realize that the policies, or rather the practices, of our first three centuries require a radical overhauling. We need to realize that our natural riches are not inexhaustible, that these riches should be held in sacred trust by each generation. We need to realize, too, that this land with its surrounding waters, and probably this land alone, belongs to our children for century after century, that this land, and probably this land alone, must provide the geographical base of our civilization forever.

Part Three

TOWARD

A NEW

CIVILIZATION

8

THE TECHNOLOGICAL REVOLUTION

1

The material foundations of a new civilization have been laid.

The peoples of the world today are leaving behind the material forms and agencies of a civilization which in its broad outlines endured for many centuries. This civilization was based on agriculture, animal breeding, handicraft, simple trade, and human energy—a civilization that in its many variants dates practically from the beginning of recorded history. The civilization which our fathers and mothers brought to this continent in the first half of the seventeenth century and molded into a special pattern during the succeeding two hundred years was one of those variants.

We can see clearly that during the last several generations this early civilization of ours has been undergoing a process of profound change and transformation. Today its material foundations are only a memory. Gone are the simple tools with which the versatile farmer tilled his soil, harvested his crops, prepared his food, fashioned his garments, made his utensils, and erected his houses and barns. Gone are the great distances, the dirt roads and trails, the rude carts and sledges, the rafts, flatboats, and sailing ships. Gone are the self-contained rural households and closely knit neighborhoods. Gone also in relative measure are the oxen, horses, and waterwheels, the long years of unrelieved human toil. Gone too in like measure are the local markets, the little stores and shops with their limited wares and services. Gone for most of us is the intimate relation with the elements—with soil, stream, and forest, with wind, rain, and snow, with sun, moon, and stars. So swiftly have these material features of our old agrarian civilization passed away that Lincoln, Grant, and even Cleveland would feel bewildered in the America of today. Indeed many members of the older generation now living experience a sense of bewilderment. And for the most part those of younger years who may feel at home in this new world really do not realize what kind of a world it is. They have experienced no other.

A new civilization is rising in America and throughout the earth—a civilization that is coming to be called industrial—a civilization so strange in its forms, so vast in its reaches, so complex in its patterns, and so mighty in its energies that thoughtful men and women fear that the control of its operations is beyond the powers of its creator. We in America are very closely identified with the rise of this new civilization. In no small measure it is a product of our genius and in some respects is perhaps further on its course here than in any other land. The fact must be emphasized, moreover, that in spite of the common reference to the "industrial revolution" as a limited series of changes in production which took place in England in the eighteenth century and in other countries at later times, the revolution has actually been gathering momentum with every decade. Industrial *civilization* is probably still in its infancy. What it will be like when fully matured, we do not and cannot know. That it will assume, at least for a time, different forms in different societies, among peoples of diverse cultures, may be confidently expected. Moreover, although certain of its broad imperatives and potentialities are already clearly discernible, we may be sure that it will bring many surprises, many challenges, many hazards, many opportunities to mankind.

The uneven advance of industrial civilization, the swift transformation of the material foundations of life and the lag in institutional, ideological, and moral adjustment, have generated the terrifying crises, the wars and depressions, the revolutions and counterrevolutions, of our time. Our world, in both its domestic and its international aspects, is out-of-joint. Our practical inventiveness, in the words of Stanley Casson, has far outrun our "moral consciousness and social organization." We have one foot in a civilization that is passing away, the other in a civilization that is only beginning to take form. Or to phrase the dilemma more aptly perhaps, as our feet tread the earth of a new world our heads continue to dwell in a world that is gone.

2

Industrial civilization releases science and technology.
Science has rightly been called, as we have noted, the most powerful force moving in the modern world. As a method of inquiry, it is man's most reliable source of knowledge about both his environment and himself. Experimental in temper and scornful alike of both sacred tradition and temporal authority, it has moved triumphantly during the past four and a half centuries from conquest to conquest. Beginning its revolutionary career in the sphere of astronomy, it has left its mark on every field of thought. It has penetrated to some degree, though by no means equally, all departments of life and overthrown countless ideas and customs hallowed by time.

The most distinctive and profound characteristic of industrial civilization is its attitude toward science. Although there is no place in the world today where the advance of science in certain fields is not blocked by fear or vested rights, our contemporary civilization is the first in history to promote scientific inquiry on a large scale and make eager use of many of its findings. In its turn, of course, science has reacted upon civilization and molded with great power man's ways of life and his outlook upon the world. It has pushed its inquiries into the farthermost limits of the universe and the innermost structure of the atom, into the origins of the earth and the succession of geological ages, into the evolution of living forms and the closely guarded mysteries of the cell, into the emergence of man, the rise and fall of social systems, the growth and decay of civilizations, and the nature of mind.

In its practical aspects, in its application to the technics of living and making a living, to the modes of livelihood, the forms of communication, the ways of waging war, the control of the life process, science is coming to be called technology. To the ordinary citizen it is this practical aspect of science that is the most striking feature of the age. Indeed, during recent generations a veritable technological revolution has swept over a large part of the world—a revolution that has brought to the astonished gaze of mankind one wonder after another and again and again made truth far stranger than fiction. So enraptured by technological advance have we become that we have tended to conceive human progress largely in its terms. We are learning today, to our sorrow, that this advance, when not accompanied by equally profound reconstruction in the realms of understanding and value, of customs and institutions, of attitudes and loyalties, can bring trouble and disaster.

The technological revolution is revealed in the many changes in our civilization to be listed in subsequent chapters. It is revealed in the changing occupations of our people. A century ago and seventy-five years after the launching of the Republic, the proportion of the population engaged in pursuits associated with the advance and utilization of technology was insignificant. In 1850, according to the federal census, to use the limited categories of the time, the country could boast but 1757 architects, draftsmen, engineers, and chemists. In 1860 the list of technical occupations was lengthened to report 12 electricians, 51 assayers, 2 astronomers, 2 explorers, and 3 geologists. In 1870 metallurgists appeared for the first time; in 1890 mechanical, electrical, and mining engineers; and in 1920 aeronauts. During the ninety-year period from 1850 to 1940, while the general population was growing from 23,191,876 to 131,669,592, the number of engineers of all kinds grew from 512 to 245,288, the number of architects from 591 to 20,376, the number of designers and draftsmen from 189 to 100,925, and the number of chemists, assayers, and metallurgists from 465 to 57,025.

The technological revolution is revealed in its most obvious and spectacular form in the march of mechanical invention. Beginning with the invention of the reciprocating steam engine by James Watt in 1765 and the invention of the cotton gin by Eli Whitney in 1793, the devising of new machines and processes gradually established itself as a cultural pattern. By the close of the nineteenth century it had assumed the proportions of a great and rising flood. This story is told in the unsentimental language of statistics by the United States Patent Office. The total number of patents issued increased from 2425 for the five-year period ending in 1845 to 180,984 for the similar period closing just one hurtdred years later. And the end is not yet. To gain perspective we should recall that the head of the Office in 1833 offered "to resign because he felt that the limit of human invention had been reached and there would be no further need for his services." We might also recall the prognostication of the United States Commissioner of Labor in 1885 at the early dawn of the automobile age and less than twenty years before Kittyhawk. "It is true," he said, "that new processes of manufacture will undoubtedly continue, and this will be an ameliorating influence, but it will not leave room for a marked extension, such as has been witnessed during the last fifty years." Today fantastic discoveries and inventions in the spheres of metallurgy and chemistry, electronics and nuclear physics suggest that the remaining years of the twentieth century will be marked by changes quite as disturbing and revolutionary as any man has ever known. As R. J. Forbes has well said, "we have picked up but a few pebbles on the shores of a great ocean that still remains to be explored."[1]

[1] R. J. Forbes, *Man the Maker* (New York, 1950), p. 329.

The technological revolution is revealed even more profoundly in the steady advance of practical knowledge in almost every field. For thousands of years man's knowledge of the practical arts, of agriculture and animal breeding, of mining and lumbering, of manufacture and communication, of medicine and hygiene, of household management and child-rearing changed but little from generation to generation. Dependable knowledge, moreover, was generally mingled with error; and the false was transmitted from the old to the young as faithfully as the true. Man pursued his occupations and met the crises of life under the guidance of folk lore and folk wisdom. As the industrial age has advanced, the body of dependable knowledge in all fields penetrated by science has grown ever more swiftly, so swiftly indeed that a great part of it remains inert and unused. Today such knowledge gushes forth in a constantly swelling stream. If anyone imagines that the volume of this stream will diminish in the coming years, he should read the "predictions" made by perfectly sober scientists in the "Diamond Jubilee Issue" of *Chemical and Engineering News*, organ of the American Chemical Society, published in August, 1951.

Finally, the technological revolution is revealed in the most fundamental and distinctive institution of the new civilization—an institution devoted solely to the advance of knowledge and discovery—the scientific laboratory. Confined almost wholly to a few great universities and a few federal bureaus and departments at the opening of the present century, the country today is literally dotted with research laboratories—laboratories maintained by institutions of learning, by private foundations, by great corporations, by trade associations, and by governmental agencies. At the beginning of the First World War the total had reached several hundred; today they can be numbered only by the thousand. Some of them are gigantic undertakings: the great laboratories of the American Telephone and Telegraph Company in New York City and New Jersey embrace a floor space of nearly one million square feet, employ more than five thousand scientists, engineers, and technicians, and operate on an annual budget of approximately seventeen million dollars. And the entire world knows of the expenditure of two billions by the federal government to develop the atomic bomb.

3

The advance of technology has been favored by the conditions of life in America.
Apparently such advance is dependent on something more than the sheer ability to make an invention or a discovery. We know that an invention or a discovery may be regarded in a given society as a mere curiosity and remain sterile for generations or maybe forever. The ancient Chinese invented gunpowder, but applied it to the making of firecrackers rather than to firearms or engineering. The ancient Greeks understood the principle of the steam boiler but failed to use it to lighten the toil of their slaves. Four and a half centuries ago Leonardo, perhaps the most versatile genius of all times, sketched designs for the making of a rifled cannon, a machine gun, a mortar, a bomb, a shrapnel, a submarine, a steamboat, an airplane, a rope-making machine, and many other inventions, but at the time nothing came of his prodigious labors. It is interesting to note that the cotton gin was invented not by a southern planter or a Negro slave, but by a Yankee school teacher out of a job. The development of technology requires a society with appropriate interests and outlooks.

In America a combination of circumstances greatly favored the advance of technology. First of all, in the course of their history the people of this land developed a hopeful, experimental, adventurous, and progressive temper. In crossing the Atlantic and moving on toward the west they broke with the past again and again and were compelled to adjust themselves repeatedly to new and strange conditions. Also they drank deep of the liberating ideas of the modern age, of the ideas of English rationalism and the French Enlightenment, of the ideas of progress and the indefinite perfectibility of man and his institutions. "Nobody," wrote Michael Chevalier of the ordinary American in 1839, "can conform so easily to new situations and circumstances; he is always ready to adopt new processes and implements, or to change his occupation."[2] This same writer, to emphasize the thought that the American is always on the make and devoted to the affairs of this world, quotes with approval a humorous passage from an unnamed American writer: "We are born in haste; we finish our education on the run; we marry on the wing; we make a fortune at a stroke, and lose it in the same manner, to make and lose it again ten times over, in the twinkling of an eye. Our body is a locomotive, going at the rate of twenty-five miles an hour; our soul, a high-pressure engine; our life is like a shooting star, and death overtakes us at last like a flash of lightning."[3] As an old adage goes, we are "willing to try anything once."

Equally important were our free political institutions, the form of our economy, and the wealth of our resources. Except for the Negro slave and the "redemptioner" during his brief period of servitude, the individual was not bound by any feudal relationship. He was free to dispose of his labor as he pleased and the opportunity of land ownership in fee simple bred in him a spirit of independence. Also the ratio of human labor to natural resources was so favorable that the workingman could demand a high reward for his services. "As to labour and labourers," said Crèvecoeur in the middle of the eighteenth century, "what difference! When we hire any of these people we rather pray and entreat them. You must give them what they ask: three shillings per day in common wages and five or six shillings in harvest. They must be at your table and feed . . . on the best you have."[4] This meant that the employer had to compete with the call of the rich land and pay high wages. And this in turn meant that

[2] Michael Chevalier, *Society, Manners and Politics in the United States* (Boston, 1839), p. 285.
[3] *Ibid.*, p. 286.
[4] J. Hector St. John de Crèvecoeur, *Sketches of Eighteenth Century America* (New Haven, 1925), pp. 82–83.

business could make a profit only if the labor employed was highly productive. Such a condition placed a premium on invention, efficiency of operation, and the most extensive use of machines and mechanical energy. It probably played an important role in developing in American capitalism its most vital and distinctive feature—its tendency to emphasize production and to share the fruits of increased productivity with workers and consumers.

This is not to say, however, that the advance of technology proceeded smoothly in America. Many of the early inventions and discoveries aroused the bitterest opposition. Toward the end of the eighteenth century the legislature of Rhode Island, according to Timothy Dwight, refused to grant permission to build a turnpike on the grounds that "turnpikes, and the establishment of religious worship, had their origin in Great Britain: the government of which was a monarchy, and the inhabitants slaves."[5] A proposal to provide for the surveying of a route for a canal "between the tide waters of the Hudson and Lake Erie," presented before the General Assembly of New York in 1808, was received by the House "with such expressions of surprise and ridicule, as are due to a very wild and foolish project."[6] The railroad was opposed as a "device of Satan to lead immortal souls down to hell." A reader of the *Western Sun* of Vincennes, Indiana, gave voice in 1830 to diverse objections to this invention:

I see what will be the effect of it; that it will set the whole world a-gadding. Twenty miles an hour, sir!—Why, you will not be able to keep an apprentice boy at his work! Every Saturday evening he must have a trip to Ohio to spend a Sunday with his sweetheart. Grave plodding citizens will be flying about like comets. All local attachments will be at an end. It will encourage flightiness of intellect. Veracious people will turn into the most immeasurable liars. All conceptions will be exaggerated by the magnificent notions of distance.—Only a hundred miles off!—Tut, nonsense, I'll step across, madam, and bring your fan!

[5] Timothy Dwight, *Travels in New-England and New-York* (New Haven, 1821), Vol. II, p. 37.
[6] John Warner Barber and Henry Howe, *Historical Collections of the State of New York* (New York, 1841), p. 41.

> ... And then, sir, there will be barrels of pork, cargoes of flour, chaldrons of coal, and even lead and whiskey, and such like sober things that have always been used to slow travelling—whisking away like a sky rocket. It will upset all the gravity of the nation. ... Upon the whole, sir, it is a pestilential, topsy-turvy, harum-scarum whirligig. Give me the old, solemn, straight forward, regular Dutch Canal—three miles an hour for expresses, and two rod jog-trot journeys—with a yoke of oxen for heavy loads. I go for beasts of burden. It is more formative and scriptural, and suits a moral and religious people better.—None of your hop skip and jump whimsies for me.[7]

The most intolerant opposition to technological advance appeared in the field of medicine. Pioneers in this realm often took their lives and reputations in their hands when they proposed radical changes in the treatment of disease. In 1721 Dr. Zabdiel Boylston of Boston inoculated his son and two servants against smallpox. When the fact became known, he "was execrated and persecuted as a murderer, assaulted in the streets, and loaded with every species of abuse. His house was attacked with violence, so that neither himself nor his family could feel secure in it. ... The enraged inhabitants patrolled the town in parties, with halters in their hands, threatening to hang him on the nearest tree."[8] The members of Boylston's own profession joined the mob in this attack. The opposition to the use of anesthetics generations later was only less bitter. And advocacy of public medicine today arouses the unreasoned wrath of many.

4

A new cultural element changes the character of both a civilization and a people.

The introduction of such an element is a serious business. It does not mean merely an

[7] Quoted by Seymour Dunbar in his *A History of Travel in America* (Indianapolis, 1915), Vol. III, p. 938.
[8] John Warner Barber, *Massachusetts Historical Collections* (Worcester, 1839), pp. 452, 453.

addition to elements already present. A culture is much more than an aggregation of distinguishable elements. It is essentially a system of functional relationships in which the diverse constituents are bound together into a kind of organic unity. A new element therefore will affect eventually, according to its strength, the entire system of relationships. And this means that it will change the character of the people nurtured by the given culture or civilization. Horace Bushnell saw all this clearly in the middle of the last century. "This transition from mother and daughter power to water and steam-power is a great one," he wrote, "greater by far than many have as yet begun to conceive—one that is to carry with it a complete revolution of domestic life and social manners."[9]

A new element may merely enrich or perfect a civilization without modifying its configuration or shifting its tendencies. But it may, depending on its nature, give a new direction to cultural evolution or even profoundly disrupt the most basic institutions of a society. The coming of agriculture to a nomadic people changes in the course of time the whole way of life, undermines certain cultural traits, and compels the growth of others. The introduction of the horse among the Indians of the great plains of North America altered the modes of livelihood, the methods of warfare, and the character of the dwellings. The invention of firearms assisted in the destruction of the feudal social structure of Europe and gave the people of the West an overwhelming advantage in their struggle to occupy the earth. The compass made possible the discovery and settlement of the New World and placed England, previously on the borders of European civilization, in a strategic and favored position. The airplane changes the relations of nations and may convert certain regions, such as the Hudson Bay littoral and northern Russia, now remote from the highways of commerce, into centers of traffic between East and West. The prohibition of ceremonial head-hunting among peoples of the South Seas, according to

[9] Horace Bushnell, "The Age of Homespun," in *Work and Play* (New York, 1864), p. 376.

one investigator, weakened their interest in life and led to rapid depopulation. And if slaves once get the idea of freedom, they will never be the same again.

The introduction of a new cultural element inaugurates a process of interaction. On the one hand, the new element impresses its special character on the culture. The cow, for example, because of its peculiar nature, will call forth appropriate cultural traits; the horse, for similar reasons, will call forth others. On the other hand, the culture will impress its special character on the new element. In one culture, the cow will be developed into a beast of burden, in another into a producer of milk, in another into a source of beef, and in still another into an object of worship. It is the same in the case of the horse. The Arabs developed a beast of great agility and swiftness, whereas the warriors of mediaeval Europe, clothed in heavy armor, evolved the powerful Belgian, Clydesdale, and Percheron breeds. So technology, while bringing the peoples of the world into ever closer relations, will take different forms and be directed toward different ends in different civilizations.

5

Technology is changing the character of both our civilization and ourselves.

Most obviously technology transforms the material aspects of our civilization—our dwellings, our tools of production, our weapons of warfare, our instruments of communication, and even our landscape. But it must never be forgotten that the people who live in the new physical setting and use the new physical agencies are themselves changed. The new conditions call forth new habits, new powers, and new attitudes, new values, new conceptions of life, new hopes and fears. The man with the tractor is not the man with the hoe, even though developed from the same germ cells. The people of the Tennessee Valley today are not the people of fifteen years ago, even though we were to

The Technological Revolution

assume neither births nor deaths, neither immigration nor emigration. The little man with the revolver is not the same as the little man with the club. A nation or a world with the jet plane or the atomic bomb is something new under the sun. And a people possessing technology with all of its revolutionary possibilities opens a new epoch in the history of mankind.

These changes which technology has brought in the realm of physical means and agencies give rise to tensions between the new and the old elements of the civilization. Thus the power-driven machine changes the status of the workman, takes the woman out of the home, encourages the growth of the factory, and modifies the system of property relations. The building of a highway or the invention of the automobile stimulates exchange, widens the scope of the market, loosens family and neighborhood ties, and weakens age-old forces of social control. The development of the machine gun, the tank, and the airplane removes military power from the hands of the people, makes impossible popular revolutions on the eighteenth century model, and places democracies everywhere under the peril of dictatorship. The point to be emphasized is that changes in such a humble sphere as the tools for producing goods will affect sooner or later the entire civilization from bottom to top and from center to circumference. Until adjustments are achieved in economic institutions, social structure, education, government, and even religion and morals, the civilization will be in a state of disharmony and crisis.

Technology impresses its special character on a civilization and on the bodies, minds, and hearts of those who use it. To think of technology solely in terms of its products, of its discoveries and inventions, would be a grave mistake. In essence it is a process, a way of working, a method of attacking problems. As such, it has a number of characteristics. First, it is marked by emphasis on precision and ever greater precision, on orderly and defined relationships. Second, it is experimental in method, guided by bold imagination and careful observation, irreverent of the past, of great names, of authority as such in every form. Third, it is practical, concerned with the useful rather than the academic, with the application of knowledge to the ways of life rather than with the cultivation of knowledge for its own sake. Fourth, it is planful, insisting on the utility of design, on the rational ordering and coordination of materials and energies in the light of purpose. Fifth, it is dynamic, ever challenging the old, ever seeking new knowledge and new and more efficient ways of doing things, ever striving to push forward the boundaries of understanding and control. Clearly, in taking such a powerful and aggressive element to its bosom, any civilization is asking for trouble and crisis, excitement and adventure without limit. The new frontier of science and technology is freighted with opportunities and exploits infinitely greater and more enduring than our old frontier in the West.

Our civilization has impressed and will continue to impress its special character on technology. Just as fire or the wheel has been put to the most diverse uses by different peoples, so technology can be directed toward the most diverse ends. It may be employed to destroy everything that is good in the world and to fasten some form of despotism on all peoples. Also, we have reason to hope, it may usher in the most glorious age of human history. At bottom the issue here is moral in character. Technology has raised anew and on a vaster scale than ever before the ancient question of the values by which men should live.

9

NEW MODES OF LIVELIHOOD

1

Technology has brought new modes of livelihood.
The importance of changes in the ways men produce and exchange the goods and services on which life depends can scarcely be overemphasized. One need not accept a crude materialistic interpretation of history to recognize the great role of economic forces in human affairs. Social relations are always profoundly molded by the existing modes of livelihood. But there is even a more fundamental sense in which economic practices affect the fortunes of a people.

Throughout history the great masses of mankind have lived on the very margin of subsistence. The lot of the many has always been hard and precarious. The ancient curse laid upon man, according to legend, as he was driven from paradise for having eaten of the fruit of the tree of knowledge, merely describes the condition under which the human race has always lived: "In the sweat of thy face shalt thou eat bread." Except for small privileged classes living on the labor of others, men, women, and children have always had to struggle and struggle without surcease for food and shelter. This was true even in our rich land in the days before the coming of the machine. "Give us this day our daily bread" has been the prayer of the common man in all ages. The demands of livelihood have been so pervasive and so consuming of time and energy that they have inevitably left a deep impress on the mind and character of every people. Any change in the modes of gaining the physical necessities for sustaining life, therefore, until the age of universal abundance arrives, must be a matter of deep significance, particularly if it lightens in any degree the burden of toil. The transformation wrought by technology in this realm constitutes a veritable revolution in the condition and prospects of mankind.

2

Technology has brought the power-driven machine.
It has displaced the simple hand tool of early America by mechanical giants which dwarf the physical powers of men. So overwhelming and impressive has been this trend that our age has commonly been called the machine age; and Clark Wissler has included the machine among the three distinctive characteristics of our culture. If we should suddenly lose our capacity to make and use power-driven machines, our entire civilization would collapse and millions would be consigned to starvation.

The story of the development of the machine is a long one, going back to the first eolith made at the very dawn of the human mind and the beginning of human culture. This entire story from the Old Stone Age down to the present industrial epoch has been told brilliantly by R. J. Forbes in his history of technology and engineering—*Man the Maker*.[1] Man has been rightly called a tool-making and tool-using animal. Certainly this trait marks him off qualitatively from all other forms of life. In the primitive cultures of the stone ages he already possessed crude hammers, chisels, awls, knives, clubs, and axes. As generations passed he increased enormously the number and quality of his tools and haltingly devised machines, or complicated contrivances coordinating several tools and increasing the power and efficiency of operations. Some of these machines were harnessed to domestic

[1] R. J. Forbes, *Man the Maker* (New York, 1950).

animals, windmills, and water wheels. But the reign of the simple tool, manipulated directly by the human hand and driven by human energy, continued to play a central role in the economy in even the most advanced countries down to the nineteenth century.

The changes which were destined to transform man's modes of livelihood throughout the world began in England in the middle of the eighteenth century in the iron, textile, and pottery industries. Here the power of steam was released and harnessed to machines with revolutionary consequences. It made England the first industrial nation and contributed mightily to the creation of the greatest empire of all times. This little island became the workshop of the world. But despite efforts to hold the new modes of production in their original home, they migrated swiftly to America and of course to other countries. Also they moved from one branch of the economy to another until all industry was brought under their sway. As the decades passed, iron gave way to steel and other metals, steam was supplemented by gasoline and electricity, and machines ever more complicated, precise, and powerful were contrived. Today we stand on the threshold of the age of atomic energy and automatic factories.

For the most part this entire transformation went forward under a regime of private enterprise. To be sure, government, through tariffs, subsidies, and concessions, through guarantees of property rights and enforcement of contractual obligations, made an indispensable contribution. But it was the class of businessmen emerging from the Middle Ages as artisans, merchants, tradesmen, and bankers that played the central and active role. Motivated by the desire for private gain, these men organized production, as well as exchange, and assembled resources for the launching of the machine on its spectacular career and for the perfecting of its operations. Whatever their faults and whatever their future, they provided the initiative, the daring, and the leadership for the most profound modification of the modes of livelihood in history. They supplied the necessary energizing principle for the advance of technology.

3

Technology has profoundly changed the role of human labor in the process of production.
The power-driven machine obviously alters the function and the responsibility of the workman. No longer does he act directly on raw materials and, proceeding at his own tempo, shape them into a finished product stamped with his own personality. Rather, following the pace set by the total productive process, he becomes a tender of machines, a stoker of furnaces, an oiler of wheels, a manipulator of levers, a presser of buttons, a feeder of materials, a coordinator of operations, and a receiver of finished products. Though the operation as a whole is an expression of the creative genius of the engineer, the ordinary workman tends to become an ever more highly specialized automaton—one of many coordinated human appendages of the machine.

But as technology advances and the miraculous resources of electronics and electrochemistry are brought into the service of the economy, the role of human labor is reduced more and more and man is pushed further and further toward the periphery of operations. First, a single machine becomes automatic, then a machine is designed to control a series or group of machines, and finally the entire process from raw material to finished product is made automatic in an automatic factory. This trend of course is still in its infancy, but it would seem that eventually any operation or series of operations susceptible of expression in mathematical formulas will be handed over to the machine. The perspectives now opening before *homo faber* leave the student of the history of human toil breathless.

Shortly after the late war two Canadian physicists painted this picture of the factory of tomorrow: "The production floor is barren of men. Only a few engineers, technicians, and operators walk about on a balcony above, before a great wall of master control panels, inserting and checking records,

New Modes of Livelihood 145

watching and adjusting batteries of control instruments. All else is automatic. Raw materials flow in by conveyer, move through automatic inspection units, fabricating machines, subassembly and assembly lines, all controlled from the master panels, and arrive at the automatic packaging machines as finished product—radios, refrigerators, tractors, fountain pens, carburetors, helicopters, or what you will." All of this, they say, is no dream of the distant future: "Nowhere is modern man more obsolete than on the factory production floor. Modern machines are far more accurate and untiring than men. Available and in use are hundreds of electronic gadgets that can do everything a workman can, and do it faster, better, and continuously."[2] "It has been said, with pardonable extravagance," observes Harold G. Moulton, "that electronic science has taught the electron to see, feel, smell, taste, hear, remember, calculate, and beat and tell time."[3] Clearly the textile mills of the early years of the nineteenth century exploiting the labor of little children, and their survivals of today, seem almost as archaic as the pyramids.

Peculiarly fantastic and fateful in their implications for the role of labor in production are the new high-speed electronic computing machines which are said to possess "rudimentary organs of memory, judgment, and mathematical logic." Recently there has been devised a machine, a giant "4000-tube brain," capable of solving "in one minute problems that would require two mathematicians six months"[4] —more than 250,000 times as fast as the human brain. According to Louis N. Ridenour this development presages a "second industrial revolution" which may be far more disruptive of established ways than the first. "Thus," he writes, "while the first industrial revolution involved the substitution of machinery for man's musculature, the second will replace by inanimate devices man's senses, nervous system, and brain." The social consequences of this development, he

[2] E. W. Leaver and J. J. Brown, "Machines Without Men," *Fortune*, November, 1946, p. 165.
[3] Harold G. Moulton, *Controlling Factors in Economic Development* (Washington, 1949), p. 243.
[4] William L. Laurence, *The New York Times*, November 22, 1950.

rightly observes, are "incalculable, and may be disastrous."[5]

It would appear that the vision of Aristotle, expressed more than two thousand years ago, may become a reality. "If every tool when summoned," he wrote, "or even of its own accord, could do the work that befits it, just as the creations of Daedalus moved of themselves, or the tripods of Hephaestus went of their own accord to their sacred work, if the weaver's shuttles were to weave of themselves, then there would be no use either of apprentices for the master workers, or of slaves for their lords." Today tools of surpassing complexity and power, almost of their own accord, can actually do the work that befits them and thus render obsolete both slaves and lords. The time may not be far distant when "drudgery in its more stupefying forms" will be as obsolete as the slave driver.

Technology has thus altered the historical relation between human labor and the tools of production. In the old agrarian economy man possessed the skills and energies which now reside in the machine. In that economy, therefore, a workman could be put to work with an astonishingly small expenditure for the necessary tools. A few dollars would have been sufficient. Indeed, with a little time he could have made most of them himself. And he learned to make and use them as he grew to maturity in family and neighborhood. Now, to put this same man to work requires in some industries an investment in plant and equipment of thousands of dollars. Indeed, in the electrical industry this figure stands at $62,000 and is still rising. Production has become a vast, complicated, and costly machine process. To insure the transmission from generation to generation of the large and growing body of skills and knowledges necessary to the conduct and improvement of this process requires a large expenditure of time, energy, and money.

The advance of the machine has been attended by a steady and rapid increase in the productivity of labor. Although this increase was particularly striking in the early stages of industrialization, it has continued with unabated strength

[5] Louis N. Ridenour, "Mechanical Brains," *Fortune*, May, 1949, pp. 117–118.

down to the present time. According to J. Frederic Dewhurst, during the ninety-year period from 1850 to 1940 the estimated productivity per man-hour of labor for the entire gainfully employed population in terms of 1940 prices rose from 17.3 to 79.3 cents. This means that the "average rate of increase over the entire period" was "18.2 per cent per decade, or about 1.7 per cent per year compounded."[6] These figures probably record the most impressive sustained economic advance in the history of nations.

The increase in the productivity of labor has been accompanied by a revolutionary reduction in the hours of work. What these hours were in the self-sustaining rural household of 1800 we can only conjecture, but they were probably between eighty and ninety per week. On the basis of available data, Dewhurst concludes that in 1850, for agricultural and nonagricultural occupations combined, the figure was 70.6. In the decades that followed, the 12-hour day gave way to the 10-hour day, which in turn was superseded by the 8-hour day. By 1940 the average work-week was 43 hours. We may confidently expect that this century-old trend will continue at least for a time into the coming decades.[7] Thus a glance at history suggests that the machine has made human labor both more productive and more precious.

4

Technology has brought mass production and enlarged the scale of operations.

In the war just concluded mass production was sometimes called America's "secret weapon." Certainly it was largely responsible for making our country the "arsenal of democracy," for the avalanche of munitions of war that flowed from our mines, shops, and factories to amaze both our friends and our enemies, and even ourselves.

[6] J. Frederic Dewhurst and Associates, *America's Needs and Resources* (New York, 1947), p. 23.
[7] *Ibid.*, pp. 20, 23.

At the peak of the war effort we produced "nearly 45 per cent of the armament output of all belligerent nations." This was achieved largely by a process of mass production, which is peculiarly an expression of American genius. "Now, for the first time in the history of the world," says Karl T. Compton, "science has given man an opportunity to secure the good things of life without taking them from someone else, and in a degree going far beyond the amount of labor he expends."[8] The full meaning of mass production, therefore, involves far more than profound changes in techniques for producing goods. It involves equally profound changes in the realm of distribution. It involves a shift from production for the classes to production for the masses. It provides a truly revolutionary means for building the economic foundations of the democratic way of life. It makes both possible and necessary the prosperity of all the people.

The idea of mass production appears early in the history of American industry. In 1799 Eli Whitney contracted with the federal government to deliver within two years ten thousand muskets. Although he required ten years to fill the order and thus failed to meet the conditions of his contract, he introduced into industry the revolutionary principle of "interchangeable parts" and the revolutionary ideal of "absolute accuracy." This achievement, combined with the invention of the assembly line which apparently came later, laid the foundations of mass production and material abundance. But before this mode of industrial operation could be applied to the commodities of popular use, the market had to be greatly extended, the scale of operations enlarged, and mass purchasing power created. In time, with the steady and radical improvement of the means of communication and transportation, all of these conditions emerged.

The extension of the market which accompanied improved highways, railroads, steamboats, automobiles, airplanes, and electrical communications, brought much more than a wider exchange of goods and services. It also brought new purposes

[8] Quoted in Christy Borth, *Masters of Mass Production* (New York, 1945), p. 14.

and interests into the economic life of the people. Whereas formerly men and women had produced for themselves or their neighbors, they now produced for a distant and wholly impersonal thing called the market, which they little understood. They became absorbed in the acquisition of money and tended to measure success increasingly in pecuniary terms. To those who were skillful in commercial transaction the possibility of wealth beyond the dreams of an earlier age entered naturally into their calculations.

The enlargement of the scale of operations was accompanied by a profound transformation in the conduct of the economy. It brought together in a single plant tens, scores, hundreds, and even thousands of workmen, each of whom performs a highly specialized function without knowing much about the total process. Indeed, the individual becomes a kind of interchangeable human part which with other parts compose the whole. While all of these developments have resulted in greatly increased efficiency, they have introduced into the economy a high degree of discipline and regimentation. The workman is required not only to begin and end his day by the clock; he is also expected to adjust all of his actions to the actions of his fellows and to the demands of the machine. The transformation of the independent and many-sided farmer into an operative in a mass-production plant is one of the most revolutionary changes in our history. Jefferson's glorified tillers of the soil would doubtless have regarded this entire process as profoundly contrary to the "American way of life," as it assuredly was in their day. The problem thus created of giving to the common man, the workingman, a sense of social status and dignity is one of the major problems of our democracy. It goes to the root of much of the popular unrest of our time.

Large-scale operations have brought together, not only the labor power of many persons, but also the financial resources of many investors. As a consequence, the corporation, which scarcely existed at the time of the founding of the Republic, has come to dominate the economy of the nation. It is difficult to realize that "up to 1830 apparently only two industrial corporations in the United States had received charters authorizing a capital subscription of as much as a million dollars."[9] Moreover, motivated by the desire for profits, the corporation has striven within the sphere of its interest to achieve a condition of monopoly. The degree to which the forces of competition have been circumvented is clearly revealed in an exhaustive study by a Congressional committee. "The major categories of business activity," says a report of this committee, "may be divided roughly into two groups. The first of these groups includes agriculture, wholesale and retail distribution, personal service, building construction, and a miscellany of smaller trades. The second includes transportation, public utilities, manufacturing, mining, and finance. In the first group business enterprises are numerous, the typical enterprise is small, the degree of concentration is low, and prices are relatively flexible. In the second, enterprises are less numerous, the typical enterprise is larger, the degree of concentration is higher, and prices are relatively rigid. Among the industries in the first group, it is probable that competition is more usual than monopoly. Among those in the second, it is possible that monopoly is as usual as competition."[10] Our giant corporations, our great monopolies and quasi-monopolies, because they represent concentrated power, have a disproportionate influence in the economy.

Mass production and large-scale enterprise have favored and even compelled the development of a new science and a new profession—the science and profession of management. The complex and far-flung undertakings of our economy, with their highly technical and intricate operations and their hundreds and thousands of personnel, do not run themselves. Nor can they be run efficiently by persons without appropriate experience and training who acquire title by purchase, inheritance, or stock manipulation. Into their successful conduct must go many special and general abilities—the ability to comprehend the given enterprise in all of its relations, the

[9] George W. Stocking and Myron W. Watkins, *Monopoly and Free Enterprise* (New York, 1951), p. 18.
[10] Temporary National Economic Committee, Monograph No. 21, *Competition and Monopoly in American Industry* (Washington, 1940), pp. 307–308.

ability to appraise the contributions of the various branches of technology, the ability to deal effectively and democratically with people, the ability to coordinate a great variety of activities and functions, and the ability to guide the formulation of short- and long-term plans and policies with some regard for the public interest. The conduct of the enormous military and economic operations involved in the Second World War is a striking demonstration of the emergence of this new science. Special proficiency in its practice and general understanding of its nature and worth must characterize democracy in the industrial age. Regardless of the institutional arrangements involved in the ownership of the means of production, a highly trained and experienced profession of managers is required in the conduct of the enterprises and the coordination of the branches of any economy resting on an advanced technology.

5

Technology has altered the contours of the economy.
In large measure technology has removed from the household most of the economic functions which were there in 1800. Among the more important may be listed spinning, weaving, sewing, and garment-making, baking, churning, canning, preserving, and butchering, building, tool construction, and fence-making, recreation and entertainment. Each of these, moreover, has been developed into a great industry or even a series of great industries. At the same time, the farmer, while continuing in some degree the tradition of versatility of his ancestors, has become more and more specialized in his economic activities, and more and more dependent on the machine. Technology has brought into being many industries that were quite unknown or that existed only in embryo in the earlier economy—industries that give to our economy today much of its peculiar character—industries associated with the production and use of steel, cement, light metals, plastics, and

mineral fertilizers, coal, oil, electricity, and water power, locomotives, automobiles, steamships, and airplanes, books, magazines, and newspapers, telegraph, telephone, cinema, radio, and television. Such an economy would confound the imagination of the generation of the fathers of the Republic.

The advance of technology is also altering the traditional conception of the nature of an economy. Although we have always defined it as a system of institutions, mechanisms, processes, and relationships for the production of goods *and* services, we have commonly assumed that the production of services is quite a secondary consideration. In other words, we have assumed that the primary and dominant purpose of an economy is to produce material things—food, clothes, houses, tools, machines, stoves, automobiles, and radio sets. This inherited conception is becoming rapidly outmoded. As a matter of fact, we can scarcely hope to achieve stability in the economy without subjecting its proportions to radical revision. With the growth of the power of the machine, the spread of the machine from one field to another, the development of electronics, the emergence of automatic processes and factories, and the radical increase in the productivity of physical labor, the proportion of our people engaged in the making of material things has already shown a marked decline. According to Lewis Corey, the proportion of people employed in "the production of physical goods fell from around 75 per cent in 1870 to 50 per cent in 1940."[11] That this decline will continue in the years ahead, and perhaps at an accelerated pace, seems certain. If we are to find employment for all, therefore, many more of us than heretofore will have to move into the service occupations—into the fields of health, education, science, communication, recreation, entertainment, and all the arts for the enrichment and refinement of personal and community life. As a noted economist has said, our economy is no longer merely a "brick and mortar" affair. The redistribution of the labor force demanded by this radical alteration of the contours of the economy will challenge profoundly our inventive powers.

[11] Lewis Corey, *The Middle Class* (Yellow Springs, 1945), p. 5.

6

Technology has transformed the system of social relations.

With the disruption of the self-contained household and rural neighborhood, the development of the power-driven machine, and the enlargement of the scale of operations under a system of private enterprise, the relations among people and the whole class structure have been profoundly changed. No longer do we have a population of independent farmers, deriving their livelihood from their own land, engaging in manual labor, and living much alike. We follow callings of the greatest diversity that number, not a score or two, but many thousands. According to the Bureau of the Census, the "total number of different occupational designations . . . probably runs well over 100,000." We make our living and we live very differently.

Although all of us, even the poorest, enjoy certain conveniences, receive certain services, and possess certain gadgets, which were unknown in earlier times, the differences in economic condition are perhaps as great as in any society of history. The total national income is divided very unevenly. The situation was summarized in the report of an inquiry by the Brookings Institution for 1929, the high point of American prosperity before the war. "The 11,653,000 families with incomes of less than $1,500," runs the report, "received a total of about 10 billion dollars. At the other extreme, the 36,000 families having incomes in excess of $75,000 possessed an aggregate income of 9.8 billion dollars. Thus it appears that 0.1 per cent of the families at the top received practically as much as 42 per cent of the families at the bottom of the scale." [12] It must be said, however, that in the meantime this condition has been modified considerably and that possibly the trend toward inequality has been reversed. According to the National Bureau of Economic Research, the "shares of the upper income groups" have "de-

[12] Maurice Leven, Harold G. Moulton, and Clark Warburton, *America's Capacity to Consume* (Washington, 1934), p. 56.

clined substantially." Yet, if Alexis de Tocqueville were to return and write a comprehensive treatise on our civilization, he would hardly begin by referring to the "equality of condition" in America.

Even more important, perhaps, is the relation of our people to productive property. The rise of the machine has been accompanied by a revolutionary change in this relationship. For the most part the individual does not and cannot, as an individual, own the tools of production. Only in relatively rare cases, outside of agriculture, does he even share significantly in the ownership. And of those who till the soil thirty per cent are tenants and about an equal percentage of the remainder own farms that are heavily mortgaged. As a consequence, the great-grandson of the independent farmer of hallowed tradition may find himself today beholden to government or to some owner or manager of capital for the opportunity of earning a living for himself and his family. At the same time we see a trend down through the decades toward the concentration of productive property in fewer and fewer hands. Those rights to the ownership of land and the tools of production which the common man fought for and won in the seventeenth and eighteenth centuries are fully exercised today by no more than twenty per cent of our people. The old economic foundations of American democracy have been largely destroyed.

7

Technology has altered the roles of the members of the family.

With the dissolution of the economic base of the family on the land and the removal to the factory of many economic activities, the husband and father increasingly found employment away from the home and the wife and mother was forced into a new economic role. Among the more favored classes, women for the most part remained in the home, shorn of many of their former functions and responsibilities and endowed with more leisure than any other large group of women in history. Among the poor, women followed their occupations out of the family and into the factory and other places of work. Today "close to 30 percent of all our workers are women."[13]

Except for agriculture in its more retarded forms the position of the young has also undergone radical transformation. From earliest times down to the rise of the machine, children and youth engaged in socially useful labor as a part of the process of growing up. This was important, not only from the standpoint of the economic welfare of the family, but also from the standpoint of occupational training and character formation. Today, for a variety of reasons, the young of town and city have little experience with work until they leave school at some time between sixteen and twenty-four years of age. Beginning in Massachusetts in 1836 we passed child labor laws designed to protect boys and girls from exploitation and from injurious and hazardous toil. Efforts to bring productive labor into the schools or into the broad educative process have generally been opposed by both businessmen and labor unions. But whatever the causes, the fact is that the vast majority of the young in our industrial society are compelled to grow to physical maturity without experiencing the discipline of socially useful work. The correction of this condition is one of the major educational problems of our time.

[13] Louis I. Dublin, *The American Population Profile* (New York, 1950), leaflet, p. 6.

10

NEW FORMS OF COMMUNICATION

1

Technology has brought new forms of communication.
In no realm has technology worked greater miracles. At the time of the settlement, except for the alphabet and the printing press, the horse, the wheel, and the sailing ship, the European immigrants were little farther advanced in the arts and agencies of communication than the aborigines of North America. Indeed in some respects, notably in the case of the canoe and sign language, the Indian held an advantage over the white man. But with the opening of the nineteenth century we, along with the peoples of Western Europe, started on a career of invention in this field that literally has transformed practically all human relations. We need only mention the steamboat, the locomotive, the automobile, the airplane, and the rocket, the telegraph, the telephone, the radio, the cinema, and television. Invention has followed invention so swiftly that we have not had sufficient time to adjust ourselves to one and incorporate it fully into our ways of life before another and more revolutionary mechanism has appeared.

The importance of communication in the evolution of the human mind and human society is beyond calculation. Language, perhaps the greatest of all the achievements of man, not only makes group life possible. It also is essential to the psychological maturation of the individual and the development of the processes of thought. It is no accident that the words *communication* and *community* have a common root. Unquestionably the boundaries of a community are limited by the modes of communication. "Of all inventions, the alphabet and the printing press alone excepted," wrote Lord Macaulay a hundred years ago, "those inventions which abridge distance have done most for the civilization of the species." If this man were alive today, he might be less confident about the exceptions. Distance has been abridged in a measure that he could scarcely have imagined: in fact, in the communication of knowledge and thought, even of feelings and sentiments, it has been destroyed. Radio transmission travels with the speed of light, the swiftest planes faster than the speed of sound. And the age of atomic energy and electronics lies just ahead.

2

Technology has created a more perfect union.

When the founding fathers met in constitutional convention in 1787, they proposed to forge a single nation out of thirteen separate states and their territories on the political foundations of popular rule. They realized fully the hazards confronting their bold experiment implicit in the facts of history and geography. Though persuaded to make common cause in the name of independence, the several states were divided by pride, ambition, and provincial loyalties. Also they were divided by great distances and the primitive state of communication. Almost fifteen hundred miles of bad roads and trails separated the northern and southern borders of the young Republic, and it was more than a thousand miles through the wilderness from Cape Cod to the upper waters of the Mississippi. In terms of communication this was an enormous territory, far larger than the entire earth today. Some conception of the situation may be gained from the fact that Washington's journey to his inauguration from Mount Vernon to New York in 1789, over one of the best highways of the time, consumed fourteen days. Even in the middle of the next century a stagecoach trip across the United States under the most favorable conditions of travel took a month and a half and was accompanied by severe hardship. The resolve to build a more perfect union out of the original thirteen states and territories on a republican basis was a supreme act of faith. The physical means essential to the success of this bold venture in statecraft were not in existence at the time.

Each of the states, moreover, was a loose aggregation of tiny neighborhoods separated from one another often by feuds of long standing and always by distances that could be traversed only by hours and days of arduous travel. Thus, when measured in miles, the world in which men and women actually lived and conducted their affairs was exceedingly small—a world in which most of the relationships among people were personal, intimate, and enduring. The government in Washington, and even in the state capital, to say nothing of the governments of Europe and Asia, were very far away. The functions of the federal government, moreover, were so limited that its actions affected but little the everyday life of the ordinary citizen. It was the activities of the neighborhood that absorbed his energies.

But the founding fathers built better than they knew. The vision of a more perfect union was brought down to earth and made actual by the march of technology and the invention of new forms of communication. With the completion of the first transcontinental railway in 1869 the coast to coast trip was made in six days. In February, 1949, a plane covered this distance in three hours and 46 minutes. Ever more powerful engines of space have shortened the great distances, loosened the ties of family and neighborhood, obliterated the boundaries of local communities, softened the lines dividing the states, halted the tendencies toward sectionalism, and all but joined the Atlantic and the Pacific. They have placed New York and San Francisco, Seattle and Miami, side by side and have brought Washington into every farmhouse and city apartment. In some respects they have reduced the whole of America to the dimensions of the rural neighborhood of a few generations ago. They have bound us all closely into a single national community in which our relationships with one another are often impersonal and fleeting while our fortunes are intimately and lastingly joined together. A union far more perfect and binding than the members of the Constitutional Convention ever imagined has been fashioned by the application of science to life.

We are bound together by the indissoluble ties of economic forces. No family, no neighborhood, no state, no region can live by itself. As the workmen of a great factory pursue their many specialties, all of which are necessary to make the finished product, so the different parts of the country contribute their special talents and resources to achieve the welfare of the whole. Technology has written for our people a declaration of economic interdependence that neither laws nor force can successfully subvert. As manufacture is dependent on agriculture, so agriculture is dependent on manufacture; as the West is dependent on the East, so the East is dependent on the West. The thread of a common interest runs through all the industries and regions of the country. And millions of us earn our living by providing the communication services that make us all of one family. So complete and pervasive is our interdependence that either fortune or misfortune arising in one sector of the economy sends its reverberations swiftly throughout the entire structure.

We are bound together, too, by the powerful ties of psychological forces. The president of the United States may sit in the White House and engage in a "fireside chat" with the people of the nation, even with those who at the moment may be on the other side of the earth. And if the president can do this, so can anyone else who succeeds in gaining access to the magic of the radio or television. As our factories meet the needs of the flesh by clothing us in the same garments from the Atlantic to the Pacific, so our agencies of communication satisfy the demands of the spirit by furnishing our minds with the same thoughts and passions from Gopher Prairie to Los Angeles and Boston. The products of Hollywood go into every American locality; the radio commentators are heard from one end of the country to another; the great news services send their dispatches to practically all the newspapers of the nation; and the popular journals and digests published in New York or some other metropolis go into the smallest hamlet. As a consequence, a new story or a new idea, a new truth or a new falsehood, a new fear or a new hope may sweep across our land in a few hours or even in a few minutes. The differences in our mental baggage are due less and less to the facts of geography and local tradition.

We are bound together and also divided by powerful voluntary organizations that span the nation. Perhaps the most influential of these organizations are those which express economic interest. We have our great associations of employers: the United States Chamber of Commerce, the National Association of Manufacturers, the American Bankers Association, the National Electric Light Association, the Advertising Federation of America, and others. We have also our great unions of industrial working people: the Railway Brotherhoods, the American Federation of Labor, the Congress of Industrial Organizations, and others. Even in the field of agriculture, the historic stronghold of individualism, we have the National Grange, the American Farm Bureau Federation, and the National Farmers Union. Certain of the professions are well organized and many white-collar workers are forming unions and affiliating with labor. Consumers, in increasing numbers, are establishing cooperative undertakings. In addition, organizations have been launched to promote almost every interest, civic or cultural, which the mind can imagine. Some of them, such as the American Legion, the American Association of University Women, the American Civil Liberties Union, and the National Association for the Advancement of Colored People, have left a considerable impress on our institutions and ways of life and thought. All of these organizations are among the stubborn realities of our society. They conduct an uninterrupted campaign of propaganda to advance their interests and ideas. Their representatives and agents constitute a kind of "third house" in Washington and exert constant pressure on state and local governments. Some of them, in their efforts to influence legislation in their favor, have employed every means conceivable to corrupt and intimidate legislators and to debase the entire democratic political process.

During the first one hundred years of the history of the Republic the federal union was continually shaken by disputes between states and by sectional rivalries. At one time it was almost destroyed in one of the bloodiest civil wars on record. Though differences associated with geography continue to this day, such differences belong for the most part to the past. The sharp conflicts of interest in the present and the future override state and regional boundaries and express alignments of forces that reach across the nation. The most turbulent of these conflicts arise out of the differentiation of economic function, the distribution of wealth and income, and the emergence of economic classes. The struggle between capital and labor, between employers and employees, has been gathering momentum with the advance of the machine, the corporation, and large enterprise. In Europe and other parts of the world this struggle has rocked society to its foundations and in some instances has taken the extreme form of revolution and counterrevolution. It has been deeply involved in the establishment of the totalitarian states and movements of our time. The survival of free institutions in America depends on our ability to resolve the deep conflicts of interest groups without resort to organized violence, bloodshed, and repression. Here it is that our Republic faces a major test in domestic affairs during the years to come.

3

Technology has created the physical foundations for one world.

The miracles of science and technology have closed a great cycle that began in the Garden of Eden. From that fabled garden in which he first ate the fruit of the tree of knowledge man slowly spread over the face of the earth. As he increased in numbers and mastered the primitive arts of locomotion, he surmounted one after another the barriers of nature. Painfully and at great hazard, he crossed plains and deserts, forests and jungles, ridges and mountains, rivers, lakes, and oceans, and ultimately came to occupy most of the land surface of the globe. In the process of migration little groups, separated from one another by vast distances and natural obstacles, gradually formed the diverse races and varieties of the human species.

For several centuries now, perhaps ever since the discovery of the New World, a reverse process has been in operation. With the advance of invention in the sphere of communication the earth has been growing ever smaller. Today we are almost back to the little garden in which man began his earthly adventure, with of course a difference. The many races and peoples, formed during the long period of migration and settlement, find themselves crowded together on this greatly shrunken planet. In the emerging air age prosperity and adversity, freedom and despotism, war and peace have become practically world-wide in their reaches. In a geographical sense the world has become one. If we are not to destroy ourselves, it must become one in spirit, or at least in law.

America is bound inextricably into this world. The great oceans which sheltered her for centuries have been mastered. The Atlantic was crossed by the *Santa Maria* in 1492 in seventy days, by the *Mayflower* in 1620 in sixty-one days, by the *Savannah*, the first steamship, in 1819 in twenty-five days, by the great ocean liner of 1950 in four or five days, by the airplane in ten or twelve hours, and by the jet bomber in slightly over four hours. In September, 1519, a fleet of five ships commanded by Ferdinand Magellan, sailed out from Spain across the western seas. In September, 1522, after a voyage of incredible danger and hardship involving the death of the commander and the loss of four vessels, one lone ship dropped anchor in Seville Roads, having circumnavigated the earth in three years. In July, 1933, Wiley Post flew around the world from New York to New York in less than eight days. In February and March, 1949, a B-50 bomber, Lucky Lady II, repeated this feat in a nonstop flight of 94 hours, starting from and returning to Fort Worth, Texas. It is freely predicted today that in the near future no point on the globe will be more than twelve hours by flight from any other point. During the great war against the Axis Powers, the planes of America and her allies literally conquered the air, making routine flights over the widest seas and the highest mountains, through fog and night and storm. By means of cable, radio, and television we are almost able to listen to the gossip and look into the backyards of the most distant peoples. And they are or will be as close to us as we are to them. Technology has written a declaration of world interdependence.

This interdependence is expressed in commerce, travel, and cultural exchange. No country, not even the Soviet Union or the United States, is self-contained. In 1790 the total value of the foreign trade of our Republic amounted to less than forty-five million dollars; in 1929, our year of greatest prosperity between the wars, it was more than nine and one-half billions; and in 1949 it reached more than eighteen billions. In 1790 our trade was confined almost wholly to Western Europe and the West Indies; today it embraces all lands—Eastern Europe, Asia, South America, Africa, Australia, and Oceania. In 1790 few citizens even thought of crossing the Atlantic to the Old World. In our period of prosperity before the great depression travel of our people abroad reached enormous proportions. In 1930 almost half a million citizens arrived from abroad and an approximately equal number departed. The volume of foreign mails has advanced rapidly for decades. In the arts and sciences national boundaries, unsupported by force and terror, have little meaning. Discoveries, inventions, ideas, and thought are increasingly the common achievements and possessions of all advanced nations. We recently discovered that even the secrets of the atomic bomb could not be held more than a few years at most. The nations and peoples of the world are bound together today both materially and spiritually in a system of mutual aid. The "iron curtain" enforced with utter ruthlessness by a vast border patrol of armed guards is known to be porous.

America is inevitably involved in the fortunes of the rest of the world. It is no longer possible, if it ever was, for her to shape entirely her own destiny, even in the sphere of internal affairs. Prosperity or depression is a world-wide phenomenon, even influencing to some extent a "closed economy" like that of Russia. We are affected by the size of the rice crop in Burma, the nationalization of the Bank of England, the production of gold in Siberia, the condition of the grass on the pampas, or the industrialization of China. Events taking place far beyond our borders may affect us more profoundly than happenings at home. Consider, for example, the Japanese invasion of Manchuria, the signing of the Munich Pact, the Fascist intervention in Spain, or the Communist assault on the Republic of Korea. There are no longer local elections without international significance anywhere in the world, and the line between foreign and domestic affairs is becoming more and more shadowy.

The ideas thrown up by revolutions and counterrevolutions abroad come quickly to our shores and leave their impact on thought and action. Both the Soviet doctrine of the equality of races and the Nazi teaching of "Aryan" superiority, as well as the theory of violence and dictatorship common to Fascism and Communism, have influenced and attracted many minds in America. In the case of war, even before the day of the atomic bomb, we found that we could not or dared not remain aloof, indifferent to the outcome of a struggle involving the great powers. Both war and peace have become indivisible on our little planet. And it must be emphasized that the unrivaled industrial might of the United States, whether we so desire or not, will play an enormous role in deciding whether the world is to have depression or prosperity, war or peace, tyranny or liberty.

Unfortunately the world remains spiritually divided. Physical space has indeed been annihilated, but formidable psychological barriers remain. Suspicions and prejudices, fears and hatreds, attitudes of superiority and inferiority, developed through the centuries, persist in almost undiminished strength. In fact some elements of this evil legacy from the past tend to grow more violent and inflexible as the peoples of the earth find themselves crowded ever more closely together. Broad psychological gulfs continue to separate American and Englishman, Anglo-Saxon and Frenchman, Latin and German, Teuton and Slav, European and Negro, Occidental and Oriental. Also Protestant and Catholic, Christian, Jew, Mohammedan, Hindu, Buddhist, and Confucianist. In addition class struggles cut across the boundaries of states and increase the tensions agitating the minds of men and women on all continents.

Yet more ominous are the profound differences in social and political philosophy, in conceptions of the future of mankind, which cast their shadow over the deliberations of every international gathering. Feudal, capitalist, and socialist institutions, attitudes, and ideas are struggling for survival or mastery everywhere in this little world. But it is the ancient conflict between liberty and tyranny, between free society and despotism, clothed in the garments of the twentieth century, that may determine the fate of the human race for centuries to come. Only yesterday peoples who love freedom made common cause with Communist totalitarianism to drive back and destroy a powerful coalition of Fascist states committed to world conquest. Today all free nations, all nations outside the folds of the "iron curtain," are threatened by an equally aggressive and ruthless adversary.

With a sense of mission rarely equaled in history, the Soviet leaders see the eventual spread of Communism over the entire earth under their inspired guidance and through the extension of Russian power. This tiny oligarchy in the Kremlin now holds sway over approximately one-third of the human race and believes with the fanaticism of religious conviction that the forces of history are working swiftly and inexorably on their side. Through the Communist Party of the Soviet Union and the network of Communist parties embracing practically all countries, they are subjecting to implacable and pitiless attack the liberal and democratic forces of the world. Guided by the ethics of battle, they are promoting both civil and national strife everywhere beyond the borders of their dominion. This division of the world is the foremost political reality of our time. It will probably remain with us for many years.

Slowly and haltingly the peoples of the world have sought to give political expression to the condition of interdependence produced by the new forms of communication. Following the formation of the International Telegraph Union in 1868, the nations proceeded to cooperate in a number of relatively noncontroversial fields: the post, weights and measures, property interests, publishing rights, freight transportation, public health, and other interests. Beginning with the establishment of the International Bureau of American Republics in 1890, many countries sought an alternative to war through The Hague Peace Conferences and the Permanent Court of Arbitration. At the close of the First World War, under the leadership of Woodrow Wilson, a truly bold and radical departure from the historic ways of man was made in the launching of the League of Nations. Following another great struggle that threatened to inaugurate a world-wide reign of tyranny, the victorious powers embarked on a second great venture in the field of international organization "to save succeeding generations from the scourge of war." If the United Nations is to be more successful than the League, the peoples of the earth will have to achieve not only a new understanding, but also a new morality. Nothing less than the future of civilization is at stake.

4

Technology has created a social fabric of surpassing sweep, complexity, and dynamism. In its patterns of organization industrial society is coming to resemble one of its own great machines, with its thousands of separate parts each performing an essential function and articulating with the others in closest harmony. To perceive all of the relationships between workman and workman, labor and management, farm and factory, region and region, industry and commerce, production and distribution, economy and government, work and play, is beyond the powers of a single mind. Even to follow the system of communication through all of its ramifications from the great centers of finance and power down to field and forest and stream, to mine and lathe and fishing boat, and back again, exhausts the imagination. When we add the interplay of social forces, of the hopes and fears and plans of people, of the designs and struggles of organized groups, of corporations, employers, farmers, labor unions, and cooperatives, we confront a condition that would have astonished and frightened the simple farmers and tradesmen of a few generations ago.

This vast system of relationships seems to be extremely sensitive and unstable. Unlike our old agrarian society, with its independent and quasi-independent neighborhoods, industrial society constitutes a single social fabric and is vulnerable as a whole. If it fails to function in any one of many of its innumerable parts, if the outlay for capital goods falls below the danger point, if speculation upsets the delicate financial balance, if purchasing power is insufficient to absorb the goods and services available, it may pass into a condition of general paralysis or crisis—loans are called, shops close their doors, wheels of production stop turning, millions of workmen are thrown on the streets, members of the middle classes consume their savings, farmers endeavor to resurrect the self-contained household of their ancestors, young men and women hesitate to marry and assume the responsibilities of parenthood, and all elements of the population become frightened and seek scapegoats for their troubles. This seems to be what happens when a great economic depression sweeps over the land.

As yet we have contrived no adequate means to operate successfully and smoothly our complex industrial economy. In spite of the repeated testimony of experience, we continue to place our trust in the so-called automatic controls of the free market which prevailed during pre-machine days. As a matter of fact such controls no longer operate generally in our highly organized economy. Also our experience with depressions demonstrates that the substitutes devised, except during the highly abnormal conditions of war, have been inadequate to keep the economy on an even keel and at a high level of production. Some measure of general planning, direction, and coordination is clearly necessary. Whether this can or should be achieved by a far-reaching fiscal policy, by the direct assumption on the part of existing governmental agencies of responsibility for stabilization, by the creation of some special federal organ to do the job, by the socialization of certain strategically situated branches of the economy, by the establishment of an economic council representative of government, management, labor, and agriculture, by the encouragement of the cooperative movement, or by some combination of these and other proposals, should be the urgent subject of bold debate and experiment. The survival of free institutions undoubtedly waits upon the achievement of success in this venture.

To those who say that general economic planning, coordination, or stabilization of any kind is certain to end in totalitarianism or serfdom, there is a simple rejoinder. If we cannot find an effective substitute for the assumed, but largely mythical, automatic controls and at the same time preserve our essential liberties, then there is no hope for free society in the emerging age. That great dangers will attend any course we may pursue is readily granted. Yet inaction is the most hazardous form of action in this critical epoch. We cannot expect even our democracy, strong as it is, to survive many depressions equal in depth and scope to the one which began in 1929 and continued until the war compelled us to introduce numerous measures of control. Those of us who love freedom should have learned during the past twenty-five years that men and women generally do not prize political liberty above all else. If they are forced to choose between liberty and bread, they will take bread, or perhaps even the promise of bread. We must not permit ourselves to be confronted with this grim and possibly tragic choice. We must find a way of uniting economic stability with political liberty.

5

The management of industrial society places heavy responsibilities on virtue and understanding.
This brings the analysis to the most difficult educational problem which the advance of technology has thrust upon us. If we are to manage this highly complex and dynamic society, we shall have to achieve a degree of loyalty to the general welfare that greatly surpasses the demands of the highly individualistic order of our fathers. Some common agreement on social purposes is clearly imperative. How far such agreement is possible or desirable is a question that can be answered only through experience. The same reasoning obviously applies with equal force to the organization of peace in the world. If the nations cannot agree upon and remain loyal to the requisite purposes, they cannot achieve even a fairly durable peace. It is in this area of purposes that the totalitarian state has a great advantage over free society. Dictatorship can impose its will upon a people by the rack, the machine gun, the forced labor camp, and the monolithic direction of all the agencies of propaganda; free society must rely on the slow process of education, political discussion, and general enlightenment to achieve a common mind. Here is one of the greatest challenges confronting our democracy in these troubled and critical times. If we fail to develop concern for the common good at home, we shall lose our liberties; if we fail to develop concern for the common good among the nations, we shall perish.

The burden placed upon human understanding by the complexities of industrial civilization threatens to overwhelm free society. Such a society rests on the assumption that the judgment of common people, of farmers, mechanics, and housewives, is sound and trustworthy. When confronted with the gossamerlike web of relationships reaching out to the borders of the nation and on to the ends of the earth the individual must often experience a sense of utter confusion and helplessness. He must be haunted with the feeling that his mental equipment was not designed to bear the heavy responsibilities of democratic citizenship in such a world. The one hope for human freedom lies in the fullest and most intelligent use of the resources which technology has placed at our disposal—the new forms of communication through which boys and girls, and men and women, might be given knowledge and understanding—the press, the moving picture, radio, and television. But as yet we have given comparatively little serious thought to directing these great engines of enlightenment to such a noble purpose—possibly because we cannot spare the time from reading our favorite comic, attending our favorite movie theater, listening to our favorite mystery play, or viewing our favorite wrestling match or baseball game!

11
NEW VISTAS OF POWER

1

Technology has endowed man with fabulous power.
All civilizations of the past, whether despotic or free, have been alike in one vital respect. They have rested almost wholly or chiefly on the physical energy of men, women, and children. At the time of the founding of our Republic, through the harnessing of wind and water, horses and oxen, the power at our disposal was perhaps twice that of primeval man. Today human energy constitutes but the most insignificant fraction of the total power sustaining our civilization.

Almost two hundred years ago in England, as we have seen, man succeeded in harnessing the power of steam and forcing this giant to do his bidding. During subsequent generations, and particularly since the opening of the twentieth century, the conquest of mechanical power has proceeded swiftly along ever more revolutionary lines. The age of steam was superseded in large part by the age of gasoline and electricity, and now we seem to be entering a perfectly fantastic age of atomic power. It should be emphasized, moreover, that the utilization of mechanical energy fails to give the full measure of our advance. Practical knowledge also is power, knowledge pertaining to the improvement of plants and animals, to the prevention and cure of disease, to the making of new materials and substances, to the forecasting, even perhaps to the making, of the weather. In this sphere progress has been no less impressive than in the realm of mechanical energy.

The increase of the power factor in human affairs is an achievement of the most profound import. This factor of course has played a central role in the transformation of our modes of livelihood, our forms of communication, and the general conditions of life. From earliest times man's standard of living has been limited by the energy at his command. As long as his chief reliance was on human muscle, the great masses of people were compelled to struggle from birth to death just to live and reproduce their kind. While the members of small aristocratic orders enjoyed a measure of leisure and luxury and cultivated both the graces and the vices of civilization, their privileges were always squeezed out of the toil and tears of the many. In the age now unfolding men and women everywhere may have power in almost unlimited abundance. What they will do with this power is the most critical question now confronting the human race—possibly the most fateful question ever faced by mankind. This question is in essence the central moral question of our time.

2

Technology has increased immeasurably man's power to produce material things.

In 1835, according to Leo Hausleiter, a German engineer and economist, just as Andrew Jackson was nearing the end of his second term of office, the total capacity of machines in the United States amounted to only three hundred thousand horsepower. The corresponding figure for England was the same, for France twenty thousand, for Germany ten thousand, for the remainder of Europe ten thousand, and for all other countries of the world combined ten thousand.[1] Thus one hundred and fifteen years ago the human race was just beginning to emerge from a

[1] Leo Hausleiter, *The Machine Unchained* (New York, 1933), p. 12.

condition that had prevailed with but little change for unnumbered centuries.

The increase in the use of mechanical power in the United States since 1835 is perhaps the best gauge available of the advance of industrial civilization. By 1875 the capacity of our machines reached a total of seven million eight hundred thousand horsepower, by 1913 one hundred six million, and by 1928 eight hundred ninety-six million, as compared with three hundred ninety million for the rest of the world. The extraordinary concentration of this development in America is exaggerated somewhat perhaps by the inclusion in the calculation of the horsepower of our motor vehicles. But with this factor eliminated the mechanical energy at our disposal almost equaled that of all other countries.

The testimony of the National Resources Committee corroborates the findings of Hausleiter and brings the record down to 1935. "The available mechanical power," says the Committee, "has increased from 70 million horsepower in 1900 to over 1 billion in 1935."[2] The committee's tables actually put the figure for the latter year at approximately one billion two hundred thirty million. In the meantime sixteen more years have passed, years that have witnessed further technological advances. It seems probable that the horsepower of our machines now must be at least one and a half billion.

The meaning of this figure can best be understood if it is converted into its equivalent in human energy. One horsepower is ordinarily regarded as equal to the power of twelve men. We may therefore say that in the form of steam, combustion, and electrical engines and motors the American people have working for them today the equivalent of eighteen billion mechanical slaves—almost nine times the population of the earth. To put the matter even more simply, these figures mean that for every man, woman, and child in the United States there are on the average one hundred twenty mechanical slaves, for every family more than five hundred.

[2] National Resources Committee, *Technological Trends and National Policy* (Washington, 1937), p. 263.

It would seem that, if man ever subsisted solely by the power of his own muscle, as he did for perhaps a million years, the economic problem in America should now be completely solved and poverty banished forever. No aristocracy or slaveholding class in history ever commanded for its own members such fabulous energies. According to the Statistical Office of the United Nations, "in 1948, the United States, with 6 percent of the world's population, produced 43 percent of the world's economic income."[3]

Our increased power to produce cannot be measured fully in terms of mechanical energy. The advances in chemistry are ushering in a new physical world and radically extending man's dominion over nature. "The present time," said J. D. Bernal seventeen years ago, "marks the beginning of a transition from the use of materials extracted out of nature to materials constructed by men. If science can be used to its full capacity, the former will become relatively less and less important." This same English scientist foresees the time, not far distant, when "we shall enter into a new world of materials . . . altogether outside our present experience"—a world in which we can "have combinations of every kind of physical property, lightness, strength, transparency, etc."—a world in which we shall make "active materials which, like living things, can change their shape and physical and chemical properties under suitable stimuli."[4] The beginnings of this age are already here.

These advances in science and technology have raised our rate of production far above that of a century ago and have given us the highest average material standard of living of any large nation in history. Yet, as a people, we did not comprehend until recently the full measure of the productive capacity of our economy. A commentator has observed that the war brought forth two great surprises: the first was the strength of the Red Army; the second, the power of the American economy. Certainly our performance in the struggle

[3] United States Department of Labor. Bureau of Labor Statistics, *50 Years' Progress of American Labor* (Washington, 1950), p. 8.
[4] Frederick Soddy *et al.*, *The Frustration of Science* (New York, 1935), p. 55.

against the Axis powers was perfectly fantastic. Within three years, as more than ten million of our most vigorous young workers were being drawn into the armed services, we increased our industrial productive facilities by nearly one-half and achieved a total national income practically double that of the best peacetime years. In 1944 we reached a level of industrial production not far below that of all the rest of the world combined. At the same time, with the farm population reduced by draft and by migration to the war industries, agricultural production advanced by thirty per cent. This was the first time that our technical knowledge was fully utilized and our productive energies fully released and harnessed.

And the end is not yet. Indeed, as the war entered its last days, mankind entered a new age—an age freighted with such revolutionary possibilities that the mind hesitates to contemplate the perspectives of the future. We are told by the most sober people of technical competence that when the problem of the release and utilization of atomic energy for peaceful purposes is fully mastered, there will open before mankind vistas of power that dwarf the dreams of the most sanguine utopians of the past. All earlier sources of power, we are told, will lose their value. Men will cease mining coal, pumping oil, and building hydroelectric stations. They will turn the wheels of industry, heat their houses, drive their vehicles, sail their ships, fly their airplanes, light their homes and cities, with incredibly tiny amounts of atomic materials. They will travel around the earth at the equator keeping pace with the sun, and perhaps take excursions to the moon and other places beyond their earthly home that they have read about. They will indeed be able to do almost anything they can imagine, if the limiting factor is energy. Also they will realize the ancient dream of the alchemist, of transmuting the baser metals into gold, should they continue their interest in this yellow substance after it has lost its scarcity value. How many years will pass before we enter fully into the new age, we cannot know. Some say twenty years, others fifty, and others a hundred or two. But of this we may be sure, the time will be too brief. We shall not be ready when it comes. The impact on our ways of life will be truly revolutionary, if not catastrophic.

3

Technology has increased immeasurably man's power to destroy himself and his civilization.
"From the dim beginnings of society, and beyond, down to this very hour," wrote James T. Shotwell some years ago, "war has been used without question and almost without interval."[5] Man seems to have given quite as much attention to the "improvement" of the instruments of warfare, to making them ever more deadly and terrifying, as to the perfection of the instruments of peace. Today we stand at the crowning point of this long evolution of the military arts. Our present situation may be thus described because we dare not proceed much further along this ancient road. We have already attained such proficiency in the ways of destruction that another world-wide struggle might either utterly destroy civilization everywhere or impose an enduring tyranny on all peoples. Mankind's most fateful hour of decision has struck.

The war recently concluded brought human society to the very edge of the abyss. As we look back now, we wonder how men, women, and children were able to survive its horrors. Even as the struggle proceeded on its course, the resources of science and technology were organized as never before to achieve victory. Building on the experience of the past men created mighty engines of death that literally dwarfed into insignificance everything and anything that had gone before—bombs of high explosive that weighed ten tons, planes that could carry these bombs four thousand miles, rockets that could be guided to their objectives by radio, steel monsters that could cross rivers and crush houses, flame-

[5] James T. Shotwell, *War as an Instrument of National Policy* (New York, 1929), p. 8.

throwers that could hurl jellied gasoline with the accuracy of firearms, giant cannons that could strike a target beyond the range of human vision, great battle fleets that could operate continuously thousands of miles from home, and a powerful industry that could pour forth these engines of death in an endless stream. But this is by no means the whole of the story.

As the struggle drew to a close, the curtain was lifted so that we might catch a glimpse of the next war, if man should lack the intelligence, the desire, and the will to establish an enduring peace. The process of destruction was brought to a climax with an atomic bomb whose power of devastation makes obsolete the rival weapons previously employed and brings in a new era of warfare. Even in its infancy this terrible weapon is capable of destroying a great city. What it might become, if permitted to grow to full maturity, only God himself could know. When combined with the resources of electronics and jet propulsion, its possibilities are literally overwhelming. General H. H. Arnold, Chief of the Army Air Forces at the time, predicted in August, 1945, immediately following the capitulation of Japan, that crewless bombers, guided from distant bases, would "home" on their targets and that greatly "improved" atomic bombs would destroy the major cities of an adversary utterly without warning. A scientist is reported as having said that "in the next war it will be possible to destroy any city in the world in twenty minutes." Already, according to report, we have perfected a new giant warplane, the B-36, which is driven by ten engines capable of developing 42,000 horsepower, which has a cruising radius of four thousand miles, and which can carry a bomb load of forty-two tons, four times the capacity of the B-29 that dropped the atomic bomb on Hiroshima. Also we are apparently engaged in the production of "atomic artillery" which will be capable of laying down a barrage of nuclear explosion, and electronic eyes and brains which can see a target and shoot more swiftly and accurately than the most skillful human warrior.

And now we are embarked on the creation of the hydrogen

bomb, which in its fully developed form, according to some of its prospective architects, might be capable of exterminating the entire population of the world and making the earth uninhabitable for centuries. Also we hear about the addition of the cosmic ray, deadly diseases, and divers poisonous substances to the arsenals of warring nations. As to what dreadful weapons may lie wholly beyond the veil that mercifully shrouds the future, even distinguished scientists can only speculate. During the present respite, how long or short we know not, man may have his last opportunity to build a lasting peace and make civilization secure on the earth.

The control of these engines of death is one of the most urgent questions facing mankind. They have made war so swift in its flight, so devastating in its impact, so total in its embrace that civilization itself, not in just one country but in all, is in gravest peril. If war is permitted to continue in this little world, the time is almost certain to come when some one nation, exalting the military virtues, guided by a policy of utter ruthlessness, and "getting the jump" on potential adversaries, will subject and hold in bondage all the rest. Once having established complete control over the means of producing these terrible instruments of warfare, over the great chemical, electrical, metallurgical, and machine construction industries of the world, a nation of even modest proportions could rule the earth indefinitely and unchallenged. These great sources of military power must be kept in the hands of those who love justice and are resolved to keep the peace, at least until the virus of war and war-making is purged from the human race. The prospect of the full conquest of atomic energy makes absolutely imperative most vigorous and sustained action toward this end. When that day arrives, as many commentators have observed, all nations standing in the first ranks of scientific advance will be of one size.

The transformation of the weapons of war contains a threat to free institutions at home. The American people must realize that the day of the "long rifle" and the "six-shooter" is past and that the power to take life no longer supports the doctrine that all men are created equal. They must realize also that the second article of our Bill of Rights, which guarantees to all of us the right "to keep and bear arms," has been repealed by the advance of technology. If a single nation could dominate the earth by gaining exclusive possession of tanks, planes, and atomic bombs, a very small minority within a nation could by the same token establish a dictatorship and hold a people in perpetual slavery. Men and women, however brave, cannot rise successfully against machineguns, tanks, and warplanes, to say nothing of atomic bombs and cosmic rays. During the period between the wars the totalitarian states demonstrated under our very eyes the truth of this assertion. If liberty is to endure in America, the people must be ever watchful to control the government and to make sure that the government controls the instruments of warfare.

4

Technology has increased man's power over the life process.

Our fathers and mothers of the eighteenth century had little more control over the life process than the people of antiquity. They multiplied without restraint, they lived on a monotonous and badly balanced diet, they were mowed down by disease, and they grew old in middle age. Childbirth was fraught with hazard for both mother and infant; smallpox, scarlet fever, measles, and diphtheria were regarded as necessary experiences of childhood; and malaria, tuberculosis, typhoid, yellow fever, and even typhus and Asiatic cholera were looked upon in many places as inevitable visitations of God. The average expectation of life at birth in the most advanced communities and regions was between thirty and thirty-five years.

Achievement of a large measure of control over the forces of human reproduction—one of the most powerful and imperious of natural forces—is laden with fateful consequences.

Through knowledge of the sexual process and through invention of contraceptives of ever-increasing potency, the human race has acquired potential dominion over its own increase and is able to flout the ancient injunction to populate the earth. If it so desires, it may commit suicide. The limitation of births has already proceeded so far in America that, in spite of the upsurge of births during the nineteen-forties, a stationary or even declining population may be expected toward the end of the century. A British scientist has described this entire phenomenon as the "invention of sterility." Unless contrary tendencies set in, he suggests that the population of England and Wales, approximately forty-five millions, "would be reduced to less than 6 millions . . . in about 200 years."[6] We are able to determine over a period of time the size and perhaps eventually the quality of our population.

The advance of medical science is one of the glories of our civilization. As a consequence, we live in a world that is far safer from the inroads of disease and ignorance than any that man has ever known. Childbirth has lost its terrors, many deadly distempers have been conquered, numerous irrational fears have been banished, and man's sense of physical security has vastly increased. Bubonic plague, yellow fever, and smallpox have disappeared in America; and typhoid fever and diphtheria have been all but conquered. Other diseases are being brought rapidly under control and yet others are the subject of carefully organized and generously endowed research. Today the average life span is between sixty-five and seventy years. At the same time we must realize that much of our knowledge is not put to use and that we lag far behind what is possible.

The prospect in this realm, as in others, is both promising and terrifying. Unprecedented power is in our possession, and more is on the way. Through knowledge of diet and hygiene and through the general advance of medical science, combined with the ability to achieve and maintain an optimum standard of living for all of our people, it is now pos-

[6] Soddy, *et al.*, *op. cit.*, p. 104.

sible practically to prevent or correct all physical defects, banish most diseases, extend still further the life span, and attain a level of physical well-being beyond the fondest hopes of past ages. The new "wonder drugs" that were put to use with such miraculous results during the war period suggest that we are still in the early stages of knowledge in this field. With further developments in chemistry and the biological sciences the time may not be far distant when man will be able to fashion himself in whatever image may strike his fancy. Given the present level of our ethics and our social organization we can view such a possibility only with deep misgivings. Science and technology have brought mankind far on its way, but toward what destination no one can say with confidence.

5

Technology has increased man's power over the mind.
From the standpoint of the future of free society here lies one of the most crucial problems of the age. Such a society rests, not only on guarantees of individual security from the violence of mobs and the arbitrary acts of governments, but also on general conditions of life that make possible the development of informed and independent judgment. In our earlier society, with its self-sufficient communities, its open frontiers, its simple face-to-face relations, its wide diffusion of productive property, its local newspapers and meetinghouses, and its relatively unorganized intellectual life, differences in outlook and independence of spirit were generally fostered. The advance of technology has transformed these conditions and greatly reduced the control of the individual over the forces which shape his opinions.

The entire process of mind-forming has become more and more organized, or at least subject to organization. The individual has become increasingly dependent for information, political ideas, and social attitudes on organized education and on the new forms of communication, particularly the daily press, the comic, the movie, and the radio, with television coming swiftly over the horizon. That these new agencies have enormous power has been demonstrated in our time by both advertising companies and totalitarian states. If conducted with a high sense of public duty, personal integrity, and devotion to truth, they may serve mightily to promote enlightenment, understanding, and good will in our country and throughout the earth. In a world as vast in its reaches, as complicated in its structure, and as dynamic in its movements as ours, they are indispensable to the successful functioning and perhaps the very survival of our democracy.

In many instances, unfortunately, they serve trivial interests, perverted tastes, vested rights, and even the ends of bigotry. Also we know, and to the sorrow of all mankind, that they may be employed to mock and destroy every good thing in the human heritage. When efficiently coordinated under the direction of a ruthless dictatorship, they may be used to keep a whole people in ignorance, force the minds of young and old into a single mold, inculcate bitter hatred and prejudice, lay the psychological foundations of war, and develop a fanatical belief in the unlimited superiority of a party, a class, a race, a nation, or a person. They may be employed to win acceptance of the proposition that black is white, that two plus two equals five, that slavery is freedom, that war is peace, or that any absurdity or falsehood the mind can contrive is true. And when they are combined with the new engines of warfare and the old methods of torture we behold the power base of the contemporary totalitarian states. What these regimes have been able to accomplish in rooting out "dangerous thoughts," in glorifying a self-appointed leader, in propagating doctrines of utter barbarism, and in educating peoples for death is one of the most extraordinary phenomena of this extraordinary age. In his *Nineteen Eighty-Four* George Orwell has drawn an imaginative picture of the totalitarian state in its "perfected" form a generation hence.

Since the war we have witnessed in the Soviet Union a vast demonstration which brings "nineteen eighty-four" very close. It seems that in the final months of the struggle the tiny oligarchy in the Kremlin made one of those unheralded and fateful decisions which the student of Soviet affairs has come to expect. It decided to reverse completely the wartime policy of friendly collaboration with the Western democracies and to revive the policy of revolutionary aggression in the spirit of 1917. This profound shift in policy was followed by a series of powerful decrees by the Central Committee of the All-Union Communist Party which commanded the entire intellectual class to participate actively in the battle with the enemies of Communism at home and abroad. The first of the resolutions was issued on August 14, 1946, and was directed at literary writers and journals. It was followed during the next two years by similar resolutions in the fields of the drama, the cinema, music, science, and humor. They all called for the unbounded glorification of Soviet institutions and the "new Soviet man" and for an equally unbounded denunciation of everything "Western" or "bourgeois." Intellectuals were told that they were "soldiers of Communism" standing in the "front line of fire" and that they should "lash out boldly and attack bourgeois culture which is in a state of emaciation and depravity." Ideological indifference or neutrality was not to be tolerated. "Art for art's sake" was condemned in most scathing terms. A humorist was warned that "his humor over the radio is nothing more than laughter for laughter's sake." Even the circus clowns were given their marching orders. No intellectual was permitted the luxury of silence. The decrees were supported without exception and with violent extravagance by the entire cultural apparatus and by all the agencies of mass communication.

Democracy everywhere rests on the freedom of the individual mind. To preserve such freedom in the present epoch is one of our most difficult and urgent tasks. We must realize that the elements in the equation of human liberty have been profoundly altered by the advance of science and technology. The problem is made the more critical and disturbing by the trend toward monopoly in the control of the media of mass communication. Morris L. Ernst, lifelong champion of the civil liberties, presents the danger succinctly in these words:

> With 2,600 dailies a few years ago are 1,700 enough today? How many will we have in 1960? . . . Five movie companies own 70 per cent of the movie income of the nation. Will there be only three in 1960? . . . Four networks have control over two-thirds of the radio stations of the nation. Will they control more in 1960? Will television and F.M. go the same way?[7]

As yet our American democracy has scarcely grasped the nature of the problem here involved.

6

Technology has made possible a rich and abundant life for all.

The physical power is unquestionably here. Yet thoughtful men and women must contemplate this power factor of industrial civilization with mixed emotions. On the one hand, it opens to our gaze the glorious possibility of at last realizing that vision of the city of God which the prophets of mankind have held before us down through the ages—a city of plenty, justice, beauty, and truth. On the other hand, we shudder in horror at the thought that this power may be used to bring in an age of utter savagery and barbarism, an age in which the most terrifying fantasies and nightmares of the race would become realities, an age on which the curtain has been lifted in our generation. Perhaps one may be comforted by the thought that so much of human misery, so much of injustice, so much of man's hatred of man, so much of the bitterness of the long struggle, may be traced to the fact that the great majority of men have always been compelled to live on the very margin of subsistence. Now, if we but have the wisdom, we can make life rich and abundant for all. The agelong struggle of classes, nations, and races over bread can be thrown into the wastebasket of history. This is the promise of science and technology.

[7] Morris L. Ernst, *The First Freedom* (New York, 1946), p. 53.

12

OLD MINDS IN A NEW WORLD

1

We enter the atomic age with minds formed largely in the day of the hoe, the horse, the spinning wheel, and the sailing ship.
The fact must be emphasized repeatedly that the strange industrial civilization which has burst upon mankind so suddenly and which is sweeping across the world so swiftly is still in its early stages, even in America. In certain of its phases it is far more advanced than in others. Our functional ideas, moral conceptions, and social organization lag seriously behind our modes of livelihood, forms of communication, use of mechanical energy, and scientific knowledge. This lag is doubtless responsible for many of the troubles and conflicts of the time. It is certainly the underlying source of the more powerful and disrupting tensions to be observed both within our American society and among the nations of the world. Today a great gulf stands between many of the stubborn realities of our industrial civilization and our customs, loyalties, understandings, and outlooks—between our closely integrated economy and our competitive spirit, between our shrunken world and our tradition of isolation, between our knowledge in almost every field and our ways of life. The task of bringing our minds and our practices into harmony with the physical conditions of the new age is a gigantic and urgent educational undertaking. Indeed, we shall

not know peace and serenity until this is accomplished. A few of the more critical instances of cultural lag will be passed in brief review.

2

We devote vast sums to the widening of this gulf that runs through our civilization.

For more than a generation now we have been supporting lavishly great laboratories, under both public and private auspices, to increase our knowledge of the physical universe and to multiply "practical" inventions and discoveries. The scientists, engineers, and technicians working in these laboratories are encouraged to break the hold of the past on their minds and engage in bold experimentation and thought. During the war we expended two billion dollars on a single research and engineering project involving the utilization and coordination of the finest scientific minds of two continents. The result was the development of the atomic bomb and the sudden precipitation of man into a new age—an age for which he is utterly unprepared. And now we are proposing through universities, industry, and government, to set aside additional funds to carry forward, on a scale greatly surpassing anything known before the war, a comprehensive program of research in physics, chemistry, and biology, as if the further advancement of knowledge in these areas would in itself bring tranquillity to a troubled world.

How different is the situation in the field of the moral and social disciplines! Here there is comparatively little financial support for the prosecution of inquiry and the advancement of understanding relevant to the problems of our time. Most of the work has to be carried on as a kind of leisure activity by persons who derive their livelihood primarily from teaching. When special funds are forthcoming for the study of social institutions, they are too commonly directed to subjects far removed from the contemporary scene—to the life of the Sumerians, the customs of the primitive Tasmanians, the voyages of Columbus, or the archaeology of the American Indian. If they are assigned to the study of some phase of our institutional arrangements, use of the new knowledge is often limited by some vested interest or purpose. Also there is little encouragement of bold and original speculation and thought. A radical proposal, however careful the reasoning, is likely to be labeled as dangerous and un-American. Until this condition is corrected, the breach will grow ever wider and the conflicts in our civilization and in ourselves ever more severe.

This of course does not mean that we should declare a moratorium on research in the natural sciences. To follow such counsel would probably mean the defeat of the free world in the present struggle to halt and turn back totalitarian aggression. The challenge of these days can be met only by supporting with equal energy and generosity research into the nature of ourselves and our institutions. Perhaps the launching of The Ford Foundation, with its vast resources, constitutes an initial step in the development of a comprehensive program to redress the balance in the sciences. The report prepared to guide the Foundation in the shaping of policy and program recommends the support of research and other activities devoted to the establishment of peace, the strengthening of democracy, the strengthening of the economy, education in a democratic society, and individual behavior and human relations.[1] It is to be hoped that this example will be followed speedily and vigorously by both public and private agencies. It is to be hoped also that we shall heed the sage counsel of an eminent physiologist and physicist, Detlev W. Bronk, tendered the House Committee on Interstate and Foreign Commerce in 1947. "I cannot think of any field of research in physical science," he told the Congressmen, "which does not ultimately lead, and usually very promptly, to new social problems. The same is true in biology and medicine. It is important, therefore, that competent social scientists should work hand in hand with the

[1] *Report of the Study for the Ford Foundation on Policy and Program* (Detroit, 1949), Chap. III, pp. 49–99.

natural scientists, so that problems may be solved as they arise, and so that many of them may not arise in the first instance."[2]

3

We disregard the methods and teachings of science in an age of unprecedented scientific advance.

The imbalance in the realm of research but reflects a general condition in our mores. Although the fabulous and revolutionary achievements of science are emblazoned on the pages of every newspaper, our minds dwell in large measure in the age of magic and superstition—the age from which we have been slowly and painfully emerging during the past several centuries. In some departments of life, in the realm of physical nature and the practical arts, as we have noted, science has achieved general acceptance. But in the spheres of social institutions and human relations it is still regarded generally as an intruder or unwelcome guest. Here we neither desire dependable knowledge nor submit to its discipline. Like the farmer who opposed the introduction of the steel plow or the physician who condemned the use of anesthesia in childbirth, we prefer to nurture our prejudices and live by ignorance.

We spend billions on armaments to halt Communist aggression. But we spend almost nothing on the scientific study of the natural history of this social disease, of the conditions which breed it, of the necessary prophylactic and curative measures. If we should devote funds to such a study and be guided by its findings, it seems quite likely that we would assign far more than thirty-five millions to the Point Four Program for assisting technically underdeveloped countries to raise their standards of living. A similar study of the social, economic, political, and cultural foundations of peace might be equally valuable as an aid to policy-making. Unfortunately, as a people, we do not turn to scientific inquiry

[2] Quoted in John R. Steelman, *Science and Public Policy* (Washington, 1947), Vol. I, p. viii.

for assistance in these domains. We choose rather to be instructed by tradition and moved by passion.

A fraction of the sums expended on the development of the atomic bomb would doubtless be sufficient to discover the road to full employment and the preservation at the same time of our civil and political liberties. But in all probability both the American people and their Congress would reject the forthcoming proposal on the grounds that it was radical, as it most certainly would and must be. That it would be as radical as the atomic bomb, however, is highly improbable. In the field of race relations the necessary knowledge is already available in some measure. We know that, while there are some differences among the races of mankind, there is no basis in biological fact for the prejudices that generally prevail in this realm. We cannot say that one people is superior or inferior to another by nature. Yet throughout wide reaches of the population in America and other countries men and women hold tenaciously to disproved conceptions and strive with striking success to transmit those conceptions to their children.

One of the anomalies of the age appears in the realm of public opinion. While large sums are devoted to the discovery of ways and means of selling both ideas and commodities to the people, little is done to develop resistance to either political or commercial propaganda. We know further that much of what the members of one political party say about those of another could scarcely stand the test of scientific analysis. In this and other departments of life, where passions so commonly rule and interests collide, both the method and the spirit of science are rigorously excluded. Moreover, it must be said that as a people we have never conducted in our schools a general campaign to educate our children in the moral and social implications of scientific advance. The present generation is in need of some of that daring and resourcefulness which their fathers and mothers exhibited in the conquest of the North American continent. The time has certainly arrived when we should abandon completely our traditional fear of the methods and teachings of science.

4

We are largely unaware of the significance of the annihilation of the economic foundations of our democracy.
Since the launching of the Republic, thoughtful men witnessing the rise of commerce and industry in America have predicted the passing of that "general equality of condition" which marked our early agrarian society. The Marquis de Chastellux, during the struggle for independence, foresaw the time when "the success of commerce . . . will introduce riches, amongst you" and prophesied trouble for our democratic political institutions. "An individual without property is a discontented citizen when the state is poor," he said to Samuel Adams. "Place a rich man near him, he dwindles into a clown."[3] Almost two generations later Alexis de Tocqueville saw in the development of manufacturing a new aristocracy "growing up under our eyes" and cautioned the "friends of democracy" to "keep their eyes anxiously fixed in this direction; for if ever a permanent inequality of conditions and aristocracy again penetrate into the world, it may be predicted that this is the gate by which they will enter."[4]

Thomas Jefferson founded his hopes for the success of the Republic on "those who labor in the earth" and remarked that "the mobs of great cities add just so much to the support of pure government, as sores do to the strength of the human body." Daniel Webster, in his address before the Massachusetts Constitutional Convention in 1820, expressed with admirable lucidity the thought of his generation concerning the relations between economics and politics:

> The freest government, if it could exist, would not be long acceptable, if the tendency of the laws were to create a rapid accumulation of property in few hands, and to render the great mass of the population dependent and penniless. In such a case the

[3] François Jean de Chastellux, *Travels in North-America, in the Years 1780, 1781, and 1782* (Dublin, 1787), Vol. I, p. 270.
[4] Alexis de Tocqueville, *Democracy in America* (New York, 1898), Vol. II, p. 197.

popular power must break in upon the rights of property, or else the influence of property must limit and control the exercise of popular power. Universal suffrage, for example, could not long exist in a community where there was great inequality of property. The holders of estates would be obliged in such case, either in some way to restrain the right of suffrage, or else such right of suffrage would ere long divide the property. . . .

The disastrous revolutions which the world has witnessed, those political thunder-storms and earthquakes which have overthrown the pillars of society from their very deepest foundations, have been revolutions against property.[5]

We know now that much of what Chastellux prophesied, Tocqueville feared, Jefferson opposed, and Webster contemplated has actually happened on a grand scale. Riches have indeed appeared "amongst" us, "inequality of conditions" has "penetrated into the world," the children of freehold farmers have helped to form the "mobs of great cities," and the "great mass of the population" has become "dependent," though far from "penniless." In spite of the fact that the average income per capita and per factory worker has more than doubled since the opening of the present century, the threat to our free institutions in this situation must be evident to anyone who has followed, even casually, the course of revolution and counterrevolution, not in distant epochs, but in our own time. Yet many of our leaders in public life prefer to ignore the facts and cultivate the illusion that our democracy continues to rest on solid economic foundations. Also our schools and colleges generally pass over lightly the threat to our American way of life resident in the concentration of economic power. The fact that we cannot return to the conditions prevailing in the pre-machine age does not prove that the problem is insoluble. If we desire to build a free society in the age of industrial civilization, we must rebuild the economic foundations of democracy. To this task we should bring all the knowledge and inventiveness, all the intellectual and moral resources in our possession.

[5] *Journal of Debates and Proceedings in the Convention of Delegates Chosen to Revise the Constitution of Massachusetts* (Boston, 1853), pp. 312–313.

5

We extol uncritically the virtues of economic individualism in an age of group action.
 In our pre-industrial society of farmers and tradesmen individual or family enterprise was the rule. Most people worked for themselves on the land and in the rural neighborhoods. This form of economic organization constituted the foundation of our free institutions and undoubtedly fostered in us our love of liberty and our spirit of independence. Many of us may regret that the old order has passed away, but such a nostalgic mood should not be permitted to blind us to the realities of the present. In the hopeful and venturesome spirit of our ancestors we must continue to love our country, not as it was, nor as it is, but as it will be.

One of the most striking and characteristic features of industrial society is cooperative and collective behavior. Only in a diminishing sector of the economy, chiefly in agriculture and small business, does the historic pattern of individualism prevail. And even here it has been notably modified. Men and women join together in organizations of most diverse character to advance their interests or achieve their purposes. Investors join together in corporations to increase the return on their savings, businessmen join together in associations to increase their profits, industrial workers join together in unions to increase their wages, farmers join together in granges to increase their incomes, professional people join together in societies to increase their salaries, and consumers join together in cooperatives to increase the power of their earnings. Most basic of all perhaps, managers, engineers, and workers of numerous types and grades join together to produce most of the goods and many of the services which appear in our markets. Also all the people are joining together increasingly through the institutions of government to achieve various economic purposes and to plan for the common welfare.

Unfortunately, the more this pattern of group action has spread through our economy and life, the more we have extolled the virtues of economic individualism. Moreover, many who engage in large corporate undertakings seem to be particularly vigorous in their defense of the philosophy of small enterprise and in their denunciation of labor unions, collective practices, and social planning. Instead of dissipating our energies in a futile effort to recover the past, we should be applying our powers to the task of bringing these new ways of life into the service of human freedom and the common good. We must assume that these new ways are here to stay and are not to be exorcised by any form of magic. That there are grave dangers in the situation is obvious. Unless the activities of the various organized groups can be coordinated in the general interest and brought under the reign of law, our society may be shaken to pieces by internal conflict. As a people we must achieve a form of social discipline under which groups as well as individuals are constrained to moderate their narrow and limited impulses. Either we shall learn to cooperate both within and among our organizations or we shall lose our democracy.

6

We tolerate material poverty and spiritual privation in an age of potential abundance.
Although we have been favored above all other peoples of the world by the richness of our resources and the productivity of our labor, we have nevertheless lived throughout the greater part of our history under conditions of relative and necessary scarcity. As a people, we have been compelled to work hard for a living. To gain material advantages and luxuries we have struggled, not only with the forces of nature, but also with one another. If some were to have enough to enjoy a rich and abundant life, others had to go without many of the necessities and live close to the margin of subsistence. Since there was not enough of

the good things to go around, we engaged in an unseemly scramble for what there was. The result was the development of a certain callousness toward both material poverty and spiritual privation among large masses of the population. Such a condition was accepted as a part of the order of nature or in accordance with the laws of God.

We know now for a certainty that we are well into an age of unprecedented abundance—of abundance for all. We know that it is now possible to lay forever the specter of poverty which has dogged the footsteps of man since the Garden of Eden. Harold G. Moulton, a cautious and distinguished economist, in appraising the "potentials of the next century" suggests that a hundred years hence we should be able to "support a population double that of the present day on a plane of living eight times as high as that now prevailing."[6] No longer is the mentality bred in an age of scarcity in accord with the facts of life. Yet in spite of the great progress made in the rise of the productivity of labor and the general standard of living, millions of our people are underfed, badly housed, poorly clad, and generally insecure; more millions live amid surroundings marked by filth, squalor, and ugliness; and yet more millions are denied from birth basic opportunities for education, guidance, and personal development. According to a study made under the auspices of the American Bar Association, "at least thirty million persons" in the United States "cannot afford the minimum cost of necessary legal service" in order to obtain justice in the courts.[7] As human beings many of us leave the world in old age as dwarfs, never having attained the physical, intellectual, and moral stature of which we are capable. We fail to bring our material resources into the service of the full utilization of the great cultural heritage which we have received from the past. Clinging timidly to personal and class privileges, we are unable to develop a conception of life that

[6] Harold G. Moulton, *Controlling Factors in Economic Development* (Washington, 1949), p. 204.
[7] Emery A. Brownell, *Legal Aid in the United States* (Rochester, 1951), p. 85.

would bring security, justice, abundance, and beauty to all. We are still under the spell of an economy of scarcity.

7

We harbor deep prejudices toward other cultural and racial groups in an age demanding justice and reconciliation among the nations.
In spite of the proclamation in our Declaration of Independence that all men are created equal, many of us have clung tenaciously to narrow and parochial attitudes and outlooks created during the ages of primitive communication and isolation of peoples. Those of us who derive from European stock assume that we are entitled to rule and exploit the races of Africa, Asia, and other parts of the world. Those of us who descend from the British migrations feel ourselves to be superior to all others. Likewise those of us who are Christians treat with a certain contempt the followers of other religious faiths, as do those of us who are Catholics, Protestants, or Methodists regard one another. These attitudes and outlooks, moreover, are expressed quite as much in the relations among our own American citizens as in our relations with the other peoples of the world. Indeed, we sometimes seem more interested in promoting the reign of justice beyond our frontiers than in correcting abuses and removing inequities in our own country.

This ancient heritage of prejudice and hatred, whose origin is easily understood, is obviously in conflict with the realities and the hopes of our time. Its perpetuation can only breed further disaster and threaten the very existence of civilization. The most urgent task confronting all mankind in the emerging age of atomic energy is the establishment of an enduring and therefore just peace. If we fail in this, we fail in all else. Such a peace, moreover, can only be built on the solid foundations of the reconciliation and equal treatment of all peoples and cultures. And our voice, the voice of the strongest country of the earth, will be vastly weakened in the councils of the nations if, while demanding justice abroad, we deny justice to racial and cultural minorities at home. Discrimination against the Indians, the Negroes, the Jews, the Mexicans, or any other group within our own borders is "heard round the world." We must learn that on our closely-knit planet few questions are purely domestic in character. We must learn also that the cultivation of a sense of racial, national, or religious superiority is one of the surest roads to the overthrow of free institutions and the establishment of despotism.

It is at this point that our American system is most vulnerable to the shafts of Soviet propaganda, and for the simple reason that here is to be found the most conspicuous failure of our democracy. The spokesmen of the Kremlin in all countries never miss an opportunity to broadcast and exaggerate all instances of racial injustice in the United States. In a world in which two-thirds of the people are colored and struggling to throw off the last vestige of European rule, such propaganda can be very effective. Every act of discrimination, therefore, is in a sense morally treasonable because it actually means giving "aid and comfort" to the enemy.

8

We cling to the myth of national sovereignty in an age of radar, the airplane, and the atomic bomb.
If national sovereignty means anything outside the realm of legal definitions, it means both the right and the power of a nation to shape its own destiny. Although no nation in modern times ever actually enjoyed this ideal condition to the full, America approximated it for generations. As long as we had no powerful neighbors and as long as the great oceans provided substantial protection against aggression from the Old World, we were able in extraordinary measure to go our own way without too much interference from abroad. We were able to main-

tain our independence without resort to conscription, huge standing armies, and a vast military establishment. To be sure, we fought a second war with England in 1812, thwarted an attempt to establish the House of Hapsburg in Mexico following our civil struggle, and lived always under economic, political, and military pressures from beyond the Atlantic. Yet, even toward the end of the nineteenth century, the great powers of Europe were so divided that no stable and sufficiently powerful combination could have been formed to threaten seriously the integrity of the United States.

Today the destinies of all nations are so closely intertwined that no one of them can determine its own destiny. We in America neither planned nor expected either the First or the Second World War. Nevertheless we were drawn into both. It was not the intention or the desire of our generation to spend three hundred billions of treasure and sacrifice a million casualties in the art of death and destruction. Yet this is what we did. Obviously we do not hold within our own hands the power of independent choice. With the development of radar, rockets, and atomic bombs, we may find ourselves a quarter century hence completely destroyed or enslaved without having much to say or do about the matter. The nation today has little more actual sovereignty than the rural neighborhood of 1800. In order to live in civilized society, mankind discovered long ago that the individual must surrender a measure of his "sovereignty" and submit to the reign of law. In order to live in a civilized world, mankind will have to learn that the nation must likewise surrender a measure of its "sovereignty" and submit to the reign of law. As a matter of fact, it is only under the reign of law that the nation can preserve whatever sovereignty is possible in the present age.

That we have been learning this lesson swiftly during recent years is one of the hopeful signs of the age. Already we have moved far from our eighteenth and nineteenth century moorings. To be sure, following the First World War we refused to enter the League of Nations and endeavored to withdraw from the world. But in the early nineteen-forties we conducted one of the most momentous debates of our history and resolved to participate actively in an effort to form an international organization to maintain peace with justice. In the light of our leading role in launching the United Nations and supporting its operations, it would seem that the ghost of isolationism has been finally laid. Yet anyone who follows closely the course of American politics cannot be certain that a great reversal may not come in the years ahead. Some of our most vocal leaders seem to be suggesting that we should flout the opinions of other peoples, antagonize our natural allies, and pursue a solitary course in the realm of world affairs. The myth of national sovereignty is still deeply rooted in our mores.

9

We enter a period of unsurpassed national prestige, power, and responsibility with a mentality bred in the days of immaturity, weakness, and isolation.
We are by no means prepared to play the role among the nations that the course of events abroad and our own amazing development have thrust upon us. Throughout the greater part of our history, in so far as we were involved in world affairs outside the Western Hemisphere, we were largely at the mercy of stronger states. What we said or did, apart from the challenge of our revolutionary ideas of life and government, carried little weight in the chancelleries of Europe.

This does not mean that we suffered from any sense of inferiority. On the contrary, in rather naive fashion we had great confidence in ourselves and our country, established a reputation for boastfulness, and proclaimed loudly on the Fourth of July that, if need be, we could "lick the world." But the rest of mankind was little impressed. Sir Charles Lyell, a friendly visitor, commented from Washington in 1845 on "the ambitious style of certain members of Con-

Old Minds in a New World 199

gress." He thus wrote of "a grave report" by the "chairman of the Post-office Committee": "After speaking of the American republic as 'the infant Hercules,' and the extension of their imperial dominion over the 'northern continent and oriental seas,' he exclaims, 'the destiny of our nation has now become revealed, and great events, quickening in the womb of time, reflect their clearly-defined shadows into our very eye-balls.' "[8] He also reported with amusement a characteristic incident from Jackson, Mississippi, in 1846. The master of ceremonies at a dinner, a general from the Tennessee militia, "first obtained silence by exclaiming, with the loud voice of a herald, 'Gentlemen, we are a great people,' and then called out the names of all the viands on his long table and sideboard, beginning with 'Beef-steak, with or without onions, roast turkey, pork, hominy, fish, eggs, &.,' and ending with a list of various drinkables, the last of which was 'tea, foreign and domestic.' "[9]

In 1846, Lyell, conscious of the might of the British Empire, could view this incident as the harmless manifestation of an adolescent spirit. But the general practice of such a ritual today would be proper cause for alarm in the most distant parts of the earth. "The United States at this moment," said Winston Churchill at the close of the recent war, "stands at the summit of the world." He then proceeded to wonder whether we would "act up to the level" of our "power and responsibility." Unfortunately, this question seems to weigh more heavily on the minds of other nations than on that of our own. To many of them we "bestride the narrow world like a colossus," and they wonder what our purposes are or whether we have any at all. To ourselves we have only the best of intentions, as clearly evidenced by the largess which we scatter so freely over the earth. But we must be watchful lest we become corrupted by our great power. As we play a central role in the defense and the strengthening of the free world, we must avoid like the plague the de-

[8] Charles Lyell, *A Second Visit to the United States of North America* (New York, 1849), Vol. I, p. 199.
[9] *Ibid.*, Vol. II, p. 160.

velopment of a messianic complex which would lead us down the road of imperialism and the forcible imposition of our policies, ideas, and institutions on other peoples.

The fact is that as yet we have not come to a clear decision on the course which we should steer during these troubled years. Our present role of leadership is an altogether new experience for us. Morally and intellectually we have not kept pace with our material strength. We do not realize that both our acts of omission and our acts of commission will shape decisively international events during the next generation. We do not realize, for example, that it is anything less than just good clean fun for our soldiers to call Koreans, friend and foe alike, "Gooks." We do not realize further, to draw an illustration from another realm, that a severe and prolonged depression in America would wreck the economies of half the world, retard immeasurably the raising of living standards everywhere outside the "iron curtain," and probably precipitate revolution and counterrevolution in many countries. Nor do we realize fully our responsibility for deciding the issue of war or peace in the decades ahead.

10

We fail to make full use of the great agencies of communication and education to equip our minds for the tasks of the industrial age.
This is not to say that the press, the radio, the moving picture, and television do not serve the cause of enlightenment and understanding. At their best they are truly magnificent; without them we would be wholly lost.

Yet no thoughtful person can view with complacency their total impact upon the minds of our people. Often they are directed by narrow partisan motives or by purely business considerations of material profit and loss. In considerable part they play the role of the "circus" during the decadent period of ancient Rome, stultifying and debauching the mind, corrupting and degrading the processes of thought. Let anyone who takes exception to this indictment listen to the radio broadcast for twenty-four hours over any one of the great networks and note the amount of drivel, misrepresentation, and downright falsehood included in the programs. The advertisement of nostrums of doubtful worth is associated with the names of distinguished commentators and the findings of "science." Much of the "output" of Hollywood can serve only as a form of vulgar escape from the realities of the contemporary world. While all of these agencies may serve to modify profoundly our sex mores and to take our minds off our troubles, they can scarcely be credited with helping us to bridge the great gulf which runs through our civilization. At any rate they are not employing their matchless resources to cultivate the virtues and develop the understandings necessary for the survival of free institutions.

The schools lag far behind the march of events. Although the service they render in their present form is indispensable to the functioning of our society, they fall well below the requirements of the age. In their programs they reveal little grasp of the character of industrial civilization, except in its more superficial aspects. They teach the findings of science, but fail to instill the spirit of science or to convey an understanding of what science is doing to the world and human institutions. They transmit the words of the tradition of human freedom, but fail to arouse concern or to apply old meanings to new conditions. They encourage the development of egoistic and competitive impulses suited perhaps to the society of yesterday, but fail to foster effectively the social and cooperative tendencies, the devotion to the general welfare necessary for successful living in the society of today. They do a magnificent job in preparing for war when the occasion demands it, but they have yet to formulate a bold and imaginative program to build a peaceful world. They have vast potentialities that remain undeveloped. They lack a generous and realistic conception of their task. They are without vision.

11

We need new minds for a new age.
The advance of science and technology is creating a new physical world. To bring our minds, our knowledge and understanding, our attitudes and moral conceptions, our institutions and social arrangements abreast of this new world will require equally daring and revolutionary discoveries and inventions. Our creative powers will be put to the supreme test. But if our forebears had the boldness to cross the oceans, to conquer a wilderness, and to launch a novel and daring form of government, we should have the courage and resourcefulness to build a civilization suited to the new conditions and commensurate with the power which science has given us. At any rate we should not shrink from the task.

All of us are disturbed by the events of our lifetime. Few of us really feel at home in this new world created by science and technology. Many of us perhaps would prefer to live in a more placid age. Indeed we might all cry with Hamlet that "the time is out of joint" and wonder why we were ever "born to set it right." Now and then we may cast the eyes of longing back to the agrarian age of our ancestors when everything seems to have been serene and secure. That we would like that age, if by some magic we were allowed to enter it, is highly doubtful. But be that as it may, this industrial civilization with its basic patterns, tendencies, and imperatives is here to stay, at least until we blow it and ourselves to bits. It is our new frontier and, like its predecessor, full of the strange and the unknown. Also, like its predecessor, it holds limitless possibilities—possibilities for good and evil.

12

Let us hold fast that which is good.
The emphasis in these pages has been placed on the profound and sweeping changes

of our time. We have spoken of wars and crises, of revolutions and counterrevolutions, of new modes of livelihood, new forms of communication, new weapons of warfare, and new vistas of power. We have dwelt on the passing of old landmarks, on the breaching of our civilization, on the coming of a new world. The reader may consequently have gained the impression that the entire human past is to be obliterated and that the wisdom of earlier ages is without relevance to these times. Such a view of course would be gravely mistaken. Although mankind never passes twice over the same road, he equally never begins the great adventure of history anew. Even our ancestors when they left their homes in the Old World, crossed the great oceans, and settled the virgin lands of North America developed, not a wholly new civilization, but rather a variant of European civilization. So as we move into the industrial age, we shall and should carry with us much from the past.

We must realize that the advance of science and technology does not render obsolete the whole of human experience. The cave man learned some things about life on the earth that are as sound today as they were in the day of the saber-toothed tiger. Every primitive people possesses certain admirable qualities—qualities which we would like to see in our neighbors in the industrial age. Every one of the great civilizations which have vanished from the earth nurtured values of universal application. The inspired prophets and teachers of the distant past—Moses, Zoroaster, Lâo-tse, and Gautama, Confucius, Socrates, Jesus, and Mohammed—are also prophets and teachers of our time. The founders of the American Republic are in many ways our contemporaries. And they were standing on the shoulders of giants who had fought for human liberty in Old England, in Mediaeval Europe, and in the Ancient World. So, as we confront the great tasks and problems of this troubled epoch, we must strive to hold fast all that is good in the human heritage.

Part Four

OUR

AMERICAN

VALUES

13

VALUES AND CHOICES

1

We are entering a new age in our history and in the history of mankind.
We are treading a course that the races of men have never trod before. We may liken ourselves to those bold mariners who in the fifteenth and sixteenth centuries turned the prows of their boats westward and discovered the New World, or to those hardy pioneers who a few generations later crossed the oceans, swept over the Alleghenies, and took possession of a new continent. But such a literary figure is inadequate and inexact. We today are engaged not in discovering and possessing, but in building a new world. And we know that in its outer aspect and in much of its inner spirit this new world will be unlike the world of our fathers.

That we are entering a new age is no longer questioned by thoughtful people. The evidence in support of such an interpretation of our times is overwhelming. To the perceptive mind it appears in the pages of every newspaper, assumes the most startling forms, and comes from the most diverse sources. Yet one event alone, tragic and ominous in its cultural and temporal setting, should be sufficient to convince the most skeptical mind that man will be compelled to build a new social and moral world or perish. The dropping of the atomic bomb on Hiroshima, when seen in all of its implications as a symbol and prophecy of man's mastery of physical nature, serves notice on the present generation that the world of the eighteenth and nineteenth centuries is gone as clearly and conclusively as the voyages of Columbus and Magellan demonstrated in their time that the traditional view of the earth and the physical universe had been shattered beyond recall. Must we not agree with Waldemar Kaempffert that the releasing of atomic energy is "the supreme scientific achievement of man."[1]

We must realize, however, that the controlled release of atomic energy did not burst upon mankind as a "bolt out of the blue," as an inscrutable cosmic accident, but rather as the natural fruit of the disinterested and inspired labors of generations of selfless men in search of truth. In the words of Selig Hecht, it was "merely the latest impact of the wave of physical science that began about fifty years ago on the ocean of knowledge."[2] And when in 1905 Albert Einstein formulated his celebrated equation which states that $E = mc^2$, that energy equals mass multiplied by the square of the velocity of light, he was continuing the work of a long line of predecessors reaching back to Democritus centuries before the Christian era. There is every reason for assuming that in the coming years the "wave of physical science" will grow in amplitude and leave other impacts of great power on the "ocean of knowledge" and on the ways of man.

We must realize also that the achievement of the Manhattan Project is but the most spectacular and revolutionary of a stream of discoveries and inventions which had been gaining volume and momentum for several centuries. The preceding chapters of the present work tell a small part of the story of the social significance of scientific and technological advance. But the data presented do not tell us whether the new world will be better or worse than the old. The issue here is the foremost item on the agenda of mankind during the second half of the twentieth century. Perhaps many of the older generation today would be happy to settle for a

[1] Waldemar Kaempffert, "The Past Century—and the Next—in Science," *The New York Times Magazine*, September 9, 1951, p. 23.
[2] Selig Hecht, *Explaining the Atom* (New York, 1947), p. 8.

world as good as the one into which they were born before the First World War. Bertrand Russell, viewing the present condition of mankind in the perspective of the centuries, concludes that "the near future must be either much better or much worse than the past."[3] Clearly, regardless of our wishes, the coming years will prove to be fateful almost beyond calculation.

2

We may be entering a new dark age.
We may be entering a darker age than any that man as a whole has ever known. Indeed, we may be facing annihilation, or something so close to it that the surviving remnants of the human race would have to begin again the long and toilsome struggle toward civilization. The magnificence of the intellectual and practical triumph symbolized by Oak Ridge must not be permitted to blind us to the perils which beset us. In a sense it has merely signalized our entry into a world in which we have been living for some time but of which we have been only dimly aware. Unquestionably catastrophe of hitherto unimagined proportions must be included among the possibilities of the emerging age. The moral gains of centuries may be obliterated.

Much evidence can be marshaled in support of the thesis that for some time now we have been moving backward along the road to barbarism. Many ramparts which Western man had erected to guard the most precious values of civilized life seem to have fallen. At any rate our consciences appear to have been dulled by the tragic experiences of the past generation. When the Lusitania was sunk by a German submarine off the Irish coast on May 7, 1915, without warning and without regard for the safety of the passengers, millions in the Western World were stunned and outraged. In the intervening years we have become inured to barbarities far

[3] Bertrand Russell, *The Impact of Science on Society* (New York, 1951), p. 64.

more terrifying and degrading. We have witnessed the emergence of the conception of total and unlimited warfare —warfare without noncombatants and directed deliberately toward the enslavement or annihilation of whole nations. We ourselves, fortunately not without some pangs of conscience, dropped atomic bombs unannounced on two great cities. The catalogue of moral atrocities already committed in the waging of war could be vastly extended. And when we endeavor to peer into the coming years we can only agree with Bertrand Russell. "Any scientific technique, however beastly," he says, "is bound to spread if it is useful in war— until such time as men decide that they have had enough of war and will henceforth live in peace."[4]

The new barbarism toward which we seem to be tending transfers to the domain of peace the ethics and methods of total war. Consequently, if it should triumph, it will be profoundly unlike its prototype in the dim beginnings of civilization. Armed with all the resources of science and technology, of physics, chemistry, biology, medicine, and psychology, it can mold, falsify, torture, and destroy on a scale far surpassing its primitive rivals of the past. The new barbarism is the contemporary totalitarian state in any of its several forms, whether labeled "left" or "right." Though their words may be different, their deeds are essentially the same. They are alike tyrannical and hostile to the spirit of human liberty and dignity. They repudiate the finest traditions of the race, convert all of the arts and sciences into weapons in the struggle for power, conscript the members of the intellectual classes to serve as obedient tools of brute will, and force scholarship to betray its genius and lend the stamp of its authority to the fabrication and propagation of falsehood. In this oft-proclaimed "century of the common man," we have watched these dictatorships revive the institution of forced labor and surpass their predecessors in tyranny in dragging common men into slavery. We have seen the Nazis restore the ghetto and launch a ruthless campaign to destroy root and branch the Jewish people—a campaign that was almost

[4] *Ibid.*, p. 31.

crowned with success throughout a large part of Europe, the historic center of Christian civilization. We have seen the Russian Communists "liquidate" national minorities by removing them from their ancient homes and sending them to labor camps in distant and inhospitable regions of the Soviet Union. In these totalitarian states political dissent and intellectual deviation are acts of treason. If totalitarianism is not "destroyed and its reappearance precluded once and forever," wrote Bronislaw Malinowski almost a decade ago, "we will have to face a period of dark ages, indeed the darkest ages of human history."[5]

The rise and spread of totalitarian doctrines and movements reveal clearly the moral weakness of Western civilization. These contemporary forms of tyranny are distinguished by the fact that in their rise to power they invariably speak in the name of the people and receive wide popular support. The Communists in particular proclaimed and continue to proclaim through all the agencies of communication that they march in the great tradition of human liberation and speak for "all progressive mankind." Their method calls to mind these prescient words of Helvetius:

Despotism, while it is gaining ground, suffers men to say what they will, while they suffer it to do what it will: but once established, it forbids all talking, writing, or thinking. The minds of men then sink into apathy: all the people become slaves, curse the breast that gave them milk, and under such a government, every new birth is an increase of misery.

Genius, there chained, drags its irons heavily along; it does not fly, it creeps. The sciences are neglected; ignorance is honoured, and every man of discernment declared an enemy to the state.[6]

We in America were wholly unprepared for the emergence of these new despotisms. At the time of the fall of the autocracies of central and eastern Europe toward the close of the First World War, we tended to assume that the only road

[5] Bronislaw Malinowski, *Freedom and Civilization* (New York, 1944), p. 15.
[6] Claude Adrian Helvetius, *A Treatise on Man; His Intellectual Faculties and His Education.* Translated from the French, with additional notes by W. Hooper, M.D. (London, 1810), Section V, Chap. X, pp. 52–53.

to the future was a road leading to an ever-increasing measure of popular liberty. When in the middle thirties the mask lost its power to conceal and this assumption was found to be untenable, many well-meaning citizens capitulated without a struggle and professed to see in one or another form of totalitarianism the "wave of the future." Even today there seem to be not a few liberals in America, spiritual descendants of Franklin, Washington, Paine, Jefferson, and Lincoln, who would make common cause with Russian Communism, hail it as a progressive and liberating force in the world, and close their eyes and ears to its denial to millions of human beings of the most elementary rights, liberties, and decencies. Succumbing to a species of moral lethargy they refuse even to hear the cry of anguish coming from the prison camps of the Soviet Union and her satellite states. How feeble have become those wellsprings of liberty which burst forth with such power in Europe and America during the seventeenth, eighteenth, and nineteenth centuries!

3

We may be entering the fabled golden age of man.

Of such a state or condition men have always dreamed, but they have rarely had the fortitude to place it at any known spot on the earth and in the present or proximate future. Rather have they located it in some mythological past, in some far distant tomorrow, or in some world beyond the seas or the skies. Borrowing from Sir Thomas More, we have very fittingly given the term Utopia or Nowhere to these literary portraits of an ideal society which from time to time have come from the pen of imaginative genius. But many are saying today that the most sublime visions of the past can now be made real on the earth, that we can build a civilization which in terms of plenty, enlightenment, beauty, and justice would surpass even the dreams of earlier times.

This optimistic outlook is not without substantial foundation, as the material already presented in these pages plainly shows. We in America at least are rapidly approaching the solution of the problem of the production of goods and services, of the establishment of a proper relationship between population and natural endowment. An age of material security and relative plenty for all is no longer a utopian fantasy. It is clearly in the realm of the possible. Also we possess the resources and agencies which, if wisely used, should enable us to achieve and sustain a level of enlightenment utterly beyond the reach of any other epoch. With the ever-increasing leisure which technological advance assures us, it is reasonable to assume a wholly unprecedented release of creative energies which could be directed toward the building of a civilization of great beauty and grandeur. Finally, under conditions of security and plenty, with the bitter struggle for bread resolved, the attainment of a high level of justice should be far easier than in the age of scarcity. The point to emphasize is that the material foundations for a golden age are today not beyond our reach in America, provided, of course, an enduring peace can be established throughout the earth. Then with the full cooperation of all nations the technically most backward peoples should not lag far behind. We must learn speedily that in our little earthly neighborhood no one land, however strong and favored, can enter the golden age alone.

The difficulty, of course, resides in the fact that the problem is by no means wholly material in character. The world today has so little of understanding, sympathy, and good will. It is so divided by ideological differences, so full of ignorance and prejudice, and so agitated by hatred, fear, and conflict that even the most optimistic can easily find ample cause for despair. Until this evil heritage of the centuries is dissipated or moderated the grounds for hope would seem to be slender indeed. Yet much of the turmoil and struggle of the period is probably the inevitable accompaniment of great changes in social institutions and human relationships. The very promise of the age arouses discontent in the hearts of men who under other conditions would meekly submit to a harsh fate. The strength of totalitarian movements is derived in no small measure from their success in appropriating the promise and in harnessing the discontent to their purposes. Submerged classes and peoples in America and throughout the world are on the march. Whether they will bring a new despotism or a new birth of freedom remains undetermined at this time. They might well be the builders of a far better society than man has ever known. The material resources and the technical knowledge are here.

4

Neither a dark age nor a golden age is fated.
It seems highly probable, moreover, that we shall get neither the one nor the other in its pure form. Even after fear, hatred, and intolerance have been banished, or largely so, error, greed, and thirst for power will remain with us, and the ideal will always lie somewhere beyond the horizon. Industrial civilization, moreover, as we have argued in a preceding chapter, holds within its broad imperatives many possibilities. It is taking and, if freedom of choice prevails, will continue to take different forms in different countries. Unless some particular pattern is imposed by force on all nations, it will be profoundly influenced everywhere by the peculiar character, the history, the heritage, and the geographical setting, of each people involved. We should be extremely skeptical of those apostles of a new order who insist that there is only one road to the future and that they alone are able to chart its course.

Perhaps the surest road to a dark age for all mankind is the fanatical promulgation of the doctrine that all nations must follow the same route in building industrial civilization. Such a doctrine, if adopted by either of the two great powers which now dominate the earth, Russia and the United States, would undoubtedly lead to war. The shadow which hangs over the world today is due largely to the fact that the Soviet leaders seem to take this position. In an authoritative article they recently stated without qualification: "The general laws of transition from capitalism to socialism, revealed by Marx and Engels, tested, applied, and developed by Lenin and Stalin on the basis of the experience of the Bolshevik Party and the Soviet state, are obligatory for all countries."[7] Clearly this is not the path to international understanding and peace. A tolerable future for mankind must rest on a common devotion to peace on the part of all great states and a readiness to tolerate differences in social, economic, and political institutions. The propagation of any system by industrial power or military force can only bring war.

This means that the character of the new age, in so far as we in America control the forces shaping our future, will depend on the choices which we make in the years ahead. And many of these choices will be grand choices—choices that go to the very foundation of things. As the present volume stresses from the beginning, we stand today at one of the great critical points in history, confronted with the necessity of making decisions that will shape the course of social evolution for decades and probably for generations. We consequently hold in our hands in unusual measure, not only the fate of ourselves, but also the fate of all who are to come after us. During the next half century we are going to modify profoundly our economy, our social structure, our cultural institutions, and even our outlook on the world. This is indeed a sobering responsibility to be placed on the shoulders of any generation. In our history only the founders of the Republic faced tasks of equal magnitude and difficulty. We can but resolve that we, like them, shall not labor in vain.

5

The character of our choices will depend on our knowledge and understanding.

Good intentions are not enough. Without knowledge and understanding relevant to the issues

[7] *Bolshevik* (Theoretical and Political Journal of the Central Committee of the All-Union Communist Party [Moscow, September 15, 1948]), p. 51.

at stake men are blind. They know neither what choices are possible nor what choice to make among the possible. The pages of recent history are strewn with mistakes made by statesmen and peoples because of ignorance of the consequences of their acts. The peoples of Europe in 1914 did not know that they were about to shatter the moral foundations of Western civilization. The Russian people in 1917 did not know what they were doing when they acquiesced in the violent dissolution of the Provisional Government and the establishment of the dictatorship. The Italian people in 1922 did not know that Mussolini intended to walk over the "decayed corpse of the Goddess Liberty." The German people in 1933 did not know that Hitler with his mad doctrines of Nordic superiority would lead them to catastrophe. The English people in 1938 did not know that when Neville Chamberlain returned to London from Munich he brought not "peace in our time" but the "buzz bomb." The American people did not know that their policy toward the civil war in Spain during the middle thirties would help to set the stage for the Second World War; nor did they know that their toleration of shipping scrap iron to Japan during the same period would take the form of bullets to kill American boys.

Many Americans today seem to think that the great oceans are as wide as they ever were, that the Russians will never be able to overtake us in nuclear physics, that wars will always be fought at a distance, that a kind Providence will continue to watch over us and protect us from our mistakes. Others seem to think that the exploitation of colored people is in the order of nature, that the organizations of working people should be destroyed, that the economic system of the time of Jackson should be restored, that women should be forced back into the home, that what was good enough for our fathers is good enough for us. The hazard of such a mentality resides in the fact that it will postpone positive choice to the point of disaster and then force hasty and ill-considered decisions. In the world today there can be no substitute for clear knowledge and understanding of the great realities of the epoch.

6

The character of our choices will depend also on our values.

Here is the heart of the question which confronts us and all mankind today. The essence of any civilization is found in its values—in its preferences, its moral commitments, its aesthetic judgments, its deepest loyalties, its conception of the good life, its standards of excellence, its measures of success, its teachings regarding the things for which and by which men should live and, if need be, die. The issue at stake in the coming years is nothing less than the birth, the death, and the survival of values.

Granted knowledge and understanding, our choices will reflect the basic values of our people at the time, or at least of those whom we place in positions of power and trust. This is not to say that values do not change, or that industrial civilization is not creating and will not continue to create values of its own. The contrary is obviously true. Yet at any moment in history a people will be moved for good or ill by the values which it cherishes. It will be largely in terms of such values that we shall make the great choices of this critical age, and thus shape the character of industrial civilization in America.

In the chapters that follow an attempt will be made to set forth briefly those values of our people which should guide us in the great creative tasks which lie ahead. That this is a task of vast difficulty is obvious. The values contained in our heritage are diverse and conflicting. They come from many different sources—from different historical epochs and social systems. The moral vestiges of feudalism and even of slavery persist in our social attitudes and relations. It would be easily possible to select from our life and history the morality of the Nazi state with all its mad pretensions—with its worship of brute power, its contempt for the common man, its cult of authoritarian leadership, its delight in torture and cruelty, its parade of arrogance, its doctrine of race superiority, its idealization of war and bloodshed. All of these ways of feeling, thinking, and acting are in us. Likewise there may be found in our heritage the moral foundations of Communist totalitarianism with its appeal to class hatred, its doctrine of violence, its subordination of the individual, its disregard for human life, its regimentation of the mind, and its glorification of the leader.

7

We must decide which values can and should survive in the new age.

It is proposed here that the major sources of such values are found in the Hebraic-Christian ethic, the humanistic spirit, the scientific method, the rule of law, and the democratic faith. In each case, to be sure, selections and interpretations will have to be made. And if the chosen values are to survive they will have to find expression in social institutions and life conditions.

It must be emphasized that the values here set down and affirmed are themselves choices—choices, it is hoped, that express the experience of our people in the long adventure of mankind. Their survival and fulfillment are not fated either by our history or by present conditions. They are believed to correspond for the most part with our professions. Indeed they are included in large measure in what a distinguished Swedish student of our civilization has called the "American Creed." "America, compared to every other country in Western civilization, large or small," Gunnar Myrdal writes, "has the *most explicitly expressed* system of general ideals in reference to human interrelations." And he adds that "this body of ideals is more widely understood and appreciated than similar ideals are anywhere else." [8]

Here are the values, we like to think, for which we have labored and fought in our finest hours. The overwhelming majority of us entertain the hope that they are the things for

[8] Gunnar Myrdal, *An American Dilemma* (New York and London, 1944), Vol. I, p. 3.

which America stands before the world today and for which America will stand in the judgment of time. When we violate them, as we do, we do not seek to immortalize our acts. On the contrary we are ashamed of such violations, devise ingenious apologies, strive to forget them, endeavor to blot them from the record. The values elaborated in the pages to follow are not taken out of the air: they are written in our history and in our conscience. Also they constitute an interpretation of ourselves which we trust will mold our emerging industrial civilization and give to it both an American and a universal quality. They constitute a heritage of "principles which *ought* to rule," according to the prevailing American opinion, and which therefore should serve as a powerful asset in the making of the great choices before us. Whether they will rule or not is the foremost moral issue confronting our people and our schools. It is to be hoped that they will rule, and further that they will neither blind us to the splendid features of other civilizations nor prevent us from making creative adjustments in the realm of values to the new and emerging conditions of life.

14

THE HEBRAIC-CHRISTIAN ETHIC

1

The Hebraic-Christian ethic is a major source of our values.

Historically our civilization is deeply rooted in the Hebraic-Christian tradition of the Western World. The extent to which we have been molded by this great tradition is but little appreciated by many of us. Even those who rebel against its contemporary forms, rituals, and doctrines often appeal to its spirit. It has become such an integral part of our civilization that we take it for granted and are consequently almost unaware of its existence. Practically all of us and our ancestors back through many generations were reared in the atmosphere, if not in the institutions, of the Hebraic-Christian faith. From the standpoint of professed allegiances, therefore, certain of the ethical conceptions of this faith are among the oldest and most generally accepted commitments of our people.

Our ethical debt to the Hebraic-Christian faith is clear. Yet it is imperative at the outset of this analysis to view the matter in historical and cultural perspective. Neither our American people nor the peoples of the Hebraic-Christian world are the exclusive inheritors of pure ethical doctrine.

Certainly the ancient Hebrews were not the recipients of any wholly special and unique moral revelation. Modern scholarship has demonstrated that they borrowed heavily from other peoples and that the ultimate origins of their beliefs are difficult to establish. Also we know that the great religious and moral systems developed through the centuries in China, India, the Near East, and the Mediterranean world hold many moral insights and teachings in common. Perhaps in our time Mahatma Gandhi has lived according to the so-called Christian virtues more fully than any other person of renown. We know too that within the limits of the clan, the gens, or the tribe certain of these virtues have been practiced by many primitive peoples. The Hebraic-Christian faith is given its pre-eminent place in the present exposition primarily because it was the medium through which we received many values from the ancient world.

One more point by way of orientation must be emphasized. There is no suggestion here that the Hebraic-Christian faith be accepted in its entirety. Our concern is with the ethics rather than the theology of this faith. We do not propose the establishment of a state church and the adoption of a common interpretation of the universe. In terms of theology our people are endlessly divided. Those who profess some form of belief in a supernatural power are organized into many scores of religious sects or denominations. And the number of such bodies increases with each generation. In addition there are many who have accepted an essentially naturalistic outlook on the world. Only about one-half of our people are actually enrolled as members of the churches of the country.

Agreement on the basic elements of the Hebraic-Christian ethic is of course far from easy. This ethic has a long history, has lived in many places and times, and has adjusted itself to most diverse conditions of life. Consequently, if considered in all of its manifestations, it will be found to contain many contradictions. Its doctrines have been employed or twisted to sanction human slavery, to sustain despotism, to justify the exploitation of working people, to support privileged orders, to hold women in subjection, to shackle the minds of scientists, artists, and philosophers, and even to consecrate the waging of wars of aggression and conquest. Yet certain elements of this great ethic constitute a basic and essential part of our social creed. That they are not derived exclusively or distinctively from this source is readily admitted. Nevertheless, in the minds of our people they are commonly identified with the teachings of the Hebraic-Christian tradition.

2

The Hebraic-Christian ethic lays the moral foundations of democracy.

It proclaims, without qualification, the supreme worth and dignity of the individual human being. Every man is precious simply because he is a man. Every man is precious also because he is unique, because he is himself and no other. Here, then, according to this ethic, is the source of all values. The development of the individual to his full stature is the purpose and the gauge of human society and relationships. As the founder of Christianity once observed, even the Sabbath was made for man, and not man for the Sabbath. So all institutions and social arrangements —family and neighborhood, industry, state, and church, social, economic, and political systems, religious and moral codes—are to be judged, accepted or rejected, preserved or modified, as they affect the lives of individual human beings.

Recognition of the supreme worth of the individual leads inevitably to the principle of equality among the members of society. If each individual is uniquely precious, there can be no moral support for privileged orders and castes. No man can be regarded as superior or inferior to another by reason of the work he does, the social rank of his family, the color of his skin, or even the altar at which he worships. Nor for any reason whatsoever does any man have the right to exploit another, to use another as a means to his ends. Hebraic-Christian writings are replete with castigations of human exploitation and the defense of the rights of common people.

The Hebrew prophet Amos, 760 B.C., in words that will never die, placed the ethical teachings of his tradition above all forms and rituals. "I hate, I despise your feasts, and I will take no delight in your solemn assemblies," he admonished the oppressors of his time. "Yea, though you offer me your burnt offerings and meal offerings, I will not accept them; neither will I regard the peace offerings of your fat beasts. Take thou away from me the noise of thy songs; for I will not hear the melody of thy viols. But let justice roll down as waters, and righteousness as a mighty stream."

Jesus himself was a carpenter, and he proclaimed in the most celebrated of his sermons that the meek would inherit the earth. The principle of equality and the affirmation of the moral worth of all men are given their most profound social application in these lines from the *Magnificat*, the Latin version of the song of the mother of Jesus, which have been chanted by old and young alike in the Western World for fourteen hundred years:

> He hath showed strength with his arm;
> He hath scattered the proud in the imagination of their hearts.
> He hath put down the mighty from *their* seats,
> And exalted them of low degree.
> He hath filled the hungry with good things;
> And the rich he hath sent empty away.

After the lapse of centuries this tradition still lives. It is therefore not surprising that men in all ages have appealed to it and gained strength from its affirmations when they have sought to overthrow tyrants and establish justice on the earth. English "dissent" since the fourteenth century has invoked the ethical teachings of the Hebraic-Christian faith in the struggle for social justice. Probably few Americans know that it was John Wycliffe who first phrased one of the most precious doctrines in their heritage of popular liberty. In his preface to the translation of the Bible into the vernacular, published in 1382, he wrote these words: "This Bible is for the government of the people, by the people, and for the people." The Levellers with their theory of inalienable individual rights contributed much to the development of both British and American democracy. Their audacious couplet, "When Adam delved and Eve span, who was then the gentleman," is an expression of militant egalitarianism. The "social gospel" of our time, which represents an effort to apply the teachings of the Bible to the correction of social evils and injustices, has left its imprint on American thought and institutions.

3

The Hebraic-Christian ethic lays the moral foundations of peace and good will among the nations.

It proclaims the sublime principle of the brotherhood, of the equality and essential unity of the races of mankind. "God hath made of one blood," the prophet declares, "all nations of men." No people is morally superior or inferior to another by reason of its physical might or its present place in history. Regardless of color, creed, or language, all men are brothers, sons of the same father, members of one human family. There are no chosen races or nations commissioned by God or entitled by their own nature to rule over and enslave their fellow men. The findings of physical and cultural anthropology corroborate this ethical insight of two thousand years ago.

This ethic also condemns war for the evil thing that it is. Jesus was the "prince of peace." His birth has been celebrated in verse, song, and prayer down through the centuries as heralding the coming of peace on earth and good will among men. He thus gave expression to one of the most ancient and persistent longings of the human heart. Although military leaders and castes have at times extolled the glories and virtues of war, the great masses of ordinary men, women, and children inhabiting this planet have always believed and known that "war is hell." While war has brought wealth to a few, fame to some, and the thrill of fighting in a great cause to many, the vast majority of the people of this world have found that it inevitably brings sorrow, suffering, and tragedy to them. Never before in the history of mankind has the practice of this teaching of the Hebraic-Christian ethic been so urgent. Many of us remember well with what a sense of ineffable yearning we listened to the Christmas carols in the dark winter evenings of both world wars as we sought to call forth the faces of loved ones engaged in mortal struggle on distant battlefields. All of this does not mean that men have not fought just wars, nor that they have not fought for glorious ends. They have indeed done these things on many a page of history. Yet we know that it is not glorious to kill one's fellow men, or to be killed by them. War is the ultimate denial of the conception of human brotherhood.

In the present volume much has been said about cultural lag, about the tendency of one segment of the culture to change more rapidly than another. It has been assumed by many that this phenomenon always takes the same form, that the "material culture" always moves in advance of the "adaptive culture," that man's "practical inventiveness" always "runs ahead of his moral consciousness and social organization." This assumption is of course incorrect. At least there are many instances in history of the contrary pattern, of moral and political ideas and even institutions running ahead of technology. The emergence in antiquity of the Christian teaching of the brotherhood of man is a remarkable example of this form of cultural lag. Conceived in an age when peoples were separated by great distances and primitive modes of communication and when nations might nurture hatred and contempt for other members of the human family without actually placing the whole future of mankind in jeopardy, it has at last entered the realm of "practical politics" for all peoples. Today, because of the reduced dimensions of the earth and the great power of the weapons of war, this ancient doctrine has become the order of the day for the entire race of men. Modern technology has laid the material foundations for its fulfillment. Indeed it seems to have made such fulfillment a condition of survival. Man's "practical inventiveness" has overtaken an ancient moral teaching.

4

The Hebraic-Christian ethic lays the moral foundations of a humane society.
It conceives man as a moral creature living in a moral order. According to this conception, the world is marked by good and evil and man is potentially capable of distinguishing the one from the other. He fulfills his nature, not by living a life of impulse and caprice, of sensual satisfaction, or of calculated expediency, or even of sacred ritual, but by striving to do good and make the good prevail in the family, the community, the nation, and the world. He is admonished to do justice, to be generous, to help the unfortunate, to show mercy toward the weak, to comfort the heavy-laden, to serve his fellow men, to be honest and truthful, to cultivate a humane and gentle spirit, to love his neighbor as himself. The man who does these things is a good man—the highest and finest expression of the creative process on the earth. Also, however much the individual may be molded by circumstance, he is judged responsible and accountable for his actions. And whatever may be the powers arrayed against him, he is always to be true to his own conscience. The good life is a life disciplined by good purposes and devoted to good deeds. When Lincoln in his second inaugural, as the bitter civil struggle was drawing to its close, uttered the words, "with malice toward none, with charity for all," he was speaking in the tradition of the Hebraic-Christian ethic.

These ethical insights are both simple and profound. Even a skeptical and cynical generation must know that the teachings and practices which flow from them are of the essence of any good society. Only as we introduce them more fully into the closer relationships of our American community and into the wider relationships of nations can we hope to build a better country and a better world. In the measure that we ignore or violate them we open the door to savagery and barbarism. Whatever may have been their original source or sanction these insights have been thoroughly validated by the long experience of mankind. At no time have their worth and truth been more fully demonstrated than in our own tragic generation. The Nazi philosophy reveals the end to which their general repudiation logically and inevitably leads. And the Communists, with their apocalyptic dogma of inevitable war, terror, and dictatorship, seem to be bent on repeating the Fascist tragedy.

In November, 1950, Bertrand Russell delivered a series of lectures before a university audience on the general impact of science on human society. Known to his generation throughout the world as a critic of supernaturalism in all its forms, he paid unqualified tribute to perhaps the most basic element in the Hebraic-Christian ethic. As he contemplated the deep distress of the human race in the current epoch, he emphasized the need for "human compassion," for the "wish that mankind should be happy," in these words:

> The root of the matter is a very simple and old-fashioned thing, a thing so simple that I am almost ashamed to mention it, for fear of the derisive smile with which wise cynics will greet my words. The thing I mean—please forgive me for mentioning it—is love, Christian love, or compassion. If you feel this, you have a motive for existence, a guide in action, a reason for courage, an imperative necessity for intellectual honesty. If you feel this, you have all that anybody should need in the way of religion. Although you may not find happiness, you will never know the deep despair of those whose life is aimless and void of purpose; for there is always something that you can do to diminish the awful sum of human misery.[1]

5

The foregoing elements of the Hebraic-Christian ethic are threatened by contemporary totalitarian movements.

This is obviously true without qualification of Fascism from the day of its

[1] Bertrand Russell, *The Impact of Science on Society* (New York, 1951), pp. 59–60.

birth. The Nazis in particular openly brand the entire ethic as a shameful betrayal of the true German spirit. The worth of the individual human being, except as a servant or an instrument of state or dictator, is flatly denied. The principle of equality as applied to peoples and races is dismissed as a fraud which the weak have endeavored to impose on the strong. Members of "inferior" stocks have no rights where the interests of their "superiors" are involved. It is appropriate to treat them as servants, playthings, or subjects for "scientific" study and experimentation. It is even meet to take delight in their torture, to shoot them down as rabbits and thus provide living space for the natural masters of the earth. In the case of members of the "superior" race, in their relations with one another, the principle of equality is also repudiated and is replaced by the principle of leadership. But it is in the realm of simple human relationships that Fascism challenges the essence of Hebraic-Christian morality. Here it is the duty of the strong to display and use their strength to their own advantage. To show mercy is to show weakness. Never in modern times has the dependence of civilization on the exercise of mercy by the strong toward the weak been so clearly and fully demonstrated. Buchenwald, Dachau, and Auschwitz should stand forever as a terrible warning to mankind and a demonstration of the worth of the Hebraic-Christian ethic.

The case of Communist totalitarianism is more complex. In its origins it was professedly a vigorous and militant movement for the achievement through harsh and ruthless means of many of the elements of the Hebraic-Christian ethic—an abundant life for the individual, the elimination of the exploitation of man by man, the application of the principle of equality to both individuals and peoples, and the establishment of a world-wide regime of peace and brotherhood. Karl Marx, with a measure of justification, has been called the last of the great Hebrew prophets. Unfortunately the means employed led to a struggle for power at home and throughout the world—a struggle marked by utter ruthlessness and the wholesale repudiation of the original promises.

As the years have passed the Communist state has assumed more and more the essential features of its rival. Today its words stand condemned beyond redemption by its deeds. Before the bar of history the Soviet leaders must be judged for such coldly calculated acts as the liquidation of certain national minorities at home and the terrible destruction and misery visited upon the people of Korea in 1950 and 1951. Communism repudiates and mocks the whole spirit of the Hebraic-Christian ethic.

6

The Hebraic-Christian ethic is challenged by the conditions and forces of industrial civilization.
If peace can be established on the earth, industrial civilization should make easily possible the fulfillment of certain of the basic principles of this ethic. With its fabulous resources it should be able to bring to all men that abundant life of which the founder of Christianity spoke. And with this accomplishment the Hebraic-Christian conception of the good man in the good society should be within reach. To be sure, the vast sweep of industrial society and the impersonal character of so many of its connections and relationships present a whole series of problems which will not be easy of solution. But, given sufficient time for experiment and invention, solutions undoubtedly could be found.

The foremost challenge which industrial civilization throws out to the Hebraic-Christian ethic is that of war. The rise of this civilization has increased immeasurably the urgency of the task of establishing a just and durable peace. It has profoundly altered our geographical relations with the rest of the world. It has greatly shortened distances, reduced the size of the earth, narrowed the oceans, and brought even the most distant nations to our doorstep. At the same time it has made war so terrifying and destructive that the imagination falters at the thought of another world war a decade or a generation hence. Also it has given war a total aspect. As no great nation can keep out of the conflict, so no locality or population group within a nation can escape its reach. Men, women, and children all feel increasingly its ruthless sweep. There have been fewer and fewer noncombatants in the wars of the industrial age. There may be none in the first and possibly the last war of the atomic age.

The spread of industrial civilization over the world is also changing the power relations of nations and peoples. During the past generation it has been moving out from its original home in western Europe and North America to the industrially backward and undeveloped parts of the earth. England, France, Germany, and Italy will probably never again know the overwhelming preponderance of power which they enjoyed for several centuries. Russia, a great Eurasian empire, still in her industrial infancy, has become the most powerful state of the Old World. America in her sheer industrial might is for the time without a close rival on the earth. The colored peoples are rising everywhere, and the speed of their rise will be determined by their mastery of science and technology. Their great numbers, their physical vigor, and the richness of the natural resources in their possession can only mean that in "God's good time" they will achieve a wholly new position in the world. The states of western Europe have had their day as arbiters of the destinies of mankind. The power to make decisions among the nations is passing into other hands. These vast and far-reaching changes place upon the American people new and heavy responsibilities.

As the rise of industrial civilization has made urgent the organization of the peace of the world, so it has made possible the achievement of the task. The contraction of the earth has been accompanied by the laying of the physical foundations of a world community. In terms of communication the earth is certainly no larger than were the thirteen American states at the time of the formation of the federal union in 1787–90. The new engines of warfare, morover, if brought into the service of the purposes of peace, could easily perform the policing function required to maintain world order. Also, for decades now mankind has been thinking about and experimenting with instrumentalities for adjusting differences and maintaining peace among the nations. While such instrumentalities have not been notably successful in dealing with the great issues, they have provided a modicum of experience on which to build. Moreover, if the nations fail to establish a peace based on cooperation, it is quite possible that some totalitarian state may take the job in hand and impose a peace on the world conceived in tyranny and dedicated to the proposition that the races of man are created very unequal. The opportunity of our generation for the fulfillment of the Hebraic-Christian promise of universal brotherhood may come again only at the close of a long and savage age of darkness.

15

THE HUMANISTIC SPIRIT

1

The humanistic spirit is one of the great liberating forces of history.

This spirit first appeared in strength in ancient Greece where it flowered with a brilliance that remains unsurpassed to the present day. That so few could add so much to the human heritage is one of the marvels of history and is at the same time a living demonstration of the capacity of man. As long as there are free minds on the earth or minds sensitive to the values of freedom, the intellectual and artistic achievements of the Greeks, provided they are not expunged from the record, will be a source of fresh and boundless inspiration. It is not surprising, therefore, that the humanistic spirit stemming from this gifted people has played a powerful role in every revolutionary and creative epoch in the Western World during the past two thousand years.

The recovery of this spirit, after it had been buried for centuries, helped to bring the Dark Ages to their close, to quicken the mind of genius, and to usher in the modern epoch. It presided over the Renaissance, challenged the authority of established institutions, and permeated the thought of the English and French revolutions. It inspired much of the great literature and art of Western Europe and contributed mightily to the development of science. It played a part in the geographical explorations and discoveries of the period.

Our indebtedness in America to this great liberating tradition is little understood by the present generation. At the time of the discovery and settlement of our country the humanistic spirit was moving with power in the whole Western World. On both sides of the Atlantic it helped to break the shackles of feudal authority, arouse men to engage in bold political speculation, and kindle the fires of protest, revolt, and revolution. It stirred the minds and shaped the visions of the founders of our Republic. It is reflected in many of our great state papers—in the Declaration of Independence, the Federal Constitution, the Bill of Rights, and the writings of Franklin, Paine, and Jefferson. It is reflected also in our universities, in our conception of liberal education, and in our free intellectual life. It is one of the authentic and precious strands of American civilization.

2

The humanistic spirit proclaims man the architect of his own destiny.

In the words of Protagoras it makes him "the measure of all things" and places him squarely in the center of the universe. For good or ill it declares that man is endowed with the capacity of choice and that his chances of salvation depend on his own powers, efforts, and decisions. It sees man as the great creator and the great destroyer, as the builder of his future and the waster of his inheritance, as the responsible architect of both his fortunes and his misfortunes. As he may glory in his successes, so he must suffer the consequences of his failures. The humanistic spirit thus rejects all doctrines of fatalism, humble acquiescence, mechanistic determinism, and cosmic caprice. It calls man to a life of effort, struggle, and creativity. It challenges him to act, to think, to surmount his infirmities, to triumph over his surroundings. It therefore affirms the dictum of Pope that "the proper study of mankind is Man."

In the springtime of the modern age the Italian humanist, Pico della Mirandola, gave poetic expression to this new conception of man. In his *Oration on the Dignity of Man* he attributed these words to the Supreme Maker in the Garden of Eden:

Neither a fixed abode, nor a form in thine own likeness, nor any gift peculiar to thyself alone, have we given thee, O Adam, in order that what abode, what likeness, what gifts thou shalt choose, may be thine to have and to possess. The nature allotted to all other creatures, within laws appointed by ourselves, restrains them. Thou, restrained by no narrow bounds, according to thy own free will, in whose power I have placed thee, shalt define thy nature for thyself. I have set thee midmost the world, that thence thou mightest the more conveniently survey whatsoever is in the world. Nor have we made thee either heavenly or earthly, mortal or immortal, to the end that thou, being, as it were, thy own free maker and moulder, shouldst fashion thyself in what form may like thee best. Thou shalt have power to decline unto the lower or brute creatures. Thou shalt have power to be reborn unto the higher, or divine, according to the sentence of thy intellect.[1]

The humanistic spirit is primarily concerned with the destiny of man on the earth rather than in some celestial realm. It is concerned with the life of sense here and now, with the span of years from birth to death. It looks at this life with all of its trials and tribulations, with all of its personal sorrows and tragedies, yes, even with the final dissolution of the bodily frame and the mournful journey to the tomb—it looks at this life and calls it good, a precious gift from the creator of all things. It would seek to make this life more secure, to make it more abundant, to make it more beautiful, to fill it with all things worthy and of good repute within the limits set by nature and the ever-expanding frontiers of knowledge and understanding. It would strive to entice paradise to descend from the heavens and establish its abode on the earth. The humanistic spirit therefore rejects asceticism in all its forms, the flagellation of the flesh, and the renunciation of

[1] Quoted in John Addington Symonds, *Renaissance in Italy*, Modern Library Edition (New York, 1935), Vol. I, p. 352.

the world. It would agree with the declaration of Martin Luther that the "stroke of a thresher in the granary was more acceptable than a psalter sung by a Carthusian."

3

The humanistic spirit proclaims a militant faith in human powers.

Above all it sees man as a rational being, as a being endowed with the ability to sense and discover the true as well as the good. It exalts in man that "divine spark of reason" which distinguishes him immeasurably from the brute and which has enabled him increasingly to penetrate the mysteries of his earthly existence and to gain control over his destiny. It promotes all conditions, agencies, and institutions designed to advance knowledge and understanding, to foster enlightenment and intellectual daring. It guards with utter devotion untrammeled inquiry into the substance of all things—into the physical universe, into the human past, into the nature of man and society, into the perspectives of the future. It conducts an unremitting struggle against all forms of authoritarianism, every species of tyranny over the mind of man, every social system, every political institution, every class relationship, every ecclesiastical order, that would cramp or degrade the human spirit. It has little respect for pomp and ceremony, for the glorification of the past, or for the deification of living rulers. It knows no master except the ideal of truth, and it realizes that truth itself grows and changes both its substance and its contours with the advance of knowledge and thought. To it the burning of books, the closing of libraries, the putting of scientists in uniform, and the regimentation of the mind constitute a degradation of the powers and a betrayal of the hopes of mankind. The humanistic spirit is the ancient, eternal, and uncompromising enemy of totalitarianism. Its vigorous rebirth is urgently needed in the present age.

The humanistic spirit was given immortal expression more than twenty-three hundred years ago in the life and death of Socrates. In the age of Pericles, the ancient Athenians, the most renowned of the Greeks in their devotion to freedom of the mind, were disturbed by the weakening of old tribal loyalties and enacted a law against blasphemy. Under this act the greatest philosopher of the ancient world, at the age of seventy, was tried, found guilty, and sentenced to death. Although Socrates might have saved his life by recanting, he chose to defend the sublime principle by which he had lived and thus left for all succeeding ages an affirmation of the central value of the humanistic spirit which should be recalled and celebrated today in every free society on the earth. In the words of Plato he spoke thus to his accusers:

If you propose to acquit me on condition that I abandon my search for truth, I will say: I thank you, O Athenians, but I will obey God, who, as I believe, set me this task, rather than you, and so long as I have breath and strength I will never cease from my occupation with philosophy. I will continue the practice of accosting whomever I meet and saying to him, "Are you not ashamed of setting your heart on wealth and honours while you have no care for wisdom and truth and making your soul better?" I know not what death is—it may be a good thing, and I am not afraid of it. But I do know that it is a bad thing to desert one's post and I prefer what may be good to what I know to be bad.

The humanistic spirit sees man as an aesthetic creature, capable of creating and responding to the true and the beautiful in art and life. It views man's struggle to achieve ever more satisfying expression in literature, drama, and music, in painting, sculpture, architecture, and community relationships as one of the most lustrous chapters of history. It wages unceasing and relentless warfare on all that is mean and ugly in both man and his surroundings. It encourages the development of artistic talents and the cultivation of all the arts by which man refines himself, ennobles his spirit, adds meaning to life, and makes the earth a more pleasing and lovely habitation. It plays a central role in lifting man from barbarism to civilization. It cherishes the distinctive insights and creative gifts of individuals and peoples. It treasures every achievement of the past as part of our common heritage which should serve both to delight and to instruct each succeeding generation. To it nothing human is alien.

The humanistic spirit admonishes man in the words of a maxim of the ancient Greeks to "know thyself." At no time in our history as a people have we been in greater need of applying this maxim. Charles E. Odegaard, Executive Director of the American Council of Learned Societies, in a recent report on the "conquest of fear" turns to it and pleads for a revival of the essence of the humanities:

We need to have as clear a conception as possible of the host of assumptions implicit in our own immediate impulses to action and belief. We need to know and understand the spiritual and moral requirements demanded of each of us in our relations with our fellow citizens and with other nationals, if we are to preserve free and liberal institutions. Such self-knowledge can be gained only through organized and persistent study of what we are, of how we have become what we are, and—may the voice of prophecy never be stilled—of what we may become. This is the business of the humanities and the social sciences. And since man is endowed with a nature which permits him not merely to seek after truth with his mind but also to love it with his heart and thereby commit himself the more to it, the arts too have their place in aiding us in the search for self-revelation. They are not a mere luxury for idle moments but a level of discourse which is an integral part of man's conversation with himself when he strives to see himself whole as a thinking and feeling creature.[2]

The humanistic spirit sees man as an inventor and contriver, as a creator of the practical arts. It sees him as an applier of knowledge to the ceaseless improvement of his estate—to the conquest of disease, to the raising of the productivity of labor, to the easing of the burden of toil, to the multiplying of the comforts of life, to the increasing of his hours of fruitful leisure. The monumental labors of the French Encyclopedists of the eighteenth century were an au-

[2] Charles E. Odegaard, "Toward the Conquest of Fear." Report to the American Council of Learned Societies (Washington, D.C., January, 1951), pamphlet, pp. 5–6.

thentic expression of the humanistic spirit and marked the opening of a new epoch in the effort to bring knowledge into the service of mankind. "The aim of an encyclopedia," wrote Denis Diderot, editor of the *Encyclopédie*, "is to gather together the knowledge scattered over the face of the earth, to set forth its general plan to the men with whom we live and to transmit it to the men who will come after us, in order that the labors of past centuries may not have been in vain in those that follow, that our children, better informed, may at the same time become happier, and that we may not die without deserving well of mankind."[3]

The humanistic spirit prizes as one of the basic values of civilization the integrity of the individual. While recognizing the dependence of the creative student or artist on the achievements of the past and the great role of collective effort in the advancement of all the arts and sciences of man, it sees the role of mind in the perspectives of time and affirms in the tradition of Socrates the right of the individual to pursue his search for truth far beyond the boundaries of wont and custom. It honors a Walt Whitman who stubbornly proclaims: "I see this my way." It would protect the individual, not only from the coercive might of state, church, and wealth, but also from the passions of the multitude. It knows that human advance comes only from those daring and prophetic minds who blaze new trails on the very frontiers of knowledge, thought, expression, and aspiration. It views their labors as precious beyond price.

4

The humanistic spirit proclaims the doctrine of the perfectibility of man and society.

It contends that faith in human powers is no idle and meaningless faith. In spite of the many reverses and catastrophes of history, it affirms that

[3] Quoted by René Hubert in his article "Encyclopédistes," *The Encyclopaedia of the Social Sciences* (New York, 1931), Vol. V, pp. 528–529.

the story of man's long adventure on the earth is glorious and full of promise, that indeed the achievements already in the record almost pass understanding. Though knowing well that peoples without number have enslaved or destroyed one another, that civilizations often have risen only to fall in ruins, that the nations of the world are now torn by strife and hatred, and that evidences of relapse into barbarism may be seen around us today, it rejects all philosophies of pessimism. It rejects alike the doctrine that the golden age of man lies in some mythical past and the doctrine that it is to be found only in some other sphere of being where we shall be freed from all our earthly trammels. It also rejects the doctrine that man, like the squirrel in a cage, merely moves in circles, repeating from age to age an essentially uniform pattern of existence. At least it finds in man's rise out of primordial "ooze and slime" to his present state sufficient grounds for hope that he will be able increasingly to become master of his earthly destiny.

For reasons which are written large on the pages of almost every newspaper, that hope may not glow so brightly for many in America today as it did in the eighteenth and nineteenth centuries, before advances in physics, chemistry, biology, geology, and astronomy had shattered the material and philosophical foundations of our civilization and catapulted us into a world for which we are unprepared. Moreover, as we contemplate the vast reaches in time and space of the physical universe which man has revealed and the vast power of the mechanical engines which he has contrived, we may feel dwarfed and overwhelmed in the presence of our own discoveries and creations. Yet the humanistic spirit proclaims now, as stoutly as it did in the Age of the Enlightenment, its belief in the possibility of human progress and the perfectibility of man and his institutions. It might even contend that the intervening years have strengthened the conviction that man can increasingly surmount his infirmities and become free. It certainly would insist that man, by his own efforts and through a process of self-discipline, may lift himself to an ever higher and finer state of being. Without this faith the terrifying events of the present epoch would appear to us, not as tragic episodes, but as acts of fate. To the humanistic spirit the golden age still lies ahead.

That the road will be rough and crooked, that disaster may lurk at every turn, indeed that the road itself will have to be carved out of a wilderness of human folly, ignorance, and passion, must be taken for granted. But man is now equipped with knowledge that no earlier generation ever possessed. If we can only make wise use of this knowledge, our hopes may not be without foundation.

5

The humanistic spirit is in grave peril today.

This of course is not a wholly novel situation. At no place in the world has the humanistic spirit been secure over any considerable period of time. It has always led a more or less precarious existence. The struggle for the liberation of the human mind in America has continued without cessation from the days of Roger Williams and John Peter Zenger down to the present moment. The victory seems never to be finally and decisively won. How uncertain the future may be is well illustrated by the statement quoted in an earlier chapter from J. B. Bury's *A History of Freedom of Thought* published in 1913. At the end of an era that had been marked by the rapid expansion of the area of freedom, he concluded tentatively that the enemy had been finally routed. We know today that he was merely reflecting the optimism of a vanishing age.

The humanistic spirit is fighting for its life today, partly because of the deep crisis in human affairs. Old institutions are crumbling and old relationships are dissolving. In consequence there is a general condition of insecurity with its usual accompaniment of fear, anxiety, and collective neurosis. We are in an age of war, revolution, and counterrevolution. Although humanistic ideals may inspire revolt, revolutionists and counterrevolutionists alike are rarely remembered in history for their devotion to the cause of intellectual freedom. Almost invariably, and regardless of their professions, they sacrifice all humane values on the altar of the struggle for power. The fathers of our Republic constitute a rare exception to the rule.

A major and perhaps enduring threat to the humanistic spirit is found in contemporary totalitarian ideologies and practices. A certain distinction, however, may be drawn between Russian Communism and German Fascism. The open and avowed repudiation by the latter of the entire humanistic tradition is well known. In Nazi Germany the intellectual and artistic life was drafted into the service of the state and the dictatorship. The forms of German scholarship, with its long tradition of academic freedom, were employed to support the doctrine of Nordic superiority and prepare the way for a return to cultural barbarism. Free minds either lapsed into silence, went into exile, or suffered imprisonment, torture, and death.

The leaders of Russian Communism, on the other hand, invoke incessantly the symbols of this great tradition, even as they slay its spirit. They proclaim daily their devotion to something called "socialist humanism." But an examination of this body of doctrine shows that it has little in common with the humanism of history. Its basic teachings are that parents should love one another and their children, that children should love one another and their parents and elders, that the peoples of the Soviet Union should love one another and the "toiling masses of the earth," that they should all love their motherland, and glorify Stalin in the highest. Also that they should obey without question the commands of the Central Committee and "hate with a burning hatred" the entire "bourgeois" world and all enemies of their "powerful socialist motherland," whether fathers or mothers, brothers or sisters, friends or relatives, individuals or classes at home and abroad. As a matter of fact, since the war the political control of the intellectual and artistic life seems to have gone further in the Soviet Union than it did under the Nazis. The blunt and powerful "decrees on ideology," issued by the Central Committee of the Party and proclaiming "truth" in all fields of thought, have forced teachers, scientists, writers, artists, and even clowns to kneel before the Party, confess their sins, and promise to mend their ways.

These cultural patterns, whether Fascist or Communist, are now widely diffused through the world. They constitute a dangerous threat to the survival of the humanistic spirit even in America. Indeed the possibility rises before us that, as we gird ourselves to meet the aggressions of Communism at home and abroad, we shall unwittingly adopt the spirit and methods of totalitarianism to protect our liberties. There are many shrill voices heard in the nation today which are in actuality proposing that we follow this course, that we outlaw all dissent and criticism, that we nullify the Bill of Rights and establish a police state dedicated to the commemoration of the signing of the Declaration of Independence on every Fourth of July! For us to listen to and obey these voices would constitute one of the tragedies of history. If in a moment of hysteria we should go down this road, it would be small cause for comfort to hope that eventually, perhaps after the passing of generations or centuries, we should at terrible cost win back our liberties and resume our march under the banners of the humanistic spirit.

6

The humanistic spirit is confronted today with an unprecedented opportunity. Industrial civilization is now placing in the hands of man the means and the resources through which he might truly be the architect of his destiny. If man had faith in himself and his powers when he was feeble, how much more reason there is for such faith today. With informed resolution he should be able to build a world without material poverty and misery, without disease and frustration. He might even be able to build a world of great beauty and grandeur in which would dwell boys and girls and men and women, finely formed in body, mind, and character, heirs of all that is best in the human legacy. He could do these things, and very much more, if he could but learn to love his neighbor as himself. In spite of the many obstacles which he faces in the coming years, in spite of the recrudescence of barbarism in so many places, industrial civilization should provide a congenial soil for the growth of humanistic ideals and the resources for their fulfillment.

16

SCIENCE AND SCIENTIFIC METHOD

1

Science is the greatest single force moving in and shaping the modern age.
Indeed, without it the modern age, as we understand it, could never have appeared. Perhaps the most profound expression of the humanistic spirit, it has marched from victory to victory during the past four centuries. No adversary, meeting it on its own grounds, has been able to prevail against it. As we have emphasized repeatedly in the present volume, it has already affected in some measure every aspect of our civilization, from the manufacture of shoes to the interpretation of the universe and from the raising of sugar beets to the conception of the origin and destiny of man. Essentially a product of Europe and the Mediterranean Basin, science enabled the peoples possessing it to extend their hegemony over all the continents.

In spite of opposition and persecution from powerful quarters for many generations, science has established itself firmly in many countries and is spreading swiftly to the uttermost parts of the earth. That it will continue on its way in the years and decades ahead must be definitely assumed, unless man himself fails to survive the present crisis or is forced by some universal catastrophe to return to a barbaric state. The human race, in a very literal sense, has become parasitic upon it. If science in all of its forms and relations were to be destroyed and forgotten, civilization as we know it would collapse and the population of the earth would be greatly impoverished and probably reduced by scores of millions within a few years.

During the past two hundred years science has become deeply rooted in America. The time of the settlement, the conditions of life here, the vast material riches of the country, the experimental temper of the people, and the outlook of some of the most influential founders of the Republic were peculiarly favorable to its development, particularly in its more practical aspects. So widely has it permeated our civilization and so impressive have been its triumphs that the very word "science" or "scientific" has come to carry great prestige and authority. Also it has perhaps influenced positively the higher levels of philosophic thought more profoundly in America than in any other country. This is not to say that science has been welcomed into all spheres of life. The contrary, as we have stressed again and again, is emphatically the case. Into whatever area of experience it has penetrated, it has always been opposed at the outset by the power of vested interests and of inherited ways of living, feeling, and thinking. During these recent years of social upheaval and crisis, some have professed to trace the troubles of the age solely to science and have suggested that a moratorium be declared on scientific inquiry. But such proposals are not to be taken seriously. Barring the spread of the totalitarian state, science is here to stay.

2

Science is an instrument of prediction and control.
From earliest times man everywhere has sought to foresee the consequences of his actions and to control the environment for the purpose of satisfying his desires. He has endeavored to survive, to procure food and shelter, to repel and overcome enemies, to ward off and cure diseases, and generally to make life more secure, pleasing, and meaningful. In this perpetual quest for sur-

vival and mastery he has followed many roads and resorted to many devices. He has postulated a world of spirits, of gods and angels, of demons, ghosts, and fairies, which could be persuaded by supplication, cajolery, or coercion to alter the course of natural events in his favor. Toward the same end he has developed and practiced innumerable magical arts founded, as he falsely imagined, on knowledge of the hidden forces and relations of nature. Down through the ages he has looked for control of his environment to astrology and alchemy, sorcery and witchcraft, clairvoyance and demonolatry, necromancy and incantation. Such bodies of practice and thought, though generally founded on error, he has always guarded with care and endeavored to transmit faithfully to each succeeding generation.

Science as an instrument of control stands in this long tradition. But in common with the humanistic spirit, it proclaims that only through the development and discipline of his own powers can man master his earthly home and shape his destiny, perfect both himself and his institutions. It assumes that man himself must be the source of whatever degree of salvation he is to enjoy in this world, that such salvation is to be gained, not by supplications addressed to supernatural forces or by the practice of magical arts, but rather by the rigorous application of his mind to the correction of error and the unraveling of the mysteries of nature. Science rests on the assumption that precise and dependable knowledge of the world is both possible and desirable, and that it is desirable, not only because it satisfies man's curiosity and enlarges his intellectual horizons, but also because it gives him power, control, and freedom. "Science," writes Benjamin Ginzburg, "may be defined as a far flung system of knowledge couched in terms which allow it to serve as a theoretical basis for practical technique."[1] It is the mightiest of all the tools that man has devised for the mastery of his environment. Its unrivaled power is revealed in the swift advance and the fabulous energies of industrial civilization.

[1] Benjamin Ginzburg, "Science," in *The Encyclopaedia of the Social Sciences* (New York, 1934), Vol. XIII, p. 591.

Man's long struggle to emancipate himself from error in his relations with his natural environment constitutes one of the most glorious achievements of the race—a struggle that still continues and doubtless will continue as long as the world stands. The beginnings of the evolution of science in the Mediterranean Basin may be traced to the mathematical achievements of the ancient Babylonians and Egyptians. Building on these foundations the Greeks perfected geometry as a rational and positive system and outlined a vast program for the development and organization of knowledge. They also contributed much to the launching of the philosophical tradition of the West on which the whole scientific enterprise rests. Breaking through the mists of mythology they liberated the human spirit from the trammels of the folkways and turned inquiring minds to a sober and eager study of the nature of things. Yet in spite of their extraordinary achievements their work was largely theoretical, speculative, and contemplative. They were little concerned with the use of knowledge to predict and control the course of natural phenomena. Nor, probably because of an aristocratical contempt for practical affairs, did they develop the instruments and techniques necessary for the collection of data and the verification of their findings. It remained for the men of the Renaissance to achieve that union of theory and practice, of mathematics and engineering, which is essential for scientific advance.

Science is knowledge, and knowledge is power. But science is far more than knowledge. In its essence it is a method of obtaining knowledge about the world of nature and man—the only truly reliable method man has ever discovered or devised. Yet, although the development of the method dates practically from the opening of the modern age, it is by no means wholly novel and strange. It has been defined as the "method of organized and critical common sense"—the kind of sense the farmer and the craftsman have always used in the successful pursuit of their callings, the kind of sense even the primitive hunter or trapper employed in the capture and dressing of his game.

Although the method of science is not easy to define, since it assumes different concrete forms in different realms and is always subject to growth and refinement, it is not difficult to understand, if broadly conceived. In a word, it is the method of intelligence. It is any method of inquiry by which dependable and ordered knowledge is acquired. According to Pasteur, it involves "systematic observation, experiment, and reasoning." The scientist commonly begins with an idea, a hypothesis, a theory, or perhaps a hunch which grows out of previous experience, knowledge, and thought. This idea, hypothesis, theory, or hunch is tested by a process of organized, accurate, and adequate observation, without prejudice or chicanery, of relevant phenomena. In the process of observation, which is supreme in all scientific work, the most precise instruments available, whether physical or intellectual, are employed. The perfecting of such instruments constitutes one of the most crucial conditions of scientific advance. Where possible the method of the controlled experiment is used. Eventually the data are assembled, correlated, and interpreted, and the idea, hypothesis, theory, or hunch, regardless of the weight of tradition, the authority of great names, or the power of vested interests, stands or falls on the basis of observed and measured fact. Here is one of the supreme achievements of the human mind. "For good or evil," according to Bertrand Russell, it is this method with its fruits that "makes our age different from antiquity and the medieval centuries."[2]

As mere instrument of human purpose, science is nonmoral. Our generation knows to its sorrow and shame that this god-like power may be made to serve any purpose whatsoever, whether good or evil. It may be the handmaiden of the "four horsemen of the apocalypse." It may be directed toward either bringing a more abundant life to all mankind or spreading war, famine, pestilence, and death throughout the earth. It may be directed toward either the curing or the propagation of disease, toward either the prolonging or the

[2] Bertrand Russell, "Nature and Origin of Scientific Method," in Lord Layton, Ed., *The Western Tradition* (London, 1949), p. 23.

shortening of life, toward either the relief or the increase of suffering, toward either the eradication or the cultivation of prejudice and hatred. The totalitarian states have employed it to break the will of alleged political dissenters and extract false and absurd confessions of guilt. It is a sad and disturbing commentary on our civilization that in the twentieth century of the Christian era our knowledge of nuclear physics first took practical form in an atomic bomb dropped on a relatively defenseless city. Responsibility for this act, to be sure, rests not on the scientists who boldly and selflessly carried their explorations to the very heart of the material universe, but rather on the controlling purposes of the great states of the world in the summer of 1945.

3

Science is a molder and bearer of values.
Science is certainly an instrument, the most powerful ever fashioned by man. But it is more than an instrument, or it would not have been included in this section on values. The development of science has both strengthened old values and brought new values into the world.

The commitment to science is therefore a great one, greater by far than most of us realize. It has modified profoundly man's conception of and his relation to the universe, not only by its discoveries but also by its emphases. In conformity with the spirit of the modern age, which it has done much to shape, science brings the existential world of time and space and matter into the focus of attention. It makes this world the sphere of its interest and the scene of its operations. It assumes that the study of the world in which man lives and dies, the world of physical nature and human society, is worthy of the greatest talents. It thus tends to turn the human mind away from speculation about and absorption in a world beyond the grave. And in so far as it is the exclusive property of an oligarchy, a class, a nation, or any minority of the human race it may tend, in Lord Acton's phrase, to corrupt its possessors and nurture in them a sense of arrogance and moral irresponsibility. Who can say that the Western peoples who developed it were not thereby corrupted in their relations with the rest of mankind?

Science, like art and philosophy, satisfies a deep craving of the human heart—the simple desire to know and understand, to look beneath the event and to explore the region beyond the horizon, to banish the veil of ignorance and fathom the mysteries of life. In the course of a few centuries an incredibly small number of men and women of genius, responding to this primal intellectual urge and employing the methods and instruments of science, tools of their own devising, have measured the heavens and recorded the birth of stars, penetrated to the innermost citadel of matter and unlocked the secrets of the atom, examined the strata of the earth and reconstructed the history of living things. Also they have formulated the laws of heredity, dug into the ruins of buried cities, studied the relics of the most distant human past, perused the documents of recorded history, mastered the symbols of forgotten languages, and painted an increasingly trustworthy picture of man's entire adventure on the earth. The story of this disinterested quest for knowledge and scrupulous rejection of error is one of the most glorious chapters in the history of the race. It clothes the human spirit with dignity, beauty, and majesty. It should give man confidence as he faces the conditions and problems of these troubled times.

Science, moreover, has developed a great moral tradition of its own. As we have already noted, the scientist in his researches must follow a rigorous and austere code. He must practice the intellectual virtues of accuracy, precision, truthfulness, open-mindedness, and absolute integrity. If he is ignorant of the work of his colleagues, if he is careless in the keeping of his records, if he permits the passions of partisanship to influence his operations, if he allows his hopes and fears to warp either his observations or his generalizations, if he tempers his conclusions to appease the wrath of either constituted or unconstituted authorities, if he clings to an untenable hypothesis in the face of contrary evidence, if he conceals from his colleagues or from the public relevant facts concerning either his method or his findings—in a word, if he allows himself to be controlled by any consideration except the disinterested and skillful pursuit and promulgation of truth, he is not a scientist. "One of the greatest benefits that science confers upon those who understand its spirit," writes Bertrand Russell, "is that it enables them to live without the delusive support of subjective certainty. That is why science cannot favor persecution."[3] Clearly this moral tradition, purchased at the cost of the blood and anguish of uncounted martyrs to the cause of truth since the death of Socrates and before, matches in social significance both the theoretical and practical achievements of science. It is one of the most precious traditions of mankind.

4

Science should penetrate increasingly all areas of life.
Although we often speak of the present age as the age of science, there are many spheres of activity and interest in which it is not welcome. From the very beginning of its modern career, its advance and spread have been bitterly resisted by vested interests and the forces of inherited ways. Today, outside the "iron curtain," the battle seems to be over for the most part in the physical and biological realms, but in the sphere of social institutions and human relations, in the sphere of economics, politics, and morals, the opposition continues. Many of the troubles, many of the conflicts and maladjustments of the epoch undoubtedly flow in some measure from this dichotomy in our civilization. They also flow from simple ignorance, the kind of ignorance that science can help to dispel. Instead of less science, as some contend, we are in need of far more

[3] Bertrand Russell, *The Impact of Science on Society* (New York, 1951), p. 58.

of it. Its method, morality, and spirit should be made general in our society.

A bold and comprehensive attack with all the resources of the scientific tradition on the major problems confronting mankind today should at least serve to point the way to a happier world, even though the peoples of the earth and their leaders should choose not to follow it. Let us list a few of the most urgent and crucial of these problems. What are the foundations of political liberty in the industrial age? Are economic security and political liberty essentially incompatible, or may the one be related positively in some fashion to the other? What is the source of the strength of totalitarian movements in general and of Soviet Communism in particular in the contemporary world? What are the respective roles of individual frustration, institutional maladjustment, and ineradicable drives for personal aggrandizement in the aggressions of classes and peoples? Can diversity of cultures and moral systems be maintained in an age of instantaneous point-to-point communication and of rocket planes capable of circling the globe in a few hours? What are the most effective methods of rooting out ancient prejudices and hatreds which were formed in preceding centuries and which now form powerful barriers to understanding and cooperation? How can the influence of propaganda conducted by power groups within a nation or by despotic governments among the nations be overcome? What are the sources and conditions of political corruption in our democracy, and how can they be eradicated? What are the necessary foundations for the establishment of a just and durable peace on the earth? How can the creative energies of a people be most fully developed for the common good? By what means and processes can the essential features of our complex and dynamic industrial society be made intelligible to the ordinary citizen? What are the conditions governing the growth and decay of civilization? Here are a few of the problems of contemporary man which the methods of science might serve to illuminate and assist in solution.

The need for the service of science in the field of public affairs is urgent. In the shaping of policy in local, state, national, and even international matters the findings and methods of science should be systematically employed to the fullest possible extent. To fail to move vigorously in this direction is to favor darkness rather than light. Equally important is the systematic cultivation in the entire population of the mentality, the methods of inquiry, and the virtues of the scientist. This is particularly desirable in the sphere of political activity. Indeed, amid the complexities of industrial society the successful conduct of the entire democratic process must depend increasingly on the measure of intellectual honesty and integrity practiced by all the citizens. Without such virtues a people can scarcely hope to maintain the democratic way of life through the generations.

These observations apply with peculiar force to our conduct of the political struggle. Not infrequently in local, state, and national campaigns for public office each candidate or party lies unconscionably about the other. To our discredit we seem to have progressed but little, if any, during the past century in this domain. The following description by Francis Lieber in 1835 of a "closely contested election" reads very much like an account of the election in New York State and in other parts of the country in the autumn of 1950:

I have stood on the evening of the 18th on the battle-field of Waterloo, when, as one of my company said, "the fun was o'er," and made my Hamlet contemplations, which forced themselves even on the mind of a lad; but nothing equals, I think, a morning after a closely contested election in a populous city. Rise early on the morning after and walk through the quiet streets. Walls and corners are yet covered with flaming hand-bills, witnesses and documents of the high-running excitement, which but yesterday seemed to roll like an agitated sea. You are told in large capitals that if the candidates of the other ticket are elected, the commonweal needs must perish; our liberty, happiness, national honour are lost: close by, sticks another huge paper, which declares, in equally measured terms, that the opposite side is composed of a set of Catilinas at least, a nest of designing demagogues, corrupt, sold, and panting for the people's money. They tell you that orphans and widows, whose money has been squandered away, call upon you to vote against the opposite candidate; they warn you to look well at your ticket before you throw it into the ballot-box, because spurious ones have been circulated by their opponents, to whom all means appear fair.[4]

Let us hope that our streets will always be quiet after an election, even though the issues reach to the very roots of our society. But is this hope sufficient justification for periodical indulgence in extravagant falsification in the name of the exercise of our "democratic liberties"? Moreover, we should realize today that the searchlights of the whole world beat upon us, and that whatever we do will be employed to judge the operation of democratic institutions. The foreign observer, witnessing our recent elections and subsequent Congressional investigations, might be justified in concluding that American politics is literally a sea of betrayal and corruption, that no loyal and honest man or woman ever runs for public office, and that perhaps there are no loyal and honest men or women in the whole of the United States, outside prison walls! We might profitably seek to apply Cicero's motto: "We who search for hypotheses are prepared both to refute without prejudice and to be refuted without resentment." At any rate a dash of the scientific spirit should improve our political brew.

5

The free development of science stands in great peril in the world today.

Freedom of inquiry, publication, and discussion is the lifeblood of scientific advance. Without such freedom the scientist is crippled and science loses its essential quality. Until recently the area of freedom was being steadily extended and the tradition of freedom strengthened from generation to generation. In those halcyon days before the First World War released the forces of violence and dictator-

[4] Francis Lieber, *The Stranger in America* (London, 1835), Vol. I, pp. 25–26.

ship it was generally assumed that this development would continue without interruption in the coming years. Now the perspectives of the future have been profoundly darkened. The dramatic and conclusive demonstration of the power of science in practical life and the waging of war during the intervening decades, and particularly since Hiroshima and Nagasaki, have aroused the desire to possess and control it on the part of every ambitious interest or group in the world. Today science is increasingly in chains over a large part of the earth. The problem here is one of the first magnitude.

The greatest threat to the morality and spirit of science is found in the totalitarian states and movements. Here control is carried to the point of compelling scientists, not only to hold findings in secret, but also to fabricate data for the support of the doctrines and policies of dictatorship. The Nazis burnt the books of Jewish scholars and forced their anthropologists to demonstrate the unqualified superiority of the Nordic "race" over all others. The Russian Communists, while making "science" a sacred word and devoting vast sums to research, require their scholars to make their findings conform to the tenets of their state religion, dialectical materialism, Marxism-Leninism-Stalinism, or the "science of the sciences," as it is variously called. In August, 1948, the Central Committee of the Party entered the realm of genetics, condemned "bourgeois science," and established "truth" by political fiat. Thereafter the free world witnessed the almost forgotten spectacle of distinguished scientists abjuring their errors, confessing their sins, suffering disgrace, losing their posts, and thanking the Party and "their great leader and teacher, the greatest scientist of the epoch, Comrade Stalin" for their loving care. Also we hear of "patriotic science," of scientists whose first loyalty is to the "powerful socialist Motherland." The conception of a science that knows neither class nor national boundaries is being relegated to the "bourgeois" past. The triumph of the doctrine that inquiry should be dedicated to the support of Party dogma and state interest constitutes the complete degradation of science and the human spirit.

This threat to science is also apparent in our own democracy. For reasons of national security in the present bitterly divided world, which can be readily understood, we have seen our government organize in secret vast scientific operations directed toward the waging of war and the development of military strength. We have seen American scientists and scientific workers betray their country and sell or give the closely guarded results of research to agents of the Soviet Union, not out of devotion to the advancement of universal science, but rather because of their commitment to Russian Communism. We have seen the development of espionage and counterespionage systems to protect or to steal the advances of an adversary in the realm of military science and technology. This entire situation has tended to generate a widespread sense of insecurity and anxiety which can be easily exploited by political adventurers and scoundrels. It would be one of the supreme ironies of history if the development of science should serve to create world tensions which would destroy science itself.

Apparently, the great conquests of science have confronted mankind with a problem of the most crucial and pressing importance. The very survival of civilization is clearly involved. It is the problem of the ends which scientific knowledge is to serve. The recent war and its aftermath put the issue in its most striking and terrifying form. Either man will learn to hold in leash his savage appetites and passions, or science will become the servant of these appetites and passions. Perhaps the scientific method, if boldly and imaginatively applied, might help to illuminate the problem. That method, moreover, obviously could not survive indefinitely the destruction of the moral supports characteristic of and essential to a highly civilized mode of life. It can attain full maturity only in a society that values, guards, and nourishes the great tradition of intellectual freedom. Today this means a world society, or at least an international order capable of moderating the tensions that now mark the relations of nations. Indeed it means a world from which war has been banished forever.

6

Science does not embrace the whole of human experience.
In conclusion the point should be emphasized that science is something less than a philosophy of life, of history, and of civilization. Although there is perhaps no realm of experience to which the scientific method cannot be fruitfully applied, it can never usurp the functions of art, ethics, religion, and politics. In a broad sense both science and scientists are subject to the moral law. This much we have learned during the past century, since those now almost forgotten days when the early devotees of science saw the gates of the kingdom of God swinging open at their magical touch. To be sure, we may still be confident that those gates will not swing open on the earth for the great masses of mankind without the assistance of science. But science alone is not enough. This truth is clearly presented in the following statement by Albert Einstein regarding the relation between knowledge and value:

It is true that convictions can best be supported with experience and clear thinking. On this point one must agree unreservedly with the extreme rationalist. The weak point of his conception is, however, this, that those convictions which are necessary and determinant for our conduct and judgments, cannot be found solely along this solid scientific way.

For the scientific method can teach us nothing else beyond how facts are related to, and conditioned by, each other. The aspiration toward such objective knowledge belongs to the highest of which man is capable, and you will certainly not suspect me of wishing to belittle the achievements and the heroic efforts of man in this sphere. Yet it is equally clear that knowledge of what *is* does not open the door directly to what *should be*. One can have the clearest and most complete knowledge of what *is*, and yet not be able to deduct from that what should be the *goal* of our human aspirations. Objective knowledge provides us with powerful instruments for the achievements of certain ends, but the ultimate goal itself and the longing to reach it must come from another source. And it is hardly necessary to argue for the view that our existence and our activity acquire meaning only by the setting up of such a goal and of corresponding values. The knowledge of truth as such is wonderful, but it is so little capable of acting as a guide that it cannot prove even the justification and the value of the aspiration towards that very knowledge of truth.[5]

Science is the most powerful instrument man has devised for the realization of his purposes. It also rests upon and nurtures a precious moral tradition of its own. But the achievement of the good life and the good society requires that it be disciplined by and integrated with the other great values of our civilization.

[5] Department of Research and Education, Federal Council of the Churches of Christ in America, *Information Service* (New York, 1939), Vol. XVIII, No. 22.

17

THE RULE OF LAW

1

The rule of law is one of the supreme achievements of Western man.

If by some strange psychological cataclysm we were to lose our entire heritage of law with its associated habits, knowledges, and attitudes, its institutions and philosophical conceptions, our political system and way of life would pass into swift dissolution. The rule of law, says Sir Ernest Barker, is *"the* foundation of foundations" of the Western political tradition.[1] Without it the political history of Europe would have no special significance.

Men who live under the rule of law commonly have little appreciation of its worth and accept it uncritically as a part of the order of nature. Only when it is interrupted or destroyed in some great social convulsion and the individual is confronted on all sides by the rule of unrestrained caprice and naked force do men fully sense its meaning and value. "Where you have the rule of law," Barker continues, "the individual knows where he is; he knows where he is to-day, and where he will be to-morrow; he lives a life, if a word may be used which is not in the Oxford English Dictionary, of expectability."[2] In like vein R. M. MacIver speaks of "the firmament of law" as a "primary condition of human life at every level." "Without law there is no order," he declares, "and without order men are lost, not knowing where they go, not knowing what they do."[3]

---
[1] Ernest Barker, "The Nature and Origins of the Western Political Tradition," in Lord Layton, Ed., *The Western Tradition* (London, 1949), p. 30.
[2] *Ibid.*
[3] R. M. MacIver, *The Web of Government* (New York, 1947), p. 61.

The term is being used here, however, in a somewhat restricted sense. The firmament of law, according to MacIver, embraces a complex gradation of practices or elements from custom through common law to statute law. Although historically the origin of law is found in custom, and although the great "lawgivers" of antiquity, such as Hammurabi, Menes, Moses, and Manu, Lycurgus, Diocles, Solon, and the authors of the Twelve Tables, probably did little more than codify custom and inscribe the results on wood, stone, or bronze, the emergence of the *idea* of law marked a new epoch in the political evolution of mankind. Law is to be distinguished from "religion, morals, and custom," writes William Seagle, as a "mode of regulating conduct by means of sanctions imposed by politically organized society."[4] It is in this sense that the term is being used in these pages.

The establishment of the principle of the rule of law in the Western World is a product of centuries and millennia of suffering and struggle, of invention and thought. And in this realm, as in the spheres of the humanistic spirit and scientific method, we are indebted beyond measure to the ancient Greeks and Romans. As human society moved out of the tribal state with its rule of custom, it was the Greeks who laid the foundations for the achievement of order, unity, and freedom through the instrumentality of law. In sharp contrast the great empires of the East, having no interest in freedom, sought order and unity by subjecting all men to the despotic will and by establishing a vast bureaucratic system for administering the affairs of the realm. Yet with all their brilliance and daring the Greeks proved incapable of extending the rule of law beyond the narrow physical boundaries of a single city-state.

If the Greeks were the bold explorers and pioneers in this new world of law, then the Romans were the architects and builders whose practical genius and enterprise bequeathed to all subsequent generations a towering structure of solid achievement. Their accomplishments during the thousand years from the Twelve Tables to the Code of Justinian stand

[4] William Seagle, *The Quest for Law* (New York, 1941), p. 7.

The Rule of Law 261

unsurpassed in the political history of mankind. They surmounted the boundaries of the city-state, extended the benefits of Roman citizenship to diverse and distant peoples, and demonstrated the possibility of a universal rule of law. They gave to the lives of the inhabitants of a large and populous part of the earth that quality of "expectability" of which Sir Ernest Barker speaks. Although they failed, as did the Greeks, in bringing government and public officials fully under the rule of law, they established an ideal that was destined to inspire those who came after them, even down to this day. "During the long centuries of chaos and impoverishment that followed the collapse of Rome," writes Frederick Watkins, "men never forgot the golden age of peace and prosperity when the whole civilized world had submitted to a common rule of law."[5]

2

The rule of law achieves its highest expression in the sovereignty of the Constitution.

A constitution is of course law, the most fundamental, the most enduring form of law. It has been called the "law of laws," the law by which laws are made and judged, the law which governs the governors, whether peoples, classes, or monarchs. It establishes the frame of government, fixes the power and scope of legislation, and defines the whole process of rule. It represents in its provisions not only the prevailing equilibrium of political forces, but also the deepest essence of the political sense and wisdom of the articulate and effective elements of a people. Thus the development of constitutionalism may be regarded as man's boldest and most imaginative attempt to bring order and stability into the conduct and administration of human affairs, and not just for a brief season but for generations and centuries. Charles A. Beard, one of our foremost students of

[5] Frederick Watkins, *The Political Tradition of the West* (Cambridge, 1948), p. 29.

political institutions, once expressed the view that "constitutionalism represents the highest type of government."[6]

The origins of constitutionalism can of course be traced back to the lawgivers, statesmen, and philosophers of antiquity. Yet, even the Romans, as we have noted, never succeeded in bringing government and public officials completely under the rule of law. It seems to have been the Christian fathers and the medieval church that first laid the moral and philosophical foundations of constitutionalism. They nourished the tradition that might is subject to right, that lords and kings should obey the divine law, that the individual may appeal to church and conscience against the commands of the state. Henry IV, mighty emperor of the Holy Roman Empire, went to Canossa in 1077! Without entering into the merits of this and other struggles between popes and kings, we can readily see that for centuries the church served as a check on the power of the secular authorities.

The triumph of the constitutional idea, however, came after the decline and disintegration of the medieval system and following an experience of several centuries with the absolute state. And if it was the Greeks and Romans who established the idea of the rule of law in the Western World, it was the English-speaking peoples who were mainly responsible for the growth of constitutionalism. When Gladstone declared that "the British Constitution is the most subtle organism which has proceeded from the womb and the long gestation of progressive history" and that "the American Constitution is . . . the most wonderful work ever struck off at a given time by the brain and purpose of man," he was doubtless indulging in a form of rhetorical license and proving that "blood is thicker than water."[7]

Yet the role of these two peoples in demonstrating the practicability of constitutional government can scarcely be exaggerated. And without minimizing in the slightest the

---

[6] Charles A. Beard, *The Republic* (New York, 1943), p. 24.
[7] William E. Gladstone, "Kin Beyond Sea," *North American Review*, Vol. 127, September, 1878, p. 185.

unique and long-sustained record of the British, we may emphasize quite appropriately in this volume the contribution and heritage of our own people. Building on the achievements of the mother country and guided by almost two centuries of experience in the New World, we flatly rejected the prevailing view of many eighteenth century leaders of thought that an "enlightened despotism" is the most desirable form of government. The decision of the founding fathers thus to "fly in the face of the teachings of history" and to establish government on a body of written law must have seemed foolhardy in the extreme to most of the philosophers and statesmen of the Old World. According to Charles A. Beard, "leaders among the framers of the Constitution regarded the resort to constitutional government instead of a military dictatorship as their greatest triumph."[8] "In my opinion," the great historian adds, "they were entitled to view their achievement in that way." The major credit for this accomplishment should obviously go to the man who beat back pressures from powerful sources favoring the establishment of a monarchy and steadfastly maintained his faith in the rule of law and the wisdom of the people—George Washington.

The Constitutional Convention of 1787 proved to be a milestone in political history. The example set there was followed, often to be sure without striking success, by many other countries in all parts of the world. "The rise of constitutionalism," writes Walton H. Hamilton, "may be dated from 1776." Then pointing to the great French Revolution this student of government observes that during the next century and a half "a count of instruments in which peoples have embodied their faith runs into the hundreds."[9] The fact that the Federal Constitution has survived these five generations is powerful testimony to the wisdom of its architects and to the political genius of the American people. But this record probably would not have been established in the ab-

---
[8] Beard, *op. cit.*, p. 21.
[9] Walton H. Hamilton, "Constitutionalism," in *Encyclopaedia of the Social Sciences* (New York, 1931), Vol. IV, p. 255.

sence of what has been called "America's unique contribution to the art of government"—"the institution of judicial review."[10] The independent judiciary, clothed with authority to declare unconstitutional and therefore null and void acts of legislatures and executives, is a powerful safeguard of the rights and liberties guaranteed to the people in the Constitution.

3

The Constitution brings government and public officials under the rule of law.

The problem of limiting the power of the state has been a central problem of liberal and humane statecraft ever since the dissolution of tribal society in which ruler and ruled alike were subject to the sway of "immemorial custom." The task confronting mankind is that of steering a steady course between the Scylla of anarchy and the Charybdis of despotism. On the one hand, if a society is to endure, sufficient power must be concentrated in the state to "establish justice, insure domestic tranquillity," and "provide for the common defense." On the other hand, if the individual is to enjoy even a modicum of security and freedom from the arbitrary actions of the agents of government, some limitation must be placed on the exercise of state power. The resolution of this dilemma is made difficult by the fact that power always tends to feed on itself and to move into every vacuum. As William Manning, the unschooled eighteenth century farmer and sage of Billerica, wrote in 1798: "Give a man honour & he wants more. Give him power & he wants more. Give him money & he wants more. In short he is neaver easy, but the more he has the more he wants."[11]

Our Federal Constitution represents an effort, certainly one of the most successful in history, to resolve this dilemma. By clearly defining the powers of government it established a government of limited powers. By distributing powers

[10] William Seagle, *Men of Law* (New York, 1947), p. 269.
[11] William Manning, *The Key of Libberty* (Billerica, Mass., 1922), p. 9.

among the several branches of the national government, by dividing powers between federal and state authorities, and by reserving powers to private persons and interests the founding fathers wrote the principle of limitation into the very structure of government. Thus did they seek to bring executives, legislators, and judges under the rule of law. "Law and arbitrary power," declared Edmund Burke in the impeachment of Warren Hastings, "are in eternal enmity." The writing and adoption of the Constitution proved to be a practical and imaginative attempt to make law triumphant over the exercise of arbitrary power by persons clothed with the authority of the state.

One can be led astray, however, by an uncritical faith in a written constitution. The British people have prospered under a constitution that was never committed to parchment at any particular point in history. And many of the hundreds of constitutions solemnly written and enthusiastically adopted since 1789 proved themselves incapable either of enduring or of keeping arbitrary power under control. The Constitution of the Weimar Republic was often characterized in the nineteen-twenties as a product of the most advanced political thought, formally superior in many respects to the constitutions of the preceding century and a half. Yet it failed to halt the rise of despotism and the establishment of a dictatorship in Germany by "constitutional" means. In divers countries governments resting on excellent written constitutions have been overthrown periodically by strong and ambitious men. It would appear that something more than a constitution is required. Laws, however wise and just, do not enforce themselves.

Even under the best of constitutions there will come times of crisis when vast power—power sufficient to destroy the law—will be lodged in the hands of a few men. What is it in these situations that holds power in leash? What is it that persuades the sword to sheathe itself? Such questions are not easily answered. Obviously men who at a given moment have at their command overwhelming military force are scarcely restrained by fear of arrest, imprisonment, and execution for treason. Moreover, few would contend that the ordinary citizen obeys the laws, as he commonly does, as a result of a careful calculation of consequences. He obeys the laws because it is his nature to do so, because his habits are law-abiding, even partly perhaps because he loves the laws.[12]

All of this means that a constitutional system, if it is to endure, must be supported by an appropriate education of the people, as Montesquieu saw clearly more than two centuries ago. "It is in a republican government," he wrote, "that the whole power of education is required." The reason resides in the fact that such a government must rest on "virtue," and virtue, involving "self-renunciation," is "ever arduous and painful." By virtue he means "love of the laws and of our country," a love which "requires a constant preference of public to private interest." To inspire such love "ought to be the principal business of education."[13] Unquestionably we see here one of the necessary supports of the constitutional system. Fundamental also of course are other social institutions and the conditions of life.

Although our American record leaves much to be desired, it is at the same time impressive. To be sure, our conduct of government at local, state, and national levels has been marked by sporadic and sometimes sustained corruption on the part of public officials. All too often persons elected to posts of trust have violated the oath of office, betrayed their constituents, and placed their private interests above the general welfare. Some American states have persistently and flagrantly disregarded constitutional provisions, and in a few instances have permitted the establishment of regimes resembling dictatorships. This cannot be denied. Yet to a degree scarcely expected by the founders the Federal Constitution has endured and guaranteed the rule of law through the generations. Although we have experienced four years of bitter civil struggle in the course of our history, no American president has ever sought to prevent an election by force of

---

[12] See R. M. MacIver, "How and Why Men Obey," *op. cit.*, pp. 73–81.
[13] Charles Louis de Secondat Montesquieu, *The Spirit of Laws* (J. V. Prichard, Ed., London, 1902), Vol. I, pp. 36–37.

arms. Nor has any unsuccessful candidate for the highest office of the land ever appealed to the sword to set aside the verdict of the polls. Neither has any politically ambitious "colonel" or great military commander flush from victory on the battlefield ever attempted to establish himself in the White House by *coup d'état*. This magnificent record augurs well for the future of constitutional government in the United States.

4

The Constitution brings the process of social revolution under the rule of law.
Throughout the period of recorded history human societies have been shaken periodically by more or less profound social convulsions. These convulsions seem to be precipitated by the failure of laws and institutions to keep pace with the advance of knowledge, the emergence of new social forces, and the spread of new hopes, ideals, and conceptions of life among underprivileged elements and classes of the population. "Laws and institutions," wrote Thomas Jefferson to a friend in 1816, "must go hand in hand with the progress of the human mind." It was the failure of the monarchs of the Old World to recognize this fact that, in his opinion, "deluged Europe in blood" in his time. "Instead of wisely yielding to the gradual change of circumstances, of favoring progressive accommodation to progressive improvement," they had "clung to old abuses, entrenched themselves behind steady habits, and obliged their subjects to seek through blood and violence rash and ruinous innovations, which, had they been referred to the peaceful deliberations and collected wisdom of the nation, would have been put into acceptable and salutary forms."[14]

Clearly, if there is an "American way of life," its essence is to be found in the attempt to bring social change and even revolution under the rule of law. Here is one of the foremost

[14] H. A. Washington, *The Writings of Thomas Jefferson* (Washington, 1853–54), Vol. VII, p. 14.

purposes of the Constitution. The founders of the Republic recognized change as one of the ineluctable facts of history. Indeed, many of them, in the spirit of Jefferson, welcomed change and saw in change the promise of an ever-improving social order and of the indefinite perfectibility of man and his institutions. The Constitution legalizes the political struggle and endeavors to direct that struggle through peaceful channels by means of the ballot and majority rule. Thus it makes possible the most profound institutional changes, even changes in the system of property relationships, without appeal to the sword. And through a process of amendment it opens the way to the gradual modification of its own provisions. Charles A. Beard was fond of saying that the American people could achieve through the Constitution any changes which they really desired.

In their constitutional system the American people reject all conceptions of the absolute state, whether idealistic or materialistic, Hegelian or Marxist, Fascist or Communist. On the one hand, they reject the doctrine that the state is above the people and that rulers are responsible only to God or to royal conscience. On the other hand, they reject with equal vigor the doctrine that the state, with all of its powers and institutions, is the faithful instrument of some assumed ruling or master class, that it is the "supreme coercive force" in society serving without qualification the interests of that class, and that "legality" is a fiction designed to becloud the minds and make easy the exploitation of the masses. It rejects also the corollary of this doctrine: that a privileged class will never surrender its privileges without resort to naked violence and civil strife, that all social systems therefore must enter and depart the world in flame, blood, and dictatorship. Here is one of the cardinal elements of our American political faith.

Many wonder today whether this faith is justified, whether the constitutional system will prove capable of carrying us through the critical years and decades ahead, whether it can survive in a world marked by violent revolution and the aggressions of powerful totalitarian ideas and movements. Almost a generation ago Lord Balfour raised this question in relation to the British constitution. "Could it long survive the shocks of revolutionary and counter-revolutionary violence?" he asked, and then proceeded to answer: "I know not. The experiment has never been tried."[15] In order to sense the values at stake the American people would do well to review periodically the terrible events of a century ago. Those events were described in 1897 with simplicity and power in approximately one hundred words by James G. Ireland, a farmer who lived through the Civil War in the border state of Kentucky:

All was peace, good will, and prosperity; and then alas! came the war—the cruel bloody war, the third war of my recollection, and the worst of all—fratricidal war, in which brother was against brother, son opposed father, neighbor was suspicious and fearful of neighbor, and the best of friends became deadly enemies; people were afraid to talk, afraid to give an opinion or express a sentiment. Men were afraid to stay at home and afraid to leave home, and no one felt safe or secure in his rights and liberties. For four long years there was anxiety, trouble, and sorrow, and the war ended.[16]

Like Lord Balfour, we cannot draw aside the veil that shrouds the future. Yet we may take hope from the record of more than a century and a half. Except for the Civil War, which was less a revolutionary struggle than a war between states which had not fully surrendered their sovereignty to the federal union, the Constitution has endured terrific strains and borne the burden of tremendous changes. Under its provisions, as amended, the nation has grown from a small outpost on the borders of Western civilization to become the most powerful state in the world. It has extended its sway to the Pacific and to the islands of the western seas, fought several minor and two world wars, absorbed almost forty million immigrants of diverse cultures and races, increased its

[15] Arthur James Balfour, "Introduction" to Walter Bagehot, *The English Constitution* (The World's Classics edition, Oxford, 1928), pp. xxii–xxiv.
[16] From a manuscript in the possession of the author, entitled "Looking Backward Through One Hundred Years" by James G. Ireland.

population almost forty fold, and grown from a loose aggregation of states and rural neighborhoods into a vast and closely knit economic empire producing almost one-half of the industrial products of the world. It has also survived the abolition of the laws of primogeniture and entail and the curbing of the power of property through estate and income taxes. This record furnishes solid grounds for optimism.

5

The Constitution brings individual rights and liberties under the rule of law.

The idea of freedom under law is an essential feature of the political tradition of the Western World. Without it no society can be said to be free. A legacy from the ancient Greeks, it repudiates the view prevailing in most of the societies of history and in many modern states that the good life for the individual is to be found in loyal and unquestioning obedience to a supposedly wise, humane, and enlightened ruler, whether he calls himself Caesar, Great Mogul, or Son of Heaven, Il Duce, Der Fuehrer, or Velikii Vozhd. To be sure, law may serve the purposes of tyranny, but without law there can be no liberty for the masses of mankind. "Political liberty, considered with relation to a citizen," wrote d'Alembert in his "Analysis of the Spirit of Laws," "consists *in that security in which he lives under shelter of the laws.*"[17] The Federal Constitution with its Bill of Rights and its other amendments provides a wide shelter for the individual citizen.

The Constitution guarantees to the citizens freedom of political and civil assembly and association. Without this right the individual cannot participate successfully in the election of public officials and the shaping of the laws. Without this right the Constitution itself could become an instrument of tyranny and the citizen a helpless subject of a tyrant. Noth-

[17] In Montesquieu, *op. cit.*, p. xxxiii.

ing impressed the young Tocqueville during his sojourn in America more than this habit of forming associations—both civil and political. "Americans of all ages, all conditions, and all dispositions," he wrote, "constantly form associations. They have not only commercial and manufacturing companies, in which all take part, but associations of a thousand other kinds,—religious, moral, serious, futile, general or restricted, enormous or diminutive."[18] He saw more clearly than most Americans do today the broad social significance of this phenomenon. "There is only one country on the face of the earth," he added, "where the citizens enjoy unlimited freedom of association for political purposes. This same country is the only one in the world where the continual exercise of the right of association has been introduced into civil life, and where all the advantages which civilization can confer are procured by means of it."[19] He rightly concluded that this relationship is scarcely the "result of accident." And if he were to return and dwell among us today, he would find this ancient habit strengthened rather than weakened with the passage of time. No society that "coordinates" the associations of men and women under state power and endows a single party or faction with a monopoly of legality can be free.

The Constitution guarantees to the citizens freedom of speech, press, and religious worship. If freedom of civil and political association is to be genuine, it must be supported by freedom of expression. And freedom of expression, if it is to have meaning, must mean freedom, within the limits of just laws of libel and slander, to criticize persons and institutions, ideas and policies, laws and public officials, yes, even the president of the Republic, the judges of the Supreme Court, and the foundations of constitutional government. This freedom is based on the faith that in untrammeled discussion truth will triumph over error and the people will know the truth. Although the dimensions and contours of the problem

---

[18] Alexis de Tocqueville, *Democracy in America* (New York, 1898), Vol. II, p. 129.
[19] *Ibid.*, p. 140.

have been changed with the rise of industrial civilization and the development of new forms of communication, the basic principles remain much the same as in the old agrarian days. No society that by the exercise of state power enforces a political or religious orthodoxy on the people through the "coordination" of all the agencies of education and communication can be free.

The Constitution guarantees to the citizens freedom from arbitrary arrest, trial, and imprisonment, and from the infliction of "cruel and unusual punishments." Without this freedom all the other freedoms mean nothing. Without it no citizen would associate freely with his fellows, and only the boldest would speak his deepest thoughts. Without it the great body of citizens would be cowed, if they would not live in a state of perpetual terror. The struggle of the English-speaking peoples over a period of seven centuries to establish this freedom in the basic law is one of the most glorious in the long history of mankind. The wonder is that they ever succeeded. Someone has said that the mark of a free society resides in the fact that when a citizen hears the doorbell ring at five o'clock in the morning he thinks the milkman has arrived. "The Habeas Corpus Act," Lord Macaulay truly said, is "the most stringent curb that ever legislation imposed on tyranny."[20] No society that endows a political police with the power to arrest, judge, and sentence the citizens can be free.

The Constitution guarantees to the citizens freedom of movement, occupation, and property. Within the limits set by legitimate professional qualifications the individual is free to choose his calling and to shift from one occupation to another and from one position to another. The law prohibits the binding of the individual to his job, restriction of travel and residence, imprisonment for debt, and the exaction of forced labor, except as punishment for crime fairly determined by the courts. It also prohibits the levying of tribute and the confiscation of property without due process. The

---

[20] Thomas Babington Macaulay, *History of England* (New York), Vol. II, p. 3.

struggle of men against bondage, serfdom, peonage, and slavery in their many forms has marked the whole history of the race. It continues today over a large part of the earth. As a matter of fact it seems probable that more men and women have been sentenced to forced labor during the last thirty years than in any like period in the past. No society that controls the movement of its citizens by the system of internal passports, prevents free choice and change of occupations, or punishes political dissent with forced labor can be free.

In conclusion the point must be emphasized that the full honoring of the provisions in the constitution and the laws regarding the rights and liberties of the citizen has by no means been achieved. There remains for the American people much unfinished business. In substance the laws may be unexceptionable, but they may not be justly administered. Destitution and cultural privation limit individual opportunity and introduce severe inequalities into the enjoyment of constitutional guarantees. The old adage that "you cannot send a million dollars to jail" has been proved incorrect again and again. Yet it is certainly easier to send poverty than riches to prison. There is more than cynicism in the oft-quoted observation by Anatole France: "The law, in its majestic equality, forbids the rich as well as the poor to sleep under bridges, to beg in the streets, and to steal bread." And the sad plight of certain cultural and racial minorities has been remarked again and again in the present volume. No society that denies to its minorities the full shelter of its laws can be wholly free.

6

The rule of law is being challenged today by the emergence of new conditions and forces.
It is being challenged in many ways by the rise of industrial civilization. It is being challenged at home by the rise of great power groups,

each influenced in its policies and attitudes by narrow and limited conceptions of the general welfare. Reference is made here particularly to the great aggregations of capital, labor, and agriculture. Engaged perpetually in a harsh struggle for advantage, they often lose sight of the common good and press ahead ruthlessly toward their objectives. Through strikes in the realm of essential goods and services, through monopoly control of vital forms of production, through pressure on wages and prices, through preferential legislation, they may win special privileges, create an artificial famine of necessities, or precipitate an economic depression or an inflation spiral that will wipe out the savings of millions and create a general condition of insecurity, misery, and anxiety. Clearly this condition of anarchy can only be corrected by the introduction of the rule of law. Failure to act may bring a condition reported in anguished voice by the President of the Norwegian Seamen's Association and Member of the Executive Council of the Norwegian Federation of Labor in the autumn of 1941, following the conquest of Norway by Nazi forces:

> We who would not or could not create security against fear and famine among the under-privileged, have seen rich and poor alike reduced to a destitution far worse than that of our most wretched slums of yesterday.
> We who squabbled in our own household over ancient prejudices of race or religion and over petty differences of politics or trade, have learned that sectional boundaries can isolate a people to the furious force of Nazi assault and persecution.
> We who saw the class struggle blind capitalist and laborer to the fury of the gathering storm, know now that both lost in their folly far more than either had ever hoped to gain.[21]

The rule of law is being challenged by the struggle among the nations. This problem has become acute in the present age for two reasons. In the first place, as we have often noted in these pages, the advance of technology has reduced the

[21] Ingvald Haugen, address in *Report of the Proceedings of the Sixty-First Annual Convention of the American Federation of Labor* (Washington, 1941), p. 451.

physical earth to the dimensions of a little neighborhood. The extension of the rule of law in some measure to the entire world has therefore become essential to the survival of civilization in its more highly developed forms. In the second place, in spite of the establishment of the League of Nations and the United Nations, there is reason for believing that Western man at least has experienced during the present century a profound reversal of trends toward an international moral and legal order which had been advancing for decades.

Max Beloff, one of our most perceptive scholars, observed that before Sarajevo "nowhere in Europe was it possible to take the same gloomy view of the future that the present generation has come to regard as almost normal" and that "the characteristic of this last period of the old Europe was something which can best be described as the rule of law."[22] This order and its promises were destroyed by the wars, revolutions, and counterrevolutions which have shaken to bits the fabric of international relations of Europe and the world. We have witnessed the rise of states which have "repudiated all law in favor of mere will." In order to realize that something terrifying has appeared in the world one need only recall the arrogant tones of Mussolini addressing his Black Shirts, the raucous voice of Hitler at his rallies in Nuremberg, or the violent language of Soviet spokesmen in the councils of the United Nations and over the air waves of the earth.

The rule of law is being challenged and threatened by the rise of totalitarian movements and states. As suggested above, we see here a complete and exultant repudiation of the essential political tradition of the West. We see the rule of law giving way before the onslaught of a philosophy of violence, dictatorship, and charismatic leadership which was foreshadowed in the utterances of thinkers and revolutionists of the last half of the nineteenth century. Karl Marx and Friedrich Engels called for the "forcible overthrow of all existing social conditions." Michael Bakunin preached a philosophy of "pandestruction" and lyrically championed the "all-destroy-

[22] Max Beloff, "Historians in a Revolutionary Age," in *Foreign Affairs* (New York, January, 1951), Vol. 29, No. 2, p. 254.

ing revolution." "Let us put our trust," he said, "in the eternal spirit which only destroys and annihilates because it is the unsearchable and eternally creative source of all life." Fyodor Dostoevsky saw "Europe on the eve of collapse, of a terrible, universal catastrophe," and had his Grand Inquisitor proclaim: "There is no equality without a tyrant to guarantee it." Friedrich Nietzsche, a prophet of totalitarianism, exalted the "will to power," predicted the "onrush of nihilism," and declared that "man must be like a lion, who says, 'I will!' and tramples to pieces everything that gets in his way." George Sorel, a harbinger of the "gospel without pity," glorified "violence erupting from the primeval cause and creating a new world."

The men of action who followed these men of the book found their ideas good. Lenin declared that "freedom is a bourgeois prejudice" and that "it does not matter if three-quarters of mankind are destroyed," if only "the last quarter should become Communist." To achieve his purposes he established a dictatorship which he defined as "an authority relying directly upon force and not bound by any laws." Mussolini glorified "danger and insecurity," "the heroic life," "the daring deed," and proudly asserted: "I am possessed by the fever of the will; it burns me, wears me down, devours me inwardly like a physical pain. I want to scratch with my will, scratch a mark on the age like a lion with his paw." Hitler, in words reminiscent of Lenin, announced without shame: "I am ready to use any method of cheating and deception if it serves my ends," for to the "extraordinary man," to the "real master," "everything is lawful," "terrorism is indispensable." Such a man, he said, "may even step over a corpse or wade through blood" for his idea.[23]

Stalin says humbly that he is merely the "pupil of the great Lenin," the "continuer of his work." He has doubtless learned much from the father of Bolshevism, but he has also sat at the feet of both Mussolini and Hitler. At any rate, though their words are different, the acts of Communism and

[23] See René Fueloep-Miller, "Dostoevsky's Prophecies," Chapter Seven in *Fyodor Dostoevsky* (New York and London, 1950), pp. 92–130.

Fascism have become more and more alike with the passing of the years. It is true that the Soviets pass many laws, that in 1936 they adopted a constitution which they declare to be the "most democratic in the world." Yet under this "rule of law" the will of Stalin remains absolute. The individual is without protection against the state; he can appeal to no writ of *habeas corpus;* and he must face a judge whose first duty is to find him guilty as charged by the political police. Nowhere in the vast Soviet empire is an independent judiciary to be found.

The struggle against this aggressive despotism, which would obliterate throughout the world the very idea of freedom under law, must be waged with power and without surcease. But it must also be waged with knowledge and wisdom. We must be ever watchful lest in this great struggle we adopt the morals and methods of the adversary. There are many in America who with the best of intentions would destroy the legal foundations of liberty in the name of national security and the defense of liberty—foundations which Western man has built painfully and fitfully since the days of the ancient Greeks. The need for an understanding of the issues involved is urgent. Here is a major task for American education, if freedom under law is not to perish from the earth.

18

THE DEMOCRATIC FAITH

1

Democracy is our American social faith.

Democracy as a word and as an ethical and political conception has an ancient and diverse lineage. Its origins may be traced back to antiquity and its basic ideas, values, and institutions to many nations. Yet in its modern development and future prospects it is perhaps more closely linked to the history and fortunes of our people than to those of any other. Since the time of the founding fathers, rightly or wrongly, we have seen ourselves engaged in a great experiment in popular government which in the course of time would have meaning for all mankind. And millions in the Old World have shared this view.

At the time of the launching of the Republic, to be sure, the term "democracy" was generally in ill repute. The word does not appear in the Federal Constitution. Even Thomas Jefferson rarely used it, although in 1816 he wrote his friend Dupont de Nemours that "we of the United States are constitutionally and conscientiously Democrats." But gradually, and particularly after the age of Jackson, we came to regard ourselves and to be regarded by others as a democracy. Today we commonly consider the democratic idea as the most distinctive and precious quality of our civilization.

This does not mean that the idea has completely routed its many opponents, or that there are no dissenters or scoffers. There are doubtless some of serious temper who would agree with Polybius that democracy is "mob rule," with Seneca that it "is more cruel than wars and tyrants," or with Edmund Burke that it "is the most shameless thing in the world." There are probably others of a cynical turn of mind who would applaud the assertion of Benjamin Disraeli that it is "that fatal drollery called a representative government," of Oscar Wilde that it "means simply the bludgeoning of the people by the people for the people," or of H. L. Mencken that it speciously exalts the common man whose "natural gait is the goose-step." Some, who pride themselves on their "realism," would say that democracy is only a beautiful dream which can never achieve substantial realization on the earth. Others, who have imbibed more or less of Marxian doctrine, loudly proclaim our American democracy a "bourgeois fraud" designed to make the exploitation of the masses as painless as possible. Yet the vast majority of us feel ourselves fully committed in principle to its basic values. When Woodrow Wilson in his "War Address to Congress" on April 2, 1917, declared, "We shall fight for the things which we have always carried nearest our hearts—for democracy," he was speaking the language of his people. Clearly, if we have a social faith, that faith is democracy.

2

Our American conception of democracy embraces many values.

The full and precise meaning of this word which is on the lips of so many millions throughout the world today is a proper subject for analysis and discussion. Democracy is a complex and dynamic conception. It has a long past; it is derived from many sources; it is always in process of change and development; it is responding today to new and strange conditions and challenges. Among the ancient Greeks, as the word itself indicates, democracy meant literally "rule by the people." The Great Emancipator, who to most Americans made the idea flesh in his own person, defined it in the words of John Wycliffe as "government of the people, by the people, and for the people." The Russian dictatorship proclaims the "Soviet democracy" to be "democracy in its highest form" and organizes "people's democratic republics" in the wake of its imperialistic sweep. And as Sidney Hook has observed, "even Hitler, Mussolini, Franco, Salazar, and Peron have made use of the term 'democracy,' with qualifying adjectives like 'higher,' 'directed,' 'organic,' to characterize their regimes!" Obviously, if the word is to have any meaning in the contemporary world, it requires clarification.

From the first our democracy has been a product of the peculiar conditions which have marked the settlement and conquest of the North American continent and the whole course of the development of our civilization. At the same time, as we have emphasized, it owes much to the spiritual heritage which we brought to the New World from the Old. Today it is generally regarded not only as a form of government, which it certainly is, but also as a way of life which embraces elements from all of the great moral commitments of our people outlined in the preceding chapters. It is indebted to the Hebraic-Christian ethic for its conceptions of human brotherhood, personal worth, and equality, to the humanistic spirit for its bold optimism and its faith in human powers, to the rule of law for its emphasis on orderly process and the curbing of arbitrary power, and to the English political tradition for its devotion to individual liberty and its recognition of the right of dissent. With the advance of industrial civilization the question of the relation of democracy to science has entered increasingly into the discussion. While some have maintained that science is neutral with respect to social systems, the position taken here is that it can develop most fully in a free society and that it can contribute mightily to the strengthening of democratic values and practices. Its rational outlook, its experimental temper, its method of inquiry, its opposition to secrecy, and its dedication to the freedom of the mind and the untrammeled pursuit of truth would seem to be essentially democratic in nature. This general conception of our American democracy will be elaborated and made more explicit in a few paragraphs.

The Democratic Faith

First of all, democracy affirms the worth and dignity of the individual. It declares that every human being is precious in his own right and is always to be regarded as an end, never as a means merely. His welfare and full development are the purpose and measure of social institutions, relationships, and doctrines. Democracy repudiates without equivocation the basic principle of all despotisms, whether benevolent or tyrannical, that the individual is a means to either power or glory. It rejects the idea that he can fulfill his nature as a lower creature designed to serve faithfully and cheerfully his "betters," as a commodity to be bought and sold on the labor market, as a pawn in the waging of a war of conquest, as an obedient slave of an authoritarian state, or even as a source of prestige and strength of some ecclesiastical order. Here is the foundation of all humane conceptions of life and probably the ultimate source of the other values of our democratic faith.

Second, democracy declares that in a most profound sense all men are created equal. This declaration flows inevitably from the idea of the worth of the individual. If every individual is uniquely precious, the very foundation of unequal treatment and consideration collapses. Democracy recognizes fully the endless differences in virtue and talent among men, but at the same time affirms the equality of all men before the law and in the moral order. Regardless of class, creed, or color they should have the same rights, liberties, opportunities, and responsibilities. Democracy is thus the social faith of common people. However glorious a civilization may appear to be, however remarkable may be the accomplishments of an aristocracy, however pleasing and gracious may be the life of a privileged class, however flourishing may be the condition of the arts and sciences, if the masses of the people do not share in the good things of a society it cannot be called a democracy. The fundamental weakness of the ancient Athenian republic lay in the fact that it rested on human slavery and was marked by the concentration of power in the hands of a fraction of the population. Democracy rejects any conception of society or human relationships founded on the assumption of the superiority of any race, caste, or order. Equality, if not purely formal and legal, breeds that pervading sense of brotherhood which must characterize any good society. Indeed, it is the only enduring base of justice, mercy, and fraternity among men.

Third, democracy regards political and civil liberty as the only dependable guardian of individual worth and equality. It therefore proclaims a profound faith in the abilities of common people—the people who do the work of the world—provided they have full access to the heritage of knowledge and thought. It declares that in the long run the masses of the people are the best judges of their own interests, that they and they alone can be trusted with both liberty and power, that they can and should manage their common affairs, that, in a word, they can and should rule themselves. This means that all men should participate actively in selecting leaders, in shaping the laws, and in discharging the responsibilities of government—that every man should be free to think and speak, to write and create, to approve and criticize, to assemble and organize, to choose an occupation, to move from place to place, to worship the God of his choice, to follow the dictates of his conscience, to pursue in his own way truth and happiness. Within the framework of democratic principles and loyalties cultural and political minorities should be tolerated, respected, and valued as creative forces in history. A "democratic" one-party state is a self-evident but dangerous fraud. The election of a single slate of candidates for public office by the unanimous verdict of ninety-nine per cent of all the "citizens" is the trademark of unadulterated despotism. The idea of freedom is the ancient, eternal, and implacable foe of totalitarianism and every form of tyranny over the bodies and minds of man.

Fourth, democracy rests on law and orderly process. It places its faith in the methods of enlightenment, persuasion, and peace in the adjustment of differences among men, in the formulation of policies great and small, and even in the transformation of the structure and basic institutions of society. It thus proclaims the most revolutionary political doctrine of all history—the doctrine that the process of revolution itself can be institutionalized and conducted without resort to organized violence and civil war. To fulfill this faith the structure and functions of government must be clearly defined in constitutional provisions, and the entire political process of elections, legislation, administration, and judicial decision must be conducted honestly and efficiently according to rules and procedures freely established by the people under the principle of majority rule. "The *lex majoris partis*," said Thomas Jefferson, "is the fundamental law of every society of individuals of equal rights." If this law is "once disregarded," he continued, the end is necessarily "military despotism." At the same time all individuals and minorities must be protected in their legal rights and liberties against the passion of mobs, the vengeance of party, the power of privilege, the tyranny of secret police, the caprice of officials, and the ambitions of madmen. Law is the indispensable guardian of both justice and freedom. It is one of the glories of our political tradition that, as we have noted, no American president or aspirant for the presidency ever turned to the sword to elevate himself to power.

Fifth, democracy rests on basic morality. It can thrive only if elementary standards of decency and humanity in all public relations and in the conduct of all public affairs are observed. In the political process, if democracy is to endure and prosper, men must be guided by the canons of simple honesty, truthfulness, and intellectual integrity; in the exercise of power they must be just, humane, and merciful. Democracy condemns in principle the doctrinal immorality of totalitarianism, whether Communist or Fascist, which subordinates means to ends and thus justifies as political "realism" the practice of falsehood, hypocrisy, deceit, and slander, of terrorism, deportations, tortures, concentration camps, slave labor, and judicial murders. Without the basic virtues democracy cannot be fully achieved. Indeed, without mutual trust and charity which rest on these virtues society itself must fall into chaos or submit to a regime of brute power.

Sixth, democracy rests on individual opportunity. Historically our democracy grew and flourished in a land of unparalleled opportunity for the common man. If America should ever lose this quality, the very foundations of our freedom would be destroyed. Democracy can live only in a mobile and progressive society in which any man can make his way according to his own talents, inclinations, and beliefs —a society which at the same time makes available to all an abundance of opportunity in work, in health, in education, in social relationships, in human enlightenment, in all the arts and sciences of life. In a word, democracy can thrive only in a society in which security is guaranteed through opportunity. In the present age, therefore, with the old foundations of opportunity profoundly changed, it must strive to insure to every individual through whatever means experience proves necessary and desirable the opportunity to develop himself to his full stature. Without opportunity to grow and to achieve, particularly for the young, the very foundations of loyalty to a society are shattered.

Seventh, democracy rests on individual responsibility. In a free society all men must be disciplined by a sense of common brotherhood, a love of truth and justice, and a devotion to the general welfare. If they employ their liberties merely to further their own selfish interests, if they are callous to wrongs and injustices, if they permit the basic supports of liberty to be destroyed, if they care not how the "other half lives," if they neglect their civic duties, if they are indifferent to the fortunes of the Republic, they will surely sink back into bondage. In the very nature of the case free men must voluntarily give of their substance for the guarding and the promotion of the common weal. If they fail in this supreme obligation, they open the gates to tyranny and dictatorship. Democracy surpasses all other systems in its demands on the time and energy, as well as the virtue and understanding, of the citizen. Individual responsibility is the final test of individual liberty. In the measure that any people fails here it demonstrates its incapacity for self-government and the exercise of political freedom.

3

Our American democracy is challenged as never before in its history.
    It is challenged first of all by fundamental changes in the distribution of power which have marked the rise of industrial civilization. Even as we have moved to extend the rights of suffrage, certain basic forms of power have become highly concentrated. In the agrarian age military force was squarely in the hands of the people. Today, owing to the development of new weapons of war, this condition no longer exists. As a consequence free institutions are everywhere in jeopardy. In our times we have seen democracies overthrown by military power in the possession of armed and disciplined minorities. If any element or class in our industrial society, even a very small class or minority, should succeed in gaining control of these new engines of death— machine guns, tanks, airplanes, and atomic weapons—it could destroy our free institutions within a few hours and render successful popular revolt impossible.

A similar change has taken place in the sphere of economic power. In its origins our democracy rested on a wide distribution of such power in the form of ownership of land and natural resources. Today title to productive property is concentrated largely in a small class and the great masses of our people are dependent on employment to earn their livelihood. Although this tendency has been checked by increasingly heavy taxation, widespread organization of working people, and bold exercise of political rights, the situation remains a serious threat to democratic institutions. When these changes in the sphere of military and economic power are linked with the development of new agencies for molding the mind—the press, the movie, the radio, and television—we can see that the problem of achieving and maintaining popular control of our institutions is far more complex than it was in the days of agrarian civilization. The fact is that the historic power foundations of our democracy have been swept away and new foundations comparable in quality remain to be built.

Our democracy is seriously threatened by the instability of our economy. As we face the future, we should realize that an ominous shadow darkens the horizon. Most of our economists agree that, unless preventive measures are undertaken we shall experience sooner or later an economic recession, depression, or crisis. Regardless of the terminology employed, if it should come, it will be a disaster of the first order. And if allowed to run its course, it may stop half the wheels of industry, throw one-fourth of our working population out of employment, wipe out the lifetime savings of millions, drive thousands of business firms into bankruptcy, reduce our total national income by forty or fifty per cent, and spread fear, anxiety, and despair throughout our entire population. The immediate result would be the undermining of the psychological foundations of our democracy. Under conditions of profound crisis men tend to abandon their rational faculties, become highly suggestible, and look about for a messiah to lead them out of the wilderness. It is in such times, in response to promises of security, that they may throw away precious rights and liberties won by generations of toil and sacrifice. The fact is that until a stable economy is established our democracy will be in perpetual danger.

Our democracy is challenged by the very complexity of industrial society. One must wonder whether the ordinary citizen can achieve the level of understanding necessary for the successful discharge of his civic responsibilities. He is called upon daily to pass judgment on men and measures, on men whom he has never seen and on measures requiring knowledge he has never gained. In considering this situation a quarter of a century ago Walter Lippmann observed: "Although public business is my main interest and I give most of my time to watching it, I cannot find time to do what is expected of me in the theory of democracy; that is, to know what is going on and to have an opinion worth expressing on every question which confronts a self-governing community."[1] How much simpler it all was in our earlier society

[1] Walter Lippmann, *The Phantom Public* (New York, 1925), p. 20.

of farmers and tradesmen! Perhaps here we have a partial explanation at least of the political indifference manifested by a large proportion of the voters on election day. Obviously there is urgent need for widespread understanding on the part of the people of the basic structure, the contending forces, and the broad tendencies of our industrial society in its historical and world relations.

Our democracy is challenged by the rise and spread of totalitarian doctrines and systems. Both at home and abroad we face Communism—an aggressive totalitarian movement which proclaims itself the vanguard of democracy in the world, even as it establishes a most ruthless dictatorship, reverses the entire conception of popular rule, and violates every basic democratic principle. This movement has gained such strength that our American democracy, for the first time in its history, is challenged by a powerful rival for the idealism of the young and the hopes of the exploited and oppressed of the earth. We also face Fascism—an equally aggressive totalitarian movement which by appealing to the worst in the human tradition would revive the military state and plunge all mankind again into war. Although the Fascist powers have been destroyed, the conditions of insecurity, frustration, and fear out of which Fascism came continue to ride the world. Each of these totalitarian movements feeds on fear of the other. Each also loudly proclaims itself to be the only practicable alternative to the other. As a consequence well-meaning but ignorant men and women in all countries are driven into Communist or Fascist ranks. We in America must repudiate this false logic and present to the world a living democracy as the answer to both. The renunciation of political liberty can only lead to tyranny.

Our democracy is threatened by war and the fear of war. The full consequences of a world-wide war in the age of jet-propulsion, guided missiles, atomic bombs, and other weapons yet to be devised we cannot know with any precision. Whether it would destroy all the great cities of the earth and set back the clock of human advance for centuries or millennia we also cannot know. But we do know that democracy would have very little chance of surviving in such a world. And the fear of war, if prolonged indefinitely, would in all probability be equally disastrous. Because of the narrowed dimensions of the earth we would be compelled to marshal and organize all of our resources, material and spiritual, against the day of conflict. We might begin with universal military service and then be driven by an inexorable logic to impose the military mind on economy, government, education, science, and art. The survival of our democracy through the long future depends on the success of the present generation in its efforts to abolish both war and the fear of war. To this task we must bend our energies and talents.

4

Our American democracy is imperiled by its failures.

The total achievement of our people in the development of democracy is substantial and impressive. Yet we must admit that we have never made a comprehensive and sustained effort to apply democratic values fully to our life and institutions. We have violated every one of these values in some measure and persistently, some of them grievously and on a vast scale. Altogether too generally and too often we have confined their observance to special days and occasions, to particular classes and elements in the population, to times of great crisis and danger. As a people we have rarely been sensitive to their full implications. We have failed to bring the deeds of our daily lives into harmony with our professions.

We have excluded the colored peoples, even the descendants of the original inhabitants, from many of the benefits and privileges of our American community. Some of us have practiced and preached "white supremacy" in its purest Nazi form. In August, 1950, a deeply troubled correspondent of *The New York Times* in Korea wrote of "a contrast of the unworthy and the finest moments of democracy." This contrast he put in the following words:

In Carolina two men fought for a seat in the United States Senate, offering as their principal qualification the ability to uphold white supremacy and oppose the program of the President of the United States. Here in Korea white, black and yellow men, under the direction of the same President, are fighting and dying to uphold the principle that men of whatever color should be free to govern themselves in a democratic society and not be subject to a totalitarian communism imposed by force of arms.[2]

Our treatment of the Negro should trouble deeply the slumbers of all who profess devotion to democratic or Christian principles. Only less flagrantly, right down through the generations, have we violated our professions in the case of nationalities of recent immigration. We have even tolerated the growth of prejudice and hatred toward those through whom we have received our highest moral and religious conceptions. Many of our people have been made to feel themselves aliens in the land of their birth. We have withheld from millions and millions of children of the less favored social classes their American birthright to healthy bodies and a decent education. We have allowed poverty and riches to grow up side by side in our democracy. We have been callous to the denial to large sections of our people of civil and political rights guaranteed by our Constitution. We have permitted private citizens to take the law into their own hands and engage in mob violence of the most savage character. We have stood by and watched man exploit man, class exploit class. We have tolerated the shameless despoilment for private gain of irreplaceable natural resources. On a wide scale we have subordinated the public welfare to personal and class advantage and privilege. The catalogue of our violations of our democratic professions might be greatly extended.

The fact remains that the democratic heritage constitutes our most precious possession. Even as we violate its principles, it disturbs our consciences and weakens the supports of our transgressions. Its power over us is expressed in our

[2] W. H. Laurence, "Journey Into War—New York to Korea," *The New York Times Magazine*, August 6, 1950, p. 7.

absurd apologies and defenses. Few of us would want to see our democratic values generally repudiated and their opposites enthroned in their stead. We all know that they lend to our civilization whatever claim it may have to an honorable and distinguished place in history. We know too that they alone can serve to guide the process of rearing our children and of preparing them to make the great choices of their generation. Without these values we would be poverty-stricken in spirit; without them we would resemble a great leviathan of the deep going nowhere with unprecedented speed, power, and efficiency.

5

Our American democracy must experience a new birth.
We must cease casting nostalgic eyes toward the past. That past, in spite of our failures and shortcomings, as we have emphasized in the present volume, is a source of just pride. Comparatively brief as it is, we would not exchange it for the past of any other people on the earth. Moreover, it was marked by a spirit which we still possess, to be sure, but which we need in full measure—a spirit of adventure, daring, and hopefulness. Instead of striving to cling to institutions suited to a society of farmers and tradesmen in the eighteenth and nineteenth centuries, we should accept eagerly the conditions and resources of industrial civilization, turn our eyes resolutely toward the future, and direct our matchless energies and inventive powers to the fashioning of a great democracy in the age of science and technology.

Of one thing we may be certain. The surest way of losing the future in the present revolutionary age is to adhere blindly to the past. It is therefore the task of our generation, inspired by the achievements of our fathers and holding fast the guarantees of the Bill of Rights, the democratic political process, the practice of constitutional government, the conception of just laws honestly administered, and the many freedoms already attained, to apply our historic democratic faith to the reconstruction of our domestic life and the building of a world order designed to bring lasting peace through justice to all men. And thus we shall conquer, not by force of arms or economic strength, but through the power of our ideas and the luster of our example. Democracy can lose in its present world-wide struggle with despotism only if it is false to itself.

Part Five

EDUCATION FOR THE EMERGING INDUSTRIAL AGE

# 19

THE RESOURCES FOR A GREAT EDUCATION

1

We need a great education.
A new age is upon us. In terms of power this new age surpasses the most extravagant fantasies of the past. It therefore presents to mankind wholly unprecedented possibilities for both good and evil. If we but possess the will and the wisdom, it can be an age of unparalleled plenty, justice, peace, and beauty. On the other hand, if we should prove unequal to the challenge, it might witness the crushing of the human spirit and the inauguration of a reign of darkness and desolation throughout the earth. Contemplation of the years ahead alternately arouses our hopes and strikes terror to our hearts. Never before in our history as a people have we in America been confronted with such awe-inspiring horizons. Indeed, never before in the history of the human race, have the peoples of the whole world been forced to make equally fateful decisions. At times every thoughtful person must share the apprehensions of a distinguished historian as he viewed the international skies in the summer of 1945. "What impends and with what portents?" he asked himself, and then responded anxiously: "Day and night I wonder and tremble for the future of my country and mankind."[1]

The fact is, as we have stressed again and again in the present volume, our minds lag dangerously behind the march

---

[1] Letter from Charles A. Beard to the author.

of events. We possess in sufficient measure neither the understanding nor the resolution necessary to meet the challenge and fulfill the bright promise of this great age. In the words of H. G. Wells, it is again a "race between education and catastrophe." But if we are to avoid catastrophe, we must have, not only an education of great power in all major countries, and particularly in our own, but also an education effectively dedicated to good purposes. We should all know only too well, after the experience of the past thirty years, that organized education conceived in violence and dedicated to despotism can speed mankind on the way to utter disaster.

2

We need an education for free men that is conscious of its worth and power. The time has passed when any society concerned about its destiny can afford to neglect its schools and other agencies involved in the rearing of the young and the enlightenment of the old. If the values of civilized life are to endure, we must come to regard education as one of our most serious undertakings. Perhaps more than anything else we do, it represents a considered effort to guard and shape our future. No longer, therefore, must we be content to hold it in a secondary position among the interests of our people. Into the framing of its purposes and the translation of those purposes into practical programs should go our finest thought, our noblest vision, and our best talents.

Such a sober approach to the question is made imperative by the clear demonstration of the great power of organized education during the period between the world wars—a demonstration made, not by the democracies, but by the totalitarian states, notably by Nazi Germany, Communist Russia, and Imperial Japan. The remarkable performances of these countries in the struggle for the world derived in considerable measure from their educational conceptions and programs.

The Resources for a Great Education

Without their agencies for molding the minds of the young to their purposes the Germans could not have waged their war of aggression, the Russians could not have halted the Nazi assault, and the Japanese could not have swept to Guadalcanal. The performance of the Soviets, because of their general backwardness a generation before, is particularly striking. Back of their military might stood a new industrial economy and back of both stood a new education—an education of great power in both its techniques and its purposes, though certainly not designed to bring peace and freedom to mankind.

Some critics contend that the experience of totalitarian states can have no meaning for a democracy. They argue that the effectiveness of education in Germany, Russia, and Japan is a distinctive expression of dictatorship. Clothed with practically unlimited power and authority and able therefore to impose on all the educational agencies unity of purpose and singleness of direction, the dictator is able to achieve miracles. In a democracy, the argument continues, because of its essential nature, because of its regard for freedom and difference, because of its respect for minorities and its fear of concentrated power, education must always be relatively aimless, dispersive, and even marked by contradictions. According to this view the citizens of a democracy can have no common interests, purposes, or loyalties beyond the defense of the fatherland against external aggression.

Such a negative attitude must be rejected if free societies are to survive in the industrial age. The weakness of our education is well expressed by a young associate professor in one of our great universities who was a captain of infantry in the United States Army and was assigned to a German prisoner-of-war camp. In his discussions with Nazi soldiers he soon learned that whereas they were "well-informed about Naziism" he himself "had only the most superficial notion about democracy." If this was true of a gifted man who had received the full benefits of our educational system from the primary grades through the graduate school, it is evident that the ordinary soldiers, even those who were wounded, tortured, and killed, had little understanding of the great political and moral issues involved in the conflict. Few of them would have been able to meet on the field of argument the representatives of any one of the several brands of totalitarianism which have struggled for mastery in our time.

That the values of democracy must be profoundly different from those of despotism is of course not debatable. But that a society of free men has no common values of its own and must therefore be equally hospitable to all values is the sure road to suicide. Only when our democracy has confronted this question profoundly and positively will our education be able to rise to its full stature. We must begin to see education as a source of both individual and national strength, as a process of building as well as expressing a great liberal civilization. And only when such a conception of rearing the young is formulated and put into practice will education succeed in serving democracy as it has served totalitarian states in the present epoch. Our difficulties doubtless arise in part from the fact that in the schools our American democracy, despite its many and great merits, remains too largely a democracy of words rather than of understanding and action. Any attempt to achieve our professed purposes in the industrial age encounters the powerful opposition of vested rights and virtuous ignorance.

3

We have the material and institutional resources necessary for building a great education.
In the development of a program for rearing the young we are limited only by our powers of conception and resolution. We possess in unprecedented abundance the resources of material wealth and educational institutions. We are in a position in the generation now unfolding to realize the finest dreams of the great teachers and prophets of the Western World from Socrates

and Jesus to Jefferson and John Dewey. No longer can any proposal be rejected on the grounds that it is Utopian, that it is theoretically desirable but practically impossible, that it is beyond our means. For the first time in history all the children of all the people can be provided with the optimum conditions for growth and the achievement of every form of excellence.

First of all, we possess the material resources. The new vistas of power derived from the advance of science and technology make clearly possible a greatly enriched and expanded educational program. If the toiling farmers of a century ago could find the means to carry the "district school" across the continent, we should be able to give to our children every good thing of body, mind, and heart. As never before, we hold in our hands the material resources essential to launch and maintain an educational program equal to our democratic professions and our social needs. Genuine equality of educational opportunity at an unprecedentedly high level for all of our children, regardless of family, race, or creed, is easily feasible. Indeed, as we have observed in an earlier chapter, the development of power-production of material goods is so changing the general pattern of our economy that we will be compelled to divert our energies increasingly to the supplying of services. Of these, education is probably the greatest and most productive of human welfare. Moreover, unlike the resources of physical nature, of soil, forests, and minerals, the resources of human nature may be improved and increased indefinitely by wise use and cultivation.

Secondly, we possess the institutional resources. To take full advantage of these resources, however, requires a radical reconstruction of our conception of the educational undertaking. Changes in the social order have greatly altered the processes and agencies of education. Even though we thought it desirable, the young could not be reared and inducted into our complex and far-flung industrial civilization as they were reared and inducted into the relatively simple and confined society of the agrarian age. In that age the school played a minor, even an insignificant, role in this process.

The major educational institutions then were the family, the church, the farm, and the rural neighborhood. The young acquired the powers, the skills, knowledges, and dispositions necessary for fairly successful living in the course of growing up and performing the activities expected of each succeeding age under the informal guidance of their elders. These old agencies, though still vital and important, have declined in either their relative or their absolute influence.

Industrial civilization has seriously disrupted the traditional ways of rearing the young. But it has also brought new agencies or radically expanded old agencies whose possibilities as yet are but dimly grasped or utilized. The list is long and impressive. It should certainly include the following: the new modes of livelihood, the shop, the factory, the mine, and the mechanized farm; the new forms of communication, the press, the library, and the museum, the moving picture, the radio, and television; the new methods of travel, the locomotive, the steamship, the automobile, and the airplane; the new patterns of group life, the club, the union, the cooperative, the religious association, the civic society, and a host of other voluntary organizations; the new agencies of recreation, the theater, the orchestra, the playground, the gymnasium, the swimming pool, the summer camp, organized sport, and children's movements. The task of fully utilizing such a wealth of institutional resources is tremendous and challenging. Industrial civilization has greatly enlarged and complicated the educational undertaking, but it has also increased immeasurably the institutional resources through which the responsibility of rearing the young and enlightening the old can be discharged.

The family, the church, and the local neighborhood must of course still be recognized as educational agencies of great significance. Studies show that the family, in spite of the loss of many functions, probably remains the most powerful single influence in the life of the young. Having almost complete control over the individual during his first six years, the period of greatest plasticity, it molds to an astonishing degree both his character and his powers. The enrichment of the cultural possessions and the improvement of the personal qualities of parents should be a major concern of all who are interested in education. The schools receive from the homes of America millions of little boys and girls dwarfed and crippled by the defective or perverted ministrations of well-meaning parents. The church enrolls today as large a proportion of the children and youth of the nation as ever before in our history. Its responsibilities, therefore, in the education of the young, particularly in the sphere of its special interest, in the shaping of moral traits, are of the first order. It is to be hoped that the various denominations will direct their resources to the softening of sectarian prejudices and the cultivation of a generous and humane spirit. The local neighborhood, like the family, continues to provide in country, town, and city, through its unorganized life and its intimate face-to-face relationships, the basic and elemental experience on which all education must rest.

The modes of livelihood have always played a central role in the rearing of the young. In the day of the self-contained rural household, with its rich and varied activities, the farm provided both occupational and moral training marked by a quality of genuineness altogether too commonly lacking today. Although it continues in somewhat weakened form to play its ancient role for a considerable portion of the population, it might be utilized far more effectively and generally than it is today. Experience on the farm should be provided in limited measure for the boys and girls of our towns and cities. The new modes of livelihood in shops, factories, mines, and the varied institutions of industry should also be utilized for all. Certainly the young should not be allowed to grow to maturity without some first-hand acquaintance with these marvelous and exciting sources of our subsistence. At appropriate ages they should be given actual work experience. To rear them in complete isolation from the means of livelihood, as now so generally happens, is evidence of a badly organized society.

In the old and new forms of communication we have educational institutions of almost unimagined possibilities.

These are the agencies on which we largely depend for knowledge about the world we live in, both past and present. The young should be inducted into the use of the press, of newspapers, magazines, and books, of libraries, bookshops, and museums, of the moving picture, the radio, and television. They should also be prepared through organized instruction to criticize and evaluate these powerful molders of the mind for the purpose of improving their quality from generation to generation. While the products of the press have long been closely identified with the processes of formal education, the moving picture and the radio are still largely neglected. Experience gained in the recent war and in other countries demonstrates their extraordinary effectiveness. Without them, and particularly without the moving picture, our program of training for both the military and the industrial front would have proceeded far more slowly than it did. Unquestionably they were in the front rank of our "secret" weapons. Television which combines the resources of screen and radio holds vast possibilities for education. All of these new forms of communication are almost miraculously adapted to the educational needs of this age. Through them ideas and attitudes can often be conveyed far more effectively and powerfully than by the printed page or by oral presentation. Through them the most complicated processes and the most distant places can be brought into the classroom. The full incorporation of these new agencies into the program of instruction will bring about a revolution in educational methods.

Mankind has always found travel an unfailing source of challenge and enlightenment. The new and swift modes of travel, if utilized intelligently, present rich opportunities for weakening the parochial spirit, extending the horizons, and enriching the lives of the young. Already the locomotive and the steamship, the automobile and the airplane have exerted a powerful influence toward these ends. But up to the present time their cultural significance has received little attention. Their use for educational purposes has been haphazard and greatly confined. Only the children of the well-to-do have had much experience with them beyond the boundaries of the locality, and that experience has often been uninformed. The time is at hand when systematic travel, designed to acquaint the young with their country through direct observation, could be made an integral part of the educational program. In the later years of youth opportunity should be extended to a considerable number to travel beyond our borders to other parts of the world. This might well be made a crowning feature of the study of other languages and cultures.

The voluntary organization, so characteristic of industrial society, is an educational agency of great power. It has been said by an eminent political scientist that the labor union should be ranked with the university as one of the major cultural institutions of the nation. The organizations of farmers, businessmen, professional workers, and consumers, of political parties and religious sects, of civic and welfare interests, and a thousand and one other groups are increasingly molding the minds of our people. Children and youth often have their own organizations in many of these areas of social life, as well as innumerable clubs and societies devoted to their special interests. It is in such institutions that they receive a large part of their social and political education. To formulate an adequate program for rearing the young without taking these agencies into consideration would be impossible. Through their own organizations children and youth should be given primary experience in group undertakings and in the promotion of the general welfare. Gradually, as they approach the age of economic and political responsibility, they should be inducted into the organizations of adult society. A major purpose of all education in this field should be the development in the young of a readiness to subordinate the narrow interest of the part to the broad interest of the whole. The survival of democracy may rest on our success in achieving this goal.

The agencies and processes of recreation have contributed powerfully to the maturing of the young since primitive times. Indeed, many contend that play is nature's method of education among both men and the higher animal forms. But, be that as it may, we have in the theater, the museum, and the art gallery, in the playground, the gymnasium, and the swimming pool, in the summer camp and the public park, in organized sport and scouting, a vast and growing body of extraordinarily effective educational agencies. Unfortunately, while we as a people have fostered with unusual generosity certain forms of recreation, particularly sport and physical play, we have lagged behind some other countries in cultivating in the young an interest in the drama, the dance, music, and art. For example, we have no children's theater and our movies are made primarily for adults. Unfortunately also, only a small fraction of our children and youth receive the full benefits of our recreational resources. The sons and daughters of the poor, for the most part, enjoy only limited opportunities in this important department of life, being restricted by the public facilities available in the local community and by the measure of the family pocketbook. They consequently often form gangs which tend to inculcate antisocial and predatory habits and attitudes. In a fully developed program every child should know the joys of scouting and camping, of wandering through public parks and forests, of climbing ridges and mountains, of canoeing on lakes and rivers, of bathing and fishing in the waters of the enveloping oceans. With the steady reduction in the hours of labor, the recreational life of our people will become ever more important.

The role of the school in the complicated process of inducting the young into the great society of the industrial age can scarcely be exaggerated. From the little one-room district school of our ancestors, supplemented by a few academies and colleges in the towns, it has grown into a vast and closely organized system of institutions reaching from infancy well into adult years. In this phenomenal expansion it has assumed many functions formerly performed by family and neighborhood and others made necessary by the advance of industrial civilization. At the same time, to its own detriment, it has tended to become more and more isolated from life. If it is to discharge effectively its greatly increased responsibilities, this condition must be corrected. Also the many other agencies enumerated above must be regarded more seriously and included deliberately in our total educational program. But this utilization and coordination of all of our resources for the rearing of the young should be achieved in so far as possible through voluntary and cooperative effort rather than through governmental intervention and direction. The latter is the method of the totalitarian state and contains a dangerous threat to political liberty and freedom of the mind. The situation calls for the assertion of leadership on the part of some element in the American community. The logical source of such leadership would seem to be the school. Completely dedicated, as it is, to the task of education, it is in a peculiarly favorable position to perform the function of coordination. Moreover, in performing this function, in relating its program to these many other agencies in which education is a kind of by-product of their activities, it would break through the barrier of isolation and identify its work more fully with the life of the community.

4

We have the resources of professional knowledge necessary for building a great education.
Since ancient times many of the best minds of all advanced nations have recognized the importance of education and have sought to understand the complex process of rearing the young. In recent generations our knowledge of this process has advanced immeasurably. With the establishment of great systems of education throughout the world, the methods of science and scholarship, of experimentation and objective inquiry, have been applied with increasing energy to the problems and tasks of education. Systematic study of the institutions and achievements of other countries and peoples, from primitive tribes to great industrial societies, has added to our under-

standing. Although much remains to be learned, our knowledge today goes far beyond our practice. We possess the material and institutional resources to put this knowledge to work.

We have reason for believing today that man is more educable than was generally thought to be the case a few generations ago. Numerous studies have demonstrated that the first years of life are supremely important. It seems that during the period from birth to the first day at school the foundations for all later development are laid. Yet we continue to assume in our conception of education and in our institutional arrangements that the child is scarcely educable until he reaches the age of six or seven years—the very period when he learns far more than he will ever learn again in the same span of time. During these most crucial years of growth, he is often left to the mercy of folkways based in considerable measure on ignorance and superstition. By the time he enters school he may already have acquired deficiencies of body, mind, and character which can perhaps never be completely overcome. A rich and wise society therefore will not long tolerate the neglect which is now so commonly the lot of little children. This of course does not mean, as we shall note later, that the family should be disrupted and that the youngster should be placed under the care of the state from birth.

Investigation has shown, too, that the individual does not abruptly and inevitably lose his mental plasticity and ability to learn on his eighteenth or twenty-first birthday. On the contrary, he seems to be able to retain these powers in amazing degree until the onset of old age. He is therefore admirably equipped in his biological inheritance to live in the strange civilization now spreading over the earth. Because of the complexity, the scope, and the dynamic quality of industrial society, the need for education, for acquiring new powers, for making adjustments to novel situations continues through practically the whole of life. The current interest in adult education is a logical and intelligent response to this condition. The necessity for a bold, rapid, and imaginative development here is obvious. The old, as well as the young, must be encouraged to learn new ways, to think new thoughts, to acquire new interests, and to formulate new purposes. The very survival of our democracy may well depend on our success in liquidating our "illiteracy" with respect to the nature of industrial civilization—its basic structure, its imperatives, its dynamics, and its potentialities. The urgency of reconstructing conceptions and attitudes inherited from the past makes full dependence on a later generation hazardous. Our free way of life may be lost before the boys and girls of today grow to maturity and take over the direction of society. Moreover, if these boys and girls are to receive the kind of education they should have, adults must be wise enough to make it possible.

We have acquired also from the school of experience and from scientific inquiry a conception of the nature of the child somewhat at variance with that of our fathers. We no longer believe that the child is born in sin, that he is perverse by nature, that his will therefore must be "broken." Likewise we no longer believe that the best education is that which is most painful. We know rather that, though education of the highest order is an arduous process, it can be on the whole a joyous adventure and at the same time achieve the kind of discipline required by a free society. Love and understanding, tempered by firmness and lofty purpose, are incomparably more fruitful than harshness and brutality. We know too that children differ profoundly from one another in every respect, that they cannot all travel the same road to maturity and life's responsibilities, that education in its most fruitful form cannot be conducted on the pattern of the assembly line and mass production. And we have learned one thing more. As the child is not bad by nature, neither is he good. Rather, as he comes from "the hand of the author of nature," he is a creature of vast, diverse, and conflicting possibilities. The same child can grow into an ardent Nazi, a devoted Communist, or a responsible citizen of a democracy, depending on the character of his total education. We should rejoice to know that, if we but have the desire and the wit, we can rear every normal American child, whatever the color of his skin or the status of his family, to be a faithful defender of human freedom and the great moral commitments of our people.

5

We have the moral and spiritual resources for building a great education.

We possess the resources of wealth, institutions, and professional knowledge necessary to support and conduct an educational program suited to these times. But those resources in themselves, though indispensable, are not enough. They merely provide the tools and materials with which the work may be done, the brushes, pigments, and canvas with which the picture may be painted. A great education requires something more than wealth, institutions, and professional knowledge. It must also be guided by a great and noble purpose, by a great and noble conception of life and civilization. For us in America such a conception should embrace the best in our heritage, confront the revolutionary forces and conditions of the present, and take into account the vast technical potentialities of the industrial age. This, and this alone, will give to our education its distinctive quality.

Our conception of civilization should be rooted in the promise of America as a land of opportunity, freedom, justice, and dignity for common men, women, and children derived from many nations and cultures. It is this promise that has given unity, power, and meaning to the life of our people. Unfortunately, in these latter days, as our civilization has moved from agricultural to industrial foundations, marked by vast complexities, inequalities, and insecurities, the old hopes have sometimes grown dim and lost some of their luster. To meet the challenge and hazards of the age now opening, the historic promise of our country, a promise that awakened to new life and energy millions around the world, must be revived and re-created. It must be revived and re-created in terms of the new conditions and possibilities produced by the rise of industrial civilization. It must be revived and re-created also in terms of the enlarged hopes and expectations of men and women everywhere. We must realize that a promise which aroused enthusiasm in the eighteenth century may lack meaning and vitality in the twentieth.

If we have the courage and imagination, we can reconstitute the promise of America on a scale far grander than that of its earlier form. It rested yesterday on the material foundation of a fabulously rich land that seemed to extend almost without limit toward the west. It must rest today and tomorrow on the material foundation of a fabulously productive industrial economy that may reach with ever-increasing power into the future. Its achievement yesterday was primarily a responsibility of individual, family, and neighborhood effort. Its achievement today and tomorrow, because of the close and far-flung interdependence of life, must be conceived largely in social and even national terms. Its benefits yesterday were fully shared only by certain favorably situated elements of the population. Its benefits today and tomorrow must be shared progressively by all of us, regardless of race, family, religion, or nationality. Its purposes yesterday were largely economic and political in character. Its purposes today and tomorrow must embrace more fully all of our great moral and value commitments. Its horizons yesterday were generally confined by our national boundaries. Its horizons today and tomorrow must extend to the farthest corners of the earth.

Such a conception of the promise of America should evoke to the full the energies of our people. Particularly should it give meaning to the lives of the young and provide the long-sought moral equivalent of war. Contrary to a common view, youth are not greatly moved by a mad competition with their fellows for material comfort and advancement. They rather crave the opportunity to work together in close comradeship for the achievement of some end that possesses recognized social value. That the continuing struggle to refine and fulfill the historic promise of American life requires labor, courage, sacrifice, and devotion only increases its appeal to the young. This psychological insight has been grasped by the great leaders of history, including not only the founders of our Republic but also, unfortunately, contemporary dictators. Indeed, the power of the totalitarian movements in our time derives largely from a stirring call to heroic action. To receive from his elders a conception of life that will demand his fullest efforts and finest qualities should be the birthright of every American child.

Such a conception should also provide an all-inclusive aim of American education. It would lend significance, not only to the program of the school, but also to the vocation of teaching and to the life of the teacher. The low quality of much of our instruction cannot be traced wholly by any means to an inferior grade of teaching personnel, to a lack of professional skills, or to the low standards of financial remuneration. It is due in no small part to the prevailing petty conception of the calling. A very large proportion of teachers feel deep down in their hearts that what they are doing is not really important, certainly not as important as running a bank or selling real estate. With a noble conception of the craft, even the routine aspects of teaching would take on life and meaning. The profession today is performing far below its possibilities. And it can achieve greatness only as it identifies its work with a great conception of life and civilization.

20

EDUCATION FOR INDIVIDUAL EXCELLENCE

1

We need an education dedicated to the achievement of individual excellence of the highest order.

It is fitting that we begin our formulation of a conception of education for America in the industrial age with a consideration of the individual. A militant affirmation of the worth and dignity of the individual human being is perhaps the most precious of our moral commitments. It is found in the Hebraic-Christian ethic, in the humanistic spirit, in the rule of law, and even in the scientific method. It marked deeply the outlook of the modern age, pervaded the revolts against both secular and ecclesiastical authority in subsequent centuries, and moved millions to seek the free shores of America generation after generation. It sustained the armies of Washington in our War for Independence and inspired our fathers and mothers in the bitter struggle to abolish human slavery, in the high resolve "to die to set men free." It is proclaimed in the Declaration of Independence and in the Federal Constitution. It has motivated every struggle to abolish special privilege and to extend economic, political, and civil rights increasingly to all of our people. It is a basic, an ancient and living, American doctrine.

Affirmation of the worth and dignity of the individual is the first article of the democratic faith. The central purpose of a democracy, therefore, is the development of fine people. And if this purpose is to mean anything substantial, it must mean the extension to the individual of the opportunity to grow to his full stature as a human being—to achieve within the limits set by a given cultural epoch, the highest standards of excellence of which he is capable. It must mean every individual, not just the individual with brown or blue eyes, the individual with white or colored skin, or the individual born on this or the other "side of the tracks," or even the individual with little or great talent. According to this basic moral commitment, all social institutions and life conditions are to be judged by what they do to individual boys and girls, individual men and women. Our educational agencies and processes in particular must be subjected to this test.

A democracy, moreover, is not only committed by its purposes to the full development of the individual. Its very survival depends on a large measure of success in the achievement of this goal. While it must have a high quality of official leadership, like any other form of society, it cannot be saved by the virtues of a small ruling group or caste. Because of its essential nature, its destiny rests in the hands of the great masses of ordinary people. If they lack the necessary virtues and talents, as Montesquieu and the founding fathers of our Republic noted long ago, it is certain to be destroyed. On the other hand, if they are fully developed as human beings, democracy is probably the most stable and enduring form of society. Under such circumstances also, since the powers of all rather than those of just a few are cultivated to the highest degree possible, it can make a maximum use of its human resources in each generation. In every society of history, even in the most democratic, a large proportion of the abilities potential in the people have remained dormant or become perverted. We know that this is true in America today.

An education dedicated to the achievement of individual excellence is peculiarly imperative in industrial society. In the day of the rural neighborhood every person was an individual and was treated as an individual. Enterprise was small, relations were intimate, and the individual could make himself felt in his little community. Today in the huge establishments of industry and government, in the vast concentrations of population, in the mass organizations of economics and politics, in the nation-wide fabric of interdependences, in the world-wide web of social relationships, he is often overwhelmed by a sense of insignificance and helplessness. In actuality, moreover, he frequently finds himself shorn of human attributes and reduced to the condition of an automaton or a part of the landscape. Under these circumstances it is not surprising that many have seen totalitarianism—ancient despotism in its modern form—as the "wave of the future." The characteristic patterns of industrial society seem to invite the political, intellectual, and personal disfranchisement of common people and the assumption of the powers of choice and direction by some dictator or oligarchy. Even certain of our practices of mass education tend to weaken the sources of individuality and to strengthen the tendency toward the robotization of life. The deliberate cultivation on a generous scale of individual excellence in all of its diversity thus becomes a crucial and urgent responsibility of democratic education. We must know that a society or a civilization is fine and great only if it nurtures fineness and greatness in its children.

2

The achievement of individual excellence is a long and arduous process.
At birth the individual is profoundly helpless, far more helpless than most other forms of life. He is incapable of locomotion, of feeding himself, of seeking shelter, of even pulling a cover over his body. Left to his own resources he would quickly starve, succumb to disease, die from frost or sunburn, or be devoured by beasts or insects.

His power of survival, apart from the automatic discharge of essential bodily functions, is largely limited to the ability to express discomfort and attract the attention of some loving and responsible guardian.

This condition of helplessness conceals fabulous possibilities. In the course of time the human offspring will leave far behind all of his animal rivals and establish dominion over them. He will not only learn to walk and swim and climb, but he will also master innumerable skills in the manipulation and direction of tools, machines, and weapons. He will learn to use the hammer, the saw, the needle, the lathe, and the automatic drill, the bow and arrow, the rifle, the machine gun, the cannon, and the atomic bomb. He will learn to ride a horse, sail a ship, run a locomotive, drive an automobile, and fly an airplane. He will acquire a language with thousands of symbols, perhaps several different languages, and learn to count and make abstruse mathematical calculations. He will grasp the meanings of such abstract conceptions as law and justice, right and wrong, self and society, family, economy, state, and church. He will learn to write, draw, and paint, to sing a song and play a musical instrument. He will learn to think and to ponder the mysteries of birth and death, of his own origin and destiny, of the purpose of life and the nature of the universe. He will learn to love and hate, to fear and fight, to struggle for ideas, to die for some cause. He may learn all of these things and many more. He may even learn to create, to invent, or to discover something new under the sun.

These mighty possibilities, however, are not realized through a process of inner unfolding. Indeed, though they may have been present in a biological sense in the age of the cave man, they would scarcely have been discernible to the most acute observer in that long-forgotten epoch. And we do not know today what they will prove to be in the far distant future when the evolution of human culture will have taken new directions and the conditions of life will have been profoundly altered. Only in our time have we caught a glimpse of how this helpless human infant may eventually respond to power-driven machines, to locomotion at the speed of sound, to flight into the stratosphere, to conquest of disease, to control of reproductive forces, to long hours of leisure, to total war on a world scale, or to a condition of peaceful relations among all peoples. Human nature is revealed, or rather perhaps created, as man through history transforms his physical environment, builds new realms of the mind, develops novel desires and powers, and changes his own self and character. As agricultural man was unlike nomadic man, so industrial man will differ increasingly from any man in history.

Neither are the possibilities of the individual fully realized through a process of unguided learning. To be sure, given the powers of the human organism, the acquisitions of the individual without any conscious tutelage whatsoever beyond provision for physical care are extremely impressive. Driven by deep-seated and imperious urges the offspring of the species takes on the behavior patterns of the group. Yet, even in the most primitive societies, long before the appearance of organized educational agencies, the young are dependent on their elders for a large amount of deliberate stimulation, guidance, and instruction. In a highly complex society, such as our own, with its vast cultural accumulations, the simple maintenance of inherited standards of conduct and performance in any sphere of life, whether it is the use of the native tongue, the pursuit of an occupation, the exercise of political rights, the management of household affairs, or the practice of any art or science, requires uninterrupted vigilance, discipline, and organized effort. If there is any desire to advance those standards and achieve higher levels of individual excellence, the processes of formal tuition must be correspondingly strengthened and improved.

In short, individual excellence is always achieved through a twofold process of guidance and learning in which the cultural heritage plays a central role. Without the mediation of this heritage, which mankind has created painfully through thousands upon thousands of years, the infant, whatever his so-called "natural" gifts and dispositions, would never rise above the level of the brute. He would not even become human in any significant meaning of the term. The quality of the cultural heritage on which the individual is nurtured, by which he is molded, and through which his powers are released and developed is therefore the essence of the problem of achieving excellence. The differences among persons of different families and social classes within the same society, as well as among persons of different racial and national origins, seem to be due largely to differences in the quality of the cultural heritage involved.

3

The achievement of individual excellence requires attention to the individual.
It is possible to produce firearms, automobiles, refrigerators, and even beef and pork by mass-production methods. Indeed, as we have seen, great benefits flow from the employment of such methods in the making of material things. Vast economies are achieved not only in production but also in consumption. To know that one Ford car is constructed precisely on the same pattern as another has great advantages. Having mastered the structure and operations of a single specimen, the driver or the mechanic is equipped to deal successfully with all other members of the same species. Having located the starter, the accelerator, and the brake, having gained understanding of the fueling, wiring, and lubrication systems of one car, he can transfer his skill and knowledge to a second without appreciable loss. Also he can replace defective or damaged parts by means of an order blank or by telephoning a service station. It has been found, however, that even in the case of automobiles and other mechanical contrivances, as well as in the case of bacon, porridge, hats, and divers commodities, the process of standardization can be carried too far. Different brands to satisfy different needs and tastes seem to contribute to the happiness of mankind and the gaiety of nations.

Education for Individual Excellence 317

In the case of human beings value appears to reside in individuality. At least this is true in free societies where people are regarded as ends rather than as means. In a totalitarian state, of course, the methods of mass production may be applied quite appropriately to the education or training of boys and girls. Here the individual as such has no value. He is but a means to the achievement of some purpose, such as military aggrandizement or enhancement of the glory, prestige, and power of state or dictator, in whose formulation he has no voice. In the new instruments of communication, which are admirably designed to mold the minds of millions to a single pattern, despotism has a powerful ally. Even free societies, in the interest of economy and efficiency, will be sorely tempted to follow the totalitarian example, propagate "democracy" in wholesale fashion, and produce little "democrats" as much alike as the automobiles which leave the assembly line of a great factory duly stamped with a serial number and the name of their maker. Although we must learn to use the press, the radio, the movie, and television in our educational program, we must never forget that the supreme value of a democracy is the unique quality of the individual human being.

The desirability of adjusting education to the powers and character of the individual has always been recognized by the favored classes in society. Within the limits of their mores and understanding they have insisted that, regardless of cost, their children be given every advantage and be treated as persons. They have provided for them nurses and tutors, special schools and academies amply staffed with well-trained teachers. Often in our American public schools classes are scandalously large and instructors are poorly prepared and overworked. Although children can learn many things in large groups through the use of visual and auditory aids, they must also receive individual attention. In the training of relatively mature young men and women for the armed forces in the last war it was discovered that successful instruction demanded small classes. Moreover, one of the most vital and persistent needs of boys and girls is to be loved, cherished, and understood by other human beings. Obviously they cannot be loved, cherished, and understood in the mass or by textbooks, moving pictures, radio sets, or television screens. At their best such mechanical helps are but tools to be used wisely and skillfully by the competent teacher. Long ago John Dewey stated simply and eloquently the principle that should guide us in all of our dealings with the young. "What the best and wisest parent desires for his children," he said, "that must the community desire for all of its children."

The great role of the culture in the development of excellence in the individual must not be allowed to obscure the fact of individual differences. When they enter the world children differ profoundly in almost every respect. While they possess in common a general pattern of possibilities characteristic of the species, each is endowed with a unique combination of qualities and powers. Within the limits set by the promotion of the welfare of all, those qualities and powers should be developed to the maximum in a free society. They constitute the most precious resource of a progressive and creative people. To fail to make the fullest use of this resource is to be content with a general standard of excellence below what is possible.

The process of achieving excellence begins at birth, or even at the moment of conception. The prenatal months and the first years of life, moreover, as noted earlier, are critical and formative. This means that the best of conditions should surround the individual from the very beginning of his existence. In order that we may advance toward the removal of the gross deficiencies and disabilities marking this early age, we must work for the abolition of material and spiritual poverty throughout the population, the radical improvement of home and living conditions, the general development of preschool agencies, the establishment of community nursing services, and the preparation of prospective and actual fathers and mothers, through the utilization of all available means, to discharge efficiently and wisely the many duties of parenthood. From the standpoint of improving the qualities of our people, it would be difficult to devise any set of social measures which in the long run would be productive of greater good. Moreover, there are probably few other areas of living where we lag so far behind our knowledge. Well-meaning but ignorant and impoverished parents perpetuate through their children their own infirmities and frustrations.

4

Our conception of individual excellence should embrace the whole person.

Such a conception is not new in the history of education. It goes back at least to the ancient Athenians and is expressed in the noblest traditions of the humanistic and liberal heritage of the Western World. It affirms the worth of the individual, stresses his creative powers, and places a high value on his integrity and independence of spirit. The fact that it has often been distorted and formalized is irrelevant. For the first time in the long human adventure it can be brought into the service of all the people.

The individual human being, as he appears in history, is a many-sided creature. He possesses body, mind, and heart. He is endowed with physical, intellectual, moral, and aesthetic powers. Few societies, if any, have ever achieved, or even sought to achieve, the full and balanced development of all of these powers in the great majority of the members. Either the emphasis has been one-sided and partial or the effort has been confined to some favored group. We in America cannot be satisfied with anything less than the achievement of the highest possible degree of general excellence for every boy and girl born into our society. Although the physical, intellectual, moral, and aesthetic powers of the individual are all closely interrelated and although the process of development is carried on necessarily in a framework of social relationships and institutions, each will be considered briefly by itself. Subsequent chapters will supply that framework and relate the process of rearing the young to the basic institutions and the great value commitments of our civilization.

First of all, our educational program should strive for physical excellence. It should endeavor to make of the individual a good animal, endowed with bodily vigor, free from defect and disease, possessing the strength and energy requisite to the discharge of the obligations of work, citizenship, and parenthood and to the full enjoyment of all that life has to offer. We know of course that no people of history has ever fully achieved this goal. The members of the human species have always lived near the margin of subsistence, dwarfed in body and prey to famine and pestilence. We know too that in spite of the miraculous advances of science we in rich America fall far short of the goal. Many of us are badly born and poorly nourished, victims of a succession of preventable maladies from the cradle to the grave.

The administration of the Selective Service Act in the Second World War gives one measure of our failure. The examination of young men from February through August of 1943 resulted in the rejection for military service of 30.8 per cent of all registrants. That this condition is not fixed by some kind of biological determinism is revealed by the great differences from state to state. The percentage ranges from 21.1 in Utah to 46.2 in Florida. Undoubtedly these figures, and the statistics of physical defect, disease, vitality, and mortality generally, reflect levels of education, medical facilities, public health provisions, and conditions of life. That we are any better prepared for the tasks of peace than for those of war is scarcely a tenable thesis.

The fact is that there is an enormous gap between our knowledge and material resources on the one hand, and our practice on the other. At no time since the great advances of science and technology revealed new horizons of the possible, have we confronted squarely the problem of putting our knowledge to work and of achieving even a moderate standard of health and bodily vigor for all of our people. Some of the totalitarian states, in terms of the productivity of their economies, have given more attention to this matter than our American democracy. It seems that the motive of strengthening the state and increasing the power of a dictator has been stronger than our democratic commitment to improving the physical quality of the individual. This condition cannot be permitted to continue.

The task immediately ahead is to incorporate our knowledge into a comprehensive program for the care and education of the individual from birth. Although the responsibility rests by no means wholly on the schools, the educational agencies must bear a major part of the burden. Every school should have a program designed to discover and correct all remediable physical defects, to develop proper habits of diet, elimination, work, play, and rest, to train in the use of all forms of medical assistance, to insure the acquisition of a modicum of functional knowledge, and to foster a sense of concern for guarding and promoting the health of the entire American community. To be indifferent to the physical welfare of any child should be regarded as a violation of the professional ethics of the teacher.

To be a good animal, however, basic and important as it is, is not enough. The individual of our species begins to assume truly human form only as he develops his intellectual abilities, his capacity to know, his power of reason, "the choicest gift bestowed by heaven." Certainly no man can be free, no man can be a responsible citizen of a democracy, who is deficient in knowledge and understanding, in critical and practical judgment, in inventive and creative thought. Moreover, our emerging industrial society, with its limitless reaches, its bewildering complexities, and its ceaseless changes and transformations, places a wholly unprecedented burden upon the mind. Today the American people, as they face a world in conflict and an age in crisis, are largely unprepared for the enormous tasks which history places before them. Even the fullest development of the intellectual powers of the individual may prove insufficient to discharge the responsibilities of a free man and avert an all-embracing human catastrophe.

The achievement of intellectual excellence is a long and

exacting process, requiring severe and sustained discipline. Left to himself and the incidental instruction of his elders, the child will advance amazingly in intellectual stature and competence by participating in the life of his group; but for his fullest development the professional guidance of organized education is essential. Such development, as the history of man and the life of the individual clearly demonstrate, requires the most complete appropriation in their life relations of certain elements of the culture. Indeed, we know that mind, both in the species and in the individual, is a cultural product. Only as man has mastered and perfected these cultural tools or processes, only as he has reshaped his mind in terms of them, has he achieved the highest levels of excellence. Only as he stands today on the shoulders of those who have wrought before him will he be able to scale the heights of possible achievement in any realm.

The first of these cultural tools or processes is language. What a marvelous achievement is language, even the most primitive! And how fortunate is the individual who is born into a civilization possessing one of the more highly developed or widely used languages of the modern world! How favored is the child who receives as a free legacy the language of Confucius, of Dante, of Cervantes, of Shakespeare, of Voltaire, of Goethe, of Tolstoi, or of Gandhi! Without language, the basic instrument or mode of both thought and expression, the individual probably would never pass beyond the mental level of infancy or be markedly distinguishable from the ape. With it and all it embraces in a rich civilization, he may in rare instances attain the intellectual stature of Socrates, Gautama, Aurelius, Newton, or Einstein. To the conquest of language in both its spoken and written forms, therefore, to the cultivation of the ability to speak and listen, to read and write, organized education must always give great attention. Mastery of the linguistic arts is one of the surest indices of intellectual excellence.

A second cultural tool or process which must not be neglected is number. Being language in its most precise form, it is an indispensable part of the intellectual equipment of

Education for Individual Excellence

the individual. In the last analysis our industrial civilization rests upon mathematics. Without it contemporary man would be forced back into some simple form of agrarian society. In its more elementary aspects it must be the possession of every individual; in its higher branches it must be vigorously and generously fostered among persons of special talent. Its devotion to precision is a quality of mind, moreover, which should be cultivated unceasingly in all relations and departments of life.

Science, broadly conceived to embrace the major branches of scholarship, constitutes a third cultural element which should be increasingly the mark of the fully developed mind. In its method it is the most mature and dependable form of inquiry and thought devised by man. To the extent that the individual fails to employ it in the fields of experience where it is applicable he becomes the victim of ignorance and superstition. Organized education should not only strive to convey to the young the major bodies of relevant knowledge and thought about the world of nature and man but also seek to develop in them the habits of mind which mark the operations of science—an experimental temper, a desire to know the truth, intellectual integrity, and tolerance of differences. Nowhere are these qualities of mind more needed in the present age than in the sphere of economics, politics, and human relations. As the ignorant can never be free, so the pooling through so-called "group processes" of the ignorances of many persons can never bring knowledge.

Physical and intellectual excellence also are not enough. By themselves, particularly if narrowly conceived, they may produce not a man but a powerful brute of highest cunning and resourcefulness. To become a man in the fullest sense the individual must also achieve moral excellence, bring his impulses under the discipline of purpose, and assume the role of a responsible member of a democratic society. He must learn to subordinate the smaller to the greater good, the more immediate to the more distant, the individual to the social. In America, as well as in the world, as subsequent pages will stress, this means that organized education will have to abandon the pretense of neutrality among values and move deliberately to nurturing in the young the great moral commitments of a free and humane society.

The development of *good* people is perhaps the supreme educational task of our age. The rise of industrial civilization, creating new life conditions, making some ancient truths uncouth, and weakening the power of family, church, and neighborhood, has brought all mankind to the verge of moral bankruptcy. In terms of our operative loyalties we are unprepared to live in the "great society" of our time. With parochial minds we undertake the responsibilities of world citizenship. Also we are unprepared to use the limitless power which science and technology have placed in our hands. Unless we achieve a veritable revolution in moral habit, attitude, and outlook we shall be destroyed. Unfortunately the sands in the hourglass are running low. Possibly the time will not wait for the rearing of a new generation morally equipped to bear the heavy burdens of this fateful epoch.

We should proceed with all energy to develop a program of organized education which will cultivate in children and youth, and even in the older generation, the virtues, loyalties, and interests necessary to insure a good life for all—virtues, loyalties, and interests which will constitute a fusion of old and new values derived from our heritage and the demands of the new age. Such a program should endeavor to cultivate in all the relationships of life the personal virtues of honesty and integrity of character, the humane virtues of kindliness, gentleness, love, and mercy, the social virtues of cooperation and neighborliness, the democratic virtues of equality and fraternity, the public virtues of interest in and devotion to the common good, and the intellectual virtues of desire for knowledge and love of truth. We should encourage the young to practice these virtues in their daily lives and to apply them imaginatively to situations beyond the range of immediate personal relations through travel, history, literature, and discussion and through all the new media of communication.

Education for Individual Excellence   325

From the standpoint of education for a democracy it is imperative to realize that the young must acquire the desired virtues through a process of self-discipline. From the earliest years the individual should be encouraged under careful tutelage to engage in activities and to undertake assignments and projects through which the appropriate qualities of character may be evoked, exercised, and strengthened. The highest goal toward which education in a democratic society can strive is that of making the learner independent of the teacher, of equipping him to weigh the alternatives of life with an informed and resolute mind. Only when the young reach this point in their development do they arrive at maturity. The ability to direct oneself and manage one's life in relations with others is the ultimate test of the education of the free man. This means that the young should be guided from infancy to acquire steady habits of work and a deep sense of individual responsibility in all that they do.

Finally, physical, intellectual, and moral excellence are not enough. If the individual is to achieve his full human character, he must develop his artistic talents, his sense of the beautiful, his powers of personal expression and appreciation. He must appropriate for himself the great aesthetic tradition and know the ecstasy that comes from losing himself in the creation or contemplation of a work of art or a thing of beauty or truth, whether it be a painting, a symphony, or a poem, a cathedral, a factory, a city, or a highway, a sunset, a river, a mountain range, or a forest of conifers.

A complete education should seek to develop in the individual his creative and appreciative powers both as a social resource and as a precious personal possession. It should encourage him, not only to appreciate all that man has sensed and contrived of beauty and truth, but also to go beyond the world of nature and society to see "the light that never was on land or sea," beyond the world of the useful and instrumental to know that which is good in itself, and beyond the world of wont and custom to explore the realm of the uniquely personal. It should encourage him to become sensitive to the finer and more subtle nuances of living, to pursue the disinterested quest of truth and beauty, to follow the lure of intellectual curiosity, to foster the growth of his own individuality, to prize the integrity of his own expression, and to insist on the right "to paint the thing as he sees it." In our industrial society, because of its mass character and its tendency toward regimentation, emphasis on individual creativity assumes special urgency. At the same time the radical increase of the hours of leisure provides a wholly unprecedented opportunity for the cultivation of all the arts of personal expression and enjoyment.

5

A conception of individual excellence is always an expression of a civilization.

The very idea of excellence is of course a cultural product, and both the contents and the standards of excellence vary from one culture to another. The achievement of excellence therefore must never be regarded as essentially a process of conflict between individual and society, even though conflict between the creative mind and the mores often does occur and is a necessary condition of cultural advance. The individual is always a child of a particular society. Even his unique qualities of mind and character, his protests and rebellions, are derived from or made possible by the social heritage on, in, and by which he is nurtured. The measure of his maturity, moreover, is found in his assumption of all the responsibilities of adult life—economic, family, civic, cultural, and religious. The nature of these responsibilities and the standards of excellence demanded vary from society to society and from civilization to civilization. In the chapters that follow we shall elaborate the social aspect of the process of achieving individual excellence in our American industrial civilization—a civilization deeply committed to the Hebraic-Christian ethic, the humanistic spirit, science and scientific method, the rule of law, and democracy.

21

EDUCATION FOR A SOCIETY OF EQUALS

1

We need an education that will preserve, vitalize, and strengthen the principle of equality in our country.
Except for our commitment to the ideal of the worth and dignity of the individual human being, from which it is derived, this is the most basic principle in our social, political, and moral philosophy. It is the practical expression of the Hebraic-Christian doctrine of human brotherhood to which the vast majority of Americans are professedly committed. It gives to the Declaration of Independence that timeless quality which makes it the most precious of our great historical documents. Lincoln in his Gettysburg Address declared without qualification that our Republic at its birth was "dedicated to the proposition that all men are created equal." Alexis de Tocqueville, profound student of our early agrarian civilization, began his great work with a reference to the "equality of condition" prevailing in the United States. And many other visitors from beyond the Atlantic during the pre-industrial age remarked again and again the sense of personal dignity prevailing among the members of what some were pleased to call the "lower orders in America." Without a pervasive sense of equality among the people democracy can have no substance. Without it liberty itself cannot be expected to endure. Without it the meeting of minds essential to the conduct of the free political process is corrupted. Without it

the joys of fraternity and comradeship are not possible. With learning and eloquence Alfred J. Snyder has contended that the fulfillment of the promise of human equality is "America's purpose."[1]

The principle of equality is in grave danger everywhere in the world today, even in America. The development of industrial civilization has transformed those life conditions which nurtured and supported this principle in the earlier period of our history. At the same time the struggle for equality on the part of oppressed and exploited classes and peoples has assumed in our generation revolutionary proportions throughout a large part of the earth. In this far-flung struggle, which is shaking the very structure of the world, privileged orders have raised the standard of Fascism and sought to defend their privileges by bluntly repudiating the principle of equality, espousing the doctrine of superiority, and turning openly to personal dictatorship. On the other hand, the underprivileged have rallied around the banner of equality, put their faith in revolutionary violence, and sought to improve their condition through the "dictatorship of the proletariat." In either case political liberty is destroyed; and history shows no instance of despotism serving the cause of equality over an extended period of time. Whatever the original promises, in the end equality as well as liberty is listed among the dead.

The hour for vigorous and enlightened action has struck. If the principle of equality is to survive in the world, it must receive a powerful affirmation in its modern home here in America. In this process of affirmation organized education must assume heavy responsibilities. Although statesmanship of the highest order in government, economy, and church is indispensable for success, it is imperative that the principle of equality be deeply rooted in the habits, the attitudes, the loyalties, and the ideas of the people. Laws have their uses, but if they have no support in popular dispositions they cannot actually function as laws, at least not in a democracy. Unfortunately we can no longer be fortified by the simple

[1] Alfred J. Snyder, *America's Purpose* (Philadelphia, 1937).

faith of our fathers that equality is a "natural" right, that it is decreed by the very constitution of the universe. Our generation knows from tragic experience that doctrines of class and racial superiority can be instilled in the young through the processes of tuition and can ride to victory on tanks and airplanes. It is our responsibility to range the power of organized education on the side of the principle of equality in this elemental battle of ideologies. It is also our opportunity and privilege.

As the principle of equality seems not to be in the original constitution of the universe, neither is it in the biological constitution of man. Few societies in history have been ordered or governed according to its provisions. It is an achievement of the race, quite as much so as technology or symphonic music. Its meaning is not easily grasped, and its practice is difficult. Each generation must learn to understand it and to live by it, if the principle is to survive. While it is true that children acquire from their elders class, national, religious, and social prejudices and hatreds, it is also true that they do not enter the world reciting the *Magnificat* and the *Declaration of Independence.* Men may be born equal in a profound moral sense, but they are not born with a love of equality. An infant may have an aversion to being dropped, but he seems not at all disturbed by the dropping of his twin brother or sister. From the moment he draws his first breath he wants what he wants when he wants it with his whole being, and he can easily grow into a tyrant. We should never forget that Cain slew Abel. If by some miracle a generation of American children left utterly alone were to survive to maturity, they certainly would not take on precisely the prejudices and hatreds of their parents; but just as certainly they would develop others and in the course of time produce a race which would repeat most of the mistakes of the species and doubtless invent others. For the most part we learn from experience in a particular group both our moralities and our immoralities.

This is not to say that men may not fight in the name of equality. They have done so in the most diverse societies since ancient times. In fact ever since the emergence of the idea that the existing inequalities of society are not ordained by God or nature, the battle cry of equality has been unsurpassed in its power to evoke the energies, enthusiasms, and sacrifices of the underprivileged orders and the idealists of all classes. In our day millions of men have wanted equality so much that they have been willing to destroy it utterly in order to get it! However, following the establishment of a regime of equality, tendencies toward inequality immediately and inevitably appear. Individual men always desire power and special privilege, and proceed to struggle by varied means to obtain them. To paraphrase the allegory of George Orwell in his brilliant satire on Russian Communism, *Animal Farm*, the citizens of the ideal republic may awake some morning to discover that to the stirring slogan of the revolution, "all men are equal," these words have been added: "but some are more equal than others." Eternal vigilance in both statecraft and the rearing of the young is the price of equality as well as liberty.

2

We need an education that will make clear the meaning and worth of the principle of equality. This is the more necessary because our people, though accustomed on public occasions to repeat in emotional tones the Declaration of Independence, the Gettysburg Address, and other eloquent expressions of our social faith, are easily confused on the basic issues involved. The fact is that the meaning of the principle of equality is little understood in America today. A bold and realistic grappling with the problem through the agencies of organized education is made clearly necessary by the condition of ignorance and indifference prevailing so widely.

To what depths our political understanding has fallen is revealed in some of the common objections raised to the principle. On the one hand, there are many in our genera-

Education for a Society of Equals 331

tion, as in the time of Lincoln, who would dispose of the "principles of Jefferson" by calling them "glittering generalities," by damning them as "self-evident lies," or by arguing that they apply only to "superior races." There are others who, interpreting equality to mean identity or uniformity of talents, pompously announce that, if the author of the Declaration had only been versed in the findings of physical and mental measurements, he would never have written that "all men are created equal." These people apparently do not realize that, certainly since the time of Plato and probably since the age of the cave man, the fact of individual differences with respect to every human trait has been known and acted upon. There are still others who maintain that the principle of equality means that anyone should be willing to marry anybody else, or at least that he should be willing to have his daughter marry a Negro, or perhaps a Chinese, a Hindu, an Englishman, a German, an Irishman, a Russian, or a man from Kansas. Such "arguments" are commonly put forward to justify the cruel and discriminatory treatment of minorities which cannot be defended on rational or humane grounds.

In our approach to the development in the young of an understanding of the principle of equality we must avoid the pitfalls of utopianism. Probably not a few are inclined to assume that it means complete equality of both material and social rewards. While there is nobility and humanity in this conception, it is obviously far beyond the range of practical consideration in the present epoch. Although great inequalities in material rewards, particularly when not clearly associated with service or merit, tend to place the values involved in serious jeopardy, substantial inequalities here may be expected to continue until the dawn of the golden age of absolute abundance. Moreover, even in that age there will be positions in society of great or little honor, and children will be fortunate or unfortunate in their parents and in the accidents of life. Also the administration of rewards will ever fall somewhat short of perfect justice, and doubtless individuals and groups will always feel that their merits are insufficiently recognized. This of course constitutes no apology for the system of rewards now prevailing in our society—for the actual distribution of income, for the condition of poverty of the lowest third of our population, for the degrading slums in which millions live, or for the allotment to a crooner, a huckster, a comedian, or a manipulator of exchanges of a salary greater than that attached to the presidency of the Republic.

The principle of equality constitutes a positive affirmation of the central value of the Hebraic-Christian ethic. While recognizing the great differences in strength and talent among men, it proclaims the unique worth of the individual and his right to unprejudiced membership in the human brotherhood. It means that each, within the limits of his powers, is entitled to the same rights, liberties, and opportunities and is subject to the same duties and responsibilities. It means equality in citizenship, in the political process, and in the general conduct of government. It means equality *in* the law as well as *before* the law, since laws can support the most flagrant forms of exploitation and discrimination. It means equality in the opportunity to make a living, to choose an occupation, to improve one's position, to launch an enterprise, to achieve security. It means equality of opportunity for health, for education, for personal growth, for leisure. Above all it means recognition of individual worth in the sphere of social relations and in the moral order, of the right to be judged without prejudice by one's own personal qualities as a human being.

The principle of equality rejects the doctrine, age-old support of aristocracy, that any individual or class should be entrenched in the law or be permitted to live above the law. In the bright lexicon of democracy there are no "superior" families, castes, races, or peoples whose members by reason of such membership are entitled or commissioned to rule, exploit, or enslave their less fortunate fellows. The principle of equality declares, in the words of the last letter Jefferson ever wrote, "that the mass of mankind has not been born with saddles on their backs, nor a favored few booted and spurred, ready to ride them legitimately, by the grace of God." As it repudiates the claim of any order of men to special rights, liberties, and opportunities apart from labors performed, so it refuses to sanction the exemption of any such order from the obligations of work and citizenship. In a society of equals, except because of age or infirmity, where equality should be tempered with mercy, there are no parasites.

In a word, the principle of equality affirms that all men are men, or, as Robert Burns put it, "a man's a man for a' that." It sees something noble or the possibility of something noble in every human being. It holds that even those who have transgressed the moral law and preyed upon their fellows may be redeemed and made men again. It recognizes the right of every man to a sense of self-respect or to the opportunity to achieve a sense of self-respect. Exploitation of the weak and unfortunate and resort to cruel and inhuman punishments constitute a violation of its spirit. In the measure that any individual is diminished in his personhood, or is made to feel himself less than a man, the principle of equality is corrupted. The members of the younger generation must be instructed in all these things.

They must also be instructed in the consequences of the denial of the principle of equality, which are written large on practically every page of history. The popular rebellions and revolutions that have shaken and remade human society periodically from prehistoric times have generally been responses to injustices flowing from inequalities imbedded in laws and institutions. "Inequality of rights," said Thomas Paine, "has been the cause of all the disturbances, insurrections, and civil wars, that ever happened in any country, in any age of mankind."[2] General repudiation of the principle of equality leads inevitably to the suppression of civil liberties and the establishment of a police state. It divides a society or a world into oppressor and oppressed, into latently or openly warring

[2] Thomas Paine, "Constitutional Reform," Appendix G in *The Writings of Thomas Paine*, collected and edited by Moncure Daniel Conway (New York, 1896), Vol. IV, p. 465.

groups, classes, nations, or races. And the young should be advised not to take comfort from the thought that equal rights once lost can be easily restored by appeal to violence. The passions aroused by the struggle make the emergence of a better social order far from certain. The Communist Manifesto, as it called the workers of the world to battle in 1848, recognized that the contending parties may destroy the very fabric of society and thus share a "common ruin." Even if the oppressed are victorious they may be so warped or deformed by bitter hatred or sense of wrong that they may be unable to bring into life the great ideals which sustained them in the struggle. The doctrine of superiority, moreover, breeds in superior and inferior alike the disposition to find ethical justification for acts of extreme cruelty and barbarism. Vengeance has always been a dangerous guide and counselor. All of this should be patently evident to those who have lived through the past half century and witnessed the general degradation of moral standards that has touched every people on the earth.

The substance of the matter is that the principle of equality, as here developed, is the only enduring foundation of peaceful relations within society or between societies. Any social order or international organization based clearly on the contrary principle carries within itself the seeds of war and violence. Genuine cooperation, now demanded on a worldwide as well as a national scale, is possible only among equals. How tragic for all mankind, therefore, is the fate of the Atlantic Charter! Forsaken by its authors, repudiated by vested interests, and torn to shreds by Soviet aggressions, its promises are almost forgotten. Justice too is a mockery if the weak must go cap-in-hand to the strong. Even the full flowering of individual liberty, which has often been set in opposition to equality, is likewise possible only among equals. When Lincoln associated the two in his most celebrated affirmation of democratic principles, he probably knew what he was doing. We may well note again the conversation which the Marquis de Chastellux had with Samuel Adams in 1780 on the form of government to be established in the states of the young Republic then in birth. With true insight he observed that "an individual without property is a discontented citizen, when the state is poor; place a rich man near him, he dwindles into a clown."[3]

This entire subject of the meaning of equality should be studied in the school. Destined to live through one of the most turbulent periods of history in which men will have to make the great choices, the young should learn how precious is our imperfect heritage of equality and be inspired to strive in their generation to fulfill its promise. Through history, biography, and literature, through the drama, the movie, and television they should be given the full story of the long struggle to establish the principle of equality on the earth. They should be introduced to the lives and teachings of the major prophets of mankind from the earliest times. They should be led in imagination through the great battles to abolish human slavery, feudal relationships, colonial domination, and the exploitation of men by men generally. They should be encouraged to look out upon the contemporary world with clear and honest eyes, to study the resurgence of despotism in the totalitarian states, and to understand that the task of achieving equality even in its crudest forms in the best of societies is far from finished. The time has come for us to realize that one of the first duties of the school is to convey to the younger generation the great conception of the nature of man which underlies the principle of equality.

3

We need an education that will reveal the deficiencies in our heritage and the dangers threatening the principle of equality in the contemporary world.

First of all, the young should comprehend the nature of the totalitarian threat

[3] François Jean de Chastellux, *Travels in North-America, in the Years 1780, 1781, and 1782* (Dublin, 1787), Vol. I, p. 270.

which in its several forms has harassed and menaced mankind for a generation. Recently we escaped by the narrowest of margins subjection to a world-wide tyranny founded on the doctrine of racial superiority. Although the assault of the Axis powers was finally crushed decisively, the raw materials out of which the Fascist systems were fashioned have by no means been destroyed. And stepping into the place vacated by the vanquished tyranny, with greater potential resources and with "fifth columns" in all countries, is a second tyranny which is to be distinguished from its rival, not by the quality of its morals and purposes, but by its professions. As they liquidate disaffected national minorities and send millions of men and women to the torture chamber and the slave labor camp, the Soviet leaders, with every breath they breathe, proclaim themselves the only true champions of equality in the world. To them equality appears to mean that all men must lie down in the Procrustean bed of Marxism-Leninism-Stalinism as framed by the Politburo, and like it. It is becoming clear that the only brand of equality which dictatorship can establish is the equality of the prison, and that the only brand which possesses moral significance is that which is established by free men under the shelter of just laws and in accord with their own consciences.

The young should also learn that the principle of equality has been imperiled by vast changes which have taken place in our society during the past century. A major threat is found in the transformation of the economic system and the entire social structure. The advance of technology, as we have seen, has grievously weakened the pattern of small enterprise and wide distribution of productive property which was the original foundation of equality in American life. We live now in a society marked by great concentration of property ownership and economic power, on the one side, and a condition of general dependence for the earning of a livelihood, on the other. These conditions tend to be perpetuated through the institution of inheritance. Great extremes of poverty and riches, of labor and leisure, of slums and grand estates, of severe exploitation and special privilege, have come to be characteristic of democratic America.[4] Also we no longer live alike and follow like modes of livelihood as we did in the agrarian age. This fact alone would create among us differences in outlook and interest.

From this economic base arises the division of society into groups and classes with unequal rights, liberties, opportunities, and duties. At the one extreme are those who have all that money can buy, and money can buy many things; at the other are those who from birth are denied full admission to our rich cultural heritage, are limited in their access to medical care, to food and shelter, to education and artistic enjoyment, even to political rights and justice in the courts. More important than moderate disparity in economic condition perhaps is the sense of dependence, insecurity, and inferiority which flows from absence of control over the source of livelihood. This condition tends to breed in the individual a spirit of servility and to destroy the psychological foundation of man's most precious possession—personal dignity and integrity. Even in days of general prosperity the individual, unless he joins his fellows in organization, is compelled to bow to the will of those who control the instruments of production; in days of economic adversity he may lose his job and walk the streets a bitter and beaten man. He may then feel that he can regain his self-respect only through violent revolt.

The program of instruction should recognize that in yet another sphere the principle of equality has been more or less grievously violated in America since the founding of the Republic, and even since the establishment of the first colonial settlements along the Atlantic seaboard. In the relations of the many national, religious, and racial groups which compose our people the doctrine of inequality has widely and generally prevailed. Broadly speaking, the earlier immigrants have looked down upon the later, the English upon the Scotch and Irish, the British upon the Europeans, the West Europeans upon the East Europeans, the Europeans

[4] See Gustavus Myers, *History of the Great American Fortunes* (New York, 1907).

upon the Asiatics, the Protestants upon the Catholics, the Christians upon the Jews, and all upon the Negroes. Our history has been marked from earliest times by racial, national, and religious prejudice, hatred, and bigotry.[5] Doctrines of racial superiority, reminiscent of Hitler and Rosenberg, have always had their advocates in America. Today, in spite of notable progress in recent years and decades, various groups, particularly the Indian, the Jew, the Mexican, the Negro, and the Oriental, suffer from severe and persistent discrimination. Here is a violation of the principle of equality which not only corrupts our democracy at home but also weakens our voice in the councils of nations. This cancer which strikes at the very heart of our democracy seriously impairs our leadership of the free world.

In the realm of the relations between the sexes the principle of equality also is not fully applied. Although we have achieved great advances since colonial days, elements of the patriarchal tradition persist. The boy still enters the world under more favorable auspices than the girl; and he is nurtured from year to year, sometimes crudely and always subtly, on the doctrine of male superiority. Our culture is permeated with double standards of personal morality, economic compensation, political rights, and intellectual and cultural opportunities. In almost all spheres of life outside the domain of narrowly "feminine" interests the woman engages in competition for leadership and recognition under severe handicaps. Dependence on and deference to the male still define largely her expected role in society.

In concluding this consideration of the dangerous threats to or the persisting violations of the principle of equality we should recognize certain assets and advances which industrial civilization has brought. Most striking perhaps is the fabulous productive power of technology. It is now possible for the first time in human history to abolish poverty and achieve relative economic security and well-being for all. Here is a material basis for equality which surpasses in its possibilities

[5] See Gustavus Myers, *History of Bigotry in the United States* (New York, 1943).

even the resources of the rich and virgin continent to which our people fell heir. Also, the social invention of popular organizations, unions, granges, and associations, which is a basic feature of industrial society, serves to place increasing power in the hands of the people and thus to limit the danger to the principle of equality resident in the concentration of the ownership of productive property. This march of the working population toward power through collective action constitutes one of the major achievements and supports of our American democracy. Another significant development which has been in process for two generations is the levying of income and estate taxes and the establishment of the principle of equality of sacrifice in the support of community and government enterprise.[6] Still another is the growing sensitivity of our people to inherited forms of discrimination against minority groups. Of like importance is the general advance of the social sciences and the dissemination of knowledge and enlightenment among all ranks of the population. Knowledge, if related to great purposes and uncorrupted by totalitarian controls, remains an unconquerable force in the world. This knowledge, as it illuminates all threats to the principle of equality, should be made fully available to the younger generation.

4

We need an education that will cultivate in the young the spirit and practice, the attitudes and loyalties of equality.
Understanding of the meaning and worth of this basic principle of democracy and knowledge of the conditions and tendencies threatening to weaken or destroy it, necessary as they are, do not encompass the whole of the educational task. To these things must be added the living dynamic of actual experience. This means that the entire educational undertaking, from its relations

[6] See Gustavus Myers, *The Ending of Hereditary American Fortunes* (New York, 1939).

with the community to the conduct of its own life, should express in so far as possible the principle of equality.

In the first place, every form of educational discrimination against any group in the American community, whether geographical, economic, cultural, or racial, should be abolished. Making due allowance for individual differences in talent, aptitude, and interest, we should set the same high standards of excellence for the children of all our people—for those who dwell in the country as well as for those who dwell in the city, for those who dwell in the South as well as for those who dwell in the North, for those who dwell on the "lower east side" as well as for those who dwell on Park Avenue—for the child of an immigrant just off the boat as well as for the descendant of the Pilgrims, for Catholic as well as for Protestant, for Jew as well as for gentile, for Negro as well as for white. Particular attention should be given to children from the economically and culturally underprivileged groups. The achievement of this goal will require funds for educational purposes far beyond the practices of the past—funds not only for buildings, equipment, and teachers but also for scholarships, maintenance stipends, and many special services. Such funds will probably have to come increasingly from federal sources. But we know that in the long run no comparable expenditure would pay greater dividends in terms of the advancement of the general welfare and the strengthening of our free institutions.

In the second place, children and youth from both sexes and from all occupational, cultural, religious, and racial groups, residing in the community, should be brought together in the common school. In the measure that any group is absent the conditions essential for the attainment of the desired educational purposes will be less than satisfactory. In the measure that any group is segregated in a special institution the opportunity for strengthening the principle of equality and for promoting mutual understanding will be limited. The job simply cannot be done effectively through theoretical instruction and the verbalization of democratic maxims. Only as children from all groups share common experiences, only as they live and work and play together *as equals*, can the ideal be given substance. Moreover, teachers as well as pupils should be representative, to the degree professionally feasible, of the various components of the population.

These proposals call for radical changes in the common practices of American education. They call for the abolition of separate schools for Negroes and whites in a considerable section of the country and the complete abandonment of the so-called "quota system" under which children of certain cultural or racial groups are deliberately held down to a given percentage of the total enrollment. Also, while recognizing the legal right of secular and religious authorities to establish and maintain private schools, we should appeal to the democratic conscience of all elements of the population and seek to persuade them to abandon the principle of separatism and join together in strengthening the public educational system. The exclusion from that system of any considerable proportion of the young encourages the growth of divisive forces and weakens the principle of equality in the nation.

In the third place, the life and work of the school should be organized in terms of the principle of equality. There must be no discrimination against any child or teacher because of origin. The young of various groups, guided by teachers of various groups, should learn together the story of the endless struggle to destroy the barriers of class and caste and to establish and maintain the great principle of equality in the world. They should examine critically violations of its letter and its spirit in the school, the nation, and the world. Rights, privileges, and duties should be enjoyed or discharged equally by all, regardless of family, creed, or color. Particular attention should be given in the social relations of the school to the abolition of existing prejudices and hatreds and to the development of tolerance, understanding, and appreciation of differences among religions, nationalities, and races. The contributions of all of the many peoples composing America to the advancement and enrichment of our civilization should be stressed. Persisting vestiges of the patriarchal tradition should be removed from the relations of girls and boys. They should also be removed from the treatment of the rise of our civilization. As Mary R. Beard has pointed out, the role of women in this great epic has been too largely neglected. The giving of marks, the making of promotions, the awarding of honors, the election of officers to pupil and student organizations, and the choosing of individuals to represent class or school in athletic, scientific, literary, and artistic activities should always be conducted fairly on the basis of merit. Needless to say, an effort should be made to nurture a proper sense of modesty in the gifted and successful. In the life of the school the members of all groups should be made to feel that they are wanted and valued. Everything possible should be done to soften and ultimately eradicate sentiments of superiority or inferiority. We should recognize that in this entire program the example set by the school and the teacher is far more important than precept.

In the fourth place, the school should endeavor to moderate the influence of social class in its own operations. Here is a task of extreme difficulty and of great urgency. It is not enough, admirable though it is, to bring together in common activities children of different family backgrounds, occupational antecedents, and financial resources. A positive program for meeting the impact of the grievous contrasts in wealth and position which children inevitably bring to school should be developed with all the wisdom available to the profession. The problem assumes particular significance during the period of adolescence, when boys and girls become sex conscious and socially sensitive. Some youths come to school from beautiful homes, dressed in the best of clothes, and ostentatiously driving expensive automobiles. In their conversations they talk about house parties, trips to bathing beaches, visits to foreign lands, where they should go to college, and what professions they should enter. Others walk to school from the slums along unsightly streets, clad always in plain and ofttimes in soiled or shabby garments. Among them may be found the sons and daughters of personal servants who work in the "big houses" in which their more fortunate classmates live. The two groups come from different worlds, with different standards of living and cultural outlooks. Particularly vicious in its psychological consequences is the fraternity and sorority system which projects into the school the injustice, the snobbery, and the social distinctions of adult society. No one unfamiliar with the facts can imagine the bitterness and heartache engendered in the minds and hearts of underprivileged youth by this situation. Many, overcome with a feeling of shame and inferiority give up the struggle, leave school, and seek employment. Others doubtless remain and harbor resentment for many years, if not for life.[7] On the other hand, it can be said that not a few resolutely surmount all obstacles, develop great strength of mind and character, and achieve positions of highest eminence in the economy, the arts and sciences, and public life. The problems raised by this whole impact of social distinctions on the life of the school should be discussed with students, parents, and board members in the light of the democratic tradition of equality. While no wholly satisfactory solution may be possible in our society today, much undoubtedly could be done to improve the situation.

In the fifth place, the social status of the teacher should be raised. Because of a quasi-servile tradition, a low level of economic compensation, and an authoritarian administrative pattern, teachers themselves often suffer from a sense of inferiority. If they are to play their part in strengthening the principle of equality in the young, their condition will have to be changed. They must be made to feel by the judgment of the community that their work is vital and necessary to the maintenance and strengthening of the American democracy. In fact, they must be made to feel that their work is as important as it actually is. This subject will be treated at some length in a later chapter.

[7] See August B. Hollingshead, *Elmtown's Youth: The Impact of Social Classes on Adolescents* (New York, 1949).

22

EDUCATION FOR A GOVERNMENT OF FREE MEN

1

We need an education that will preserve, vitalize, and strengthen the principle of political liberty in our country. The situation is critical. At no time since the English, American, and French revolutions in the seventeenth and eighteenth centuries has this precious possession been in greater danger in the world. The advance of industrial civilization has transformed the social, economic, and military foundations of human freedom. The rise of vigorous totalitarian movements which mock political liberty has brought the first living and vigorous challenge to democracy in more than two centuries. A powerful and uncompromising affirmation of the spirit and practice of political liberty in the mightiest of the democratic states is therefore imperative. In this context it is appropriate to quote again the prophetic words of Washington in his first inaugural: "The preservation of the sacred fire of liberty and the destiny of the republican model of government are justly considered as *deeply*, perhaps as *finally* staked, on the experiment intrusted to the hands of the American people." Today it seems even more probable that, if we fail, political liberty will disappear throughout the earth.

Education for a Government of Free Men

The educational problem arises from the fact that the spirit and practice of liberty must be acquired anew by each generation. The individual, we know, is not born free. He is born more helpless and dependent than the beasts of field or forest. Whatever freedom he ever enjoys is a product of a long and difficult process of learning through which he develops his own powers and learns to participate with his fellows in the shaping of the conditions under which he is to live. "The qualifications for self-government in society," wrote Thomas Jefferson near the end of his life, "are not innate. They are the result of habit and long training." More than two generations later, decades before industrial civilization had reached its present state of complexity and dynamism, Herbert Spencer expressed the same thought. "The Republican form of government," he observed, "is the highest form of government; but because of this it requires the highest type of human nature—a type nowhere at present existing."[1] But freedom of the individual is far more than an individual achievement. It is also a social product, and rests on social foundations. Only in a free society, only under a government committed to liberty and the defense of liberty, can the great masses of men know and enjoy freedom.

Although there is probably a deep longing in the human heart for freedom in all times and places, there have been few free societies in history. Despotism being "the simplest form of government," wrote Edmund Burke, "is infinitely the most general."[2] Like the individual, society is not free by nature. Rather is such a society one of the highest and most difficult achievements of mankind, the product of a long historical process involving struggle, thought, and invention. Freedom never appears full blown on the stage of history. On the contrary, as someone has said, it "broadens down from precedent to precedent." Moreover, like every form of excellence, it is always in a precarious state, it is always in danger of decay and dissolution. This is due to the fact that

---

[1] Herbert Spencer, "The Americans," in *Essays Scientific, Political and Speculative* (New York, 1892), Vol. III, pp. 478–479.
[2] Quoted in *The Manual of Liberty* (London, 1795), p. 83.

it makes most rigorous demands on the energy, courage, virtue, and understanding of the people. Should any single generation falter in these qualities, liberty might be lost for centuries. Millions in the free countries of Western Europe during the years immediately following the last war, as they faced the fresh threat of totalitarian assault and felt the full impact of the Communist "strategy of terror," seemed to lose the will to struggle. As a distinguished European remarked paradoxically to the writer in the spring of 1948: "In the Old World today only the brave are frightened; all others have seen fit to surrender before the battle." The young must learn in idea and in deed that freedom divorced from responsibility cannot survive.[3]

If we would preserve, vitalize, and strengthen this great heritage, we must see clearly, therefore, that it does not automatically and surely reproduce itself from generation to generation and that its fortunes are always in the hands of the living. Only as the necessary qualities of mind and heart are rigorously and successfully cultivated in the young can liberty be expected to endure. Unfortunately, at no time in our history has this truth been fully recognized by our people. Never have our educational institutions directed their energies deliberately and imaginatively to the performance of this task. The crisis now enveloping human affairs demands the abandonment of this historic mood of indifference and complacency. Without the loss of an hour we should proceed to the reconstruction of our entire educational program from the earliest years, embracing both the school and other agencies, for the purpose of developing in children and youth the qualities and powers essential to the perpetuation through the years of our heritage of freedom. We should recall today the sage counsel of Jefferson that "no nation is permitted to live in ignorance with impunity."

The young must learn, too, that political liberty does not grow in every soil and that it flourishes only under certain conditions. To establish and maintain a form of government

---

[3] See Carl L. Becker, *Freedom and Responsibility in the American Way of Life* (New York, 1945).

that places political power squarely in the hands of the people is of course essential. But more is necessary. The foundations of liberty are diverse. And as they may be swept away suddenly in some great social convulsion, they may also be undermined slowly and imperceptibly through the process of cultural change. More basic in a sense perhaps than political power is military force. Consequently, if the weapons of war ever come to be lodged in the hands of any class or caste, the people will sooner or later lose their liberties. Next in order probably is economic power—power over the means of livelihood. In the absence of military force, as the founding fathers knew well, political power tends to gravitate into the hands of those who own the property. If such ownership should become the monopoly of a small and united faction, the actual operations of government would tend to fall under the control of an aristocracy of property. Knowledge is yet another form of power which the friends of liberty must ever watch with a jealous eye. In the measure that the masses of the people are ignorant and uninformed, in the measure that their minds are molded by false propaganda, they are automatically removed from the seats of power, even though they may go through the motions of the entire democratic political process. The only secure foundation of political liberty and popular rule is the wide distribution of power in its several forms among the people. Every generation must learn this fundamental truth.

2

We need an education that will make clear the meaning of political liberty.

Political liberty is one of the most revolutionary conceptions ever formulated by mankind. It is founded, not only on the affirmation of the worth of the individual human being, but also on a sublime faith in the powers of common people. It assumes that farmers, mechanics, and housewives can be prepared to rule themselves, that "hewers of wood and drawers of water" can achieve the qualities of mind and character necessary to participate in the framing of the highest policies of state, that all men, and not just the "well-born," are potentially capable of taking part in the selection of governors and the passing of judgment on the conduct of government. Clearly, those who are not permitted or equipped to do these things can in no sense be called free men and women.

Political liberty therefore means direct or indirect participation of the individual in the entire process of rule, in the selection of public officials, in the framing of the laws, in the discussion of political affairs. In the measure that this great democratic process is closed to any element of the population the exercise of political liberty is denied. Likewise, in the measure that the process is controlled, manipulated, or corrupted by any class, party, group, or authority through organized propaganda, resort to bribery, threat of reprisal, or display of physical force, it becomes a cloak of tyranny. The so-called popular elections of totalitarian states which invariably issue in an almost unanimous approval of the policies, programs, and henchmen of a dictator should deceive no one. Also in the measure that the democratic process is directed to deliberate falsification, misrepresentation, and vituperation with respect to persons, platforms, and parties it is employed to undermine its own foundations. The young of America should be educated to an understanding of all these things.

Political liberty must be expressed in the laws of society and the conditions of life. The individual must be guaranteed, not only the right of suffrage, but also certain basic assurances, freedoms, and opportunities through which he may achieve intellectual maturity and integrity. First of all, he must enjoy a large degree of material and spiritual security. He must be guaranteed the right to labor and to enjoy the fruits of his labor, the freedom to think, to speak, and to worship as he pleases. He must be guaranteed security under the laws against mob action, police surveillance, arbitrary arrest, and cruel and inhuman punishments. He must be guaranteed full access to knowledge through all the agencies of communication, through a free press, a free radio, a free library, and a free school, generously conceived, supported, and administered. Within the limits set by reasonable considerations of national defense in times of "clear and present danger," he must be guaranteed the right to move about, to associate with his fellows, to organize for the purpose of guarding his own welfare or of promoting any public cause or cultural interest whatsoever. He must be guaranteed the right to learn, to investigate, and to engage in the untrammeled pursuit of truth in any field. There is no place in a society of free people for a secret police, a passport system, thought control, or forced labor camps designed to suppress, ferret out, and punish political dissent.

All of this means that a free society will always be marked by recognized and tolerated differences—differences in economic interest, in political doctrine, in world outlook, and in conceptions of public welfare. Such a society will also be marked by diverse and competing economic, civic, and cultural organizations. The conduct of free government is consequently characterized at all times by open struggle and by loyal opposition to the party in power. Where there is no such struggle or opposition, there is no political liberty in any fundamental sense. Whatever a one-party state may be, it is not a free state. As diversity is one of the marks of liberty, so it is one of the great assets of a free society. Dissenting minorities constitute a great creative force through which the old order is challenged and the new is fashioned. A free people therefore must learn, not only to tolerate, but also to respect and value differences. Here is a major educational task.

Finally, a free society is a society of equals. The two great principles of liberty and equality are the twin supports of democracy. Together they constitute the essence of the democratic spirit. If a democratic society should lose either, its conception of life would enter a regressive and counterrevolutionary phase. Moreover, if it should forsake either, the other would be in danger. Certainly a society of free people could not long endure if it became marked by gross and persisting inequalities in basic rights, opportunities, and responsibilities. Likewise, if a society of equals should lose its civil and political liberties, life would immediately take on the pattern of caste, special privilege, and concentrated power. No totalitarian state can tolerate either liberty or equality.

3

We need an education that will give understanding of our American heritage of political liberty.

This legacy of course belongs to all mankind, as it has been the achievement of many peoples in many ages. We in America owe an incalculable debt to the prophets and lawgivers of the ancient world, to the giants of liberal political thought and statesmanship of the intervening centuries, and to the millions of ordinary men and women who from generation to generation have carried on the struggle against despotism. During the colonial period, drawn to these shores by the desire for freedom in one or more of its varied forms, our fathers proceeded to weld into a single liberating synthesis elements from many sources and to fashion our institutions in the name of liberty. Then at the end of the eighteenth century, guided by the long experience of mankind with freedom and tyranny, they established the Republic and framed a great political charter under which we have ruled ourselves with marked success for more than a century and a half. Every child should know this story from its earliest beginnings on the other side of the Atlantic down to the present hour. He should also know its meaning in terms of the price paid in courage and sacrifice for all of our political rights and liberties.

The young should acquire full understanding of the nature of democratic constitutional government, of government by law and orderly process, of government of, by, and for the people. The Constitution, as noted in an earlier chapter, establishes, on the foundation of guaranteed rights and liberties, a framework of political institutions, of legislative, judicial, and executive authorities, through which the laws, expressing the considered judgment of the citizens and their chosen representatives, can be enacted, interpreted, administered, enforced, and changed. For the adjustment of differences among groups, sections, and classes it substitutes the ballot for the sword and makes the will of the majority expressed in law generally supreme over the action of mobs, the ambition of rulers, and the power-thirst of fanatics and madmen. By making possible the most profound changes in economy, government, and even its own provisions, it creates a peaceful alternative to the method of violent revolution. The magnitude and the worth of this achievement should be clearly grasped by the members of the younger generation. They would then see that Election Day, focus and symbol of democratic constitutional government, should ever be regarded as a veritable "holy day" by our people.

They should learn too that the successful operation of government founded on liberty places the heaviest burdens on the powers of all the people. They should learn that laws neither make nor enforce themselves, that the ability to make laws and the disposition to obey them are not an expression of untutored "human nature," that acceptance of majority decision and respect for minority rights are not a gift from the germ plasm to free society, that the entire process of democratic constitutional government requires a long period of carefully guided learning, that only by some fortunate chance can the quality of the laws and their administration rise above the wisdom and devotion of the citizens. If they should lack the necessary powers of mind and heart, if they should fail to understand the world of their time, if they should cease to share great common loyalties and purposes, if they should become divided into irreconcilable factions and classes, if they should lose faith in the essential justice of their institutions, if they should refuse to accept the verdict of the ballot, if they should grow indifferent to or unskilled in the discharge of their civic responsibilities, if they should be unable to hold political passions in leash, if they should grossly degrade the political process by sustained resort to dishonesty and falsehood, if they should lose courage in the presence of danger, they might dissipate their entire heritage of democratic constitutional government and open the gates to despotism. They should be instructed fully in the responsibilities of their generation.

The young should be encouraged to examine critically our record of constitutional government, including the many failures and delinquencies noted in this volume. But they should also be taught to take pride in our triumphs. They might well study two recent demonstrations of the strength of our tradition of political liberty. The conducting of a vigorous presidential election in the midst of the Second World War, without any effort by the party in power to coerce opinion or intimidate the voters, must have seemed a wholly incredible event to millions living under dictatorship. The spectacle of our people going calmly to the polls on November 7, 1944, of our fighting men marking their ballots in the "fox holes" of Europe, Asia, and the islands of the sea, to decide some of the greatest issues of history, doubtless appeared to our friends abroad a bit unwise or even foolish. It certainly made them uneasy. But it also must have conveyed to people everywhere a sense of the confident strength and vitality of our tradition of political liberty.

Similar comment might perhaps be made regarding the great debate over foreign policy in May and June of 1951 which was precipitated by the dismissal of a great military commander by the supreme civil authority. In this case, however, many American citizens probably were disturbed by the "terrifying frankness" with which the secrets of our military position and strategy were made public. One unusually perceptive commentator expressed this sense of uneasiness in the following words: "In response to the Senators' uninhibited probing, the service chiefs told about all that is to be known about our military strength and weakness, our plans and doubts, to friends and enemies alike. No such act of self-revelation was ever before committed by a great nation in the shadow of war." [4]

The young should be brought to realize, however, that the record of past and present should not breed a sense of complacency. We have been vastly favored by history and geography. Moreover, we have often badly mismanaged our inheritance and permitted the growth of tendencies in our society which, if not halted, would eventually destroy both equality and liberty. As a people we have never made complete use of our political institutions for the achievement of our avowed purposes. We have rarely discharged nobly and intelligently our full responsibilities as free men and women. Even in a hotly contested presidential election approximately one-half of the eligible voters fail to go to the polls and exercise rights bought with the blood of heroes. To meet successfully the dangers and trials which clearly lie ahead we may be called upon to surpass in virtue and understanding any earlier generation. The young should learn that he who refuses to discharge his civic duties to the best of his abilities is not a free man but rather a political parasite living on the body of liberty.

4

We need an education that will reveal the dangers threatening the life of political liberty today.

That the prospects of the survival of democratic freedoms in the industrial age are critical beyond expression is one of the fundamental theses of the present volume. On every hand the rights for which people fought with unsurpassed heroism in the eighteenth and nineteenth centuries are gravely imperiled. At many points the conditions of life are tending to support the resurgence of authoritarianism and despotism. Only a generation that is clearly aware of the hazards in the situation

[4] Anne O'Hare McCormick, *The New York Times*, June 4, 1951.

can achieve the level of understanding and concern necessary to preserve and strengthen our heritage of freedom. The sober study of these hazards through the use of all the resources of history and the social sciences should be one of the first obligations of the school.

The sweep and tempo of industrial civilization create a task of understanding that staggers the imagination. The individual, whether he lives on a farm in Nebraska or in a great industrial city in New York or California, is caught in a vast maelstrom of change and interaction embracing all institutions, all regions, and all nations. His fate may be decided by events taking place in some remote part of the earth about which he has never heard. Where is the man who at a moment's notice can pass informed and reasoned judgment on Soviet policy in Sinkiang, the admission of Communist China into the United Nations, the support of the Franco regime in Spain, the rearming of Western Germany, or the control of the atomic bomb, not to mention such homely matters as the tariff on sugar, the closed shop in the coal industry, or the voting record of a congressman! And yet, if our people are to remain free, they must find some way of making accurate and dependable knowledge function in the shaping of public policy. They must learn in both attitude and understanding to become good citizens in the great society of the industrial age.

Certain forms of power, as we have stressed at several points in these pages, have been removed from the hands of the people. Military force which in the early years of the Republic hung over the fireplaces of the cabins and homes of farmers and mechanics is now concentrated in great engines of destruction of incalculable power—machine guns, tanks, airplanes, warships, poison gases, and atomic bombs. The time when common people armed with axes and corn knives, or even with rifles and shotguns, could rise against tyrants has long since passed away. Also economic power which in former days was widely distributed among the people in the form of land and little shops has become concentrated in vast establishments owned by a small fraction of the population.

Education for a Government of Free Men   355

We have become a nation of employees, of hired men and women, of dependents beholden to the few for the opportunity of making a livelihood. Through organizations of farmers, industrial laborers, and clerical and professional workers, this tendency toward concentration of economic power has been checked, but the threat of aristocracy still remains. Even control of the dissemination of knowledge tends now to be lodged increasingly in the great corporations which own and administer the press, thé radio, the moving picture, and television.

Industrial society is also marked by divisions of interest and function which commonly reach across the nation. In many instances the people involved band together in organizations. Some of these aggregations of citizens, notably the United States Chamber of Commerce, the National Association of Manufacturers, the American Federation of Labor, the Congress of Industrial Organizations, and the American Farm Bureau Federation, exercise far more influence in the shaping of policy than the entire populations of some of our states. Moreover, the coercive power of the organization over the member, particularly where the means of livelihood are involved, raises in a new sphere the issue of individual liberty. This is profoundly true in those cases, and there are many, where the conduct of the organization violates the most elementary democratic principles and approaches the pattern of dictatorial control. Also these various organized groups, being frequently in conflict with one another, often override the interests of the unorganized and place the immediate welfare of a class above the common weal. The loyalties of our people are as yet not sufficiently broad, except in times of war, to support loyally the good of the nation. Unless this condition is changed through the establishment of the rule of law and the fostering in the young of appropriate dispositions, the country may be literally torn to pieces by warring classes and interests. Preparation to participate effectively in these voluntary organizations and at the same time remain sensitive to the general welfare, should be regarded as an essential and vital part of training for citizenship.

An even more serious threat to the survival of political liberty during these times is a chronic condition of insecurity both at home and in the world. Periodically our economy passes into deep crisis marked by the partial paralysis of the whole process of production and exchange, the wiping out of fortunes and savings, and the discharge of millions of workers. Inflation and deflation, moreover, may from time to time exact their tribute, erasing the hopes and blighting the lives of multitudes. No one can expect human liberty to endure indefinitely under such circumstances. At least no one who loves freedom would want to see the democratic loyalties of our people put again to the terrible test of the years following the crash of 1929. Also the shrinking of the earth, the obliteration of the geographical barriers which in the past have sheltered our country, and the invention of atomic bombs and radar-guided rockets which threaten the destruction of all civilizations, combine to create a state of insecurity in the world that as yet is only dimly sensed and understood. All of these conditions must be moderated or removed if the American people, or people anywhere in the world, are to feel secure in their liberties. As long as they continue, free society will be exposed to the attacks of that ancient enemy of republics—the demagogue.

The war cloud which hangs over us today and which may hang over us for years and even decades threatens the survival of political liberty in yet another respect. Our system of government was founded on the principle of the subordination of the military to the civil authority. This has rightly been regarded as one of the foremost achievements of the fathers of the Republic, an achievement which was strengthened through the generations by the sense of security fostered by our geographical position. It appears now that for an indefinite period we shall be forced to maintain a large military establishment and possibly a program of universal service. The full impact of the pursuit of this fateful course on our free institutions is difficult to foresee. Yet that it may greatly increase the power of the military interest in our society and tend to create a military caste would seem quite possible.

Fortunately we have succeeded in developing a tradition which even our greatest commanders share and respect. The case of General Dwight D. Eisenhower, the most popular of the military leaders produced by the last war, deserves far more attention than it has received. Confronted with the invitation to accept the nomination for the presidency in 1948, and with the practical certainty of election, he issued a public statement through a letter to a friend which has few precedents in history. In refusing to run for the highest office in the land he affirmed with simplicity and strength our American tradition in these words: "It is my conviction that the necessary and wise subordination of the military to the civil power will be best sustained and our people will have greater confidence that it is so sustained, when lifelong professional soldiers, in the absence of some obvious and overriding reason, abstain from seeking high political office." Let us hope that his more ambitious successors will be influenced by his example. And even if the author of this letter should at some time yield to popular pressure and enter the political arena, his clear statement of principle will find an enduring place in our heritage of freedom.

As industrial civilization has advanced in our country the functions of government have been increased and enlarged. During the past generation this tendency has moved swiftly and inexorably. And we may expect the trend to continue until we achieve a large measure of economic security or come face to face with disaster. That there is a threat to human freedom in this aggrandizement of government is clear to anyone who has followed the course of events in the world since the opening of the present century. Such concentration of power in the hands of the state would have frightened the founders of our Republic, even as it should cause us many anxious moments. On the one hand, through some form of collective action we must achieve a large measure of economic security; on the other, we must strive to preserve political liberty. This twofold task may be as difficult as squaring the circle; yet it must be attempted. The burden which it places on civic virtue and understanding surpasses anything which our people have experienced at any time in their history. The widespread corruption in the conduct of government, revealed by congressional investigations in 1950 and 1951, demonstrates our moral unpreparedness to administer public affairs in a complex and far-flung industrial society.

The task is gravely complicated and made more difficult by the totalitarian movements—Fascism and Communism. Both would destroy at the roots the entire liberal and humanist heritage of the Western World. Each is prepared to seize the opportunity to come to power when in time of economic crisis men and women are rightfully fearful and anxious about the future, when their loyalties to inherited values and ways of life are badly shaken. The one falsely promises security without either equality or liberty; the other security and equality without liberty. To anyone reared in the great tradition of the rights of man stemming from the English, American, and French revolutions it is difficult to believe that the masses of men anywhere would succumb to the totalitarian madness, as it has been revealed in both the words and the deeds of Hitler and Stalin. Yet we know that this can happen. We know too that in the present mood of mankind, if liberty is to survive, those who love it will have to find some way of combining it with security as well as with equality. All of these perils to liberty should be studied by the younger generation as soberly and thoroughly as any subject was ever studied in our schools and colleges.

5

We need an education that will cultivate in the young a deep sense of the worth of political liberty.
Perhaps the most effective way of achieving this end, in addition to a study of the historical record, is to get them to see what life is like when political liberty has been extinguished. And perhaps the

most effective way of doing this is to introduce into the schools a thorough and realistic inquiry into the morals and practices of the contemporary totalitarian states. The entire system for holding a people in bondage in the age of advanced technology should be passed in review and clearly understood—the concentration of absolute power in the hands of the dictatorship, the outlawing of all political dissent, the absence of the writ of *habeas corpus*, the huge army of political police, the vast network of forced labor camps, the resort to torture in obtaining confessions of guilt, the entire pattern of abject obeisance to the "great leader," and the all-embracing system of mind control. Fortunately the data necessary to present a relatively complete and trustworthy picture of life under dictatorship are rapidly becoming available. There is no longer any defensible excuse for ignorance.

Stefan Zweig was a great German writer, and one of the great writers of his generation. Following Hitler's rise to power, he went into voluntary exile, and in 1942 died in Brazil by his own hand. There was found among his possessions after his death an unpublished article which has been called "one of the greatest and most moving essays on the tragedy of Europe." It should be read and pondered by every high school student and by free men everywhere. "Never before in history," he wrote in his last hours of spiritual agony, "has violence of this kind been practiced so widely, so methodically and so systematically." And he wondered whether he was "really living in the twentieth century of human history." The essence of this last will and testament of a great spirit follows:

You all know how the tragedy began. It was when National Socialism arose in Germany, National Socialism whose motto from the very first day was: stifle everything. Stifle all voices but one. Eradicate all manifestations of free speech, in whatever form, artistic, literary, journalistic—even in the form of simple conversation. Destroy, root out all freedom of expression.

A few days later this appalling doctrine was translated into practice. Books were burnt, scholars were driven from their laboratories, priests from their pulpits, actors from the stage. Newspapers and the right of assembly were suppressed. Men who had enriched European culture by their ideas and works were hunted like wild animals.

It was the sudden unleashing of a hate that was all the more odious since it was nowhere spontaneous, but was calculated and coldly worked out into the smallest details. The whole world was struck with horror. . . .

But the smothering of freedom of thought, the violence used against the intellectuals of Germany was only a prologue. You all know the blood-stained calendar of Hitler's attacks on individuals and peoples. The victims varied, the method remained the same. Always the same sharp assault against a weak country, an already half-stifled cry for help—and then silence. Icy silence, complete silence. No longer the gentlest moan, no longer the faintest sob. As if this country with its towns and villages, with its millions of human beings had sunk below the surface of the earth. No more letters, no reliable news. Dead the voices of relations and friends, dead the voices of poets and writers; not another sign from them, silence. . . . A silence that today lies heavy as lead on so many nations, on so many peoples who yesterday were still free and whose voices were for us the voices of brothers.

This silence, this terrible, impenetrable, endless silence, I hear it by night and by day, it fills my ear and my soul with its indescribable terror. It is more unbearable than any noise; there is more horror in it than in the thunder, than in the howling of the sirens, than in the burst of explosions.

It is more nerve-racking, more oppressive than cries or sobs, for at every second I am conscious that within this silence is enclosed the thraldom of millions upon millions of human creatures. In no way does it resemble the silence of solitude.

When there is peace over a mountain, a lake, a wood, then it is as if the landscape were holding its breath in order to rest or to dream. This calm is a natural one.

But of this silence which torments and weighs upon me I know that it is an artificial silence, a silence of terror, enforced, commanded, imposed, extorted by threats. Under the vast shroud woven of lies I perceive the desperate convulsions of men unwilling to be buried alive; beneath this silence I sense the humiliation and anger of these millions of choked and strangled voices. Their silence pierces my ear-drums and storms my soul night and day.

Sometimes I forget. I sit with friends, I talk and laugh. But

Education for a Government of Free Men 361

suddenly, like a person waking up with a start, I hear above our friendly conversation the horrible voice of this silence—and the laugh freezes on my lips, I stop short and become mute.

To speak while these millions of people are gagged and are groaning in their death-agony, is shame for me, and I strain my ears to hear them. I then remember those who are perhaps at that very moment calling on me in their thoughts; I conjure up their distant souls before me. . . .

Through the impenetrable distance I begin to see them. I think of Prague, of a laboratory there, of the chemist who explained his researches to me. The laboratory is empty; the bottles, the beakers, the retorts are broken; my friend has disappeared.

I think of a certain poet in Vienna, I know that he is in a concentration camp. I see the University of Cracow; I remember the hum of happy voices that I have heard in its corridors; the voices are stifled, the corridors abandoned and dumb.

I try hard to recall the faces, the attitudes and the gestures of those friends who are incarcerated in the giant prison of the German occupation, but I know that I am deceiving myself. I know that they no longer have the faces that were once theirs, but grey and weary masks; I know that they have lost the free and spontaneous movements of free men and that they are hiding in their houses under the shadow of the terror. They dare not go out, the street is guarded by soldiers in steel helmets. Their ears are ever alert. At the slightest step on the stairs they wonder if it is not the Gestapo, come to arrest them. Sitting together at the family table they do not dare to speak a word: for perhaps the maid is spying on them. It is silence, therefore, silence, silence.

The same silence in the neighboring house, in the house opposite, in all the houses of the town, in all the houses of all the towns and villages in Poland, Czecho-Slovakia, Austria. And still new tortures in the midst of tortures; all these human beings know that the waves of the ether carry the friendly voices which come from France or England, and the comforting voices of the neutrals.

These voices are so near to them, so easy to catch—one only has to turn the knob of the wireless set, and thus men could learn in Poland, in Czecho-Slovakia, what tremendous efforts are being made so that they may regain their freedom and so that all Europe may not fall into the servitude which has been imposed upon them.

But the tormentors have forgotten nothing in order to make the torture even more cruel. They have confiscated the wireless sets.

... It was not enough to have made their victims dumb, they must also be made deaf, deaf for every sound of hope. Only when night falls do they begin to whisper in broken voices: "When will they give us speech back, when will this torment of silence end?" —the most cruel mutilation of the soul that was ever invented in this world below.

Sometimes one of them escapes from this iron prison and, amidst a thousand dangers, sets across the frontier. He is welcomed, his friends embrace him. "Speak," they say to him. "Describe what is happening."

But he has not yet learnt to speak again. A jumble of nerves, he looks about him, terror in his eyes, as if he were still in the grip of his merciless gaolers. He is pressed for news of one person or another. He knows nothing certain. This man has disappeared, is perhaps dead. That other man is in prison. The brother has no knowledge of his brother. The mother no longer knows what has happened to her son.

The silence, the terrible silence has broken off all contact between people. It is useless to press him further: what one single man can relate is no more than a drop in this ocean of misery that has flooded a quarter of our Europe.[5]

In these short paragraphs Stefan Zweig tells of the degradation of spirit which follows the hushing of the human voice. But this is only the first step taken by dictatorship in its effort to command the soul of man. The next step is more terrifying and also more degrading. All members of the intellectual class, teachers, writers, artists, and scientists are *ordered* to speak, and to speak, not the truth as they see it, but the "truth" as defined by the all-powerful state. The decrees on ideology issued by the Central Committee of the All-Union Communist Party immediately after the close of the Second World War attacked without mercy those who sought the refuge of silence or pursued the course of "political neutrality." They were told over and over again that they were "soldiers on the front line of fire" and that they should direct their "weapons" against the enemies of the Party. The famous Chinese philosopher, Hu Shih, put the

[5] Stefan Zweig, "Europe's Terrible Silence Haunts Conscience of Remaining Free World," *The New Leader*, New York, March 14, 1942.

issue in these words: "In Communist countries there is no freedom of silence. We know of course that there is no freedom of speech. But few persons realize that there is no freedom of silence either. Residents of a Communist state are required to make positive statements of belief and loyalty." [6] If the young of America are awakened to the terrors of dictatorship they may then appreciate the blessings of liberty.

6

We need an education that will cultivate in the young the spirit and practice of political liberty.

Such an education should be placed squarely in the framework of the present age—an age of revolution and counterrevolution, of unparalleled violence and bloodshed, of dictatorship and authoritarianism. So widespread is the repudiation of orderly processes of government, so closely knit are the nations of mankind, that the totalitarian way of feeling, thinking, and acting has spread like a malign contagion throughout the earth. Moreover, the strains and tensions among classes and peoples, the dislocations and maladjustments of institutions, the fears and anxieties of men and women occasioned by the birth-throes of a new age tend to undermine and weaken those rational faculties on which the successful conduct of democratic processes rests. Also the strangeness, the infinite complexity, the dynamic quality of a world committed to science and technology place a wholly unprecedented burden on the capacity for understanding of even the most gifted and devoted.

Only a concerted and sustained effort on the part of all who love liberty can be expected to carry our form of government safely through the coming years and decades. This requires first of all a far more comprehensive program of civic education, embracing the entire period from birth to maturity and beyond, than anything we have ever known. The process of education, of acquiring the appropriate habits,

[6] *The New York Times*, September 23, 1950, p. 4.

loyalties, and understandings, cannot begin too early or continue too long. In our rapidly changing society the citizen can never assume that he has completed his preparation for the discharge of his civic responsibilities. More than in earlier ages, eternal vigilance is the price of political liberty and all the other fine things for which men and women have labored and fought down through the centuries. In the emerging age of atomic energy such an educational program should not be beyond our means.

The life of the school and other educational agencies should be organized to develop in the young the habits and dispositions, the attitudes and loyalties of free people. They should learn by democratic procedures under wise and careful tutelage to make rules to guide their work and play and to obey the rules they make. At the appropriate age they should be introduced, through numerous activities and organizations, to all the processes and institutions, rights and responsibilities of democratic citizenship. They should be led to acquire the basic loyalties of free men, the virtues of honesty, truthfulness, and fairness in debate and discussion, the ability to value and judge leadership, to select and depose officers in the conduct of their common affairs. They should be disciplined in the sharing of decisions, in the service of others, in the subordination of private to public good. From early years they should be encouraged to develop interest in and establish active relations with the institutions and processes of democratic citizenship in locality, state, and nation. Ceremony and pageantry, drama and screen, artistically commensurate with the grandeur of the conceptions involved, might well play an important role in this program. Greatly needed is a series of powerful moving pictures designed to dramatize the heroic and sustained struggle for democratic political rights and liberties through the centuries and in all countries.

In its practices the school should exemplify the spirit of freedom. Children should be encouraged to think, to investigate, to criticize, to pursue without compromise the quest for truth. This can be achieved through a forthright study of the great issues of government and civilization. There are the old issues, issues as old as the ancient world, the issues of honesty and efficiency in the conduct of public affairs. There are next the issues that must appear in one form or another in every free society, the issues set forth in the preamble to the Federal Constitution. There are also the many issues raised by our great moral commitments and the revolutionary conditions of these days, the issues of freedom and tyranny, of equality and caste, of cooperation and competition, of prosperity and depression, of security and liberty, of beauty and ugliness, of war and peace, of progress and catastrophe. The educational program should be designed to give to the young, in terms of their growing powers, some understanding of these and many other issues, without any effort to deceive or mislead them, to blind them to the weaknesses and deficiencies of our society. A government of free people is the sole political system whose stability and improvement depend on the encouragement of honest and informed criticism, on the steady advance and the general dissemination of knowledge and thought. It alone gives institutional expression to the faith that only truth can make and keep a people free.

Finally, if this program is to be effective, the teacher will have to set an example of a free person in school and community. He will have to participate with his fellow teachers, administrators, and citizens in the formulation of educational policy; he will have to express himself freely in matters pertaining to the conduct of the school; he will have to show in the classroom a genuine devotion to the pursuit of truth; he will have to assume in the community the full responsibilities of active citizenship; and he will have to reveal in his own life deep devotion to the principle of human liberty. Only a free person can lead the young in the ways of freedom. But to achieve this goal the members of the teaching profession will have to acquire a far greater measure of security, social and economic, than they have enjoyed at any period of their history. They will also have to know more about the world in which they live than they know today or have ever known in the past.

23

EDUCATION FOR AN ECONOMY OF SECURITY AND PLENTY

1

We need an education that will be directed toward the achievement of an economy of security and plenty.
Our industrial economy, based on science and technology, holds out to the American people for the first time in all history the promise of a life of material security and plenty for all. The responsibility for the fulfillment of this promise rests immediately on the shoulders of the members of the mature generation. At least they must succeed in warding off the threat of profound economic crisis which will impend until the foundations of a stable economy are firmly laid. But the completion of the task will absorb a large measure of the creative energies of our people for decades. It is imperative, therefore, that the problem be attacked in the schools broadly, thoroughly, and imaginatively. This means the launching of a well-rounded educational program designed to develop in the young an understanding of the nature of the task, the necessary special and general skills and knowledges, and the appropriate social and moral attitudes, traits, and outlooks.

Education for an Economy of Security and Plenty 367

The importance of the question is evident to all who have followed the course of events of the past half-century. One need not accept the doctrine of historical materialism to realize that economic forces always play a powerful role in human society. Although the worth of a civilization is not to be measured in material possessions, a truly great civilization requires an adequate and stable material base. For the achievement and maintenance of a democratic civilization of the highest order this is peculiarly and emphatically true. No democracy can expect to endure if the masses of the people are compelled to live, even for a limited period, under conditions of economic insecurity and misery. Moreover, the bitter and tragic struggles of our time, the wars and rumors of war, the revolutionary and counterrevolutionary movements which have shaken the foundations of domestic and world society cannot be understood apart from the play of economic forces. Until we make a bold and successful attack on the problem of livelihood in terms of the realities and potentialities of industrial economy, all of the values of our civilization will be in peril.

2

We need an education that will make clear the full nature of the task of developing an economy of security and plenty.

First of all, the young must be brought to sense the urgency of this task. The economic foundations of our democracy in pre-industrial times consisted in the natural abundance of our country, the wide distribution of land ownership, and the relatively self-contained rural household. These foundations have disappeared for the most part and comparable new foundations are yet to be constructed. As we confront this task we should realize that the factor of security or stability is far more crucial than that of plenty. The extreme fluctuations in our economy, the violent swings from prosperity to depression, from inflation to deflation, simply will not be endured indefinitely by any free people. No appeal to the tradition of private enterprise when millions are unemployed and all are prey to fear and anxiety will be able to prevail against the extravagant and irresponsible promises of the totalitarians. A measure of economic security, a minimum of material well-being, and a general condition of occupational opportunity are the indispensable supports of both equality and liberty.

The emphasis in our educational program, however, should be positive. The young should be given a vision of the glorious possibilities which lie ahead, if we but have the courage and the wisdom required to make use of all of our resources —natural, technical, cultural, and human. In terms of economic welfare an age is opening that will mark a revolutionary break with the entire human past. From earliest times, except perhaps in a few spots favored by nature, the overwhelming majority of the men, women, and children who have inhabited this planet have lived on the very margin of subsistence with both bodies and minds undernourished, waiting to be carried away by pestilence and famine. Even here in America, in this golden land of opportunity, many have suffered in every generation from severe physical privation. Today, despite the fabulous advances in the productivity of our economy, a considerable part of our population still experience hunger and want. In 1949 one family in every eight had an income of less than one thousand dollars a year.[1] The hard lot from which man seemed destined never to escape led to the designation of political economy as the "dismal science."

Today wholly new prospects are being presented to the eyes of mankind—prospects so beneficent in character that they pass the bounds of credibility. Through the contriving of machines and the harnessing of energy it is now technically possible to maintain from generation to generation a level of production sufficient to drive from our land forever poverty, material distress, debasing toil, and economic insecurity. It

[1] Bureau of the Census, *Current Population Reports—Consumer Income* (Washington, 1951), p. 1.

Education for an Economy of Security and Plenty 369

is also possible to guarantee even to the poorest a life rich in all the good things of the spirit. At last man stands at the gates of a paradise in which the conditions of livelihood should place no limitations on his achievement of full human stature. The idea of course is not new. It has been proclaimed by prophets in all ages, and it has been anticipated for several generations by the steady rise of the productivity of labor. Today the possibility is definitely present. The coming generation should be challenged to undertake the task, not only of achieving an economy of security and plenty, but also of ridding the world of those cruel offspring of scarcity—the exploitation of man by man, the struggle of classes for bread, and the mortal clashing of nations and peoples for land and resources. These things are possible.

The fact must be emphasized, however, that the difficulties are many and grave. To be sure, in terms of production the scientific and technical means for the most part are already present in America. Yet the actual attainment of the goal of economic security and plenty still eludes us. We lack not only the techniques of distribution but also essential social dispositions and institutions. The latter wait upon the sloughing off of old habits and attitudes, the development of an appropriate mentality among our people, the formation of high resolve and determination, the making of necessary social inventions, and the achievement of political leadership and statesmanship of the first order. That the inventions, however, would be speedily forthcoming, if the problems were clearly grasped and social acceptance were assured, may be confidently assumed. We have never experienced great difficulty in devising new ways of doing things that we want to do. All of this means that we are confronted with a large task of popular enlightenment. We need to formulate an educational program that will bring the understanding of our people abreast the material world in which they live and that will equip them to solve the many problems involved in building a stable and abundant economy.

Equally vital is a recognition of the hazards that beset the way to the goal. It will not be easy to keep all the values concerned in balance. If we were prepared to make material security the overruling purpose of our civilization, the task might not seem too difficult. We could take the totalitarian road and transfer the entire burden of thought and decision to some "all-wise and beneficent" dictator. This is the short and easy road which many tired souls, both "left" and "right," are saying all industrial societies are destined to follow. To the spiritual descendants of Locke and Condorcet, of Jefferson and Lincoln, such a proposal is the counsel of despair. It seems highly improbable, moreover, that any police state could actually succeed in achieving any of its promises. We must see clearly that, while material security and plenty are critically important and not to be postponed indefinitely, we have other values which we want to preserve and realize more fully. It is true that democracy is in urgent need of a solid and enduring economic base; but it is also true that liberty can be exchanged for the security of slavery. This means that our approach to the economic problem should be made within the framework of all the great values we cherish. As we proceed experimentally to the reconstruction of our system of livelihood, therefore, we must hold firmly to the ideals of political liberty, intellectual freedom, and personal dignity and integrity. The young should be led to understand that, aside from establishing a just and durable peace, this is the most crucial task of our age. And quite possibly peace itself may depend on our success.

3

We need an education that will provide occupational guidance and training of the highest order.
The operation of our economy requires first of all the mastery by the younger generation of the vast body of specialized skills and knowledges which has been accumulating slowly but ever more rapidly through decades and centuries. The richness of this

heritage, its complexity and variety, almost passes comprehension. The *Dictionary of Occupational Titles* for 1949 defines more than twenty-two thousand jobs, practically all of which are essential to the successful operation of our productive system. If this heritage were lost, even in certain of its parts, our entire economy would collapse. In pre-industrial times, except for a few so-called professions, it was transmitted by the old to the young through a formal or an informal system of apprenticeship, or through the simple process of growing up on the farm or in the neighborhood. Today the task must be discharged increasingly by educational institutions organized for the purpose.

The basic resource, in addition to the heritage of skills and knowledges, is the reservoir of talents and aptitudes resident in the young. In order to achieve the highest possible level of occupational proficiency it is essential that all obstacles to the wisest and most complete utilization of this resource should be removed. Such an obstacle, and one of major proportions, is the limitation of choice set by social tradition and divers inequalities. Many youth are barred from certain occupations because of family, race, or religion, or because of economic condition. Some children are destined by circumstances of birth, having no relation to talent, to enter the ranks of the unskilled and semi-skilled workers. Others are destined by the same token to become lawyers, physicians, engineers, and scientists. Clearly we must work steadfastly to abolish all forms of social discrimination involving preparation for and admission to occupations. Also, until the rate of compensation of the lowest-paid callings is greatly increased the state should provide stipends and subsidies sufficient to surmount every economic barrier to the full development of the talents of the young.

With the removal of these limiting factors, rooted in the very structure of our society, the way is open for a comprehensive program of occupational guidance which should begin in the early grades. This process of inducting the young into the bewildering variety of vocations of industrial society requires far more attention than it has received. The choice of occupation, even though it may not be irrevocable, is one of the most important choices the individual ever makes. It will affect profoundly all his later life—his associates, his marriage, his standard of living, and perhaps even his political outlook and affiliations. Likewise, since it may make of him either a contented or a discontented citizen, it will affect the social welfare, quite apart from his qualifications to perform efficiently the duties of his calling. But only through a systematic survey of the possibilities can the individual find his way among the extraordinary complexities of the economy. The school should place before him, through excursions, readings, moving pictures, and personal counseling, the demands and hazards, the satisfactions and frustrations, the rates of compensation and conditions of work associated with each of the major types of occupation. In a free society the individual will make his own choice, but the school should help him to make it in the light of knowledge.

By growing up in industrial society, by having direct experience with many kinds of tools, machines, and processes in home and neighborhood, the individual acquires without formal tuition many useful skills and knowledges. But this experience only lays a foundation for systematic occupational training. Society should therefore provide for youth a comprehensive program of vocational preparation, embracing all the callings for which such preparation is necessary. Through subsidies and transportation every state should bring to the individual, regardless of economic condition or place of residence, the opportunity for occupational training which he desires and for which he is fitted. Moreover, a concerted and imaginative effort should be made to raise the qualifications of the lower grades of labor, or even perhaps to eliminate them. Many forms of unskilled work are survivals from our agrarian or early industrial society. We know today that, in the emerging age of electronics and the automatic factory, work which requires only the exercise of human muscle and the mastery of routine skills can for the most part be performed by the machine. Within the limits of human endowment and the necessary conditions of industrial production we should aim to raise the qualifications of every worker to the level of the technician or engineer and to enlarge the opportunities for genuinely creative labor.

As an integral part of the process of occupational guidance and training, provision should be made for genuine work experience under the conditions of production for the market. Ever since industry was removed from the home and child labor laws were passed, our program of vocational preparation has tended to lack an essential element or quality. Work experience is necessary, not only to achieve effective coordination between theory and practice, but also to give the training a spirit of reality. Moreover, there are many things that can be learned only on the job. But entirely apart from its vocational value, work experience should be recognized as an indispensable element in all education. Serious work, as our life in the agrarian age demonstrates, makes a unique contribution to the moral and social development of the individual. A successful attack on this problem will be possible only when the present gap between school and society is bridged. This will require the active and generous cooperation of labor, management, and government with the educational authorities.

4

We need an education that will insure general economic understanding.

For too long we have conceived the problem of economic efficiency solely in terms of narrow occupational proficiency. Reflecting an extremely individualistic philosophy, fairly well suited to the pre-industrial age, we have assumed that if each individual is prepared to do well his particular job our economy as a whole will prosper. The fact is that general competence and understanding are quite as necessary as specialized skills and knowledges. Indeed, it may well be that in terms of the obligations of the school the former are more important than the latter. Not being immediately necessary on the job, they are certain to be neglected if society as a whole through some special agency such as the school does not assume responsibility. For economic efficiency, as well as for intelligent citizenship, responsible parenthood, and personal fulfillment, industrial civilization demands a radical extension of the period of general education.

The younger generation should see our industrial economy in the perspective of history. They should know the story of the development of science and technology and their impact on social institutions and modes of livelihood. The basic features of the old agrarian and mercantile economy should be passed in review. Then the transformation of this economy through the march of the machine, the growth of capital goods, the invention of new agencies of communication, the widening of the market, the coming of mass production, the harnessing of mechanical energy, the raising of the productivity of human labor, and the general integration of the economy should be thoroughly studied. The difficulties, the dislocations, the crises, accompanying these revolutionary changes in the modes of livelihood, should all receive close attention. Such a historical survey should be directed toward illuminating the tasks and problems of the present.

The program of general economic education should include a study of the system of institutions, relationships, and processes by which we now gain our livelihood. The approach should be, not through abstract principles and laws formulated in the pre-industrial age, but rather through an examination by means of readings, excursions, and moving pictures of the actual structure and functioning of our economy. The individual should see his specialty in relation to the whole. He should know something of the great branches of the economy—agriculture, forestry, mining, and fishing, manufacturing, transportation, and communication, medicine, education, and recreation, money, banking, and trade. He should know something, too, of the basic institutions and arrangements through which the several branches of the economy are administered—private and public enterprise,

Education for an Economy of Security and Plenty 375

individualistic and collective operations, partnerships and corporations, employers' associations and labor unions, chambers of commerce and farmers' organizations, monopolies and consumers' cooperatives. He should also know the basic facts concerning economic awards and power—the distribution of wealth and income among the American people. And as we train the young in the skills, attitudes, knowledges, and understandings necessary for the efficient operation of our great power-driven machines, so we should train them in the conduct and management of the emerging social arrangements and institutions which the machines have called and are calling forth.

Close attention should be given in the school to the education of the consumer. In the vast world of goods and services provided by our industrial economy the ordinary individual must experience a sense of bewilderment surpassing that of the young when confronted with the problem of occupational choice. He is largely unequipped to distinguish the good from the bad, and as yet society has developed no effective agencies designed to help him make informed choices among the offerings of the market place. At the same time he is bombarded on every hand and almost throughout his waking hours with carefully framed appeals to purchase this or that commodity, to dine in this or that restaurant, to invest in this or that enterprise, to patronize this or that place of entertainment, to turn to this or that cure for some malady or infirmity. He may even be enticed to spend his money on "illth" rather than wealth. Obviously, if he is to find his way among the snares and pitfalls of high-pressure salesmanship, he must have assistance in the acquisition of elementary standards of judgment. Also he should be encouraged to demand the closest possible approximation to truth and simplicity in all the media of advertising. In this sphere lies one of the most vital sectors of economic education.

The foundations of our economy in the natural resources of our country and the world should be emphasized. The condition of our American land at the time of the first colonial settlements should be a part of our common knowledge—the diversity of climate, the fertility of soil, the wealth of stream and lake, the expanse of forest, the abundance of game and fish, the richness of mineral reserves, the beauties of landscape. We should also be familiar with the shameful record of waste and exploitation—the mining of the soil, the destruction of watersheds, the burning and slashing of forests, the slaughter of animal life, the depletion of mineral reserves, the neglect of aesthetic values. On the other hand, we should know the story of the heroic struggle on the part of public-spirited and far-sighted citizens to conserve and renew the natural heritage. Instruction in the present condition of this heritage and our dependence on other countries for essential raw materials should be a part of any adequate educational program. The time has come when we must realize that an economy of security and plenty rests of necessity on an adequate and continuing base of natural resources.

The technological foundations of our economy should be made the subject of systematic instruction. It is not enough for technicians and engineers to know their specialties. All of us should be familiar with the broad sources of our livelihood. We should become technology-minded and sense the romance in this new and powerful arm with which man is lifting himself out of privation and transforming the material world. As an essential part of our liberal education we should probe the mysteries of matter and the harnessing of energy, of chemistry and the making of new substances, of metallurgy and machine construction, of agrobiology and the farming of the sea, of electricity and electronics, and of the whole complicated process of planning, organizing, and managing the production and distribution of goods and services. Here is a form of subject matter for the liberation and the quickening of the mind which is not surpassed by the language or literature of any people, ancient or modern.

Underlying and nourishing technology, without which technical advance would be limited to superficial manipulation of haphazard hunches and experiences, is the whole domain of science. An education therefore designed fundamentally to serve and guard the long-time economic interests of our people must bring science, scientific method, and mathematical processes squarely into the center of its program. Here is a force that has played the central role in creating the modern world and the strange civilization which is sweeping the earth in our time. Yet we in America probably know less about it, in some of its wider implications, than certain other peoples who entered the scientific age at a later time. Also throughout our history we have tended to concentrate our energies on the practical applications of science and to leave to others the development of "fundamental science." For the ordinary citizen, however, chief attention should be placed, not on an encyclopedic knowledge of the sciences but rather on method, ways of thought, and the general impact of science on the life and condition of man. The young should be reared in the spirit of science. They should be led to see that science is the basic instrument by which man understands, subdues, and harnesses the forces of nature. They should be prepared in mind to support on a wholly unprecedented scale scientific research into all realms of nature and existence.

In the upper levels of the educational system the younger generation should be brought face to face with the central social problem involved in the building of an economy of security and plenty—the problem of achieving a sufficient degree of coordination among the several branches of the economy and between production and consumption to prevent economic crises and depressions and to insure a steady advance in the standard of living of all the people. That this will require substantial change in the structure and operation of our inherited economic and political institutions is now generally recognized. As a minimum, a minimum which already is in process, we shall have to establish some kind of economic council in which labor, management, agriculture, and government are all represented. The young should be encouraged to study critically in terms of our experience the strengths and weaknesses of the nineteenth century system of free enterprise, the dangers and possibilities in collective action, in organizations of working people, in associations of businessmen, in consumers' cooperatives, in social and economic planning, in government intervention in the economy. In the same spirit they should examine the competing economic and political systems in the world today—capitalism, socialism, and mixed economy. Fullest opportunity should be provided for free discussion and debate on the many issues which all of these practices and proposals suggest. In view of the extraordinary complexity and dynamism of industrial society the task of gaining understanding is critical and urgent. No phase of this emerging society should be barred from most searching and critical study by the young of each generation.

5

We need an education that will develop the moral foundations of an economy of security and plenty.

This will require achievement of a synthesis of moral values which will embrace both old and new elements. Among the old are the dignity of labor and the right and obligation to work; among the new are regard for the means of livelihood, cooperative attitudes and practices, and devotion to the general welfare.

In our pre-industrial society, except for the slave-holders of the South and a small commercial, landlord, and professional class in the North, we were for the most part freehold farmers. This meant that preponderantly we earned our livelihood in essentially the same way. We labored on the land, tilling the soil, tending domestic animals, and practicing the many practical arts of farm and household. Under these conditions labor assumed a dignity that has rarely been equaled anywhere else in the world. Although much of this tradition remains, the manifold forms and gradations of occupation characteristic of industrial society are slowly undermining the old pattern. Children are beginning to sense that many indispensable kinds of labor are actually regarded as disgraceful or lacking in dignity by community opinion. The school can do something directly in preserving the precious legacy from the past by emphasizing in its entire program of instruction and human relations the idea that all forms of socially useful labor are worthy. It can perhaps do more by working for better compensation, higher qualifications, and improved conditions of work for the less favored occupational groups.

In the earlier society the right and obligation to work, while not written in the laws, were largely guaranteed by the conditions of life. There was little place for any leisured class, and the individual who did not work was looked upon with suspicion and aversion. As Benjamin Franklin put it, a person "who has no other quality to recommend him but his birth" cannot carry such a "commodity . . . to a worse market than that of America." Closely linked with the idea that every able-bodied man or woman should pay his own passage through life by means of useful labor was the notion that the individual also has a right to work. If he really wanted employment, he did not have to go to a private employer or to the government. The rich land extending seemingly without limit to the west offered him a means of livelihood. The rise of industrial society has greatly changed this situation. On the one hand, we have a comparatively large leisure class and, on the other, at times, a vast population of unemployed denied by the circumstances of our economy the opportunity to work. The school should present this whole problem to the young and challenge them to apply to present conditions the democratic ethical principle of the right and obligation to work. The idea that "really smart people" live by their wits and that "only saps work" is profoundly un-American.

A major moral weakness in our civilization has been the persistence from generation to generation of an exploiting attitude toward the sources of our livelihood. Most peoples view with deep regard and even with reverence the material base of their earthly existence, whether it be the soil, the sea, or the forest, the horse, the salmon, or the buffalo. Probably because of the very abundance of our natural riches, the swift course of our migration across the continent, and the individualistic pattern of the economy, we have behaved as if North America were merely a temporary abode. We must endeavor to instill in the young a new sense of stewardship toward our rich natural endowment. In similar fashion we should seek to develop a deep appreciation of technology, of our fabulous power-driven machines, of our magnificent factories and production plants from which we increasingly derive our subsistence and by which we are easing the burden of toil carried on the backs of men and women. The Russians, possibly because of their nearness to the age of dependence on human energy, emphasize in their educational program far more than we do the liberating power of technology.

The development of cooperative attitudes and practices is another urgent task of education in our industrial economy. The moral value here involved is both new and old. The very term "society" implies group life. And group life implies cooperation and mutual aid. Without some measure of these things no society can exist. Yet the degree of cooperation and mutual aid has varied greatly from society to society and within a given society from time to time. In the agrarian age of our fathers American society was a loose aggregation of families and neighborhoods. Although the level of social cohesion was high in the household and the locality, it was low in the region and the nation. In the rural community neighbor helped neighbor and cooperative activity was common; but in the country as a whole integration was feeble and national unity was generally called forth only in the waging of war. Federal and even state government was weak, distant, and almost foreign. We have entered a period in which a higher degree of general cooperation and mutual aid is necessary for the welfare of all and perhaps even for survival. Clearly the appropriate attitudes and skills should be systematically cultivated in the young.

Industrial civilization, as we have noted, is marked by interdependence on a vast scale, by group and collective

Education for an Economy of Security and Plenty 381

action in many forms, by increasing government participation in economy and life. Prosperity or depression sweeps all of us in varying measure into its embrace. One of the most characteristic patterns of American society today is the voluntary economic organization, whether corporation, chamber of commerce, trade union, farmers' grange, or consumers' cooperative. Another is social planning on local state, and national bases. These patterns of social organization and behavior, which undoubtedly inhere in the very texture of industrial economy, require a morality that is more social, more cooperative, and more wide-reaching than the morality of the past. The young should receive careful training in mutual undertakings, in organizational work, and in social planning so that they may form the desired habits and dispositions. Also, as they mature, they should be brought increasingly into functional relationships with such operations in adult society.

Finally, the new morality must include greater concern for and devotion to the general welfare. We have a long and deeply rooted heritage of rugged individualism and of grievous neglect in some areas of the public interest. The motive of individual success, commonly conceived in material terms, has been a basic driving force in the education of the young. The average citizen has been reared in the tradition that it is far less reprehensible to defraud the government than to cheat a private citizen or enterprise. Our long record of political corruption, even in times of national danger, is one of the darkest blemishes on our democracy. Liberty has ofttimes been regarded as insuring the right of the individual to concentrate all his energies on the advancement of his personal interests. But this subordination of the common good which in the past has merely been blameworthy may prove fatal in the future. Today, moreover, it is not merely the individual against the public but rather the powerful organized group against other groups and even against the community. If these groups are disciplined by no common conception of the general welfare, they will develop separate and conflicting moralities. The problem here is fundamentally one of education, and not of law, even though laws may be required. Through all of its resources education should strive to develop a sense of loyalty to the total community. Also it should place great emphasis on the high worth and dignity of public service. Without a generally accepted conception of the common welfare we shall find ourselves unable to build and sustain an economy marked by either security or plenty. A morality conceived largely in terms of family, neighborhood, or some limited group is scarcely sufficient to govern the actions of the individual in the great society of the industrial age.

24

EDUCATION FOR A CIVILIZATION OF BEAUTY AND GRANDEUR

1

We need an education that will prepare the young to build a civilization of beauty and grandeur. As life is more than the bare physical necessities of food, clothing, and shelter, so civilization is more than economics. It is also more than politics. Although the forms of food, clothing, and shelter, the quality of farms, machines, and factories, the conduct of the processes of economy and government may reveal beauty and grandeur in a civilization, these things do not encompass the potentialities of the human spirit. Men may be free, equal, secure, and well-fed, they may fly around the earth in a few hours and to the moon in as many days, they may even be able to remove mountains and change the courses of great rivers, yet they may fail in some realms of the mind to reach the heights scaled by the ancient Athenians or the men of the Elizabethan age. The central purpose of economic and political institutions is to provide the material base and social conditions essential to the release and fulfillment of the creative powers of the species.

The emphasis on aesthetic interests in our educational program is especially necessary because of a long-standing deficiency in our civilization. We have had comparatively little time or energy to devote to the perfection of the artistic tradition. We have been engrossed from early colonial times in theology, morals, economics, and politics. To be sure, there is grandeur in many of our social conceptions and achievements. There is an aesthetic, as well as an ethical, quality in the timeless eloquence of the Declaration of Independence, in the conception of popular rule set forth in practical form in the Federal Constitution, and in the very idea of a society of free and equal people affirmed with poetic simplicity in the Gettysburg Address. There is grandeur, too, in the heroic march of our people through the wilderness to the Pacific, in the epic struggle of man against nature recorded on almost every page of our three centuries of history. The seemingly inexorable advance of technology and the conquest of energy have in them something of sublimity. But after all this is said the fact remains that there has long been a deficiency in our heritage.

2

We need an education that will reveal the deficiency in our aesthetic tradition. America was settled in the colonial period largely by Englishmen in whom, except for literary expression and certain arts of practical life, the aesthetic interest was weak. And the Englishmen who crossed the Atlantic came in considerable measure from Puritan and dissenting sects whose members followed a stern and austere moral code, abhorred idleness and luxury as lures of Satan, and looked with not a little suspicion on the refinements of life, considering them sinful and worldly. "Literature and art," says Thomas Cuming Hall, "had little place in their rather starved imaginations."[1] Moreover, like the Protestant

[1] Thomas Cuming Hall, *The Religious Background of American Culture* (Boston, 1930), p. 119.

Education for a Civilization of Beauty and Grandeur 385

English, the immigrants who represented other national stocks and religious sects came largely from the lower ranks of European society. This means that the less skilled in the practical as well as in the humanistic arts came to America. Certainly there were few gifted artists among the immigrants, and even master craftsmen were rare. In general, therefore, those who came from the Old World were quite incapable of bringing to the New the full artistic heritage of their peoples.

The neglect of the arts was fostered by the severe conditions of life in America. Though the land was rich and abundant, it was untamed and uncultivated. Men, women, and children had to work hard and long to obtain the bare necessities of living. On the early frontier they had to fell the forests, build houses and barns, break trails and roads, fight the Indians, guard against the depredations of wild animals, and establish the institutions of worship and government, even as they struggled to perform the manifold economic tasks of the self-contained household. Later when they passed the Allegheny mountains and beheld the boundless riches of the west they were beckoned ever forward by the promise of physical possession. Moreover, the War for Independence and the launching of the Republic created another compelling interest in the life of our people. "I must study politics and war," wrote John Adams to his wife, "that my sons may have the liberty to study mathematics and philosophy." And even Thomas Jefferson, whose wide-ranging mind embraced all the arts and who confessed music to be the "favorite passion" of his "soul," remarked that, while architecture was worth the serious study of American youth, painting and sculpture were "too expensive for the state of wealth among us. They are worth seeing but not studying." The full development of the arts had to await the conquest of the continent and the establishment of the economic and political foundations of our civilization.

One of the favorite sports of Europeans since colonial days has been to remark this deficiency, often in superior and exaggerated tones, and to attribute it to the inevitable operation of democratic institutions. A young English writer of inconspicuous talents reported approvingly from Georgetown, South Carolina, in 1799 the "supreme contempt for *American* genius and *American* literature of a compatriot residing in America at the time." Apparently this man observed, on the basis of personal experience, that "as no snake exists in Ireland," so "no poet can be found in America."[2]

Even Sydney Smith wrote thus of the Americans in 1820: "During the thirty or forty years of their independence they have done absolutely nothing for the Sciences, for the Arts, for Literature. . . . In the four quarters of the globe, who reads an American book? or goes to an American play? or looks at an American picture or statue?" Thereafter he added a few more rhetorical questions which have a strange ring today: "What does the world yet owe to American physicians and surgeons? What new substances have their chemists discovered? or what old ones have they analyzed? What new constellations have been discovered by the telescopes of Americans? What have they done in the mathematics? Who drinks out of American glasses? or eats from American plates? or wears American coats or gowns? or sleeps in American blankets?"[3]

Charles Dickens, as is generally known, was little impressed by the qualities of the Americans whom he saw on his visit in 1842, except perhaps their unsurpassed skill in tobacco-spitting, truly a filthy habit. When he sought to interest them in the development of a literature, the universal answer was: "Our people don't think of poetry, sir. Dollars, banks, and cotton are *our* books sir." He then observed: "And they certainly are in one sense; for a lower average of general information than exists in this country on all other topics, it would be very hard to find."[4] These thoughts doubtless led him to sum up the American character in these words: "And I am quite serious when I say that I

[2] John Davis, *Travels of Four Years and a Half in the United States of America During 1798, 1799, 1800, 1801 and 1802* (New York, 1909), pp. 49–50.
[3] Sydney Smith, *Wit and Wisdom* (New York, 1901), pp. 27–29.
[4] John Forster, *The Life of Charles Dickens* (Philadelphia, 1872), Vol. I, p. 410.

Education for a Civilization of Beauty and Grandeur 387

do not believe there are, on the whole earth besides, so many intensified bores as in these United States. No man can form an adequate idea of the real meaning of the word, without coming here."[5]

Thomas Colley Grattan, British consul to Massachusetts from 1839 to 1846, expressed the same idea, but with more regard for the canons of diplomacy and perhaps with greater insight into the nature of our institutions. The United States, he wrote, is "a paradise of mediocrity," the reason being: "Genuine Democracy can produce nothing more. To be consistent with itself, it wants nothing more for its disciples than a medium quality in mind and manners, respectability of talent, moderate acquirements, unpresuming tastes; no meretricious ornaments nor luxurious displays; homely living, plain attire, industry, integrity, and truth."[6]

In these appraisals from the Old World, and they could be multiplied indefinitely, there was of course a measure of truth. Yet the fair-minded and intelligent critic must concede that from colonial days we have been engaged, perhaps unknowingly for the most part, in a venture that goes far beyond popular control of economic and political power, a venture that places the entire cultural heritage largely in the keeping of the people. In Europe, until very recent times, the patrons and molders of the great arts of aesthetic expression have been members of a favored and limited social class. We have sought to break this monopoly and open the gates to the masses. Our effort thus to democratize the artistic tradition constitutes a major feature of our civilization and has had consequences which our critics have little understood.

It must be said also that during our first two hundred years in the new homeland we did succeed in developing a fine, though limited, artistic tradition. This tradition flowered in the handicrafts which were rooted in a vigorous folk art and grew out of the household industries as occupational specialization became possible. Although we produced no great painting, music, or poetry, we did evolve ever finer pat-

[5] *Ibid.*, Vol. I, p. 376.
[6] Thomas Colley Grattan, *Civilized America* (London, 1859), Vol. I, p. 222.

terns of things of ordinary use. Testimony to the excellence of the colonial craftsman survives to this day in wooden, textile, metal, earthen, and glass ware, in chairs, tables, cupboards, counterpanes, candlesticks, pitchers, tea sets, and bottles, in colonial homes dotting the landscape from the Carolinas to Massachusetts, in churches, occasional public buildings, and chastely designed communities along the entire Atlantic seaboard. While this tradition has long since vanished, its canons of utility, simplicity, integrity, and beauty should serve to inspire the youth of today as they carry on the task of building an equally sound tradition for the new age.

The first half of the nineteenth century witnessed the "flowering of New England" in the literary arts and also the swift dissolution of the colonial culture. The leisurely development of the sheltered life along the Atlantic was interrupted: the nation marched west over the Alleghenies, across the basin of the Mississippi, and on to the Golden Gate. In this same period our people felt the first impact of the rise of industrialism, of the age of coal and iron and steam. Under the stress of the new forces the household economy melted away, the community lost its integrity, the machine destroyed the craftsman, an exploiting individualism rose to economic dominance, money-making became a ruling passion in the minds of men, and a new privileged order, product of the commercial spirit, displaced the limited landed aristocracy of colonial times. Increasingly, things were produced, not for use, but for the market, for profit. Thus the foundations of an artistic tradition, the fruit of two centuries of life in the new land, were demolished. The task had to be undertaken anew.

The initial reaction of our most sensitive minds was to join the ranks of European critics and lament the degradation of American culture. During the "gilded age" which followed the Civil War and reached well into the twentieth century many artists and writers turned to Europe for inspiration. Some abandoned their native land and formed colonies of expatriates in London, Paris, and other cultural

Education for a Civilization of Beauty and Grandeur 389

centers beyond the Atlantic. In 1922 thirty Americans joined forces in a general appraisal of their civilization which for the most part would have gratified Sydney Smith and Charles Dickens. In his prefatory note Harold E. Stearns, editor of the volume, presumably expressed the common sentiment in these words: ". . . the most moving and pathetic fact in the social life of America to-day is emotional and aesthetic starvation."[7] Shortly thereafter this member of the "lost generation" journeyed to France and remained twelve years. There on the boulevards of Paris, "watching with a set, gloomy expression a world of wastrels drift past," he apparently rediscovered America. Returning home in the middle of the "great depression," he expressed the following judgment: "At whatever point you touch the complex American life of today you get a sense of new confidence, new pride, and even new hope."[8]

3

We need an education in the arts that will make full use of our resources.

In spite of certain deficiencies in our artistic heritage, in spite of the handicaps deriving from the character of the early migration, the conditions of life in the new world, and the impact of the machine on our entire cultural life during the middle part of the nineteenth century, we possess a substantial and even rich endowment for building a civilization of great beauty and grandeur. The magnificent land, though scarred and ravaged, is still here; the later migrations are adding much to our cultural heritage and human talents; the building of a new and vigorous artistic tradition is well advanced; and industrial civilization itself is bringing new materials, energies, conditions, and perspectives. All of these resources should be fully utilized in the educational program.

[7] Harold E. Stearns, Ed., *Civilization in the United States* (New York, 1922), p. vii.
[8] Harold E. Stearns, *America: A Re-appraisal* (New York, 1937), p. 11.

We have a land of unsurpassed beauty and grandeur. It is not necessary here to dwell on the loveliness of such a detail as the simple perfection of dogwood and redbud blossoming in chorus in the Ozarks, or on the majesty of the land as a whole with its eastern and western mountains, its central basin and coastal plains, all set between the great oceans. But it is necessary to awaken in the young a deep and reverent sense of appreciation of this glorious legacy from nature, and to develop in them the high resolve to transmit this legacy unimpaired to their children. "In Europe," wrote Tocqueville long ago, "people talk a great deal of the wilds of America, but the Americans themselves never think about them: they are insensible to the wonders of inanimate nature, and they may be said not to perceive the mighty forests which surround them till they fall beneath the hatchet."[9] And Thomas Colley Grattan caustically observed: "The greatness of the country strongly contrasts with the deficiencies of the people. The magnificent scale of creation seems unsuited to the beings who possess it."[10] Except for a few of our poets and others of poetic mind, most of us of all generations have dwelt unknowingly in a natural paradise. If we could but build a civilization equal in beauty and grandeur to this land of ours, it would be unexcelled in all the history of mankind.

The gradual change in the national sources of our people during the past century has greatly increased our artistic endowment. The deficiency of the English in most of the arts except literature, architecture, industry, and community design has been corrected by substantial migrations from many other countries. In a unique sense today we are the heirs of the artistic traditions of all the peoples of the Old World, reaching back to the ancient Greeks and even to the ancient Chinese. Descending from most of the races and cultures of the earth, we have within our American family the heritage, not only of the British, but also of many other peoples,

---

[9] Alexis de Tocqueville, *Democracy in America* (New York, 1898), Vol. II, p. 90.
[10] Grattan, *op. cit.*, Vol. II, p. 105.

some possessing an extraordinarily rich experience in the arts. We are fortunate indeed that we have among us the children of Europe, Africa, and Asia, of France, Italy, Spain, and Belgium, of Germany, Austria, Holland, and Scandinavia, of Poland, Bohemia, Hungary, Russia, and Palestine, of Egypt, India, China, Japan, and other lands. Even our unenlightened efforts to "Americanize" all who have come to our shores have failed to destroy the precious cargo of aesthetic tradition which they have brought with them, even from early colonial days. The fact is revealed in the names of those Americans who have achieved greatness in literature, painting, sculpture, and music, in architecture, engineering, community planning, and many of the other arts. We possess the talents needed to adapt the great artistic heritage of the entire human past to the new materials, processes, possibilities, and life conditions of the industrial age. The school should utilize fully the rich resources residing in the diversity in cultural origin of our people.

It would be unwise, however, to attempt to rely wholly on ourselves. Through new modes of travel, distances have been vastly reduced; through new instruments of communication such as the radio, distances have been annihilated; through new agencies of representation such as the cinema, the most remote scenes and events are brought swiftly before our eyes. These developments open to us and to all mankind revolutionary possibilities of cultural exchange and fertilization. And since all peoples are entering the industrial age together, though some are more advanced or retarded than others, they all face similar artistic problems. Although each nation, including our own, will want to make its own choices and pursue a distinctive course into the future, we should seek to establish the closest possible cultural relations with all peoples. From the pursuit of such a course we are certain to derive many fruitful ideas, suggestions, and challenges. Much can and should be done here by individual teachers and artists on their own initiative and with their own resources. But much should be done also in organized and systematic fashion by the great quasi-public foundations and by governmental action and subsidy. Already we have our Fulbright Act for promoting cultural exchange and our Point Four Program for providing technical assistance to underdeveloped countries. In addition we are participating actively in the work of the Educational, Scientific, and Cultural Organization of the United Nations, from which in time much may be expected. In building our educational program we should take full advantage of the opportunities which come from close contact with the other great civilizations of the world—civilizations which have been and which will continue to be our teachers.

The final great resource to be utilized is found in the marvelous new materials, energies, conditions, and perspectives of industrial civilization. The first consequence of the coming of the technological revolution, as we have seen, was disastrous. Much of the old artistic tradition was destroyed. To fill the resulting vacuum the initial tendency was to imitate with the machine designs evolved in the age of handicrafts. The inevitable result was the degradation of all values. But gradually, under the leadership of such men as Louis H. Sullivan in architecture, John Roebling in engineering, Thomas Benton in painting, Bertram Goodhue in sculpture, George Gershwin in music, and Ebenezer Howard in social planning, a new artistic tradition, true to the nature of the new age, began to emerge. The spirit and outlook of this tradition are well expressed by Frank Lloyd Wright's emphasis on the development of a "new sense of the nature of materials":

A stone building will no more *be* nor *look* like a steel building. A pottery, or terra cotta building, will not be or look like a stone building. A wood building will look like none other, for it will glorify the stick. A steel and glass building could not possibly look like anything but itself. It will glorify steel and glass. And so on all the way down the long list of available riches in materials: Stone, Wood, Concrete, Metals, Glass, Textiles, Pulp, and Pigment; riches so great that no comparison with Ancient Architecture is at all sensible or in any way essential to Modern Architecture.[11]

[11] Frank Lloyd Wright, *An Autobiography* (New York, 1933), p. 356.

Education for a Civilization of Beauty and Grandeur 393

The new artistic tradition is still in its infancy. Its full development will require vigorous and sustained creative effort. But the direction and certain guiding principles are clear. Instead of seeking to imitate the forms of the past we must gather inspiration from their spirit, resolutely face the future, and strive to discover the genius of the new age. When we do this we shall find that with the materials and energies provided by science and technology we shall be able to build a civilization which in beauty and grandeur will certainly equal and possibly surpass in its own way anything that the age of handicraft and human muscle ever achieved. The development of the automobile may serve to illustrate simply the course which we should follow. As soon as we stopped trying to make of it a horseless carriage and labored honestly in terms of material and function, it was on its way to becoming a work of art. The same may be said of the airplane when we abandoned the idea of making a kite with a combustion engine.

The achievement of an economy of security and plenty for all, which is now clearly possible, will create an opportunity for the almost unlimited refinement of our civilization. Already the advance of technology has so increased the productivity of labor that the working hours of the average man or woman have been reduced far below what was thought possible and even "proper" a few generations ago. A thirty-hour working week, contrasted with seventy-five, eighty, or ninety hours in our old agrarian society, is already above the horizon and will reach the zenith in the proximate future, if peace is established among the nations. The time and energy thus released for leisure activities and interests constitute something new under the sun. There has been nothing remotely resembling this condition in any place or time. The opportunity afforded for the development of people, provided the individual is no longer harassed by a sense of profound insecurity, presents one of the greatest challenges of the age. Education must do all in its power to make sure that the hours away from work will be employed, not to cheapen and degrade taste and character, but to introduce a finer quality of being into the lives, relationships, and material surroundings of all the people. Through the cultivation of the traditional arts and crafts the school might well encourage the production of things of use and beauty as an avocational interest both to release the creative energies of individuals and to enrich the economy of the industrial age.

4

We need an education that will foster a broad and catholic artistic tradition.
First of all the marked distinction between the fine and the practical arts, a strange phenomenon of the past one hundred and fifty years, must be erased. "Let us recognize," writes Paul T. Frankl, "that our period —the Machine Age—is practically the only one in the long history of humanity, during which there has been so sharp and distinct a division between the 'Industrial Arts' and the so-called 'Fine Arts.' This division has worked to the detriment of the full and satisfying maturing of the creative spirit,"[12] In Periclean Athens artists and craftsmen cooperated to build a city; in the Middle Ages they cooperated to build a cathedral; in early New England they cooperated to build a town; today they must cooperate to build a great civilization. While the so-called "fine arts" may be regarded as the crown of the edifice, they constitute but a part of the total artistic achievement of a people.

The art of America must be a living art, a function of the very texture of the ongoing economic, social, and cultural processes. Museums and galleries have their place as custodians of the artistic tradition of both past and present. They should be generously supported by society and fully utilized in the rearing of the young. But in the measure that a people comes to identify art with halls where relics are kept and pictures hung the conception is made narrow and sterile.

[12] Paul T. Frankl, *Machine-Made Leisure* (New York, 1932), pp. 48–49.

The position taken here is that art should be conceived in universal terms. On the one hand, it should be regarded as the rightful possession, not of a privileged or esoteric order, but of all the people. On the other, it should be viewed as an aspect of every department of life. All things, even the most humble and commonplace, can be marked by grace, beauty, and truth. It is therefore a responsibility of education to strive to develop in each child or youth some degree of artistic sensitivity toward every phase of our civilization. Special effort should be made to arouse concern with respect to the many aesthetic incongruities in our society—a beautiful park by the side of ugly and degrading slums, a limpid stream polluted by the offal of mine or factory, a lovely square cluttered with filth and debris, a noble conception of government administered by a coterie of ignoramuses or a gang of scoundrels. The schools should bring nearer the day when artistic gains can be measured in terms of a rising level of appreciation and performance of all the people in all their relations and activities.

Education should strive to raise the standards of appreciation and performance in the arts of individual expression and communication—in language, in drawing and painting, in modeling and sculpture, in music and the dance. In these arts our achievements have rarely been of the highest order. Although we have made notable advances in our schools during the past generation, particularly in music, much of this great world of beauty is closed to our people. Even in language, in spite of the unparalleled expansion of education at the secondary and higher levels, the quality of command of the vernacular on the part of the ordinary citizen is certainly below that achieved in certain other countries. We face the task here of correcting deficiencies of long standing in our cultural heritage. Systematic attention to all the expressive and communicative arts for the purpose of attaining a higher standard of performance is called for. Also, through the many aids now generally available the young should be led to acquire, as a precious personal possession, appreciation of great literature, great painting, great sculpture, and great music. The "pulp" magazine industry, to take an illustration from one field, is a standing disgrace to the American people. Education should strive to raise the standards of appreciation and performance in the arts of home and community. The young should learn to look for art and to criticize current designs in the objects of ordinary use—in food, dress, utensils, machines, automobiles. They should be guided in the development of canons of judgment so that they may distinguish the good from the bad, and always insist on the good. "Made in America" should come to mean something fine and honest, even in the world beyond our borders. In the same way the young should become architecturally-minded and able to view with an informed and critical eye their dwelling places, their homes and apartments—their places of work, their shops and factories, and even their schools—their public buildings and monuments. Likewise they should learn something about landscaping and community planning, about the laying out of streets and highways, about the utilization of all the resources of nature. They should see through travel or moving picture how beautiful a town or city can be. Perhaps if every child could ride with an intelligent guide over one of the magnificent highways leading out of New York to the north the time might come when there would be no ugly roads in America. Before the members of the younger generation leave the high school they should know that even that part of America which comes from the hand of man, from a saucepan to the capitol at Washington, might match in beauty and grandeur that other part that came from the hand of the author of nature. And they should be outraged to learn that "more than 3,400 cities and towns inhabited by 29,000,000 persons discharge into our waterways a volume of $2\frac{1}{2}$ billion gallons of raw sewage plus $3\frac{3}{4}$ billion gallons of industrial waste each day."[13]

Education should strive to raise the standards of appreciation and performance in the arts of personal enjoyment and cultivation. Industrial civilization, as we know, provides a radically new foundation for these arts through a revolution-

[13] Harold L. Ickes, *New York Post*, Sept. 25, 1946.

Education for a Civilization of Beauty and Grandeur 397

ary increase in the resources available to the ordinary individual for the enrichment of his personal life. We have with us still the old resources of reading, religion, politics, drama, sport, travel, and simple human association. Some of these, notably reading and travel, have been raised to a new order of magnitude by technological advance. Then there have been added those fabulous agencies through which the mind and soul of man might be immeasurably enriched and civilized—the cinema, the radio, and television. The artistic standards marking performance in these new agencies and in some of the old can only arouse feelings of anxiety and foreboding in the conscience of any thoughtful and loyal citizen. The sensationalism of much of the press, the cheapness of so many of the movies, and the utter banality of a large part of the radio and television programs give a false and sordid view of American life and civilization. Yet these agencies provide in increasing measure the aesthetic as well as the intellectual and ethical nourishment of boys and girls and youth in our country. The schools should make the critical study of these things a major responsibility in the years ahead.

Education should strive to raise the artistic standards of appreciation and performance in the arts of social relations. Perhaps the most precious part of life is embraced by the individual's relations with his fellows and associates of both sexes, all ages, and all sects, races, and occupations. There are involved not only the ordinary human relationships, but also group relationships and public services of many kinds. Because of the character of industrial society, with its close integration, its vast reaches, its tendency toward organization, its unprecedented mobility, and its dependence on cooperative and collective action, these relations are far more numerous and varied than in any earlier age. The problem is the more important because so many of our contacts among people are casual and fleeting. Here is a field for the development of aesthetic sensitivity that is all too commonly neglected. Today the relations among people are often marked by vulgarity, and sometimes by intolerance, arrogance, and bigotry. At this point aesthetics and ethics should be brought into harmony. Social relations should always be conducted not only with grace and charm and dignity, but also with truth and honesty. Although the idea that uncouth manners express a contempt for aristocracy, a democratic spirit of equality, and a ruggedness of character is in our American tradition, the time has arrived when we should realize that it does not reflect a high level of civilization. The schools have an admirable opportunity to raise the level of taste and behavior in this entire domain of social relations.

5

We need an education that will discover and encourage the development of creative talents in all the arts.
In this sphere, as in all others, we should be constantly in search of that "natural aristocracy" to which Jefferson referred, that aristocracy of "virtue and talents . . . the most precious gift of nature for the instruction, the trusts, and government of society." There is no suggestion here that art is in any sense different from the other interests of man, that it is the possession of a few "queer" people. It seems probable that capacity in any one of the arts is distributed through the population in approximately the same manner as capacity in language or manual dexterity. We all possess some ability in each of the arts. But there are some who possess unusual or great talent. So whenever we discover a mind of rare sensitivity or perception in any one of the arts, we should be quick to provide it with all the opportunities for development that our society affords, regardless of family, creed, or color. If such attention to the gifted is accompanied by a broad program of artistic education for all, we may be confident that we are on the way to building a civilization of true beauty and grandeur.

25

EDUCATION FOR AN ENDURING CIVILIZATION

1

We need an education that will be dedicated to the building of an enduring civilization.
The time has clearly arrived when we should face squarely, soberly, and profoundly the question of the qualities or conditions necesssary to enable our civilization to endure, not just for a few years or decades, but for generations and centuries. The era for uncritical and exuberant optimism is over. We must realize that the fairest hopes and promises of America may prove to be as fleeting as the glories of Nineveh and Babylon, of Angkor and Chichen Itza.

For three hundred years we have been building in North America a unique civilization, a civilization founded on faith in the common man and dedicated to the conquest of the forces of nature. We have vanquished many foes, overcome many hazards, weathered many storms, survived many mistakes, and prospered mightily. Although we have often violated in larger or smaller measure our deepest moral commitments and rarely fulfilled the highest expectations of our friends, we have generally discomfited our enemies. We stand today the most powerful state in the world, dwarfing in material strength the proudest empires of the past. Our good fortune has naturally bred in us unlimited confidence in our institutions and an uncritical conviction that our civilization is destined to endure forever. To have doubts is taken as evidence of disloyalty and weakness.

That the future is secure, however, is by no means certain. The paths of archaeology and history are strewn with the wrecks of great empires and civilizations which had endured for centuries. And the earth today is littered with small states and feeble cultures which are but pale shadows of their former greatness. A feeling of confidence in the future, moreover, is no trustworthy index of the power to survive. It may be merely a reflection of past triumphs. A long and uninterrupted record of success inevitably breeds in a nation a false sense of power and security—a certain blindness to impending decay and danger. A people may stand on the brink of doom and be wholly unaware of the abyss yawning at its feet. Those who lived through the last days of the Roman Empire apparently had no comprehension of the magnitude of the disaster about to overwhelm their world. They noted the events which presaged the coming catastrophe, but they did not know their meaning. It is to be hoped that with our greater knowledge of history and human society we may be wiser in the ways of statecraft and education than the ancients. We should all be studying the theme presented with power and erudition by Arnold J. Toynbee in his monumental *A Study of History*—the theme of the rise and fortunes of the twenty-one great civilizations which man has built on the earth, only five of which are living today.

2

We need an education that will stress the critical nature of the present age.
Today, as much of the analysis in the present volume makes plain, we are passing through deeply troubled times. Science and technology have released such

Education for an Enduring Civilization

revolutionary forces and created such revolutionary life conditions that nothing should be taken for granted. The time for complacency has long since passed.

We must help the younger generation to understand that the first great epoch in our history is closed and that our good fortune in the past has not always been of our own making. As a matter of fact, although we have tended to live hopefully in our tomorrows, during much of our history we have given little sober thought to the future. We have rather assumed that a kind and beneficent Providence watches over our destinies and ever saves us from our blunders. And in this assumption there has been not a little of truth. A beneficent Providence has existed in the benign forces of both geography and history—in our rich land, in our sheltered position in the world, and in the great cultural heritage, product of thousands of years of struggle and achievement, which we were able to apply to bold political experimentation and to the exploitation of a virgin continent.

A wholly new orientation on the part of our people is necessary. We must know that powerful guardians of the past have largely forsaken us. During these troubled years we are entering the second epoch in our history. Whether it will be short or long, only the uninformed or unconcerned would be so bold as to speak with assurance. The geographical conditions that protected us in considerable measure from the quarrels and ambitions of the Old World have been blasted away by electricity, radar, and atomic energy. For the moment the mightiest state on earth, we stand in the very center of the world exposed to all the winds that blow and equipped to loose forces of incalculable power on ourselves and all mankind. The conditions amid which we must live are new and strange and changing; the road to the future is unexplored and uncharted; mankind has never been this way before. Since the kind Providence which has watched over us in the past has departed never to return, we must watch over ourselves. No nation in history was ever in greater need of wisdom and understanding, of sobriety and humility.

In 1937 a distinguished English archaelogist, Stanley

Casson, published a small but prophetic volume in which he discussed the question of progress and catastrophe in the light of all we know about the human past and brought the discussion to bear on the present condition and prospects of mankind. So prescient is this book, already proven by events, that the following passage merits quotation here:

> But now again the end is in sight, unless we take measures to prevent its coming. Blithely we consider the possibility of vast cities being ruined by flame and violence. The mere fact that we are prepared even for a moment to consider such destructions is eloquent of the distance we have gone on the pathways of Retrogression. To consider London or Paris in ruins is a reversion itself to barbarism. To say that it may yet happen is an admission of defeat. Yet we are not living in a world fringed vaguely by barbarism, the extent of which we cannot gauge. . . .[1]

The barbarism, Casson wrote, is here and now, with us, inside the gates all the time. The symptoms are strangely similar to those which accompanied the collapse of Rome. Freedom of speech, tolerance, and justice have completely vanished in all lands except France, Britain, and America and in some of the politically powerless smaller states. The first step on this decline was the World War. With the dead who perished in that cataclysm there also perished the major part of international morality, which neither the eloquence of the high-minded nor the organization of the League of Nations can do anything to atone for. The raging afflictions that the war engendered have now reached their pathological crisis:[2]

> I wonder exactly how long it will take us to awake to the fact that before our very eyes the world we lived in in our youth has passed away, and with it the main props of civilization. I wonder what can be salved from the wreck. At all costs let us avoid the easy optimism of 'it will all come right in the end', for the end is now so very imminent.[3]

[1] Stanley Casson, *Progress and Catastrophe* (New York and London, 1937), p. 182.
[2] *Ibid.*, pp. 182–183.
[3] *Ibid.*, p. 185.

Education for an Enduring Civilization

The awesome perspectives which this situation reveals for the rearing of the young are thus outlined by Casson:

Were we still engaged in the rigours of a fight against Nature, were we still living in caves from which our children had to emerge to help combat the mammoth and the sabre-toothed tiger, as soon as they were able to wield an axe, it would be comprehensible that we should launch our boys and girls into life at the age of puberty. Otherwise I can see no explanation for such suicidal folly. That any prospective citizen should be considered ready for his State, a finished product at fourteen, seems to me to suggest that our conception of the State still belongs to the Palaeolithic Age.[4]

In the meantime, according to Norman Cousins, a thousand years have passed. At any rate, as he contemplated the dropping of the first atomic bomb on a great city in August, 1945, he observed that a full millennium had been "compressed in that brief fraction of a second during which Hiroshima was leveled." He then declared that "modern man is obsolete."[5] Unfortunately this is only a half-truth. The fact is that modern man with all of his deficiencies in mind and character is still here, even as the physical conditions of his existence have marched on through the centuries. Today, six years after the end of a war waged in the name of the Four Freedoms and the promises of the Atlantic Charter, an aggressive despotism holds dominion over one-third of the human race, the nations are bitterly divided by a great ideological conflict, a good part of the earth is smoldering or in flames, and men speak despairingly of the Third World War. Even if we count the launching of the United Nations as a substantial gain, few would be bold enough to say that the prospects of mankind in general and the American people in particular look any brighter now than they did in 1937. Whether this organization will be more successful than its predecessor will depend far less on the words of its charter than on the purposes and understandings of those who wield power in the great nations of the world.

[4] *Ibid.*, p. 226.
[5] Norman Cousins, *Modern Man Is Obsolete* (New York, 1945), p. 40.

3

We need an education that will instruct the young in the sources of civilizational decay and death. Unfortunately this is a matter about which we know too little, even though it has been a subject of inquiry and speculation by philosophers and statesmen since ancient times. Here is the supreme challenge to American science and scholarship. We have had authoritative investigations of recent social trends and diligent studies without number of our history and of this or that phase of our life and civilization. Also we have at our disposal similar investigations and studies of other civilizations past and present, from the most ancient to the most modern and from the most primitive to the most advanced. But never have we sought in systematic and comprehensive fashion to bring this vast store of knowledge and thought to bear on the problems of our time through the channels of education and statesmanship. We do know, of course, that there is no simple and dependable formula by which the condition of civilizational vigor or decay can be judged. We know also that geographical, biological, social, psychological, and military factors all play their respective roles in the grand drama of the life and death of societies and cultures. In their later years of study the young in all seriousness should be brought face to face with this problem.

Civilizations have decayed because of profound changes in their geographical foundations. The advance of the ice sheet in Europe and Asia during the Pleistocene epoch brought death or migration to many primitive peoples and cultures. The decline of rainfall and the progressive desiccation of vast regions in the Middle East and Central Asia destroyed forests, closed caravan routes, and contributed to the decay of great civilizations. And we in America know how the "dust-bowl" of the nineteen-thirties impoverished the lives of hundreds of thousands of our people. The loss of some important natural resource, such as soil fertility, timber, or minerals, has often

Education for an Enduring Civilization 405

been disastrous to a people. The leadership of the English in the development of industrial economy, which was founded in no small measure on the abundance and accessibility of coal, is now challenged because of the depth of the seams and the difficulties of mining. In some of the older parts of the United States may be seen farms, once rich and prosperous, now abandoned because of erosion and loss of soil fertility. Even a favored geographical position may be undermined by the emergence of new modes of communication, the shifting of trade routes, and the modification of the international economic structure. We think at once of Basra, Tyre, and Athens, of Venice and Cadiz. The airplane will doubtless vastly reduce the value of certain locations as it will enhance that of others. Our own geographical position in the world, as we have noted again and again, has been profoundly altered by the advance of technology.

It has been said that in the long run biological forces determine the destiny of a civilization, that the vigor and quality of the human stock constitute the most crucial factor in the history of a people. Without accepting the more extreme doctrines of biological determinism we must recognize the importance of this question. On the quantitative side the issue is clear up to a certain point. If a people fails to reproduce itself, its civilization dies with it. Moreover, the issue of many a struggle between two tribes, nations, or races has been decided in the "battle of the loins." One has simply outreproduced the other. A striking illustration of our time is the rivalry of France and Germany. In 1800 France was the most populous state in Europe west of Russia, surpassing Germany by almost six millions. When the Nazis marched into Poland in 1939 the total German population of the continent was almost twice the French. The climb of the United States to the position of a great power is reflected in the growth of population. In 1800 we could boast but six million people. During the next century and a half we passed and left far behind all the leading countries of western Europe—Austria, Britain, France, Germany, Hungary, Italy, and Spain. But our period of rapid growth seems to be over. Our birth rate, which in 1800 was probably more than fifty per one thousand of the population, has declined to approximately twenty-two. The corresponding figure for Russia today is forty-four. On the other hand, in many parts of the world the advance of medical science is creating a condition which threatens the stability of institutions everywhere. Through the control of disease and the improvement of infant care the death rate is being greatly reduced. As a consequence, according to Robert C. Cook, "the same birth rates that once merely balanced deaths have now become a destructive force." "Today," he goes on to say, "there are nearly two and a half billion human beings on this earth, and the number is increasing some sixty-eight thousand every twenty-four hours. This increase is not distributed equally over the earth. In many areas that are already densely populated growth is most rapid, and other areas are filling fast." He is of the opinion that "next to the atom bomb, the most ominous force in the world today is uncontrolled fertility" and that this force "is ravaging many lands like a hurricane or a tidal wave."[6] Thus a people may reproduce itself into poverty, disease, starvation, physical misery, and cultural stagnation. This of course is not happening in America. But who can say that excessive birth rates elsewhere may not set off political explosions that sooner or later will reach our shores?

On the qualitative side the issue of population remains obscure because of deficiencies in our knowledge of genetics. There is some reason for believing, however, that great civilizations have decayed because of decline in the quality of the stock. Many are convinced that such a process of deterioration is going on among us through the differential birth rate. According to the report of a British Royal Commission issued in 1949, "the average intelligence quotient of the British people was declining about 2 points every generation." An American scientist declares that "the same pattern exists in the United States, where the experts consider a similar decline to be a 'moral certainty.'"[7] Obviously

[6] Robert C. Cook, *Human Fertility* (New York, 1951), p. 5.
[7] *Ibid.*, p. 6.

the matter is so fraught with the gravest of consequences that, if we have any concern for the future of our country, we should take steps immediately to discover and act upon the facts. Without a sound population policy no civilization can expect to endure.

The social and moral factors essential to an enduring civilization are not easily unraveled. History is full of prophecies of degeneration due to such factors that have been disproved by events. Often changes in the mores necessary to survival under altered conditions of life have been interpreted as harbingers of disaster. Until recently practically each major scientific or cultural advance was viewed with alarm by powerful elements in society, often quoting scripture and invoking ancient tabus. Yet we know that every civilization does rest upon a social and moral foundation. If the necessary loyalties are seriously weakened, if social consciousness or social conscience decays, if a spirit of indifference or corruption comes to pervade public relations, if essential standards of conduct and performance are seriously lowered, if the masses of the population become pauperized through the concentration of wealth, if society is divided into bitterly contending classes and factions lacking a common conception of welfare, if a people loses faith in itself or hope for the future because of some terrible defeat or catastrophe —if such conditions appear and become chronic, then we may be sure that a civilization is facing evil days. Whether it will fall never to rise again, as in the case of ancient Crete, Persia, Greece, or Rome, or pass through a period of eclipse to emerge later in the full light of day as China or India has done a number of times, we do not know. We should obviously strive to save our own civilization from such a hazardous ordeal.

Closely related to the social and moral factors is the psychological factor of inventiveness and adaptability. Because of changes in external relations or uneven development within, a civilization may face the issue of life or death. Many peoples have been overwhelmed by being brought into contact with more powerful and dynamic cultures developed in other parts of the world. Such has been the fate of innumerable societies during the past four hundred years as European civilization has moved out across the oceans to the New World and on around the globe. Even the great civilizations of China and India have had difficulty in making the adjustments necessary to survival. Moreover, in no country of the West, the birthplace of science and technology, has any people yet succeeded in bridging the vast gulf that separates the fruit of its practical inventiveness from its inherited moral sense and social organization. Certainly, in some respects the ethics, politics, and religion which we *practice* lag centuries, possibly a thousand years, behind the atomic bomb. If we fail to bridge this gulf, our American civilization, along with the other great civilizations of the age, may be destroyed in a single all-embracing catastrophe. If we fail to lift ourselves to the necessary level of intellectual comprehension and moral resolution, we may lack that vision without which both peoples and cultures perish. The psychological factor, the inability to understand, to think, to imagine, to invent, to change, to venture, may prove to be the final and decisive frailty of the human family. Because of deficiency here a people may be unable, to employ Toynbee's formula, to respond successfully to a profound challenge, whether the challenge comes from within or from without.

This brings the analysis to the fifth great threat to the survival of a civilization. The history of mankind is marked on almost every page by peoples and cultures going down before military aggression and the thirst for power and empire. Here perhaps is the greatest danger that survival has faced through the centuries and millennia. To take a few examples, Athens whose cultural achievements stand unrivaled in the long course of the human adventure never recovered from her wars with Sparta; Carthage and Palmyra were obliterated forever by the Roman legions; even Rome herself ultimately became a victim of her devotion to the art of war; the Aztecan and Incan civilizations perished by the swords of Cortez and Pizarro; and in our day the Jews of Europe and the Tartars of the Crimea have received blows

Education for an Enduring Civilization 409

from which they may never wholly recover. Clearly, in a world in which military power is a possession of the tribal or national state, pacifism can scarcely be regarded as the dependable guardian of a civilization. On the other hand, so long as this condition persists, the way is open in any society for the emergence of the most dangerous enemy of human freedom and of every constituent of high culture—the military caste and the military adventurer. Against these destroyers of civilization we must ever be on our guard. Hitler, Mussolini, and Tojo brought untold suffering not only on the world but also on their own peoples. And Stalin, with greater craft and vast patience, seems to be advancing along the same road. Total war, war to the death, is perhaps the surest and quickest way of destroying a civilization.

4

We need an education that will stress the study of the future.

Heretofore we have studied the past with a good deal of care and have looked out upon the present. But never in our schools have we sought to awaken in the young a sober and thoughtful interest in the future of their country and mankind. Before we can undertake this task intelligently, however, our society will have to renounce its relatively complete absorption in the immediate, abandon root and branch every vestige of "after-us-the-deluge" psychology, and proceed to organize its resources for bringing knowledge to bear on the shaping of the future.

Reference has already been made to the necessity of making fuller use of the findings of science and scholarship. We should move at once to organize on a comprehensive scale our intellectual resources for the prosecution of bold and fundamental inquiry into the foundations of national health and strength. Such an undertaking would certainly be no more difficult, and probably much less expensive, than the marshaling of forces to create the atomic bomb. If our historians, our scientists, our students of society, our philosophers, and our creative minds generally have nothing significant to say on this question, the layman may well ask what they are good for, beyond being an ornament to our culture. It is not too much to hope that they might have something very helpful and instructive to tell us. One of the tragedies of our civilization is that we have not learned how to make full use of our intellectual resources. Perhaps if the ancients had possessed the knowledge about man and human society which remains too largely inert and unused in the minds of our scholars and on the shelves of our libraries, they would have been able to save themselves.

The thing needed is neither an academy established to honor individuals nor a commission of scholars and scientists appointed for a term of months or years to prosecute a limited inquiry, but rather a great national institute generously endowed and staffed with the best minds of each generation and designed to put genius to work in the realm of statesmanship. Such an agency, by serving directly the government and people of the United States, would bring all the resources of scholarship and science to bear on the initiation, the formulation, and the appraisal in terms of probable consequences of the highest and most far-reaching policies of the nation. Our present methods in this domain of statesmanship are as archaic as the oxcart, and as inadequate for the purpose involved. The placing of such responsibilities on scientists and scholars would not only tap a great reserve of national strength but also bring them face to face with the implications and consequences of their work. They could no longer "refuse to defend their own value, nobly and dispassionately preserving their 'objectivity' even if firebrands should be thrown into their ivory towers."[8] Nor would they be content to remark with a lofty disdain of all values, as did a British scientific writer in 1935, that "an attack by gas is another form of the effect of environment to secure the survival of the fittest and the elimination of decadent and un-

---

[8] Emil Lederer, *State of the Masses* (New York, 1940), pp. 54–55.

worthy persons and races."[9] Fortunately, our physical scientists, profoundly disturbed by the consequences of their work, are becoming morally conscious and vocal. But they should remember that their achievements do not endow them with all wisdom, with the right to speak with authority in fields in which they know no more than the ordinary well-informed citizen.

5

We need an education that will foster in the young a deep and enlightened love of country.

If our civilization is to endure, each generation must possess an abiding affection for, a faith in, and a devotion to their native land. The fact must be recognized, however, that this great end can be achieved, neither by a refusal to recognize our weaknesses and deficiencies nor by an uninformed and uninspired practice of formal ritual, but rather by active and intelligent identification with the task of fulfilling the historic promise of American life. The young should be fired with the resolve to remove every blemish from our democracy and to make their country a better place to live in for all the people.

To those who fear that such an emphasis would breed a narrow nationalism, the reply can be made that everything depends on the moral ideas embraced by our civilization and cultivated in the young. The national state is one of the stubborn realities of our age, and will probably remain so for many decades. It will indubitably be the architect of any better world that the future may bring. If an enduring and just peace is to be established on the earth, the *nations* loving peace and justice, and not some nebulous body of internationalists, must be its responsible creators and defenders. Let us hope that the American people will constitute one of those nations. There is no necessary conflict between love of country and love of mankind. The issue rests with the actual moral commitments of the country involved.

[9] Casson, *op. cit.*, p. 189.

If the young are to love their country and shape its future, they must have knowledge of its history—of its moments of greatness and its moments of shame and weakness, of its achievements and failures, of its triumphs and defeats, of the troubles it faces today. They should come to know and admire the persons, the men and women, humble as well as great, who have built and are building democratic America, who have framed and are framing our free institutions and ideals. In this way they should be inspired in their turn to labor and sacrifice for the improvement of their country and for guarding and fulfilling its finest traditions. Also by books, moving pictures, television, and extended travel they should become acquainted with the rich and beautiful land which belongs to them and their children forever, however short or long that "forever" may prove to be.

They must be imbued with a deep sense of responsibility for conserving and developing the resources of their country. They should be taught to think of our natural reserves of soil, forest, water, minerals, and beauty as a great heritage which they are to transmit unimpaired and even enriched to future generations. They should become sensitive to the importance of developing to the full the richest of all our resources—the talents of the boys and girls, of the men and women, of the many races, nationalities, and religions comprising our people. Every child, regardless of class, creed, or color, should be regarded as holding within himself something of the destiny of America. In the words of a Norwegian national song, "every child's soul we unfold, is another province added to the country." At any rate a strong, intelligent, and virtuous generation is the surest guarantee of the endurance of a civilization. To the rearing of such a generation the school and the teacher should be deeply dedicated.

26

EDUCATION FOR A WORLD COMMUNITY

1

We need an education dedicated to the building of a world community.
To speak of such an education today requires both hardihood and faith. The disastrous course which world affairs have taken since the close of the Second World War is well-nigh enough to discourage the most optimistic. The grand alliance of Britain, Russia, and America, supported by China, India, France, and the smaller states, formed to conduct the struggle against the Axis powers, has long since dissolved. The world appears to be as bitterly divided, as consumed with fear, suspicion, and hatred, as at any time in the past. This division splits and paralyzes the United Nations whose birth was hailed so recently as the hope of mankind.

That the present picture of the world is dark and forbidding must be granted. Yet the fact remains that the supreme task of the present and the coming generation in all countries, surpassing in its urgency any domestic issue, is the development of the institutions, the outlook, the morality, and the defenses of a world community. The material foundations of such a community, as we have noted repeatedly in this volume, have already been laid through the development of new forms of transportation and communication. All geographical barriers, including distance, have been surmounted. Retreat into the past is impossible; perpetuation of the present means chaos and disaster. The only sane course for all nations today is the building on existing and potential material foundations of a comparable superstructure of social arrangements, practices, and ideals. Although this superstructure is already in process of development, the difficulties in our way are vast and terrifying. The peoples of all countries are largely unprepared in mind and heart for the fateful decisions which they are compelled by events to make. Their attitudes and understandings reflect an age that is gone. Many simply do not see the realities standing starkly before them, while others lack the resolution necessary to meet conditions which they freely acknowledge. And in a large part of the world, unfortunately, the people have no voice in the shaping of national policy.

Failure to adjust to the new material conditions can only bring catastrophe surpassing in depth and sweep anything that man has experienced. We know in our rational moments that total war waged with the rapidly advancing military technology and with that spirit of ruthlessness which in our lifetime has greatly weakened the sense of mercy and brotherhood threatens all the ways and values of civilized life. Unless this terrible scourge is driven from the earth, no civilization worthy of the name can be expected to endure. Otherwise, with the earth growing ever smaller and the engines of death ever more destructive, war and preparation for war may become the all-absorbing passion of mankind until that fateful day when the nations are consumed in the purple and orange holocaust of atomic explosion. During this respite of leashed fear and hatred, how long or short we know not, the enrichment of civilization through the friendly and unrestrained intercourse of peoples will be rendered impossible. War and the threat of war tend to weaken and destroy the great civilizing conception of a common humanity. In spite of all discouragements and defeats, therefore, we must strive with every resource in our possession, and particularly through the agencies of organized education, to establish a lasting and just peace within the next quarter of a century. This may be our last chance.

2

We need an education that will foster a sustained sense of urgency and responsibility. The task of building a world community fit for human habitation will be exacting and prolonged. It will encounter seemingly insuperable obstacles and be marked by many bitter disappointments. Success will consequently require that steadfastness and toughness of spirit which flow from deep conviction and concern. These indispensable qualities of mind cannot be developed through the repetition of slogans and prophecies of impending doom. They can come only out of a clear understanding of the values at stake and the elements in the situation. Our education should strive to convey such understanding.

The conquest and annihilation of distance through the transformation of the modes of transportation and communication must be thoroughly understood by the coming generation. The young should see and ponder this transformation in historical perspective—the invention of the sledge, the wheel, the cart, the locomotive, the automobile, the airplane, and the rocket, of the raft, the canoe, the sailboat, the steamship, and the atomic-driven vessel, of the messenger, the drum, the signal fire, the telegraph, the telephone, the radio, and television. But the emphasis here should be placed, not on the mere record of technical advance, romantic as the story is, but rather on the impact of these inventions on the life and institutions of man—on the conquest of natural barriers, the development of trade, the expansion of markets, the specialization of production, the clash of strange cultures, the exchange of ideas and customs, the formation of nations, the extension of state boundaries, the advance of imperialism, the bringing of distant peoples into close association, the reduction of the earth to the dimensions of a neighborhood, the creation of a condition of world-wide interdependence, and the widening of the sweep of war to the point of embracing the entire planet. The meaning of this development for the future of mankind should be the object of careful study and sober reflection in all educational agencies. The transformation of the modes and instruments of warfare should be treated in similar fashion. To look out upon the contemporary plight of the human race is not enough. The history of warfare and of weapons from the earliest times should be passed in review, with emphasis on their consequences in terms of human suffering and the spread of cultures, the rise and fall of peoples, the setting of national boundaries, and the modification of class structures and class relations. But chief attention should be given to the revolutionary changes of the past generation and particularly since that fateful morning of July 16, 1945, when the first atomic bomb in history exploded over the deserts of New Mexico—changes which have made war an utterly intolerable method of settling disputes among nations.

The young should be given a realistic understanding through the generous use of moving pictures of the meaning of total war as waged from 1939 to 1945—the sinking of ocean liners, the bombing of cities, the slaughter of armies, the massacre of peoples, the enslavement of labor, the torture of prisoners, and the explosion of atomic bombs that vaporize steel and turn sand into green glass. In so far as the techniques of instruction make possible, nothing of the horror and the tragedy of war as already waged should be left to the imagination. *This Is War!*, a pictorial account of the war in Korea by David Douglas Duncan, a talented and courageous news photographer, might well be introduced into the high school program of studies—a book which contains, according to a seasoned reviewer, "the best photographs of men at war and of battle action which I have ever seen."[1] But we should go beyond past and present and bring under study and contemplation the vast "advances" in the engines of death which will be employed if the great nations ever again appeal to physical force—the "hell bomb," the guided rocket,

[1] David Douglas Duncan, *This Is War! A Photo-Narrative in Three Parts* (New York, 1951).

Education for a World Community

and all the resources for destruction potential in physics, chemistry, and biology. The young should know that man has possibly reached the point in his earthly career when he must choose between peace and extinction.

The responsibility of the United States of America in this moment of destiny must be clearly perceived. The unrivaled industrial power of our country need not be reviewed here except to say that it equals approximately that of all the rest of the world combined and that in the realm of military science and technology we stand at least temporarily in the vanguard of the nations. Whether we continue to take an active part therefore in the effort to organize peace or withdraw completely from international councils, we shall profoundly affect all decisions and programs, unless we should transport ourselves to some other planet. While neutrality on the great world issues of our time might be possible for a small or weak nation, it is quite impossible for the most powerful and advanced industrial state on the earth. We must realize, moreover, that we probably stand at the very apex of our power in relation to other peoples. In another generation or two the situation may be greatly changed. The opportunity and the responsibility of today may be gone tomorrow. This fact alone should sober us and breed a resolve to prepare ourselves for this most crucial test of history.

The pre-eminent position of America in the world at the present time has direct bearing on the central issue involved in the building of an international community. That a world order of some kind will emerge in the proximate future has already been decided by the facts of technology, provided mankind survives. The only living option before the peoples of the earth is the character of that order. Hitler believed in and fought for a world society in which peace would reign for a thousand years. But, if he had triumphed, it would have been a world dominated by the Nazi philosophy and violently hostile to every great moral commitment of the human race. Today Stalin, with far greater potential resources and with allies in all countries, is directing a mortal struggle for the world under the banners of Communism and in the name of peace. Profiting from the mistakes of his predecessor, equipped with the atomic bomb and a far more effective propaganda, he might succeed where Der Fuehrer failed. And if he should succeed, the world which he would build would scarcely be more humane than the vision of Hitler. Ruled by Communist morals, it would be a world bereft of even the hope of individual freedom and political liberty. The young of America must be inspired to work with all haste to build a world-wide community founded on the principles of justice, equality, freedom, and security. If this should prove impossible, they must at least struggle for a more limited order of great strength under which such principles may be able to survive until conditions change and mankind can resume the march toward world order and peace under freedom.

3

We need an education that will give a sense of the magnitude of the task of building a tolerable world order.
This is not the place to discuss ways and means of achieving a just and lasting peace on the earth. We know that the undertaking is perhaps the most difficult ever faced by the human race and that it will require all the knowledge, wisdom, faith, courage, and good will of which statesmanship is capable. We know that it will require the abandonment of ancient and cherished traditions, the blazing of new trails on the unexplored frontiers of civilization, and the development of institutions, ideas, and attitudes as revolutionary as the new weapons of war and modes of communication. We know that it will require the formation of a measure of world law and government which will set limits to national sovereignty and bring adequate military force to the support of the peaceful adjustment of differences among nations. The fact is that today we have an emerging world community with precious little law and no government. The smallest state would be

torn by rapine and civil strife under similar conditions. The Charter of the United Nations would be only a beginning, even if its provisions were firmly established in the institutions and mores of the peoples of the earth. The great task would still lie ahead. The young should have some knowledge of the difficulties and hazards to be encountered and overcome along the way.

They must realize fully how formidable is the foe that they would vanquish. Few peoples in any age have loved war for its own sake. From earliest times the great prophets of mankind and all who have been sensitive to human suffering have condemned this monster as the devourer of civilization. In the seventeenth century Fénelon expressed truly the reasoned judgment of all ages when he declared that "war is the most dreadful of all evils by which heaven has afflicted man." And yet, despite almost universal condemnation, it has endured from century to century, taking its periodic toll of wealth, life, and happiness. Even Christian peoples, who for two thousand years have proclaimed themselves devout followers of the Prince of Peace, have an unsurpassed record of war and conquest. Indeed, as they have gone forth to destroy their enemies, they have invariably invoked the name of Jesus. So ancient and so persistent is the pattern of war in history that many have concluded that it is rooted in the biological constitution of man and is therefore ineradicable. For this position there is little support, since some peoples have been proverbially peaceful and others have become so after long records of military adventure.

But to say that war is not fated by the very nature of man is not to imply that its eradication will be easy. Its basic causes and sources are many and powerful. It is deeply rooted in the facts of geography and history, in the cultures, the institutions, and the acquired dispositions of the human race. Any given war is a product of the complex interaction of a large number of factors. Among such factors are the distribution of resources and populations, the instabilities of economic systems, the selfish drives of interest groups, the exploitation of man by man, the bitter cleavages and struggles of social classes, the thirst for power of ambitious and ruthless men, the dialectic of revolution and counterrevolution, the clash of conflicting philosophies and social systems, the injustices, the tensions, the fears, the hatreds, and the historic aspirations and rivalries among the nations and peoples of the earth. The long practice of war, moreover, has left a heritage which leads to further war. The breaking of this vicious circle will demand of the coming generation a more general and profound understanding of the sources of military conflict than people generally possess today. The schools must deal with this question with boldness and realism.

The organization of peace requires also a clear grasp of the changing power patterns of the world. It is extremely difficult for an American to see the world as it is or as it is becoming. We can scarcely accept the reasoned judgment of an American historian of German origin that in the Second World War the "collapse of the traditional European system became an irrevocable fact" and that "what is commonly called the 'historic Europe' is dead and beyond resurrection."[2] Conditioned for centuries to look upon Britain, France, Italy, Germany, and the West generally as the great centers of power on the earth, we tend to think in terms of conditions that have passed away, probably forever. Our educational program should awaken the young to certain great political realities of our time—the shift of the center of power from Western Europe, the rise of the United States of America, the swift transformation of Russia into an industrial state, the emergence of China from her long sleep, the liberation of India from British control, and the spirit of unrest and bitter discontent agitating the minds of the colonial and colored races and peoples of the earth. We in America can scarcely accept these revolutionary changes in the patterns of power as accomplished facts. Indeed, we find great difficulty in believing that we stand today as the mightiest state of history. To act wisely upon this belief is still beyond our capacity. Yet, if we are to participate effectively in the build-

[2] Hajo Holborn, *The Political Collapse of Europe* (New York, 1951), p. x.

ing of the world community, we must base our policies on the realities of our time and not on those of the past.

A central factor tending to thwart all attempts to build a free and peaceful world community is the economic condition of vast populations. It has been estimated that approximately two-thirds of the people of the earth are caught in a vicious circle of ignorance, poverty, disease, and hunger. Except for small privileged minorities, they are engaged from birth to death in a grim and often losing struggle for sheer existence. For them malnutrition is chronic, actual starvation is frequent, medical care in the modern sense is unknown, illiteracy is the general condition, modern science and technology are mysteries, and the average span of life is about thirty years. Their vocational skills, knowledges, and implements are primitive, and remain practically static from generation to generation. Their economies rest almost entirely on the energy of human beings and domestic animals. When this condition is combined with political discontent, racial hatred, and revolutionary expectations, as it commonly is, we have an ideal situation for the spread of totalitarian ideas and movements. The Point Four Program for assisting technically underdeveloped countries constitutes a statesmanlike proposal to build a solid economic foundation for a world community. But, if not supported by an enlightened education, it will remain only a dream. Indeed, it may bring violent explosions.

Among the many hazards and difficulties blocking the road to understanding and peace there is one that stands out above all the rest and casts its shadow over every international gathering—the present division of the world into two rival and hostile camps—the one led by the Soviet Union, the other by the United States. The two camps have existed in some form ever since the Bolshevik Revolution of 1917 and, except for the period of the war, have been engaged in open or concealed conflict. It was hoped that the union formed by the struggle against the Axis powers would hold together during the years to follow. Today that hope is gone. Yet if the present trend continues, if no basis of reconciliation or toleration can be found, the prospects of building a world order in the proximate future are extremely slender. The educational program should provide the greatest possible illumination of the foundations of this conflict which may in time set the world aflame. The stakes in this issue involve the whole future of mankind.

4

We need an education that will convey to the young an informed understanding of the Soviet Union and world Communism.

The educational task is shaped by the critical importance of the issues involved and by the fact that the American people today, thirty-four years after the Russian Revolution, are profoundly ignorant of the Soviet Union and world Communism. Although we expected the revolution, as we expected revolts against monarchies, autocracies, and despotisms everywhere, and although we greeted with unrestrained enthusiasm the revolution of March, 1917, we had little knowledge of either Russia or Marxism and were quite unprepared for the triumph of the Bolsheviks in November. Indeed, even now the word "Bolshevik" carries no precise meaning to the American mind. It is not surprising, therefore, that we have made mistake after mistake in our appraisal of the Russian Revolution, the Soviet Union, and world Communism. A review of a few of these mistakes will reveal something of the magnitude of our intellectual deficiency.

At the time of the revolution a small company of Marxists and near-Marxists saw it in purest Marxian terms. To them it meant the swift fulfillment of a man's fondest dreams—the establishment of socialism, the building of a classless society, the achievement of complete political democracy, the closing of prisons, the withering away of the state, and the liberation of men from every form of bondage. A much larger group of liberals interpreted the events of 1917 as a delayed democratic revolution. They saw the Russians following the path blazed by the countries of Western Europe and America during the seventeenth, eighteenth, and nineteenth centuries. They were disturbed by the violent language and methods of the Bolsheviks—the seizure of power by force of arms, the establishment of the dictatorship, the resort to mass terror, the attack upon religion, the church, and the family. But they tended to view these developments merely as excesses which were a natural response to the despotism and brutality of the tsars. They knew in those days that all roads were leading to democracy. The great body of conservatives were generally convinced that the Bolshevik regime was merely a passing phase of the revolution. Though outraged by the attack on the institutions of private property, they comforted themselves with the thought that Lenin and his associates would soon be swept away by crisis, famine, and pestilence. It was clear to them that the Soviet system violated the universal laws of economics and human nature. Obviously such a system could not endure.

Events proved all of these expectations to be mistaken. The reality today is a social system marked by great inequalities of condition, a political police numbering hundreds of thousands, the outlawing of all political dissent, the consignment of millions to forced labor camps, an all-embracing system of mind control, a ruthless dictatorship by a small oligarchy heading the Communist Party, and a worship of Stalin surpassing in its sweep and intensity the practices of German Fascism. Although the Soviet leadership proclaims every day complete devotion to the interests of the people of Russia and the "toiling masses" of the entire world, the Soviet state is to be found nowhere in the writings of Karl Marx or in the thought of nineteenth century socialists. At the same time the Bolsheviks have maintained their rule and today hold sway over one-third of the population of the earth.

Since the revolution we have continued to make one mistake after another. When Lenin launched the New Economic Policy in 1921 many believed that the Bolsheviks had abandoned their collectivist ideas and were on their way back to the "time-tested" principles and practices of capitalism. And when Stalin launched the First Five-Year Plan in 1928 under the slogan of "socialism in one country," we were sure that they had abandoned the doctrine that had disturbed most profoundly their relations with other states—the doctrine of world revolution. Following the Nazi attack in June, 1941, we hailed the Soviet Union as "our great democratic ally" and the man who had sent his old comrades to the execution chamber and millions of men and women to forced labor camps, as "Uncle Joe," or even as "good old Uncle Joe," wearing a benign and fatherly smile. Finally, throughout these years many held tenaciously to the view that the "national Communist Parties" of the world were merely expressions of popular revolt and were guided primarily by the interests of the working classes in their several countries. We know today that all of this, and much more besides, was thinking compounded in varying measure of wish and ignorance.

Clearly the time has come, if it is not already too late, for us to marshal all of our educational resources for the purpose of achieving understanding of this strange and complex political phenomenon which threatens to overwhelm free societies throughout the world. We must recognize Russian Communism for what it is. We must learn that it is neither Marxism nor Russian absolutism, but a powerful and dynamic synthesis of the two. From Marxism it takes in their harshest and most inflexible form the so-called "scientific" laws of transition from capitalism to socialism. From Marxism also it takes the vision of a new heaven and a new earth where peace will reign forever and man will no longer exploit man. It is this union of "science" and Utopia, propagated throughout the world by means of all the agencies of the Soviet state and "international" Communism, that appeals to the oppressed and desperate classes and peoples of the earth. The Soviet leaders also appropriate the worst elements from the imperial heritage of Great Russia, elements which, to be sure, have their counterparts in some measure in many countries of the West. The decisive political reality of the entire Communist world, the All-Union Communist Party and its Central Committee of seventy-two members which rules the Soviet Union and directs the Communist movement in all countries except Yugoslavia, comes not from Marx but from a century-old Russian revolutionary tradition. Imperial Russia also contributes the principle of absolutism and the person of the autocrat, the all-wise, the all-good, and the all-powerful father and teacher, Joseph Stalin, before whom the faithful "bow down to the ground" with assurances of praise "forever and ever." Finally, the Bolsheviks appropriate the Great Russian messianic mission of bearing salvation to the "putrescent West," bring it into a powerful synthesis with the Marxian apocalypse, and promise the establishment of a Communist paradise of peace, plenty, and justice throughout the earth.

Fanatical, ruthless, and corrupted by unlimited power the Soviet leaders can be halted short of their goal only by the economic and military strength, the moral and political strength of the free world. The task of achieving the necessary strength in the coming years rests in considerable measure on the American people and their educational program. At the same time we must strive by every means possible to reach the Russian people and assure them that we are utterly without aggressive designs against them and would welcome beyond measure the establishment of friendly and peaceful relations with them. If we could thus bring the Soviet leaders to abandon their messianic mission and their aggressive policy, the building of a world community of free and equal nations living under a rule of law would then become possible. This should be the great object of American statesmanship and of the statesmanship of the entire free world. But we must also resolutely renounce all wishful thinking and prepare for a struggle that may last for years, decades, and even generations. The Soviet leaders have not changed their ultimate goal of world domination since 1917. The situation confronting the free world was stated with utter bluntness in the autumn of 1946 by Konstantin Simonov, a distinguished Soviet dramatist. "A most ferocious ideological struggle between two systems," he said, "between two world outlooks, between two conceptions of the future of mankind has been, is being, and will be waged in the world." Unfortunately he was probably speaking the truth.

5

We need an education that will prepare positively for world citizenship.

Men must acquire the knowledge, develop the loyalties, and make the sacrifices necessary to discharge the political responsibilities required for the establishment of an international order. They must become familiar with the efforts of the past several generations to build the institutions of peace. Then, as the necessary arrangements and processes are established and strengthened, they must learn to participate effectively in their operation. Most important of all, they must develop a sense of responsibility for creating the necessary institutions and for making them serve the purposes of justice and peace. If they should fail to make substantial progress in this direction, the terrible sacrifices of the last war will seem a bitter mockery in the coming years. Only as the peoples of the world develop common understandings and interests can the international political order rest on solid foundations.

A basic element in world citizenship is knowledge of the efforts of nations to establish peace on the earth. Along with our heritage of war we also have a heritage of peace. From the Achaean League to the United Nations, from the early Christians to the modern Quakers, states and peoples have sought in many and diverse ways security from the ravages of war. This entire story should be a part of our common knowledge. Particular attention should be given to the various methods which have been put to the test in modern times —the development of national strength, the resort to balance of power, the formation of alliances, the making of pacts of nonaggression, the reduction of armaments, the establishment of regional agreements, the creation of federations, the declaration of neutrality, the profession of pacifism, and the founding of international courts of justice. The unique experience of the American people in forming a federal union out of thirteen separate and jealous states is worthy of careful study. The causes of the failure of the League of Nations should be thoroughly explored. Finally, the latest attempt to establish peace through the United Nations and plans for the control of atomic energy and the limitation of armaments should be examined in detail.

The question of national sovereignty is the rock on which all efforts at world organization may be wrecked. Unless a people is prepared to surrender some measure of sovereignty, unless it is prepared to bow before the international will on some matters, there can be no rational hope for peace and order on the earth. The young should be encouraged to confront this problem with all the resources of scholarship and good will. They must be led to see the issue, not in abstract or ideal terms, but rather in terms of the historical reality. The close integration of the world has as a matter of fact already placed severe limitations on the actual sovereignty of every nation. At the outset of each of the two world wars the American government expressed a resolve to keep out of the conflict. Nevertheless, with the inexorability of fate we were dragged into the struggle. When the sovereignty of a people has been so diminished that it is not really free to declare war or remain at peace the term has certainly lost much of its meaning. The younger generation must understand the changed foundations of sovereignty and be prepared to make sacrifices to the building of genuine world order.

The creation of an international political organization designed to keep peace among the nations calls for informed and responsible citizenship on the part of the peoples of all the democracies. Because of our great power this obligation rests with peculiar weight on us. The young, therefore, should become familiar with the structure and operation of the institutions of the United Nations, even as they should become familiar with the government of their own country.

In similar measure they should develop the loyalties and assume the duties of world citizenship. They must learn to keep a very watchful eye on foreign policy, knowing that what we do abroad through our representatives in the United Nations may be quite as important for our general welfare as what we do at home. Indeed, where issues of war and peace are involved, even an important domestic issue may actually be insignificant in comparison. An understanding of international problems therefore constitutes an indispensable element in the equipment of the individual for the discharge of the duties of world citizenship.

As a support for the practical activities of world citizenship must go a broad and sympathetic understanding of the great peoples and cultures of the earth. Here it will be necessary to overcome a narrow and parochial spirit which we share with all nations. Because of the great geographical barriers which have separated us from Europe, Asia, Africa, Australia, and even Latin America we know altogether too little about the inhabitants and institutions of these continents. Indeed much that passes for knowledge is replete with error and colored by prejudice. Through the study of history, geography, and anthropology, through the cinema and organized travel, we must make a gigantic effort to overcome our deficiencies in this realm. We should also strive to correct the many misunderstandings about ourselves which are widespread in the world today. It should be noted here that the moving pictures which we send abroad and which inevitably convey an interpretation of American life should be subjected to critical scrutiny. We would do well to follow the counsel of J. E. Morpurgo, an Englishman who knows us well. Speaking in the name of Europe, he writes: "We need the voice of Thomas Jefferson and we have been given the voice of Hollywood."[3] Every form of cultural exchange should be encouraged—newspapers and radio programs, books and periodicals, art exhibits and industrial expositions —delegations of workers, farmers, and businessmen, of stu-

[3] J. E. Morpurgo in *The Impact of America on European Culture* (Boston, 1951), p. 60.

dents, teachers, and scholars, of artists, scientists, and clergymen. It is of course critically urgent that every effort be made to break through the "iron curtain" and establish such contacts with the peoples of the Soviet Union. The provisions of the Fulbright Act constitute a resource of incalculable value in promoting the mutual understanding of peoples.

Understanding, though invaluable, is not enough. An effort must be made to develop in the young a love of mankind and a feeling of kinship with all peoples. Our emphasis on the great principle of equality at home must be made to govern increasingly our relations abroad. If we use our vast power with wisdom, justice, and humanity, if we defend the rights and interests of the weak and oppressed peoples of the world, we shall keep filled to the brim that great reservoir of good will of which Wendell Willkie spoke so eloquently. The foundations of such a role are well laid in our history— in our Hebraic-Christian ethic, in our humanistic affirmations, in our tradition of welcome to the poor and the downtrodden of the earth, and in our comparatively enlightened treatment of the Filipinos and other colonial peoples. The young should be taught to cherish and nourish this heritage as one of our most precious possessions, removing every blemish that any imperialistic adventures may have placed upon it. For the development of this love of humanity we have another valuable resource in the many religions, cultures, and races composing our own nation. The application of the principle of equality in our schools to all of our people would establish a firm foundation for an enlightened and humane policy in the world. If we strive honestly to fulfill the promises of the Declaration of Independence at home, we shall be powerfully armed to support the Declaration of Human Rights of the United Nations throughout the world.

Finally, through a well-conceived and carefully organized program of language instruction we must strive to overcome a severe cultural disability from which we have long suffered. In spite of the fact that we have had far more youth in our secondary schools and colleges studying foreign languages than any other country, we are noted the world over for our incompetence in this field. The truth is that for the most part neither students nor teachers regard the work seriously or expect to achieve mastery. Another defect in the program is the concentration on three West-European languages to the virtual neglect of all others. Provision must be made for the mastery by appropriate numbers of gifted children and youth of the more important languages of mankind. This means that, at least for those who have the talent and the interest, language instruction in America must become a serious undertaking. Powerful motivation could be developed through generous awards of travel and study in foreign countries to students achieving a certain level of proficiency.

6

We need an education that will keep America strong in every way.

It must of course be understood that a world organization capable of maintaining peace among the nations on foundations of justice is today only a hope. Moreover, any world organization, if it is to be successful, must have the support of popular loyalties and understanding in all the great powers. No one country can move forward to this difficult and hazardous task by itself. We must therefore prepare ourselves for a long and sustained effort. Years and even decades may pass before the hope of today approaches realization. In the meantime, as we strive earnestly and resolutely to realize this hope we must always be ready, in collaboration with other free nations, to oppose aggression in every form. We should all have learned in our generation that peaceful intentions are not enough. Unless and until overwhelming physical strength stands behind the enforcement of peace, no nation, however abhorrent of war, can feel secure. As we move boldly to build our world community, therefore, we must remain strong—strong in our economy, strong in our military might, strong in our statesmanship, strong in our commitments to freedom and justice.

Part Six

EDUCATION

AND

SOCIAL

FORCES

27

THE AMERICAN COMMUNITY

1

The conduct of American education proceeds in the American community. The central argument of the present volume is that every educational program expresses, either unreflectively in terms of wont and custom or deliberately in the light of knowledge and clear purpose, some conception of life and civilization. If such a program is to be more than an expression of individual preference, if it is to affect practice anywhere in the world, it must be rooted in the history and culture of some living society, unless it is imposed by force from without. But even if thus imposed, to be effective it must articulate in some measure with the traditions and institutions of the people involved. An education conceived in Utopia, though it may challenge and stimulate in the manner of an education conceived in another age or place, can actually function only in Utopia, that is, nowhere.

In its present form our American educational system is a product of the American community, of the American people in their social and historical relations. With all of its deficiencies and excellences, and it has many of both, it is an authentic expression of our democracy. Yet that it is the only possible such expression must be rejected, if we are not to accept the doctrine that all history is fated and that men are but the helpless pawns of destiny. The conception of education developed in the foregoing pages is presented as an equally authentic expression of our civilization in the present epoch. Some will doubtless call it quite Utopian. If they are correct, it will prove relatively sterile. The assumption of the author, however, is that it represents the best in our traditions, the inescapable realities of the present, and the reasonable promises of the future—that it therefore lies within the limits of the possible. Some of our people will probably reject it wholly, because they have never fully reconciled themselves to democratic institutions and the ways of liberty. Many will reject it in some of its parts, because they will take exception to certain historical interpretations or value judgments. But the author believes that most will accept its major provisions as they understand them. Differences of course will emerge as interests come into conflict and meanings are made explicit in practical proposals.

As an education always expresses a conception of civilization, so the conduct of an educational program always proceeds in some human community. And American education is carried on, not in some Utopia beyond experience, nor in ancient Athens, mediaeval Italy, or colonial New England, nor in contemporary Britain, Germany, Russia, China, India, or Brazil, but in the American community of the mid-twentieth century. This fact has two important consequences. On the one hand, the community through its activities and institutions gives vitality and meaning to the whole process of rearing the young. If our education is to be effective, it must be related intimately to the environing life conditions. Children and youth cannot be inducted into any society by the most systematic instruction administered in a cloister. On the other hand, the community in its organized capacity controls this process. What education may actually become here in America, whether it is to serve the cause of freedom or the cause of despotism, whether it is to liberate or enslave the mind, whether it is to civilize or brutalize the heart, depends on the community. In the last analysis the great choices involved in the shaping of the future of American education will be made outside the school. The teaching profession, as we shall emphasize in the final chapter, must of course bear heavy responsibilities of enlightenment, counseling, and leadership, but the power of decision resides in the community. Certain relevant features of our American community must therefore be understood.

2

The American community reaches from the Atlantic to the Pacific and from the Lakes to the Gulf.
Here is a major reality affecting the organization and conduct of American education. The time has long since passed when we could think of the school community in terms of a geographical unit embracing a few square miles. The relatively isolated and self-contained rural neighborhoods of the pre-industrial era have vanished under the impact of steam, gasoline, and electricity. No locality can pretend to live to itself. Even state and regional boundaries have lost much, if not most, of their former meaning. Although the political divisions inherited from the past still have value as administrative units, they rarely express distinctive economic and cultural interests, and they sometimes constitute a heavy tribute exacted by tradition. As a matter of fact, families, localities, counties, states, and sections are all closely bound together into one great American community by a fantastically complex and intricate system of communications and interdependent relationships. Consequently, an educational program focused narrowly on the immediate surroundings might be as limited in its own way as was the bookish school of recent memory. And this might be done under the banners of the "community-centered school."

The fabric of communications which holds our American community together staggers the imagination. Besides our city streets we have more than three million miles of rural roads over which travel approximately forty-five million automobiles, buses, and trucks, driven by fifty-six million operators. The amount of movement by these means alone is a subject for speculation. But if every car runs ten thousand miles per year and carries on an average but two persons, the total passenger mileage would reach the astronomical figure of nine hundred billions. We have almost a quarter million miles of railroads which in the course of the year carry about two million passenger and freight cars a distance of approximately one billion train miles. We have a network of commercial airlines which in its domestic department transports sixteen million persons annually seven billion passenger miles. We have a postal service which delivers each year more than forty billion pieces of mail. Far beyond any other society past or present, we are today a nation on wheels. And who would say that in some tomorrow we may not be a nation on wings!

We have a telegraph service which handles annually two hundred million messages and a telephone service which arranges daily more than one hundred and thirty million conversations, over five million being long distance. And of course this figure does not include those who "listen in" over the "party line." We have ninety thousand motion picture theaters with a total seating capacity of almost fifty million, showing for the most part identical films produced in Hollywood. We have ninety-five million radio and eight million television sets presenting much the same programs from coast to coast. We have over seventeen hundred daily newspapers, five hundred Sunday newspapers, and eight thousand weekly newspapers with combined circulations of more than fifty million, forty-five million, and thirteen million respectively, served largely by a few great news-gathering agencies. If to all of this we add communication through the book and periodical press, as well as by means of the spoken word in face-to-face relationships and through apartment walls, by means of crawling, walking, and swimming, by means of the ox, the horse, and the pigeon, the wagon, the trolley, the sled, the boat, and the bicycle, one gains the impression that the American people are solely engaged in communicating with their fellow citizens. Even gossip today may be conducted on a national scale.

The American Community

Each school is of course located at some particular point in the far-flung American community. And there are differences from place to place in geographical factors, in economic functions, in political traditions, in life conditions, in morals and customs, and even in language. The complete absence of any central authority in the sphere of organized education, however, probably tends to exaggerate in the minds of many the significance of these differences. Although the federal government is not wholly without influence over the schools, responsibility rests overwhelmingly with the forty-eight states and the approximately one hundred thousand school districts, each with a board of education which presumably expresses the outlook and the desires of the people of the district. Yet the fundamental fact remains that no school can long operate under a condition of complete isolation. Social forces beat upon it perpetually, not only from the immediate neighborhood, but also from the most distant borders of the nation, and even from beyond the seas. The locality is no more independent in the domains of educational and cultural interests than in those of political power and means of livelihood.

The people living in the American community are in almost ceaseless motion. In a sense the locality into which one is born or in which one dwells is merely the point of entrance into or of contact with this vast community—a sort of home base from which one may sally forth on all kinds of exploits. "Except in isolated areas," wrote C. Warren Thornthwaite almost two decades ago, "population has achieved a remarkable mobility. Fewer than half of the families of the United States are bound to a locality by the ties of home ownership, and the automobile has destroyed all respect for distance."[1] According to a report of the Bureau of the Census made public in March, 1950, "twenty-eight million persons, or about 1 out of every 5, in April, 1949, were living in a different house from the one they had lived in a year earlier." Of this number, "19 million had moved within a county, 4 million

---

[1] C. Warren Thornthwaite, *Internal Migration in the United States* (Philadelphia, 1934), p. 3.

had changed county of residence within a State, another 4 million had moved from one State to another, and half a million had been living abroad a year earlier."[2]

People travel from one place to another for business, pleasure, or the advancement of the public interest, for any reason whatsoever or for no reason at all beyond the desire to be in motion. They may cross the continent to "put over a deal," to watch a prize fight, to attend a convention of the American Federation of Labor, to lay plans for the election of a president of the United States, or to solemnize a reunion of the "Blizzard Men of 1888." They may drive fifty or a thousand miles or more to take a swim, to see a tree, to climb a mountain, to catch a fish, to shoot a rabbit, or just to turn round and drive back. District, county, and state boundaries mean nothing to them, except as they may signify changes in traffic laws, the alertness of policemen, the tax on gasoline, or the price of cigarettes.

Individuals and families, in the tradition of their ancestors who crossed the ocean and followed the frontier westward, leave their homes behind them and move out in all directions to improve their condition. Some doubtless migrate to escape the law or to make a clean break with the past. But most respond to the lure of occupation, climate, cultural opportunity, or simple adventure. Children move away from place of birth, cross county and state lines, settle in distant regions, and found families of their own which in their turn will be scattered to the four corners of the land. The young, moreover, may begin their formal schooling in one place, continue it in another, and perhaps complete it in yet another. Consequently, when we consider the question of organized education we must think of the entire American community and not some small fraction thereof. Only then can we have an education that is firmly grounded on the social and cultural realities of the industrial age.

This of course does not mean that local responsibility for the conduct of the school is an anachronism and should be

---

[2] Bureau of the Census, Current Population Reports, *Population Characteristics* (Washington, March 17, 1950), p. 1.

abolished. The result of such action would be a vast bureaucracy administered from forty-eight state capitals or from Washington which would tend to crush all initiative and enforce a uniform pattern throughout the land. But if local responsibility is to be fruitful, it must be discharged with an informed sense of the transformations wrought in America by the new modes of communication. Moreover, the centrifugal forces operating at every point in industrial society make necessary a special effort to maintain the vigor of local institutions. As a democracy must always stimulate enterprise, encourage diversity, and cherish individual excellence and integrity, so it must foster participation in civic activities at the local as well as the state and national levels. Such an emphasis is peculiarly imperative in the field of education because of the basic and central role of personal relations in the rearing of the young. Yet all who are involved in the shaping of the program of the school must realize that the closely knit neighborhood of earlier times is probably gone forever and that every locality is meshed into a far-flung system of interdependences—the total American community.

3

The American community is marked by innumerable voluntary and quasi-voluntary organizations differing greatly in scope, solidarity, purpose, and power.

Although individuals may seek to stand alone in a position of splendid isolation amid the welter of conflicting forces, eschewing all formal association with their fellows, the American people generally and increasingly live by the maxim, "in union there is strength," or perhaps "in union there is fun." Even self-styled "independents" not infrequently join together to proclaim and demonstrate their independence. This predilection on the part of our citizens to form organizations for the achievement of both civil and political ends, as we have noted, deeply impressed Alexis de Tocqueville long ago.

The situation, however, has changed profoundly since the old agrarian days. Given the "habit of forming associations," a distinctive feature of free society, the number, the sweep, the cohesion, the course, and the purpose of organizations are influenced by life conditions. The complexity of industrial society, with its vast fabric of diverse occupations and conflicting interests, provides an opportunity for the unlimited flowering of the tendency. The new modes of communication make easily possible the development of closely knit organizations of thousands and even millions of like-minded persons residing in all parts of the country. The dynamism of the technological age stimulates unceasingly the abandonment of old and the formation of new associations. The productivity of the economy and the reduction of the hours of work give men both the resources and the leisure to engage in personal, civic, and political activities. As a result of the operation of all of these forces and factors the American community today is the scene of a perfect phantasmagoria of associations forming and reforming in endless variety and profusion. The inquirer, whatever his prejudice or interest, can usually find some organization suited to his taste. He could probably even find or form an organization committed to the abolition of all organizations.

The World Almanac for 1951 lists approximately twelve hundred "societies and associations in the United States." Although the list includes many organizations operating largely in New York, most of them are nation-wide in scope and influence. At the same time it omits the several political parties, the two hundred sixty-five religious denominations, the manifold large-scale business enterprises and corporations, and a vast multitude of local and regional bodies. Almost three-fourths of the organizations listed were launched since the beginning of the present century. Of the remainder, fifty appeared before 1850, and only twelve were here when the Constitutional Convention opened in 1787. The oldest is the American Philosophical Society which dates from 1743. This entire phenomenon seems to be closely linked with the advance of industrial society under a regime of liberty.

The American Community

The range of these organizations is fantastic. No purpose, whether serious or trifling, seems to have been overlooked, even though we know that in the next ten years many new associations will be formed. Today, if properly qualified or interested, the citizen may join the Guild of Former Pipe Organ Pumpers, the American Affiliation of Tall Clubs, Automobile Old Timers, the American Goat Society, or the Cave Men of America. But if these are not to his liking, he may turn to the American Bible Society, the Euthanasia Society of America, the American Council of Learned Societies, or the League for Industrial Democracy. If he so desires, he can throw his energies into an organization dedicated to the prevention of hay fever or cruelty to animals, to the abolition of the poll tax or capital punishment, to the promotion of world government or skeet shooting, to the saving of children or redwoods, to the advancement of science or sunbathing, to the propagation of atheism or the gospel, to the reduction of taxes or tuberculosis, to the prohibition of the use of alcohol or profanity, to the protection of wild life or the foreign-born, to the guarding of the civil liberties or the honor of Texas, to the advancement of colored people or colonial dames, to the commemoration of the battle of Bunker Hill or the adoption of the Bill of Rights, to the perpetuation of circus street parades or the American way of life, to the increase in the use of cotton or educational tests, to the giving of aid to crippled children or anti-Communist China, to the honoring of grandfathers or grandmothers, to the encouragement of horse shows or historical research, to the abatement of noise or traffic accidents, to the limiting of population or the use of contraceptives, to the dissemination of socialist or capitalist ideas, or to any one of hundreds of other causes. One can only marvel at this restless urge of the American people to form associations. And the individual citizen may identify himself much more fully with some organization whose members dwell in all parts of the nation than with the locality of his legal residence.

Many of these organizations have few members and limited resources. Others exceed in membership the populations of some of our states or command material resources greater than the riches of large geographical regions. The National Association of Manufacturers, through its fifteen thousand member companies, represents a large part of the corporate wealth of the country. The Chamber of Commerce of the United States, though somewhat loosely organized, is an authentic voice of American business interests. The American Federation of Labor and the Congress of Industrial Organizations, with a combined membership of approximately fourteen million working people, representing through their families perhaps one-fourth of the population of the nation, constitute a great and growing force in the American community. Two million farm families are organized and articulate in the National Grange, the American Farm Bureau Federation, and the Farmers Union. The Protestant and Catholic churches issue pronouncements on diverse subjects through the Federal Council of Churches of Christ in America and the National Catholic Welfare Conference respectively. The American Legion, numbering three million veterans and armed with the prestige of defenders of the Republic, speaks with great authority on questions of patriotism and the American way of life. The American Medical Association, though enrolling only one hundred fifty thousand physicians, has often demonstrated great strength on matters close to its interests. Women, through such organizations as the American Association of University Women and the League of Women Voters, are perpetually active in public affairs. Mention should also be made of the taxpayers' groups, the real estate bodies, the consumers' cooperatives, the advertising fraternity, the racial and national organizations, the hate-mongering factions, the service clubs and brotherhoods, the so-called patriotic societies, and the innumerable civic and professional associations which together have millions of members and seek to shape the course of thought and action in our great American community. This practice of forming associations is both an exuberant expression of our free way of life and a central factor in the dynamic of our society.

4

These organizations generally are engaged in a perpetual struggle to guard and advance their purposes. Except for the minor associations which are dedicated to the propagation of good fellowship or the cultivation of some talent, art, science, or idiosyncrasy, they battle for goals which touch directly and immediately public policy. Some, such as the National Association for the Advancement of Colored People, the National Conference of Christians and Jews, the American Civil Liberties Union, and the League of Women Voters, commonly seek no advantage for their members. Others, such as the National Association of Manufacturers, the American Federation of Labor, the American Farm Bureau Federation, and the Cooperative League of the United States of America, while serving many purposes, some of which are highly praiseworthy, are inspired primarily by economic self-interest. Yet others, such as the Communist Party and various native brands of totalitarianism, are engaged in a conspiratorial struggle for power and the overthrow of free institutions.

Ofttimes these organizations find themselves in bitter and violent conflict over matters of economic interest and public policy. As a result the whole of society may be the scene of an unprincipled campaign of misrepresentation, vilification, and falsification. In the pursuit of its ends an organization may seek to form or capture a political party or maintain a powerful lobby in Washington, the state capital, or the city hall. It may strive by divers means to influence in its favor any or all of the great media of mass communication through which opinion is informed and molded. It may employ public relations counselors to apply the resources of psychology to persuade the people of the justice and righteousness of its cause. It may, by means of strategic control of some key industry, paralyze the economy and lay heavy tribute on the entire nation. Indeed this struggle of organized interests may shake society to its foundations. According to the chairman of the Buchanan Committee of the House of Representatives, appointed to investigate "expenditures by corporations to influence legislation," the "business of influencing legislation is a billion-dollar industry."[3]

With the possible exception of extra-legal gangs of hoodlums, criminals, gamblers, and purveyors of narcotics, which are patently predatory in purpose, these organizations invariably present their policies and programs in terms of the public good. They stand before the people as the true defenders of the Declaration of Independence, the Federal Constitution, and the American way of life. And this is not to be understood as hypocrisy, even though a measure of hypocrisy is sometimes involved. Every organization, if it is to have faith in itself and be effective in its appeal, must incorporate its special concern in some conception of the general welfare. Organized business, as it opposes governmental restrictions on its operations, sees unregulated private enterprise as the true guardian of liberty and unlimited profits as the sole guarantor of prosperity for all. Organized labor, as it demands the closed shop and strikes for higher wages, contends that it is really fighting for all the people, for social justice, for the American standard of living, for democracy and economic stability. Organized farmers, as they struggle for governmental subsidies to maintain prices of agricultural products, argue that the land is the source of all wealth, that the farm is the nursery of democratic virtue, and that rural well-being insures an indispensable market for industrial goods. And the various organizations committed to the propagation of this or that reform commonly regard themselves as saviors of the nation. Radical and conservative alike go to battle under the banners of the fulfillment of the promise of America or the preservation of American ideals and principles. Opponents therefore are often, and sometimes from honest conviction, presented as enemies of the people, as propagators of foreign ideologies, as subverters of the government and institutions of the United States.

[3] Karl Schriftgiesser, *The Lobbyists* (New York, 1951), p. 147.

The American Community

In structure and operation many of these associations violate the basic principles of democracy. Since they are dedicated to the guarding or advancement of some cause or interest, they are strongly tempted to develop forms of organization and procedure designed for battle. Also in every one of them there appear strong and ambitious men motivated by a thirst for position and power. As a consequence, emphasis tends to be placed on the suppression of individual differences, on the establishment of discipline, solidarity, and loyalty to the leadership. Authoritarian or quasi-authoritarian practices emerge and become crystallized in rules and customs. In not a few organizations, even including some labor unions, the members have little voice in the determination of policy, while power is concentrated in some small body of officials, an executive board, or a national committee. This small body may exercise relatively complete control over the press, the technical staff, and the financial resources of the organization. Conventions composed of representatives of the rank and file may not be called for years, and when they are called they may merely endorse resolutions introduced by the official leadership. Thus policies formulated at headquarters in Washington, New York, Chicago, or some smaller city may be imposed on a great organization and carried throughout the nation by an obedient and disciplined membership. The greater the crisis and the more bitter the struggle, the stronger the tendency toward the authoritarian pattern.

5

Voluntary organizations are essential to the vital functioning of our American democracy.

Many citizens, outraged by their pressures on public officials and governmental bodies, by their campaigns of misrepresentation and intimidation, by their debasement of the agencies of communication, and by their disruption of the economy, hold that they vitiate the entire democratic political process and therefore should be abolished root and branch. Such critics, pointing to the disasters which in our time have overwhelmed certain countries of the Old World, contend that the struggles between organized interest groups may become so bitter and irreconcilable that they may completely destroy free institutions and open the gates to dictatorship.

The indictment is severe, and undoubtedly contains an element of truth. Yet the proposal to abolish private associations is both utopian and undesirable. It is utopian because they reside in the very structure of our society and could be abolished only by the destruction of that society. We may be sure that under the conditions of the industrial age men, if they are free, will combine with others of like interest and like mind for the achievement of common purposes. The proposal is undesirable because these organizations assure that distribution of power which is essential to the preservation of liberty. The alternative is not, as the critics believe, the isolated and independent individual, but the police state. One of the first measures taken by a totalitarian party after the seizure of power is the outlawing of every rival body and the "coordination" of all organizations in a monolithic structure. Regardless of differences in their declared purposes, the rival totalitarian movements follow the same course. The Communists, proclaiming their devotion to the interests of the proletariat, actually put the working class in chains and convert the labor union into a servant of their will. And the Fascists, appealing to businessmen as guardians of the institution of private property, rule by the sword and send former supporters to prison or into exile.

Here it is necessary to note that democracy is not a social and political order from which all struggle is banned. On the contrary, it is an order in which the struggle of interests is subjected to the rule of law and is conducted by non-violent methods. As a matter of fact, it is only in a democracy that struggle is tolerated. Wherever men are free, they will differ on matters great and small, and will strive to make their views prevail. He who would avoid struggle and the burden of decision should not look to democracy as the ideal state. Rather should he turn for refuge to the jail or the dungeon, to slavery or some other form of despotism. Democracy, as we have emphasized again and again in this volume, is a system under which the most profound changes, even revolution itself, can be achieved by peaceful means, by persuasion, enlightenment, compromise, toleration of differences, and majority decision. In our day much of the political struggle is carried on through organized groups and interests. And the politically active association seems to be spreading.

This does not mean, however, that all is well in our American community. Great organizations may use their power to exploit the people and violate the long-time interests of society. Rival organizations in their fierce struggles may trample on popular rights and arrogantly proclaim in the words of a famous "rugged individualist," "the public be damned." They may even act thus in times of great national peril. Or they may actually bring the nation to the verge of civil war. The remedy, however, is not to abolish associations, but to discipline them. This may be achieved in some measure by encouraging the organization of the unorganized and thus insuring a more equitable distribution of power. But sooner or later in both their internal structure and their external relations they must be brought more fully under the rule of law and under the searchlight of publicity. On the one hand, they must be organized and run according to democratic principles, with the policy-making authority squarely in the hands of the members. On the other hand, they must be prevented from jeopardizing vital public interests and be made to understand that they are but a part, and not the whole, of society. But laws are not enough. Hand in hand with the enactment of legislation must go a comprehensive program of education designed to build in the minds of the citizens appropriate moral and intellectual supports of the law—a national conception of the general welfare, a sense of social responsibility, loyalty to democratic values and processes, a spirit of tolerance of differences, and a tradition of fairness and honesty to govern the conduct of the struggle.

The preparation of the young to participate in the life and activities of private associations constitutes an indispensable part of education for citizenship.

6

These organizations advocate differing and conflicting educational conceptions, policies, and programs.
According to our official American theory, the conduct of public education is a responsibility which under the Federal Constitution is reserved for the most part to the state. In its turn the state generally delegates this responsibility in large measure to the local school district. And the citizens of the district, either directly or indirectly, establish by popular vote a board of education. The assumption seems to be that the members of the board, free from outside interference or pressure, shape educational policies during their terms of office in response to the clearly expressed mandates of the people.

As a matter of fact, the actual process is quite different. The organized groups interested in public education do, to be sure, participate in the elections. But thereafter they do not leave the board alone. In fact, from day to day and week to week throughout the year they seek to influence the members in their behalf, whether it be a matter of the use of a textbook, the employment of a teacher, the letting of a contract for the construction of a building, or some much larger consideration. Also these pressures are brought to bear continuously on members of the educational profession both individually and collectively. Thus, far from being isolated, the school is increasingly the center of the play of most diverse social forces.

The interest of organized groups in the conduct of the public school seems to have increased greatly during recent decades and promises to increase much more in the years ahead. Apart from the influence of the probable growth and spread of the pattern of voluntary association, this tendency appears to be due primarily to two conditions. In the first place, the school has developed into a major social and educational institution during the past two or three generations. Today it guides the maturing process and constitutes a major factor in the lives of the young from six to eighteen years of age and even beyond. In the second place, with the upward expansion of the school and the broadening of the curriculum it has become much more than an agency for the teaching of the tools of learning. Through history, the social studies, the natural sciences, and literature it introduces the young to new attitudes, ideas, values, and conceptions of life. As a consequence the school has become a considerable factor in shaping the course of American society and the destiny of the American people. As organized groups have become aware of the importance of the institution, they have sought increasingly to shape its policies. And some citizens have founded associations expressly for this purpose.

The demands which these organizations make upon the school are often in conflict. Also, while some of them may be well conceived, some may be narrow and partisan, formulated in terms of the special and limited interests of the groups concerned. Organized business has insisted that classical economic doctrine be taught in the schools, that the "virtues" of individual private enterprise be extolled, that the "fallacies" of government ownership of public utilities be exposed. Organized labor has sought to have labor's "story" told in the history textbooks and to have labor represented on boards of education. Organized farmers have opposed the consolidation of school districts and the introduction of "fads and frills" into the curriculum. Various national and racial groups have fought for more recognition in the program of studies. The so-called patriotic societies have advocated the flag drill, the study of the Constitution, the teaching of patriotism, and loyalty oaths for teachers. Many organizations have opposed the study of socialism, Communism, and the Soviet Union. Others have waged war on the use of "progressive" methods of teaching. Not a few, as diverse as the Civitan International and the Advertising Federation of America, have practically forced upon the schools essay contests designed to propagate some idea or outlook close to their interests. The Chamber of Commerce has consistently opposed federal aid to education, even as the American Federation of Labor has supported it. The Catholic Church has demanded public support for parochial schools, while the Protestant and Jewish denominations have generally taken the opposite position. In summary, one may say that there is some organized group committed for or against practically every proposal that may be advanced with respect to public education.

This battle over the schools threatens to destroy the integrity of public education in the United States. The basic difficulty probably resides in the fact that the American people as a whole lack a comprehensive understanding of the role of education in a free society. Since the "great educational awakening," since the founding of the common school more than a century ago, they have actually given little serious thought to the problem of rearing the young, possibly on the assumption that the issues were all satisfactorily decided by their ancestors during the agrarian age. The time has come for them to probe the question of education to its very foundations. Perhaps the present interest, expressed in widespread and largely uninformed attacks on the schools, may herald the coming of a genuine effort to raise the level of popular understanding. In the development of such understanding the teaching profession should play a leading and responsible role. It is hoped that the present volume will contribute something of value toward the defining of the function of public education in our free society during these troubled and fateful times.

28

THE AMERICAN TEACHER

1

The conception of education developed in the present volume makes heavy demands on the teacher.
It requires far more than the following of a set of prescribed rules and techniques, the practice of a body of esoteric knowledge regarding the learning process and the maturation of the young. It even requires of him far more than a mastery of his specialty and methods of teaching. It requires of him also, as a frame and guide for all that he does, a deep understanding of our developing civilization in both its historical and its world setting. It requires finally that he be sensitive to the profound moral implications of his calling—that he strive to express in his own life and work, both as teacher and as citizen, a great and noble conception of the life and destiny of man. All training of teachers, all administrative procedures, all methods of instruction, and all aspects of the curriculum, if not illuminated and inspired by such a conception, are destined to mediocrity and confusion of purpose, perhaps to futility and obscurantism.

The task of the teacher is made more difficult by the condition of cultural transition which marks the current epoch. It is of course commonplace to speak of the present as a period of swift social change. Yet the scope and depth of this change, with its implications for education, are insufficiently recognized. The fact is that the very foundation and framework of our civilization and social institutions are being profoundly modified. For some time now, for several generations at least, we have been moving with growing speed and momentum from the agrarian civilization of the founding fathers to a new civilization which we are coming to call industrial. As in all transitional epochs, men are being compelled to make the great choices. Education must be geared to the task of assisting our people in the making of these choices. If we are not to experience a prolonged period of trouble, bordering on catastrophe, education must give understanding of the conditions and bring clarification to the issues involved. It must play a central role in building the new minds required by the new age. It must engage in the perpetual reconstruction of its own methods and purposes. Although the teacher cannot and should not discharge this responsibility alone, he will have to provide much of the leadership required.

The task of the teacher is made more difficult also by the sweep, complexity, and dynamism of the American community. The surface of this community is always agitated, while in times of national crisis storms of political passion may penetrate its lowest depths. Local and nationwide organized interests, as we have seen, struggle incessantly to achieve their diverse and conflicting purposes. Powerful groups play upon the school, each striving to impose its will on the substance and processes of education. To surrender to these pressures would rob the school of its integrity and convert it into a kind of weather vane which would show the direction of the wind at the moment but would scarcely bring the ship of education to any port, except by chance. Some perhaps would seek tranquility by having the school retire from the world, renounce all controversial matters, and devote itself to the teaching of the "fundamentals" and the "training of the mind." Unfortunately for this proposal an educational program cannot be launched without confronting and making decisions regarding the most fundamental issues of value and purpose. And modern psychology has demonstrated that the training of the mind does not take place in a social and cultural vacuum. This can only mean, at least in a free society, that the teacher must be more than a tool or a "weapon," to use Stalin's term, of political power.

The task of the teacher is made yet more difficult by the presence in the American community of many other agencies and influences which mold mind and character. While the school is the one institution that is wholly dedicated by society to the work of education, it is by no means entirely responsible for the rearing of the young, even though irate citizens often charge it with failure to eradicate ignorance, stupidity, delinquency, corruption, and other ills common to humanity. The fact is that the school has supervision over children and youth from birth to eighteen years of age during only about one-eighth to one-seventh of their waking hours, if they are in attendance every day the school is in session. During the remaining hours they are subjected to the influences of family, neighborhood, and church, street, gang, sport, camp, and industry. And in these days of advanced technology we must add the powerful agencies of mass communication—the comic, the movie, the radio, and the video whose controlling purposes are not education, but profit, entertainment, and perhaps propaganda. With all of these forces competing with and often ranged against the school, it is astonishing that the teacher is able to accomplish as much as he does in the civilizing of the young. Yet this challenge must be confronted, and it can be confronted successfully only by making the work of the school so vital that its influence will pervade in some measure the entire life of children and youth.

2

The teacher is inadequately equipped to discharge the duties of his profession in the present age.

Although great advances have been made during the past two generations, the teacher is the victim of a severe cultural lag. While the demands made upon the school by the changed conditions of life have greatly increased, the popular conception of the calling remains rooted largely in the pre-industrial epoch.

The difficulty may be traced in part to the origins of our system of common schools. That system was not imposed from above by a strong central government or an influential intellectual class. Rather were its foundations laid by relatively untutored farmers who established one-room district schools in rural neighborhoods as they moved across the continent. In their eyes the school was a minor social and educational institution. Its work was encompassed by "book larnin," and "book larnin" was a simple matter of reading, writing, and arithmetic. They could therefore see little reason for an elaborate program of teacher training. To them it seemed entirely appropriate to ask a bright boy or girl graduate of the eighth grade to return to school and teach the things he or she had just learned. Thus there developed in the United States the tradition of the professionally untrained teacher. In a later generation many of our people viewed with scorn and ridicule the proposal that farm boys and girls should study agriculture and housekeeping.

Under these conditions teaching was not taken too seriously. It ranked low among the occupations as a life career. It was poorly paid, marked by insecurity of tenure, and hedged about by all sorts of petty restrictions and annoyances. It was regarded as a task suited to the undeveloped powers of youth approaching manhood and womanhood, as a steppingstone to marriage or some adult calling or profession. As late as the middle of the nineteenth century many teachers in the most progressive states were under twenty-one years of age and the great majority departed the school after one, two, three, four, or five years of teaching. Those who remained longer were often looked upon as a "little queer," as human culls who could not "make the grade" in the rough and tumble of life, as women who failed to find husbands or as men who feared to compete with their peers in the economic struggle.[1] This conception of the teacher was given

---

[1] See Willard S. Elsbree, *The American Teacher* (New York, 1939), Chaps. XXI–XXII, pp. 271–305.

satirical expression by Washington Irving in the character of Ichabod Crane. Many an American citizen doubtless has greeted with a chuckle of approval the observation of Henry L. Mencken: "The average schoolmaster . . . is and always must be essentially an ass, for how can one imagine an intelligent man engaging in so puerile an avocation?"[2] And how often have we heard a banker, a physician, or even a teacher evoke condescending laughter with George Bernard Shaw's famous gibe, "He who can, does: he who cannot, teaches!" But how many know that the great dramatist also said, "He who can do, does: he who can think, teaches"?[3]

More than a century ago when we were building the common school Francis J. Grund described the status of the teacher in America in words that in some respects remain true to this day. An extended quotation from the pen of this naturalized citizen and ardent defender of our free institutions is both fitting and illuminating:

> Much as the Americans appreciate the services of a teacher, they neither reward or esteem him according to his merits, and are hardly ever willing to associate with him on terms of fair reciprocity and friendship. The same feeling exists, in a still higher degree, in many parts of Europe, especially in England; but then there is no reason why it should continue in America, in a country in which no disgrace ought to attach to any honest pursuit; but in which, on the contrary, men should be honored, in proportion as they contribute to the moral and intellectual advancement of the State.
>
> The correctness of this doctrine, however, is so well understood in the United States, that the people are ashamed of their own sentiments, and leave no opportunity unimproved to evince that respect for the vocation *in private*, which they are most deficient of showing on all public occasions. Many a fashionable gentleman of the large cities would be glad of the company of the instructor of his children to a *family* dinner; but would be unwilling to introduce him to a party of friends, and would think himself disgraced, were he to be seen with him on 'Change. . . .

[2] Henry L. Mencken, *Prejudices* (New York, 1922), Third Series, p. 244.
[3] *The W. E. A. Education Year Book* (London, 1918), pp. 20-21.

The salaries of teachers in the public schools in most of the States are mere pittances, when compared with the remuneration of professional men, or clerks in the counting-rooms of respectable merchants. . . .

This inadequate compensation of the most arduous labor, is not only unjust and ungenerous, but productive of the most serious consequences to the public. The profession of teacher is embraced by a large number of men, who, though qualified for the office, resort to it only as a temporary means of subsistence, which they quit as soon as an opportunity of preferment offers itself in some other quarter. The immediate consequence is an almost annual change of instructers, and the succession in office of novices unqualified by age or experience. . . .

But the greatest evil arising from the too frequent changes of instructers in the United States is the unavoidable contempt to which it exposes the veterans in the profession.—Many of the most eminent lawyers, ministers, and physicians of New England have, during a certain period of their lives, been obliged to resort to teaching, either to finish their collegiate education, or to obtain the necessary means for the study of their respective professions. They have thus been in a habit of considering the employment of an instructer as a sort of relief from the most pressing necessities; but not as *an end* to be proposed by a man who aspires at honorable distinction. This creed, once established in the minds of professional men, has communicated itself to all ranks of society; so that, instead of the thanks of his fellow-citizens, an ancient instructer is only sure of being considered as a man of inferior talents; else he would have followed his colleagues in their professional career. As long as this opinion of instructers is entertained in the United States, the schoolmaster's task will be degraded. Those whom necessity shall reduce to it, will look upon it as defaming their fair reputation, and embrace the first opportunity to leave it with disgust and detestation.

But with what zeal can a man devote himself to a profession, at once laborious and difficult, in which the greatest success is incapable of procuring distinction?—which exposes him to unmerited contempt and reproach? And why should a pettifogging lawyer or a quack, consider himself better than an honest and successful instructer? [4]

[4] Francis J. Grund, *The Americans, in Their Moral, Social, and Political Relations* (Boston, 1837), pp. 125-128.

The American Teacher 457

This of course is not the whole story. From earliest historical times the word teacher has generally carried a lofty connotation. The great prophets of mankind have been called teachers. According to an old Chinese saying, which reflects the high regard for learning of this enduring civilization, "a great teacher is like a spring breeze and seasonal rain." Cicero inquired: "What greater or better gift can we offer the republic than to teach and instruct our youth?" Franklin, Washington, Jefferson, and others among our founding fathers regarded teaching as a noble profession. And throughout our history men and women of highest idealism and talents have given themselves unsparingly to the cause of education. Moreover, the improvement of the preparation and the raising of the status of the teacher have advanced notably during the last several generations. Today, in terms of social idealism and devotion to the general welfare, teachers as a group are unsurpassed by any other comparable body of citizens. Yet, as we shall see later, much remains to be done. The old heritage lingers on. In 1947–48 many teachers in the American common schools had received no college training whatsoever, and less than fifteen per cent held the master's or a higher degree.[5] Moreover, in five states more than forty per cent of the teachers received less than fifteen hundred dollars a year.[6] Clearly the task of building a profession capable of discharging the heavy responsibilities of public education in the present epoch is only well begun. Our American conception of the teacher still lags far behind our expressed convictions regarding the worth and power of education.

3

As a people we are inadequately prepared to support the teacher in the discharge of his essential functions in a free society.

That we are far from ready to provide the financial and material resources necessary to the fulfillment

[5] The Council of State Governments, *The Forty-eight State School Systems* (Chicago, 1949), p. 70.   [6] *Ibid.*, p. 209.

of our democratic faith and professions in the field of education need not be elaborated here. It is well known that the common rate of compensation is quite insufficient by itself to attract the more talented of our youth, to justify the long period of arduous training required, and to enable the teacher to live a rich and full life. It has often been remarked that we seem to be more interested in the condition of our school buildings than in the excellence of our teachers.

The most conspicuous failure of our people, however, is found in the realm of understanding. We lack a clear and comprehensive understanding of the nature of education in a free society. Boards of education seem to regard the teacher as something less than a first-class citizen or a complete person. They are inclined to frown upon teachers accepting fees for speeches, living in apartments if unmarried, failing to attend church, playing pool or billiards, going to public dances, or joining a teachers' union. They are very much opposed to teachers smoking in public, playing cards just for fun, teaching controversial issues, making a political speech, or running for political office. Also they are decidedly of the opinion that a woman should not teach after marriage.[7] That the teacher should be expected to live by higher moral standards than the ordinary citizen is readily granted. The fact that an individual is able to keep out of jail scarcely qualifies him for the high calling of supervising the rearing of the young. Yet there is undoubtedly much in the treatment of the teacher that not only consigns him to an inferior status in the community, but also impairs his qualities as a guardian of the tradition of human freedom. It would seem, moreover, that boards of education sometimes think that he should be compelled to live in an earlier generation, if not in the agrarian age itself.

The teacher is the natural prey of busybodies and pressure groups, partly perhaps because of his weakness. Without shame they often act as if the school belonged to them and

[7] See Lloyd Allen Cook and Elaine Forsyth Cook, *A Sociological Approach to Education* (New York, 1950), p. 447. Also Howard K. Beale, *Are American Teachers Free?* (New York, 1936).

the teachers were their liveried servants. They strive to throw out textbooks, to determine methods of instruction, to force their special interests into the curriculum, and to secure the discharge of qualified teachers of independent mind. Individuals and organizations professing the highest purposes seek to influence through political pressures and propaganda campaigns the program and personnel of the school. Sometimes bigots and ignoramuses gather people of like qualities around themselves and launch wholly vicious and irresponsible attacks on members of the profession in the name of the preservation of American liberties. That such assaults upon the teacher rarely arouse the wrath of the general body of citizens is evidence of political and intellectual immaturity in the realm of the conduct of public education.

There is of course a problem here. It is not suggested that a "law be passed" to protect the school. The cure would certainly be worse than the disease. Moreover, the informed interest of citizens in the schools in both their individual and their organized capacities is to be desired and encouraged. Such interest is indispensable in order to keep education in touch with changing conditions of life. And toleration of the "lunatic fringe" is doubtless a part of the price which men must pay for a free society. Yet much of present practice reflects a lack of understanding on the part of both teachers and citizens of the nature and function of education in our democracy.

4

The training of the teacher must be greatly broadened and deepened.
The central theme of this volume is that education always expresses some conception of civilization and that, regardless of the efficiency of its procedures, it can rise no higher than the conception of civilization which determines its substance and purpose. Since the teacher must ever be the living embodiment of this conception, it follows that

the education of a society can rise no higher than the qualifications, physical, intellectual, aesthetic, and moral, of its teachers. The conception of civilization developed in these pages obviously requires profound changes in the program of professional preparation.

First of all we must abandon or enrich much that is in our heritage. We must abandon completely the idea that teaching at any level is a simple process whose elements can be mastered in a few months or even several years by bright boys and girls in the period of late adolescence. We must abandon completely the tradition derived from our simple agrarian past that teaching is a matter of keeping order and transmitting verbal skills to embellish the genuine education acquired in the home and on the farm. We must abandon also the tradition derived from the class societies of the Old World that teaching in the common school involves merely giving to the offspring of the "hewers of wood and drawers of water" the narrow training required by that humble station in the social order to which they are called by the laws of God and man. We must abandon too the idea derived from the early period of industrialization that teaching has as its main object the preparation of ambitious youth to "get ahead" of their fellows in the race for preferred positions in the economic and social order. We must abandon likewise the assumption that teaching is essentially a process of passing on to the young various bodies of knowledge and that the level of teaching bears a direct relation to the abstruseness of the knowledge involved. We must abandon finally the idea derived from business management that the teacher is merely a semi-skilled worker in the assembly line who is expected to follow without question the orders of his immediate superior in a mass-production enterprise.

We must see teaching as the tremendous and difficult task that it is. We must see that it involves nothing less than the guiding of the individual to full maturity and freedom, of inducting him into the most complex and dynamic society of history, of preparing him to assume the heavy duties of managing that society and of transmitting its heritage of liberty unimpaired and even enhanced to his children. The assumption of the post of teaching at any level of the school system is indeed a sobering and challenging responsibility, and hardly to be assigned to the ill-prepared or the ill-disposed. Who can say that the task is easier in the kindergarten than in the university, in the guiding of the total personality of the child than in the teaching of the higher mathematics? About this we need not quarrel. We know that either requires not only professional skill and knowledge of the first order, but also charity, understanding, and wisdom.

Since the days of Samuel R. Hall and James G. Carter, who toward the close of the first quarter of the nineteenth century founded the first institutions to prepare young people for "school keeping," the need for the professional training of the teacher has been increasingly recognized in America. With the unparalleled expansion of the common school during subsequent generations, and particularly since the opening of the present century, the program for the training of teachers has been greatly extended. Today the need for such a program is generally accepted. Yet the actual practice lags far behind the evolution of American civilization and the conception of education. The professional training of the teacher continues to bear the stamp of its humble origins in the agrarian age. It is severely limited in both scope and content. In terms of depth and breadth of preparation teaching remains today a skilled or at best a semi-professional occupation. The emphasis is still on the mechanics of education, on methods of teaching, on "school keeping," on mastery of narrow subject matter, on financial and material operations. All of these things are of course necessary, but they are scarcely sufficient to equip even the most gifted to discharge the obligations of rearing the young in the atomic age. The time has come for us to consign to the wastebasket of history the idea that teaching requires less severe selection and training than the practice of medicine, law, engineering, or theology. Indeed, from the standpoint of the values and responsibilities involved teaching is probably the most difficult and important of all the professions.

In addition to the mastery of techniques and specialized subject matter, every teacher should be expected to acquire a basic understanding of the nature of the child and of man. This would of course mean knowledge of the biological constitution of the species, of the role of hereditary forces, of the laws of growth, learning, and maturation, of the development of character and personality, of the whole process of the induction of the young into the life of the group. It would mean also the acquisition of those insights and perspectives which can come only from some acquaintance with man in the natural order, in history, and in diverse cultures. The value of knowledge of psychology has of course long been recognized, and with the revolutionary advances in the science during the past two generations it has thoroughly established itself in the program. However, even today the emphasis is placed too largely on the relation of the individual to the learning of "subject matter." The educational psychology of the future must be increasingly social in character. It must devote far more attention than heretofore to the relation of the individual to the group and the entire field of human relations. The complexity and dynamism of industrial society, as well as the moral commitments of democracy, make this shift in emphasis clearly necessary.

At this point we come to the central and crucial deficiency in our program of teacher training—a deficiency which is derived from the limitations of our traditional conception of education. According to that conception education should and can be conducted in conformity with the universal laws of the organism and its own nature. Adequate understanding of the process can therefore be gained through the study of the child and the school. The thesis of the present volume, on the other hand, is that the whole enterprise of education is a function of a particular society at a particular time and place and must express some conception of life and civilization supported by the social group involved. This view vastly complicates the task of the teacher in a free society and, if consistently applied, would call for nothing less than a revolution in the program of professional training.

If the education of the young involves in some measure not only the fortunes of individuals, but also the future of our society and civilization, of our democratic institutions and free way of life, as it clearly does, then the selection and preparation of teachers should be recognized by all as a major concern of the Republic, certainly as important as the production of material things or even the maintenance of the national defense. Indeed, if conceived in appropriate terms and with adequate vision, it is the most basic and decisive factor in survival and progress. Johann Valentin Andreae, seventeenth century humanist, long ago gave voice to an ideal which free society should always cherish. "Their instructors," he said of teachers in his mythical community of Christianopolis, "are not men from the dregs of human society nor such as are useless for other occupations, but the choice of all the citizens, persons whose standing in the republic is known and who very often have access to the highest positions in the state."[8] In these words Andreae was merely saying that our children, all of our children, constitute our most precious resource.

For a teacher to be ignorant of the history of his people, of their triumphs and failures, of their basic ways and institutions, of their points of weakness and strength, of their moral commitments and ideals, of the great patterns of their civilization, of the dangers which threaten them, and of the opportunities which confront them is to invite catastrophe in the present age. Yet it must be conceded that our program of teacher training today must plead guilty in considerable measure to this indictment. The fact is that few American teachers are able to outline except in most superficial terms the basic features of our civilization or our way of life. Fewer still have reasoned and informed convictions regarding the foundations of free society and the forces at home and abroad which place in jeopardy our entire heritage of human liberty. And yet fewer have more than a most superficial knowledge of the great ethical, aesthetic, philosophical, and religious

[8] Johann Valentin Andreae, *Christianopolis*, edited by Julius Goebel (New York, 1916), p. 207.

traditions of Western man on which our entire civilization rests. The explanation of this situation undoubtedly must be attributed largely to deficiencies in their training. They are simply not expected to be interested in or to probe deeply into such questions.

Whatever may be said about other forms of professional preparation a teacher-training institution should make central the study of our American civilization in both its historical and its world setting, from its origins in antiquity to its relations with all nations and peoples. Whether the individual is to practice his calling in the kindergarten or the university, in the teaching of literature or science, he should know both the society and the culture which the school is supposed to serve. To aspire to less than this in the contemporary world is certain to provide an education of inferior quality and possibly to court catastrophe. Clearly, if teachers are to assist effectively in the rearing of a generation of free men, they must themselves have the knowledge and the loyalties necessary to set and keep men free. This of course does not mean that they should be required to transmit to the young an official body of doctrine or a set of fixed allegiances beyond the reach of informed criticism. The adoption of such a policy would be disastrous and would mark the end of liberty in America. The spirit of freedom cannot be evoked on command, even by the highest authority. On the contrary, it is a tender plant that can be nurtured in the young only by those who practice, understand, and love it.

The central purpose of our program of training should be the development of a teacher who would adopt as his own the pledge framed and signed by the teachers of Norway when on April 9, 1942, they defied their German conquerors. Under the threat of torture and death they openly repudiated the Nazi conception of life and affirmed their own moral commitments in words that will live and enrich the heritage of our profession as long as the love of freedom and justice endures on the earth. With unsurpassed heroism and understanding they thus defined the obligations of the teacher to his children and his people:

... The teacher's duty is not only to give the children knowledge. He must also teach the children to have faith in, and to earnestly desire that which is true and right. Therefore he cannot, without betraying his calling, teach anything against his conscience. He who does so sins both against the pupils he is supposed to lead and against himself. This, I promise you, I shall not do. I will not call upon you to do anything which I regard as wrong. Nor will I teach you anything which I regard as not conforming with the truth. I will, as I have done heretofore, let my conscience be my guide, and I am confident that I shall then be in step with the great majority of the people who have entrusted to me the duties of an educator.[9]

These Norwegian teachers refused to evade personal responsibility by bowing to the will of brute power. In simple language they proclaimed their loyalty to both a great conception of education and a great conception of civilization. We in America, without being called upon to face corresponding hazards, can do no better during these uncertain times than follow their example. Our teachers must be prepared to teach the children of America, by example as well as precept, that which is true and right. But we can do this with confidence and strength only as we mature a great and noble conception of our civilization and of the dignity of man. In so doing we, like our Norwegian colleagues, can be sure that we then will be fulfilling the wishes of the vast majority of our people. We shall know too that we shall be marching in the great tradition of human liberation—a tradition which our fathers in their finest hours have helped to build and guard.

5

The life of the teacher must be greatly enriched.

First of all the teacher must be relieved from excessive demands on his time and energies. He must be assured those working conditions which

[9] Norwegian Teachers' Pledge to Their Pupils of April 9, 1942. "Norway's Teachers Stand Firm," published by The Royal Norwegian Government's Press Representatives, 2720 34th St. N. W., Washington, D. C.

are essential to the successful discharge of his heavy responsibilities. This means the reduction of class size and teaching load to the point that makes it possible for him to know his pupils individually, to become acquainted with their parents and home surroundings, and to participate effectively in the formulation of school policy and the development of the curriculum. It means also the complete abandonment of the tradition that the teacher is merely a more or less high-grade servant who may be called upon at will by members of the board of education or private persons of power and influence in the community to perform manifold duties ranging from the teaching of Sunday school to the administration of an essay contest on the virtues of advertising. Only when an individual feels that he is doing his job well can he experience that sense of personal dignity and satisfaction in his calling which is the highest reward of socially useful and creative labor. It is only then, too, that the community is likely to appreciate fully the work of the teacher.

In the second place, the teacher must be free to participate as a mature person in the life of the community—local, state, and national. Indeed, such participation should be encouraged and rewarded. This calls for the abandonment of the tradition that the teacher should be something less than a whole human being, that he should lead a cloistered existence, that he should always remain as immature as the boys and girls who wielded the "hickory stick" and taught "readin', 'ritin', and 'rithmetic" in the one-room district school of hallowed memory. Teachers today, whether men or women, should be expected to engage in courtship, to marry, and to have children of their own. They should be expected to join and aspire to leadership in organizations devoted to the promotion of the general welfare, the advancement of the arts and sciences of life, or the simple enjoyment of good fellowship. They should be expected to pursue avocational interests of the greatest variety, from hiking to music and from stamp collecting to horticulture. Through appropriate conditions of work and adequate remuneration they should be assured leisure and funds necessary for travel, purchase of books, attendance at the theater, and general cultivation of personal interests. Perhaps even more than other citizens they should set an example to the young by taking an active part in civic affairs and exercising responsibly all the rights of citizenship. They should join political parties, make political speeches, and run for public office. There is of course no suggestion here that every teacher should do all of these things. Like others of his generation he should be allowed freedom of choice. The point to be emphasized is merely that by living a full and rich life he will be a better teacher. No one can truly understand our American community by reading books and following the role of a spectator.

In the third place, teachers should be as free to form their own organizations as any other group of citizens. This right is implied in the foregoing paragraph. But the issue is so important that it merits special consideration. It is of course well known that teachers today have many organizations. They are organized at all levels and in all specialties, and they have several organizations which aspire to embrace and represent the profession as a whole. Yet the fact remains that as yet they are not effectively organized to present their case as a whole to the American community.

The object of an adequate organization, aside from the improvement of the processes and purposes of education, should be threefold. It should strive to remove the many disabilities and frustrations under which the teacher labors and to which attention has already been directed. In a world marked by organized pressures, no group is likely to be heard or even respected if it lacks the resources which come from association. Also the organization should battle for the common school, for the welfare of the younger generation, and for a conception of education appropriate to the present age. Being closer to these interests than any other group of citizens, teachers naturally have a special obligation here to the whole community. Finally, through their organization they should endeavor to express with power their special point of view with respect to all the great issues confronting the American people. In their varied struggles teachers will inevitably work with other groups which share their values and purposes. Whether they should affiliate organically with any one element in the population, such as organized labor, is a highly complicated question whose merits will not be discussed in these pages. The point to be emphasized here is that teachers need a powerful organization and that they will find themselves closely associated with those groups which are devoted to the cause of public education and democracy.

6

The American people must achieve a more comprehensive and profound understanding of the nature of education in a free society.
Throughout our history as a nation we have had great faith in the school and have assumed that in some way it is a dependable guardian of democracy. Yet, with the exception of small minorities in the population, we have never been fully aware of the fact that a free society requires a very special kind of education. Since civil and political liberty is one of the basic values of our civilization and since it is under great threat in the world today, these concluding paragraphs will be devoted to a consideration of certain aspects of this issue.

In a democracy the people rule themselves, either directly or indirectly. In a democracy power rests ultimately in the hands of the citizens. Under appropriate constitutional guarantees and provisions they control the state and may alter it in accordance with their wishes. In a democracy political liberty and the process of revolution itself are institutionalized. It is assumed that the most fundamental changes in the social order can be achieved peacefully through education and enlightenment. In such a society, therefore, the exercise of control over the schools by the state would appear to constitute something of a contradiction or at least a hazard. Potentially there is always the danger that the political authority may seek to convert the entire educational process into an instrument dedicated to the rearing of a generation of subjects or slaves. In the present industrial age, with the trend on the one side toward the concentration of power in the hands of government and the trend on the other toward the expansion of the institutions of organized education, the threat to the perdurance of a society of free men is evident. The totalitarian pattern for the molding of the mind might make its way unobtrusively in the most democratic state. The American Federation of Labor, peerless champion of public education and ardent defender of free institutions, by convention action in 1950 formulated in these words the principle which should guide us: "Enlightened citizens of free nations should, through their thinking, control their government; but a democratic government should never attempt, through legislation, to control the thinking of its citizens." The traditional fear on the part of the American people of federal control of education is not without significance here. The same may be said of their invention of the independent board of education.

The resolution of this contradiction or difficulty, however, requires much more than institutional safeguards. It requires the development of powerful supporting traditions. And this requires the acquisition by the people of a clear conception of the nature of democratic education. According to the position developed throughout the present volume. such an education is not necessarily one which the people at a given time may want, even though they do constitute the final authority. The current epoch has amply demonstrated the truth of the proposition that in a moment of crisis or passion they may approve unwittingly measures which will destroy their liberties and reduce them to bondage. The old adage that "the voice of the people is the voice of God" is true only with reservations. Unsustained by reasoned loyalties and uninformed by relevant knowledge, the people may respond to the violent shouts of the demagogue and open the gates to despotism. A truly democratic education is one that is designed to guard and strengthen the free way of life through the generations. We in America lack a clear grasp of the nature of the educational problem in this relationship.

If education is to serve the ends of democracy during the troubled years ahead, the American people will have to achieve the necessary understanding. First of all, democratic education is committed to the basic values and processes of democracy, to the conception of human equality, dignity, and worth, to all the civil and political liberties. It must therefore be designed to bring the individual to full maturity as a free person, to foster enlightenment and release creative energies and talents. It must be earnestly committed to the transmission, cultivation, and enrichment of the great tradition of intellectual inquiry and artistic expression. A democratic education must be sensitive and responsive to the changing foundations, the deep-flowing currents, and the emerging conditions and potentialities of industrial society in both its domestic and world relations. At the same time it must be removed in some measure from the passions and narrowly partisan struggles of the moment. Amid the present confusion of tongues and conflict of ideologies the school should be a stabilizing force, a place of calm and serenity, a center for the nurture of the intellectual virtues. It should be a place where the honest questions of the young may be raised with the assurance that they will receive honest consideration. We must always remember that the school is a temple erected to the future, a shrine dedicated to the *long* future of our society and mankind.

An education so conceived is not to be attained by responding to every wind that blows, nor by remaking itself after every election. On the contrary, while it can never be autonomous, it should enjoy a large measure of independence from the pressures of private persons, minorities, classes, organizations, parties, churches, and even government officials. The establishment of this condition of freedom and independence for the school should be a major responsibility of the state in a democratic society. This means that members of boards of education must not only protect the school from external demands but also voluntarily restrain themselves in the exercise of power. The desired condition, moreover, cannot be achieved by the passing of laws, but only by the development of an appropriate tradition shared alike by both citizen and teacher.

The citizen, on his side, must be willing to place his trust in the teacher. The current attacks on teachers and the furore over loyalty oaths are much to be regretted and scarcely augur well for the immediate future. Long ago William Godwin, at a time when Englishmen were fighting the battle of human liberty, made an observation that many of our citizens should ponder today. "Wherever men of uncommon energy and dignity of mind have existed," he wrote, "they have felt the degradation of binding their assertions with an oath."[10] Such men will always be much needed in the schools of a free society. Moreover, that the overwhelming majority of the members of the profession are loyal to their country and the cause of democracy cannot be doubted by any soberminded citizen. And that they may be trusted, within the limits of their knowledge and understanding, to pass fair judgment on all colleagues who would betray their people can hardly be questioned by anyone who knows the great body of American teachers. If persons born and reared in our society, formed by our institutions, nurtured in our ideals, and educated in our schools and colleges from childhood to manhood and womanhood cannot be trusted to guard and fulfill our heritage of liberty, then indeed has our democracy fallen on evil days. Certainly very few Americans believe in their hearts that such a condition has actually come to pass. The American Federation of Labor, also at its 1950 convention, thus set an example of confidence in the teacher which the community as a whole could wisely follow: "We must prevent not only any attempts to control educational content, but we must protect the freedom of the teacher. We recognize the right of government to require loyalty of all public employees, including teachers, but we would oppose singling out any one group as distinct from other public employees."

[10] Quoted in *The Manual of Liberty* (London, 1795), p. 182.

The teacher, on his side, must be sensitive to the great trust which the American community places in his keeping. He must be loyal to his country, to the children under his care, and to the values of democracy. This of course does not mean that he should not criticize our institutions and way of life. Indeed, if he is to be loyal to the finest traditions of his people, he must engage in criticism and teach his pupils to do likewise. Yet the point must be repeated here that the average American teacher is inadequately prepared for his task. His weakness is to be found, not in his loyalties, but in his knowledge and understanding. Unfortunately he shares with his fellow citizens generally ignorance of the time and the world in which he lives. He believes in democracy, but does not know precisely what it is. He believes in liberty, but he does not know the foundations and conditions of liberty in the industrial age. Obviously this weakness cannot be corrected by loyalty oaths or rules of conduct. It can only be corrected by a greatly expanded and enriched program of professional preparation. In the meantime the teacher should strive earnestly to know his social heritage and his local and national community in its world setting.

In conclusion a word should be said about the responsibility of the teacher in raising the level of popular understanding with respect to the nature of democratic education. Clearly the profession should take a position of vigorous leadership here. Working with parents, public-spirited citizens, and representatives of all organizations devoted to the cause of democracy, teachers should strive to assist the public in achieving a mature and informed vision of the entire enterprise of organized education. As an indispensable part of their task they should acquaint the younger generation with the development of the common school as a basic institution of our democracy. To give to the American people, young and old alike, a conception of education commensurate with the best in their traditions and their civilization should be regarded as a major obligation. Success in this venture will both ennoble their calling and justify the faith of our fathers in the power and the beneficence of the common school.

Index

INDEX

Absolute state, conceptions of, 268
Achaean League, 426
Adams, John, on intellectual interests, 385
Adams, Samuel, 66; on economic threat to democracy, 190
Adirondack Mountains, 116
Aesthetic interests, long-standing deficiency in, 384
Aesthetic tradition, education to reveal, 384; impact of industrialism on, 388
Agrarian civilization, and mercantile, 10; foundation of, being transformed, 127
Agrarian society, our early, 87
All-Union Communist Party, 16
America, developed in modern age, 46; populated by greatest migration in history, 58; land of unequal peoples, 67; settled by common people, 70; settled by poor, oppressed, and persecuted, 71; land of opportunity, 73; haven of refuge, 74; a fabulously rich land, 104; a beautiful land, 114; sheltered geographical position of, 118; power of, 417; responsiblity of, 417; keeping strong, 430
American Affiliation of Tall Clubs, 441
American Bar Association, on cost of legal service, 194
American community, education in, 433; role of, in education, 434; sweep of, 435
American democracy, 22; optimism of, 4; failures of, 45
American education, foreign travelers on, 23, 25, 34
American Federation of Labor, on government and citizens, 469; on oaths for teachers, 471
American Goat Society, 441
American people, diversity of, 59; composition of, 64, 68; progressive temper of, 133; contribution to rule of law of, 263
American Philosophical Society, essay contest of, 37; 440
American Revolution, 55
American Telephone and Telegraph Company, laboratories of, 132
American way of life, 81, 149; essence of, 267
Amos, 223
Anburey, Thomas, on diversity of American people, 59
Andreae, Johann Valentin, 463
Animal Farm, 330
Animal life in United States, 108
Appalachian highlands, 116

Aristocratic visitors to America, 84
Aristotle, on automatic tools, 146
Arnold, General H. H., on new weapons, 177
Art, need for functional, 394; to be conceived in universal terms, 395
Artistic tradition, development of, 393; broad and catholic, 394
Arts, need for comprehensive program of education in, to make use of our resources, 389; of individual expression and communication, 395; of home and community, 396; of personal enjoyment and cultivation, 396; of social relations, 397
Athens, 405
Atlantic Charter, 403; consequences of forsaking, 334
Atomic age, coming of, 175
Atomic energy, release of, 175
Auschwitz, 5, 228
Autocracies and despotisms of the Old World, 12
Automatic, factory, 144; machine, 144; controls, trust in, 169
Automobile Old Timers, 441
Axis powers, 11
Azalea, 116

Baily, Francis, on destruction of trees, 120
Bakunin, Michael, philosophy of "pan-destruction" of, 275
Balfour, on British Constitution, 269
Barker, Ernest, on rule of law, 259
Basra, 405
"Battle of the loins," 405
Bauxite, 110
Beard, Charles A., 39, 71; on constitutionalism, 261; on framers of Constitution, 263; on flexibility of Federal Constitution, 268; on the future, 295
Beard, Mary R., 71; on role of women in history, 342
Belgian Congo, 113
Belgium, 13
Beloff, Max, on breakdown of rule of law in Europe, 275
Benton, Thomas, 392
Berkshires, 116
Bernal, J. D., on making new substances, 174
Bible, translation of, 223
Bidwell, Percy Wells, on trade in rural New England in 1800, 94; on division of labor, 96; on education, 102
Bidwell, Percy Wells and Falconer, John I., on costs of transportation in 1800, 96
Bill of Rights, 51; second article of, 79; first article of, 83; 233
Birth rate, differential, 406
Black Mountains, 116
Blake, William, on liberating influence of America, 119
"Blizzard Men of 1888," 438
Blue Ridge Mountains, 116
Bolshevik, on roads to future, 215
Bolshevik Revolution, 43, 421
Bolsheviks, 14
Bolshevism, 15
Boylston, Dr. Zabdiel, 136
Bradbury, John, on "good neighborship" in early America, 91
Bread, ancient struggle for, 141
British Royal Commission, on decline of intelligence quotient, 406
Brogan, D. W., on American education, 34; 68
Bronk, Detlev W., on relation between physical and social science, 187
Bryce, James, on classes in America, 55
Buchanan Committee, on lobbying, 444
Buchenwald, 5, 228
Bulgaria, 13
Bullitt, William C., on prospects of mankind before First World War, 13
Burke, Edmund, on law and arbitrary power, 265; on democracy, 278; on despotism as simplest form of government, 345

INDEX

Burns, Robert, on meaning of equality, 333
Bury, J. B., on freedom of thought, 13; 240
Bushnell, Horace, on "age of homespun," 89; on "transition from mother and daughter power," 137

Cadiz, 405
Caesar, 270
Cain and Abel, 329
Calaveras grove, 115
California, 115
Canossa, 262
Capital offenses in Britain in 1800, 74
Capitalism in America, distinctive feature of, 135
Carter, James G., 461
Carthage, 6
Cascade Mountains, 117
Casson, Stanley, 10; on uneven advance of civilization, 129; on critical nature of present age, 402; on education of the young, 403
Cathedral of Seville, 116
Catskill Mountains, 116
"Causes" of the success of our democracy, 7
Cave Men of America, 441
Central purpose of economic and political institutions, 383
Chastellux, Marquis de, on cooperation in early America, 91; on economic threat to democracy, 190; on consequences of inequality, 334
Chevalier, Michael, on adaptability of ordinary American, 134
Child, nature of, 307; understanding of nature of, 462
Child labor laws, 155
Chinese saying, on "great teacher," 457
Choices, character of, 215; role of knowledge in, 215-216; role of values in, 217
Christian fathers, contribution to rule of law of, 262
Christianapolis, 463
Christians, early, 426

Church, role of, in education, 102; as educational agency, 301
Churchill, Winston, on power of America, 199
Cicero, on hypotheses, 254; on teaching, 457
Citizen, responsibilities of, in education, 471
Civil liberties, 271
Civilization, agrarian and mercantile, 10; great conception of our, 39; agrarian, foundations of, transformed, 127; uneven advance of, 129; rise and fall of, 400; biological foundations of, 405; psychological foundations of, 407; study of our, in teacher training, 463
Civilizational decay and death, study of, 404
Civilizations destroyed by sword, 408
Class composition of early immigrants, 71
Class structure, and English migration, 62; transformation of, 153
Classes, study of division of society into, 337
Cleveland, Grover, on government, 100
Climate, in America, favorable to release of human energy, 105; changeableness of, 106; range of, 106
Coal reserves, richness of, 112
Colored peoples, rise of, 230; discrimination against, 288
Colt revolver, inscriptions on, 79
Columbus, Christopher, 47, 50
Combe, George, on American education, 38
Commager, Henry Steele, on watershed of eighteen-nineties, 7
Common man, hope for better life for, 50
Common people, America settled by, 70, 71, 73; story of rise of, in America, 76; storm citadels of power, 77; conquer military power, 78; conquer economic power, 79; conquer political power, 80; win right to

knowledge, 81; win right to freedom of conscience, 82; achievements of, in America, 86
Common school, desirability of, for all children, 340
Communication, primitive character of, 94; and human mind, 156; and community, 157; use of new agencies of, 181; control of media of mass, 183-184; failure to make full use of agencies of, 200; debasement of agencies of, 201; media of, as educational agencies, 301-302; fabric of, 435
Communism, advance of, 19; spread of, 165; and Fascism, 276-277
Communist conception of revolutionary elite, 37
Communist imperialism, 165
Communist Manifesto, on "common ruin of contending parties," 334
Communist Parties, 16
Communist totalitarianism, 228
Compton, Karl T., on science and productivity, 148
Computing machines, high-speed electronic, 145
Condorcet, Marquis de, 52
Confucius, 203
Congressional investigations, 254
Conservation of natural resources, education for, 376
Constituent Assembly, dispersal of, 14
Constitutional Convention of 1787, 263
Constitutionalism, as highest achievement in rule of law, 261; justification of faith in, 268
Consumer, education of, 375
Continental shelf, resources of, 122
Contributions of various peoples to American civilization, 65, 66
Cook, Robert C., on uncontrolled fertility, 406
Cooperative action, in rural neighborhood, 91
Cooperative attitudes and practices, development of, 380
Cooperative behavior, tendency toward, 192

Cooperative patterns of social behavior, 381
Copper deposits, 110
Cordilleras, 117
Corey, Lewis, on development of service occupations, 152
Coronado, 115
Corporation, development of, 149
Cosmic ray, 178
Counterrevolutions, 4
Cousins, Norman, on obsolescence of modern man, 403
Coxe, Tench, on rural household, 89
Creative talents, development of, 398
Cresswell, Nicholas, on social rank of Washington, 75
Crèvecoeur, 68; on migration to America, 77; on spiritual transformation of immigrant, 77; on American farmer, 89; 93; on scale of distance, 119; on high wages of American labor, 134
Criminals sent to colonies, 71
Critical nature of present age, need to stress, 400
Criticism, value of, 352
Cultural change, nature of, 137
Cultural element, disruptive effect of new, 137
Cultural exchange, 163; importance of, 391
Culture, role of, in developing excellence, 318

Dachau, 5, 228
D'Alembert, 52; on law and political liberty, 270
Dark age, possible new, 209; or golden, not fated, 214
Dark Ages, 232
Davis, John, on "*American* genius," 386
Death rate, reduction of, 406
Declaration of Human Rights, 429
Declaration of Independence, 44; signers of, 66; 195, 233, 429
Declaration of world interdependence, 163

INDEX 479

Decrees on ideology of Central Committee of All Union Communist Party, 183
Demagogue, dangers from, 468
Democracy, "causes" of success of our, 7; economic foundations of, 190; economic threat to, 190; threat to, in concentration of economic power, 191; 218; as American social faith, 278; Oscar Wilde, on, 279; as bourgeois fraud, 279; values of American, 279; Woodrow Wilson, on, 279; origins of American, 280; and equality, 281; and worth of individual, 281; and rule of law, 282; and liberty, 282; and morality, 283; and individual opportunity, 284; challenged in America, 285; challenged by concentrated economic and military power, 285; threatened by economic instability, 286; challenged by complexity of society, 286; challenged by totalitarianism, 287; threatened by war and fear of war, 287; imperiled by its failures, 288; need for rebirth of American, 290; role of people in, 468
Democratic heritage, our most precious possession, 289
Democrats, German, Hungarian, and Italian, 72
Democritus, 208
Depression, 19
Der Fuehrer, 270, 418
Despotism, on the march, 3; emergence of, 211
Destruction of animal life, 120
Dewey, John, 39; on aim of education, 318
Dewhurst, J. Frederic, on increase in productivity of labor, 147
"Diamond Jubilee Issue" of American Chemical Society, 132
Diaz, Bartholomeu, 50
Dickens, Charles, on American "bores," 386
Dictatorship, of Stalin, 15; use of new agencies of communication by, 182

Diderot, Denis, 52; on aim of encyclopedia, 238
Diocles, 260
Disease, conquest of, 179
Disciplines, neglect of moral, 186
Discrimination, abolition of educational, 340
Disraeli, Benjamin, on democracy, 279
Dissenters, religious and political, 72
Distance, at time of Constitutional Convention, 157; impact of railway and airplane on, 158; study of conquest of, 415
Dostoevsky, Fyodor, on collapse of Europe, 276
Duncan, David Douglas, on war, 416
"Dust-bowl," 404
Dwight, Timothy, on qualities of emigrants, 75; on opposition to turnpike, 135

East, exploitation of, by West, 11
Economic, depression, 3; stability, 18, 20; forces, ties of, 159; interests, conflicts of, 161; council, 168; stability, study of difficulties and hazards in achieving, 369-370; education, comprehensive program of, 374
Economy, scale of operations, enlargement of, 149; productivity of, 174; study of transformation of our, 367; study of potentialities of our, 368
Educability, of man, 306; of child, 306; of adult, 306
Education, 21; faith in, 22; power of, 22; beneficence of, 22; William Graham Sumner, on, 23; foreign travelers on, 23, 25, 34; 24; uncritical nature of faith in, 24; in totalitarian states, 26; H. G. Wells, on, 27, 296; and catastrophe, 28; for mechanical efficiency, 30; and the interests of children, 31; and the "great books," 32; and conceptions of civilization, 33; great, source of, 36; in rural household and neighborhood of early America, 101; role of church in, 102; for general eco-

nomic understanding, 373; need for great, 295; conscious of worth and power of, 296; power of totalitarian, 296; and values of democracy, 296; challenge of totalitarian, 297; weakness of our, 297; resources for building great, 298; material resources for, 299; institutional resources for, 299; resources of professional knowledge for, 305; moral and spiritual resources for, 308; as process of guidance and learning, 315; mass production methods in, 316; for physical excellence, 320; for intellectual excellence, 321; for moral excellence, 323; for aesthetic excellence, 325; to reveal deficiencies in our heritage of equality, 335; and political liberty, 344; and meaning of political liberty, 347; and dangers threatening political liberty, 353; and cultivation of sense of worth of political liberty, 358; and cultivation of spirit and practice of political liberty, 363; and economic security and plenty, 366; and occupational guidance and training, 370; for conservation of natural resources, 375; to guard long-time economic interests, 376; and civilization of beauty and grandeur, 383; and an enduring civilization, 399; of the young, Casson on, 403; in American community, role and sweep of, 433, 434, 435; geared to present age, 452; inadequate understanding of nature of, 458; limitations of traditional conception of, 462; in free society, nature of, 468; moral commitments of democratic, 470; freedom in, 470; citizen's responsibility to, 471
Educational agencies, old and new, 300
"Educational ladder," 23
Educational program, formulation of, 36
Educational reform, proposals for, 29
Educational, Scientific, and Cultural Organization of the United Nations, 392
Educational system, origin of American, 433
Einstein, Albert, celebrated equation of, 208; on knowledge and value, 257
Eisenhower, Dwight D., on subordination of military to civil authority, 357
Election day as "holy day," 351
Election during Second World War, 352
Emancipation Proclamation, 68
Emerson, Ralph Waldo, on feudalism in America, 54; 63
Encyclopedia, The, 52
End of an era, 7
Energy resources, richness of, 111
Engels, Friedrich, 275
England, politically most advanced, 53
English Bill of Rights, 44
English Cavaliers, 72
English Puritan migration, 71
English Puritans, 72
English rationalism, 133
English revolution, 232
English-speaking peoples, contribution to rule of law of, 262
Enlightenment, Age of, 52, 55, 239
Epoch in our history closed, first, 401
Equality, of races, Soviets on, 58; principle of, 83; aggressive spirit of, 84; in America, 85; principle of, 222; education and, 327; principle of, endangered, 328; need to affirm principle of, 328; not in biological constitution of man, 329; struggle for, in history, 330; education to clarify meaning and worth of, 330; misunderstanding of principle of, 330; avoidance of pitfalls of utopianism concerning, 331; as affirmation of central value in Hebraic-Christian ethic, 332; meaning of, 333; story of struggle to establish principle of, 335; study of totalitarian threat to, 336; imperiled by social changes, 336; study of viola-

tions of principle of, 337; sex and principle of, 338; organization of school according to principle of, 339-340
Erie, Lake, 115
Ernst, Morris L., champion of civil liberties, 184
Erz Mountains, 113
Europe, recent elections in, 12
European system, collapse of, 420
Everglades, 115
Expatriates, colonies of, 388
Expectation of life, increase of, 179
Exploitation, of our mineral resources, 121; of natural riches, 120

Falangism, 15
Family, role of, in early America, 88; role of, in education, 102; as educational agency, 300
Farmer, "jack of all trades," 89; transformation of independent, 149
Fascism, 12, 14, 15, 227; attack of, on art and scholarship, 241; and Communism, 277; and Communism, tactics of, 358
Fascist conception of a master race, 37
Fatalism, humanistic rejection of doctrine of, 239
Federal Constitution, 44, 51; on citizenship, 67; 233; as government by law, 264; on social revolution, 267; growth of America under, 269; and individual rights and liberties, 270
Federated American Engineering Societies, 9
Fénelon, on war, 419
Filipinos, treatment of, 429
First Five-Year Plan, 27, 424
First World War, 4, 13, 14, 209
Florida, 114
Forbes, R. J., on history of technology and engineering, 142
Forced labor, 6
Ford Foundation, program of, 187
Foreign trade, 163
Foreign travel, 163

Foreign travelers, on American education, 23, 25, 34
Forests, in United States, 108; extent of, 116-117
Four Freedoms, 403
France, 13, 50
France, Anatole, on justice of laws, 273
Frankl, Paul T., on "Industrial Arts" and "Fine Arts," 394
Franklin, Benjamin, 37; on migration to America, 73; on the "way to wealth," 99; 233; on value of birth, 379
Fraternity and sorority system, 343
Free institutions, danger of prejudice to, 196
French aristocrats, 72
French Encyclopedists, 237
French Enlightenment, 133
French Huguenots, 72
French Revolution, 52, 53, 232
Fulbright Act, 392, 429
Fundamental science, need for development of, 377
Future, the, diverse roads to, 214; study of, 409

Gama, Vasco da, 50
Gandhi, Mahatma, 221
Garden of Eden, 161
Gautama, 203
General welfare, devotion to, 381; need for loyalty to, 169
Genocide, 6
Geographical base of civilization, 104; 404
Geographical exploration, 49
Georgian princes, 72
German Nazis, 5
Germans, incursions of, 61
Germany, 11
Gettysburg Address, 44
Ginzburg, Benjamin, on nature of science, 246
Gladstone, on British Constitution, 262; on American Constitution, 262
Glories of Nineveh, Babylon, Angkor, and Chichen Itza, 399

482 INDEX

Godwin, William, on oaths, 471
Gold, 110
Golden age, possible, 212; not fated, 214
Good, holding fast that which is, 202
Good people, development of, supreme educational task, 324
Goodhue, Bertram, 392
"Gooks," 200
Government, limited role of, in early America, 100
Grand Canyon, 115
Grattan, Thomas Colley, on America as a "paradise of mediocrity," 387; on deficiencies of American people, 390
"Great American Desert," 115, 117
Great Charter, 44
Great Emancipator, 279
Great Mogul, 270
Great Russia, 15
Great Smokies, 116
Great tasks, 17
Greece, 13
Greeks, role of, in developing humanistic spirit, 232; achievements in law of, 260
Green Mountains, 116
Grund, Francis J., on education in America, 23, 34, 38; on origin of American people, 44; on genius of liberty of America, 66; on dignity of labor, 83; on love of country of Americans, 119; on status of teacher in 1837, 455
Guild of Former Pipe Organ Pumpers, 441
Gulf of Alaska, 118
Gulf of the St. Lawrence, 116

Hague Peace Conferences, 166
Hall, Samuel R., 461
Hall, Thomas Cuming, on aesthetic tradition, 384
Hamilton, Alexander, on economic foundation of personal integrity, 98
Hamilton, Walton H., on rise of constitutionalism, 263
Hamlet, 202

Hammurabi, 260
Handicrafts, colonial tradition in, 387
Hapsburg, 13
Harrington, James, on power, 79
Haugen, Ingvald, on Nazi conquest of Norway, 274
Hausleiter, Leo, on growth of capacity of machines, 172
Hebraic-Christian ethic, 218; major source of our values, 220; diverse and conflicting elements in, 221; source of, 221; moral foundations of democracy in, 222; moral foundations of peace in, 224; moral foundations of humane society in, 226; threatened by totalitarian movements, 227; repudiated by Fascism, 228; repudiated by Communism, 229; challenged by industrial civilization, 229; challenged by war, 229
Hebrews, exodus of, 61
Hecht, Selig, on release of atomic energy, 208
Hedges, Henry P., on self-sufficient rural household, 90
"Hell-bomb," 6
Helvetius, on despotism, 211
Henry IV, 262
Heritage, influence of, 43; of America, unique and glorious, 44; of the ancient world, rediscovery of, 48; of nations and peoples, our rich, 390–391
High Sierra Mountains, 115
Hiroshima, 6
Hitler, 19, 275, 276
Hohenzollern, 13
Holland, 50
Hollywood, products of, 159; 428
"Holy day," election day as, 351
Hook, Sidney, on use of term "democracy" by dictators, 280
Hours of work, reduction in, 147
House of Hapsburg, 197
Household, the, removal of economic functions from, 151
Howard, Ebenezer, 392

INDEX 483

Hu Shih, on Communism, 362
Hudson River, 116
Hugo, Victor, on twentieth century, 14
Human energy, 98
Human labor, role of, affected by technology, 144; and the tools of production, 149
Human muscle, role of, in past, 171
Human offspring, helplessness of, 313; potentialities of, 314
Human reproduction, control of, 179–180
Human resources, barriers to development of, 371
Humanistic spirit, 218; as liberating force, 232; conception of man in, 233; basic concern of, 234; faith in human powers in, 235; enemy of totalitarianism, 235; inspirer of creative life, 236; in grave peril today, 240; threatened by instability of institutions, 240; threatened by totalitarian ideologies and practices, 241; confronted with unprecedented opportunity, 242
Humanities, essence of, 237
Hydrogen bomb, 177–178

Ignorance, dangers of, 216
Ignorance and prejudice, heritage of, 213
Il Duce, 270
Immigrants, composition of early, 71; qualities of, 76
Income, division of national, 153
Indentured servants, 71
Indians, American, 20, 59
Individual, the, supreme worth of, 222; attention to, in education, 316
Individual excellence, as aim of education, 311; and democratic faith, 312; needed emphasis in industrial society on, 312; achievement of, long and arduous process, 313; and whole person, 319; an expression of a civilization, 326
Individualism, of the farmer in early America, 93; of enterpriser, rise of, 99
Individuality, as source of value, 317
Indivisibility of war and peace, 164
Industrial civilization, in its infancy, 127; need for understanding, complexities of, 169; new materials, energies, conditions, and perspectives of, 392
Industrial production in Second World War, 175
Industrial revolution in England, 143
Industrial society, complexity of, 166, 354; dynamism of, 166; sweep of, 166; instability of, 167
Infancy, importance of years of, 318
Inner unfolding, process of, 314
Insecurity, dangers in widespread economic, 367
Institute of scientists and scholars, national, 410
International Bureau of American Republics, 166
International Telegraph Union, 166
Inventions, opposition to, 135–136
Ireland, James G., on Civil War, 269
"Iron curtain," 164
Iron resources, 109
Irving, Washington, on teacher, 455
Isolation, persistence of mentality bred in age of, 196
Issues, need for study of great, 365
Italy, 11, 13; as cultural center, 48; 50

Jameson, J. Franklin, on economic democracy, 80
Jamestown, 58
Japan, 11, 13
Japanese military caste, 6
Jefferson, Thomas, father of American democracy, 22; 37; on "those who labor in the earth," 98; on government, 100; on economic threat to democracy, 190; 233; on laws and institutions, 267; on democracy, 278; on majority rule, 283; on the many and the few, 332; on qualifications for self-government, 345; on

ignorance, 346; on aesthetic interests, 385
Jesus, 203, 223; as "prince of peace," 224, 419
Jews, 20
Judgment, informed and independent, 181
Judicial review, institution of, 264

Kaempffert, Waldemar, on release of atomic energy, 208
Kalm, Peter, on separate homesteads, 88; on "carelessness of futurity," 120
Kennan, George F., on sense of security in America, 7
Knowledge, need for, 170
Korea, 18, 229
Kremlin, "men of the," 15

Lag, cultural, 185, 225; in physical education, 320
Land, arable, in United States, 107; impact of, on institutions, 118
Language, master of, 322
Lâo-tse, 203
Law, need for reign of, among organized groups, 193; reign of, necessary among nations, 197; source of obedience to, 265; violations of, 273
"Lawgivers" of antiquity, 260
Laws of transition, Marxian, 215
Lazarus, Emma, 74
Lead in the United States, 110
Leadership, our present role of, 200
League of Nations, 166, 197; failure of, 427
Lederer, Emil, on "objectivity" of scientists, 410
"Left," extreme, 12
Legacy from slavery and colonialism, 58
Leisure, ever-increasing, 213; utilization of, for refinement of life, 393
Leith, C. K., on mineral resources, 109
Lenin, on freedom as "bourgeois prejudice," 276
Levellers, the, 223

Liberty, political, and British people, 43; anthology on poetry of, 65; British contribution to conception of, 66; and tyranny, conflict between, 165; 168; and equality interdependent, 349–350; cultivation of spirit of, in young, 464
Lieber, Francis, 38; on scale of time, 119; on elections in 1835, 253
Limited government as foundation of political liberty, 101
Lincoln, Abraham, on the American Union, 45; second inaugural of, 226; on equality, 327; on "principles of Jefferson," 331; on liberty and equality, 334
Lippmann, Walter, on complexity of society, 286
Literacy, in Japan, 26; in Nazi Germany, 26
Local responsibility in education, 438
Locke, John, 51, 52
"Long rifle," 78
Lord Acton, on power, 78, 250
Love of country, fostering of, 411
Lucky Lady II, 163
Lusitania, The, 209
Luther, Martin, 235
Lycurgus, 260
Lyell, Sir Charles, on American education, 34; on equality in America, 85; on hardships of travel in 1846, 95; on "ambitious style" of members of Congress, 198

MacIver, R. M., on "firmament of law," 259
McCulloch, John, 81

Macaulay, on Habeas Corpus Act, 272
Machine, power-driven, 142
Magellan, Ferdinand, 162
Magnificat, 223, 329
Malinowski, Bronislaw, on political liberty, 19; on interests of children, 32; on possible dark age, 211
Mammoth Cave, 115
Management, development of profession of, 150

INDEX

Manhattan Project, 208
Mann, Horace, father of the common school, 22
Manning, William, on knowledge, 81–82; on nature of man, 264
Mansfield, Edward D., on American education, 38
Manu, 260
Mariculture, 122
Market, feebly developed in early America, 94; extension of, through communication, 148
Marx, Karl, on revolution by peaceful means, 45; as last of Hebrew prophets, 228; 275
Marxism, 14, ignorance of, 422
Marxism-Leninism-Stalinism, as "science of the sciences," 255
Mass production, as America's "secret weapon," 147; appearance of idea of, 148
Mathematics, role of, in industrial society, 323
Mayflower, The, 162
Meany, George, on feudalism in America, 55
Mechanical, invention, march of, 131; power, conquest of, 171; slaves, number of, 173
Medical science, advance of, 180
Melish, John, on independence of farmers, 97
Mencken, H. L., on democracy, 279; on schoolmaster, 455
Menes, 260
Mesabi Range, 110
Messianic complex, dangers of, 200
Michaux, François A., on costs of transportation in 1802, 95
Migration, to America, greatest in history, 58; composition of early, 59; composition of later, 60; diversity of, 62; impact on new civilization of, 60; westward 63
Military commander, dismissal of, by civil authority, 352
Military power, control of, 178
Military service, rejection of young men for, 320

Military threat to civilization, 408
Mind-forming, process of, 181
Minds, need for new age, 202
Mineral resources, richness of, 109; deficiencies in, metallic, 110, nonmetallic, 111
Minorities, liquidation of, 211; discrimination against, 289; role of dissenting, 349
Mittelberger, Gottlieb, on voyage to America in 1750, 72
Mobility, ceaseless, of American people, 437
Modern age, birth of spirit of, in America, 53
Mohammed, 203
Molotov, on Communism, 15
Molybdenum, 110
Monarchs, 12
Money, absorption in acquisition of, 149
Monolithic direction, reliance of dictatorship on, 169
Monopoly, tendency toward, 150
Montesquieu, on laws of education, 25; 52; on republican government, 266
Moral degeneration, 6
Moral education in the "great society," 324
Moral foundations of civilization, 407
Moral foundations of economy, study of, 378
More, Sir Thomas, 212
Morpurgo, J. E., on voice of Jefferson, 428
Morris, Richard B., on redemptioners, 71
Moses, 203, 260
Moulton, Harold G., on electronic science, 145; on economic potentials, 194
Mountain laurel, 116
Moving pictures, need for, in political education, 364
Mussolini, 275, 276
Myrdal, Gunnar, 68; on "American Creed," 218

Nagasaki, 6
Napoleon, 53
National resources, attitude toward, 379
National Resources Committee, on mechanical power in America, 173
National Socialism, 15
Nationalism, narrow, 411
Nations, as architects of better world, 411
Natural beauty, neglect of, 121; appreciation of, 390
Natural gas resources, 112
Natural riches, need for changing attitude toward, 123
Nazi dictatorship, 6
Nazi Germany, 241
Nazis, 228
Neglect of natural beauty, 121
Negro, 20, 68
Negro slaves, 71
Neighborhood as educational agency, 301
New age in our history, 9
New civilization rising in America, 128
New Economic Policy, 423
New England, "flowering of," 388
"New Soviet man," 183
Niagara Falls, 115
Nietzsche, Friedrich, on "will to power," 276
Nineteenth century, hopes of, 13
Nineteen Eighty-Four, 17, 182
Nordic superiority, 57
Norway, national song of, 412; pledge of teachers of, 464
Number, mastery of, 322

Oak Ridge, 209
Oaths, loyalty, 471
Occupational designations, number of, 153
Occupational division in early America, lack of, 97
Occupational guidance and training, comprehensive program of, 371–372
Occupations, changes in, 130; development of service, 152; number and variety of, 371
Odegaard, Charles E., on "conquest of fear," 237
Oil-bearing shales, in United States, 112
Old Stone Age, 142
Opposition, to Erie Canal, 135; to railroads, 135; to inoculation and anesthetics, 136
Optimism of American democracy, 4
Organizations, voluntary, 160; as educational agencies, 303; influence of voluntary, 355; voluntary and quasi-voluntary, 439; number of, 440; diversity of, 441; resources of, 441; struggles among, 443; impact of, on public affairs, 443; all defending American way of life, 444; violation of principles of democracy by, 445; essential to democracy, 445; indictment of, 445; destruction of, in totalitarian states, 446; subject to rule of law, 447; preparation of young to participate in, 447; advocacy of conflicting educational conceptions by, 448; increase of interest in education by, 448; demands made on school by, 449
Orientals, disabilities of, 20
Orwell, George, 17, 182, 330

Paine, Thomas, on government, 100; 233; on consequences of "unequal rights," 333
Pasteur, on scientific method, 248
Peace, just and durable, 18; urgency of struggle for, 231; knowledge of efforts to establish, 426
Pearl Harbor, 8, 58
"Pennsylvania rifle," 78
Peoples and cultures, understanding of, 428
Perfectibility of man and society, 238
Pericles, age of, 236
Permanent Court of Arbitration, 166
Pessimism, humanistic rejection of philosophies of, 239
Petroleum reserves, richness of, 112

INDEX

Phosphates reserves of, largest on record, in America, 111
Pico della Mirandola, on "dignity of man," 234
Planning, general, 168
Plant life in United States, 108
Pleistocene epoch, 404
Pocono Mountains, 116
Point Four Program, 188, 392
Policy of national isolation, 7
Political liberty, 19, 20, 101; endangered today, 344; personal and moral foundations of, 346; social foundations of, 347; a revolutionary conception, 347–348; elements in practice of, 348; laws and life conditions essential to, 348; and tolerated differences, 349; understanding heritage of, 350; burden placed on individual by, 351; danger to, in condition of insecurity, 356; and war, 356; and expansion of government, 357; and corruption in government, 358; eternal vigilance as price of, 364
Polybius, on democracy, 278
Pope, on "study of mankind," 233
"Popular despotisms," 12
Portugal, 50
Post, Wiley, 162
Potash, recent discoveries of, in United States, 111
Poverty, in age of potential abundance, 193; and riches, study of extremes of, 336; of vast populations, 421
Power, to produce material things, 172; to destroy civilization, 176; over life process, 179; over the mind, 181; removal of, from hands of people, 354; patterns of world, changing, 420
Practical knowledge, advance of, 132, 171
Prayer of common man, 141
Prejudice and hatred, our heritage of, 195
Primogeniture and entail, abolition of laws of, 83

"Prince of peace," 224, 419
Private enterprise, role of, 143
Private property in early America, 93
Production, of American industry, 8; approaching solution of problem of, 213
Productive property, distribution of, 154
Productivity of labor, increase in, 146
Promise of America, 21; fulfilling, 69; in industrial age, 309; and education, 309
Propaganda, resistance to, 189
Prospects of mankind, new, 142
Protagoras, on man the "measure of all things," 233
Protestant Reformation, 51
Providence, beneficent, 401
Provisional Government, Russian, 14
Psychological forces, ties of, 159

Quakers, 426

Racial injustice, Soviet propaganda on, 196
Radio commentators, 159
Reconciliation among nations, need for, 195
Recreational institutions as educational agencies, 303
Red Army, strength of, 174
Reform, study of proposals for economic, 377
Regimentation in production, 149
Renaissance, 232
Resources, failure to make full use of, 194
Responsibility, development of deep sense of, 412
Revolutions, 4
Rhododendron, 116
Rich and abundant life for all, possibility of, 184
Rich land, lure of, 118
Ridenour, Louis N., on "second industrial revolution," 145
"Right," extreme, 12
Rittenhouse, David, 37

Rocky Mountains, 117
Roebling, John, 392
Roman Empire, 61; last days of, 400
Romanov, 13
Romans, achievements in law of, 260
Rome, 6
Rousseau, 31
Rule of law, 218; as supreme achievement of Western man, 259; Barker on, 259; Christian fathers' contribution to, 262; English-speaking people's contribution to, 262; American people's contribution to, 263; American record in, 266; challenged by new conditions, 273; threatened by totalitarian movements, 275; extension to entire world of, 275; Beloff on breakdown of, in Europe, 275
Rural household, relatively self-sufficient, 89
Rural neighborhood, role of, in early America, 88; personal relations in, 92; role of, in education, 102
Russell, Bertrand, 16; on future of mankind, 209; on use of scientific techniques in war, 210; on "human compassion," 227; on scientific method, 248; on science as foe of persecution, 251
Russia, 13; transformation of, 420
Russian, Communism, 12, 16; absolutism, 14, 15; Communists, 15; expansionism, 15; revolutionary doctrines, 15; Messianism, 15; revolution, 14; landlords, 72; revolution, mistakes in judging, 422

Santa Maria, 162
Scarcity, heritage of, 193
Schlesinger, Arthur M., 71
Schools, weakness of, in early America, 103; lag of, 201; role of, in education, 304; spirit of freedom in, 365; location of, in American community, 437; battle over, 450
Science, and technology, 10; development of, 49; and technology, release of, 129; as method of inquiry, 129; conquests of, 130; support of physical, 186; neglect of social, 186; neglect of teaching of, 188; greatest single force, 244; product of Europe and Mediterranean Basin, 244; dependence of our civilization on, 244; deeply rooted in America, 245; instrument of prediction and control, 245; as knowledge, 247; as method, 247; as nonmoral, 248; as molder and bearer of values, 249; as satisfier of desire to know, 250; moral tradition of, 250; need for more, today, 251; need for, in public affairs, 252; free development of, in peril, 254; question of control of, 255; "patriotic," 255; threat to, in democracies, 256; limitations of, 257; and the good life, 258; and scholarship, role of, in education for excellence, 323
"Science of the sciences," 255
Scientific laboratory, 132
Scientific method, 248; elements of, 248; need to apply, to problems of mankind, 252
Scientific spirit, need for, in political struggle, 253
Seagle, William, on nature of law, 260
Second article of Bill of Rights, repeal of, 179
Second World War, 4, 9, 14, 15, 151, 352
Sectional rivalries in United States, 161
Security, importance of material, 366
Self-discipline, in a democracy, 325
Seneca, on democracy, 278
Separate schools, abolition of, 341
Shaw, George Bernard, on teaching, 455
Shotwell, James T., on war, 176
Silence, outlawing of, in Soviet Russia, 362
Simonov, Konstantin, on "ferocious ideological struggle," 425–426
Slavophils, 15
Smith, Preserved, on science, 49

Smith, Sydney, on aesthetic poverty of America, 386
Snyder, Albert J., on equality as "America's purpose," 328
Social and political philosophy, differences in, 165
Social class, moderation in school of influence of, 342
"Social gospel," 224
Social problems, need for scientific study of, 189
Social research, fear of, 187
Social revolution, in modern age, 52
"Socialist humanism" of Communists, 241
Socrates, 203; death of, 236
Soil, fertility of, 107
"Soldiers of Communism," 183
Solon, 260
Son of Heaven, 270
Sorel, George, "gospel without pity" of, 276
Sovereignty, myth of national, 196; national, 427
Soviet espionage, 5
Soviet leaders, character of, 425
Soviet Russia, education in, 27; First Five-Year Plan in, 27, 424
Soviet state, 5
Soviet Union, and World Communism, ignorance of, 422; study of, 422; mistakes in judging, 423–424
Soviets, on equality of races, 58
Spain, 50
Spencer, Herbert, on Republican form of government, 345
Spiritual division of world, 164
"Squirrel rifle," 78
Stable economy, 18
Stalin, dictatorship of, 15; as "leader of the toiling masses," 15; as "pupil of Lenin," 276; directing struggle for world, 417
Standard of living, highest average, 174
Statue of Liberty, inscription on, 74
Stearns, Harold E., on civilization in America, 389

"Sterility, invention of," 180
Struggle, role of, in democracy, 446
Subject matter, mastery of specialized, 462
Sullivan, Louis H., 392
Sulphur reserves in United States, 111
Sumner, William Graham, on education, 23
Superiority, doctrine of, 20; doctrines of class and racial, 329
Switzerland, 13

Teacher, raising of social status of, 343; as example of free person, 365; heavy demands on, 451; task of, today, 451; task of, made difficult by battle over school, 452; task of, made difficult by nonschool agencies, 453; inadequate equipment of, 453; tradition of untrained, 454; status of, in agrarian age, 454; Francis Grund on status of, in 1837, 455; Washington Irving on, 455; social idealism of, 457; inadequate compensation of, 457; people lack understanding of work of, 458; restrictions on, 458; attacks on, 459; training of, 459; development of professional training of, 461; enrichment of life of, 465; improvement of working conditions of, 466; participation in life of community by, 466; right of, to form organizations, 467; responsibility of, 472; loyalty of, 472
Teachers' organizations, purposes of, 467
Teaching, George Bernard Shaw on, 455; Cicero on, 457; abandonment of inherited ideas of nature of, 460; recognition of arduous nature of, 460; techniques, mastery of, 462
Technological foundations of our economy, study of, 376; tensions from changes, in, 139
Technological revolution, evidence of, 130
Technology, nature of, 130; conditions favorable to advance of, 133; oppo-

sition to advance of, 135; impact of, on our civilization, 138; characteristics of, 139; moral issue raised by, 140; and new modes of livelihood, 141; and mass production, 147; and new industries, 151; impact of, on family, 154; and new forms of communication, 156; role of, in forming more perfect union, 157; and one world, 161; and power, 171
Third Estate, 52
Third International, 15
Thornthwaite, C. Warren, on mobility of population, 437
Thucydides, on power, 78
Tocqueville, Alexis de, on "causes" of the success of our democracy, 7; on education in America, 23; on American education, 34; on growth of America, 47; on migration to America, 61; on westward migration, 63; on who migrates, 72; on equality of condition, 80, 154; on cooperation among Americans, 92; on the valley of the Mississippi, 107; on America's geographical position, 118; on economic threat to democracy, 190; on American habit of forming associations, 271; on equality, 327; on American insensitiveness to wonders of nature, 390; on forming organizations, 439
Totalitarianism, 5; morals of, 210; as "wave of the future," 212; tendency in America to adopt spirit of, 242; need for study of, 359
Toynbee, Arnold J., on rise and fortunes of great civilizations, 400
Transportation, costs of, in 1800, Bidwell on, 96
Travel, as educational agency, 302; purpose of, 438
Trollope, Anthony, on equality in America, 85
Turkey, 13
Turner, Frederick Jackson, 89; on conflict between capitalist and pioneer, 99
Tyre, 405

Unemployment, 19
UNESCO, 22, 392
Unguided learning, limitations of, 315
United Nations, 18, 21; educational, scientific, and cultural organization of, 22, 392; Charter of, 419; 427; study of, 428
United States, rise of, 420
Uranium reserves, in United States, in Canada, 113
Utopia, 212

Values, nature of, 217; of our people, 217; diverse and conflicting, 217; of Nazis, 217; of Communism, 218; survival of, in new age, 218
Velikii Vozhd, 270
Venice, 405
Vergerius, Petrus, 48
Vinson, Fred M., on productivity of the economy, 9
Virginia Gazette, 50
Virtue and understanding, need for, today, 353
Virtues, Hebraic-Christian, 226; worth of Hebraic-Christian, demonstrated, 227; cultivation of, 324
Vogeler, Robert A., 17
Voltaire, 52

War, costs of, 18; condemnation of, 224; and threat of war, dangers of, 414; general condemnation of, 419; causes of, 419
Warfare, study of history of, 416
Washington, George, Farewell Address of, 7; first inaugural of, 45; contribution to rule of law of, 263; on experiment in republican government, 344
Waste in industry, 9
Water resources, 113
Watkins, Frederick, on Roman law, 261
Weapons, in Second World War, 176; of the future, 177; threat of, to free institutions, 178
Webster, Daniel, Bunker Hill oration of, 45; on power, 79; on economic

INDEX 491

threat to democracy, 190
Weimar Republic, constitution of, 265
Weld, Isaac, on hardships of travel in 1795, 95
Wells, H. G., on education, 27; on "race between education and catastrophe," 296
West, free people of the, in their relations with the East, 11
Western man, horizons of, in modern age, 48
White Mountains, 116
Whitman, Walt, on personal integrity, 238
Whitney, Eli, and mass production, 148
Wilde, Oscar, on democracy, 279
Williams, Roger, 240
Willkie, Wendell, on reservoir of good will, 429
Wilson, Woodrow, 166; on democracy, 279
Wissler, Clark, 23; on the machine, 142
Women in industry, 155
"Wonder drugs," 181
Woods, John, on cooperation among American families, 92

Work experience, importance of, 373; as educational agency, 301; attitudes toward socially useful, 378; right and obligation to, 379
World Almanac, 440
World, building new, 207; community, building of, 413; community, material foundations of, 413; division of, 413, 421; community, moral and political foundations of, 414; community, urgency of building, 415; order, task of building, 418; citizenship, preparation for, 426
Wright, Fanny, on practice in use of musket, 79
Wycliffe, John, 223, 279

Yellowstone River, 115
Yosemite, 115
Yugoslavia, 425

Zenger, John Peter, 240
Zinc, resources of, in United States, 110
Zoroaster, 203
Zweig, on life in Nazi Germany, 359–362